Religious Pluralism in South Asia and Europe

Religious Pluralism in South Asia and Europe

Edited by

JAMAL MALIK AND HELMUT REIFELD

OXFORD
UNIVERSITY PRESS

OXFORD
UNIVERSITY PRESS

YMCA Library Building, Jai Singh Road, New Delhi 110001

Oxford University Press is a department of the University of Oxford. It furthers the University's objective of excellence in research, scholarship, and education by publishing worldwide in

Oxford   New York
Auckland   Cape Town   Dar es Salaam   Hong Kong   Karachi   Kuala Lumpur
Madrid   Melbourne   Mexico City   Nairobi   New Delhi   Taipei   Toronto   Shanghai

With offices in
Argentina   Austria   Brazil   Chile   Czech Republic   France   Greece   Guatemala
Hungary   Italy   Japan   South Korea   Poland   Portugal   Singapore   Switzerland
Thailand   Turkey   Ukraine   Vietnam

Oxford is a registered trade mark of Oxford University Press
in the UK and in certain other countries

Published in India
by Oxford University Press, New Delhi

ISBN 019 566975 4

Typeset in Calisto MT 10/12 by Jojy Phillip
Printed by Pauls Press, New Delhi 110 020
Published by Manzar Khan, Oxford University Press
YMCA Library Building, Jai Singh Road, New Delhi 110 001

Contents

Preface

None of the great religions of the world grew and developed in isolation. The exchange, the encounter, and the togetherness with other religions was more the rule rather than the exception. In return, these experiences with other religions always had and have some kind of impact on the understanding of one's own religion. It is not only in history, but in the world of the 21st century as well that we find manifold ways how these experiences are perceived and accepted. They may be perceived in a more positive or in a more negative way. On the negative side, reactions vary from the lack of respect for the other religion, over the sweeping and malicious generalizations and prejudices up to the perception of the other religion as a thread which might stamp out one's own religion of existence. The worst reaction certainly is any form of violent interference or even the desire to erase our own neighbour's religion. On the positive side, however, there are equally many ways to react, and it is these which deserve—certainly for the future—our main attention.

The experiences of plurality between and within religious traditions which we know from the European context may be different from those in South Asia, but there are also similarities. The options for dialogue between Europe and South Asia and for understanding contemporary controversies will certainly be enhanced if we search for their respective traditions of religious plurality. For sure, many questions can be posed and discussed with comparative intent and, therefore, invite and challenge comparative answers. For instance: What do we mean by plurality? Does plurality necessarily lead to pluralism? How is plurality embedded in everyday life and in popular culture? What is the position of an individual who belongs not only to one religion but shows multiple religious identities? How is plurality considered within a church, within a community or within national ideologies? While these questions certainly promote comparative discussions, others point more to differences rather than to similarities. What are the main characteristics in the historical handling of plurality? How did and do different states deal with religious differences? How is religious plurality integrated in secularism, multiculturalism, and increasing individualization? How are great traditions of plurality enculturated into daily life and where are the fault lines in the affirmation of plurality today? But also these kinds of questions may lead to comparative answers.

There can be little doubt that great traditions of plurality can be traced in all religions. If we look for them we will find them in many different forms, with regional variations and sometimes perhaps even in disguise. But in any case, the knowledge about them can be regarded as precious, and today, they are probably of as much importance as they have been in the past. On the one hand, the world of the 21st century opened up with intense discussions about the universality of human rights, about the character of civil societies and about different concepts of secularism. On the other hand, we face even more intense discussions about religious fundamentalism, not only in Islam, but in most of the world's great religions. How shall we react to these manifold forms of violence, based on fundamentalist ideas and resulting in horrible acts of terror? Perhaps there is some legitimate hope in the attempt to counterbalance religious fundamentalism with religious pluralism. If this is true, traditions of religious pluralism are more important than ever before.

It is with these considerations in mind, that the German Konrad Adenauer Foundation launched and developed a series of workshops under a programme called 'dialogue on values'. The essays of this volume emanated from one of these workshops which was held at the Gajner Palace in Bikaner between 23rd and 26th October 2002. It was the common interest of all participants, not to state and re-state one's own conclusions but rather to find new ground for dialogue by negotiating different points of view. Thus, the opinions and judgements expressed in the following articles are those of individual authors and neither of the Konrad Adenauer Foundation nor of any Indian organization. The articles were written with the idea to promote and carry forward the spirit of dialogue rather than end it with a final statement.

The success of this endeavour is not only due to the pleasant atmosphere of the Gajner Palace. Inputs have come from many sides, in the process of preparation as well as of publication, and it is difficult to name them all. The initial idea to jointly organize this workshop came from Professor Jamal Malik, from the university of Erfurt in Germany. His patient and reliable collaboration, his profound knowledge about both sides, the European as well as the South Asian, and his firm but friendly way to incorporate new ideas into the programme from time to time were indispensable for the outcome. Therefore, it is him who deserves our first and main word of thanks. In the process of conceptualization many discussions have taken place in the course of which decisive inputs have come from Professor T. N. Madan, Professor Ashis Nandy, and Dr. Margrit Pernau. We are also particularly grateful to all those, who not only presented a paper and participated in the discussion, but who made the effort to revise their paper in the light of these discussions. All their efforts are reflected in this book.

For the implementation of the workshop the Konrad Adenauer Foundation is particularly proud of the collaboration with and grateful to the *Fondation Maison des Sciences de L'Homme* in Paris which contributed the air-fares for two French experts. Last, but certainly not least, we would like to thank Oxford University Press for handling the problems of publication. The responsibility for organization and administration was mainly in the hands of Manu Emmanuel, while all the paperwork before and after the workshop was done by Ashvini Thakur and Mohita Bhansali. Without the help, imagination, and friendship of all mentioned, this book would never have come out.

New Delhi
September 2004

HELMUT REIFELD

Contributors

SUDHIR CHANDRA retired as Professor from the University of Baroda. He is the author of *Continuing Dilemmas: Understanding Social Consciousness* (2002), *Enslaved Daughters: Colonialism, Law and Women's Rights* (1997, paperback 1998), *The Oppressive Present: Literature and Social Consciousness in Colonial India* (1992, paperback 1994, 1999). He is currently working on *Religion, Culture and the Nation: Upper Caste Converts to Christianity.*

MICHAEL DUSCHE, Senior Assistant Professor, received his doctorate in Philosophy from the University of Frankfurt (Main), Germany, in 1999. He teaches Philosophy and European Cultural History at the Centre for German Studies of Jawaharlal Nehru University, New Delhi. He is the co-editor of *Justice: Political, Social and Juridical* (forthcoming), the author of *Der Philosoph als Mediator* (The Philosopher as a Mediator), Passagen Verlag, Vienna 2000, and of numerous articles in journals such as *Ethical Perspectives* (Belgium) and *TRANS — Internet Journal for Culture Studies* (Austria).

CLAIRE DE GALAEMBERT is a researcher in Political Sciences at the Centre National de la Recherche Scientifique (CNRS). She is a member of a laboratory specialized in the study of Public Policies (Groupe d'Analyse Publique). Her research topic is Religion as an object of Public Policy and the comparison of the relationships between State and Church in France and in Germany. She is currently involved in a survey about the way the different French public actors approach the Muslim issue in France.

MARK HAEBERLEIN has taught early modern and North American history at the University of Freiburg, Germany, since 1991 and has recently accepted a call to the chair in early modern history at the University of Bamberg. He has published a number of books and articles on migration, trade, elite networks, and religious minorities in the early modern period.

SAIYID ZAHEER HUSAIN JAFRI is Reader in the Department of History, North Campus, University of Delhi. He has authored *Studies in the Anatomy of a Transformation: Awadh from Mughal to Colonial Rule* (1998) and *Masnad-e Faqr-o Irshad: Tareekh Khanwadae Karimia Naeemia Salon* (2003), and has published numerous articles on Awadh's economic, cultural, and social history by exploring archival sources, family documents, and Awadhi folk literature extensively. His present research interests revolve around the documentation of the history of ecclesiastical institutions, Awadhi literature, and mystic traditions in northern India.

MONICA JUNEJA is presently attached to the Institut für Geschichte, University of Halle, Germany. Her publications include *Peindre le paysan. L'image rurale dans la peinture française de Millet à Van Gogh* (1998), *Architecture in medieval India. Forms, contexts, histories* (2001), *Exploring alterity in pre-modern societies*, (special issue of *The Medieval History Journal*, 5 February 2002). She is the co-editor of *The lives of objects in the pre-modern world* (forthcoming 2005).

T.N. MADAN is Honorary Professor at the Institute of Economic Growth where he was earlier Professor of Sociology and Director. His most recent publications are *Modern Myths, Locked Minds: Secularism and Fundamentalism in India* (1997) and has edited *India's Religions: Perspectives from Sociology and History* (2004).

JAMAL MALIK, studied Bonn/Germany (M.A. 1982), acquired the degree of Doctorate from Heidelberg (1989), and he completed his postdoctoral work at Bamberg (1994). In 1998 he was appointed Head of Religious Studies at the University of Derby. Since February 1999 he is Chair of Religious Studies - Islamic Studies at the University of Erfurt, Germany. His publications include *The Colonialization of Islam* (Delhi and Lahore 1996, second edition 1998), *Islamische Gelehrtenkultur in Nordindien* (Leiden: E.J. Brill 1997), and the edited volume *Perspectives of mutual encounters in South Asian History 1760–1860* (Leiden: E.J. Brill 2000).

SALIL MISRA is a faculty member at the Department of History, Indira Gandhi National Open University, New Delhi. He has published a monograph, *A Narrative of Communal Politics, Uttar Pradesh, 1937–39*, and has also published articles on themes related to communal politics, languages, Hindi, and Urdu

ASHIS NANDY, a political psychologist and cultural theorist, is at the Centre for the Study of Developing Societies, Delhi. His recent books are *An Ambiguous Journey to the City: The Village and Other Odd Ruins of the Self in the Indian Imagination* (2001), *The Romance of the State and the Fate of Dissent in the Tropics* (2003), *Time Warps: The Insistent Politics of Silent and Evasive Pasts* (2002) and *Bonfire of Creeds: The Essential Ashis Nandy* (2004).

MARGRIT PERNAU is Research Assistant Professor at Erfurt University; research fellow at Bielefeld University. Her recent publications include *The Passing of Patrimonialism. Politics and Political Culture in Hyderabad 1911–48* (2000). She is the co-editor of *Family and Gender. Changing values in Germany and India* (2002), *C.F. Andrews: Zaka Ullah of Delhi* (2003), and *Regionalizing Pan-Islam. Documents on the Khilafat Movement* (forthcoming).

HELMUT REIFELD is presently Head of division, planning, and concepts, in the head office in Berlin of the Konrad Adenauer Foundation. He was representative of the Konrad Adenauer Foundation to India from 1997 to 2003. He recently co-edited *Pluralism and Equality. Values in Indian Society and Politics; Peace as Process. Reconciliation and Conflict Resolution in South Asia; Family and Gender. Changing Values in Germany and India; The Public and the Private: Issues of Democratic Citizenship; The Value of Nature: Ecological Politics in India; and Lived Islam in South Asia: Accommodation, Adaptation and Conflict*.

CHRISTIAN W. TROLL is Hon. Professor for the Study of Islam and Christian-Muslim Relations at the Philosophisch-Theologische Hochschule St. Georgen, Theologische Fakultät SJ, Frankfurt/M. Among his books may be mentioned *Sayyid Ahmad Khan, A reinterpretation of Muslim theology* (Delhi, 1978 and Karachi, 1979) and *Muslime fragen, Christen antworten* (Regensburg, 2003). He has edited four books in the series *Islam in India: Studies and Commentaries* (Delhi 1982–9). In 1998, together with John J. Donohue, he edited the volume *Faith, Power and Violence: Muslims and Christians in plural society, past and present* (1998).

MONIKA WOHLRAB-SAHR is Professor for Sociology of Religion at the University of Leipzig. She is on the board of the German Sociological Association and on the council of the International Society for Sociology of Religion. She was Visiting Scholar in Sociology at the University of California at Berkeley, where she did research on American Islam. Her current research is on generational change in religiosity and worldviews among families in post-socialist East Germany. She also works on the role of Islam in European societies. Her latest publications include *Konversion zum Islam in Deutschland und den USA* (1999) and the edited volume *Atheismus und religiöse Indifferenz* (2003).

Introduction

JAMAL MALIK

This edited volume is a modest attempt to promote comparative discussion on traditions of religious plurality in Europe and South Asia.[1] Plurality—social, political, ethnic, linguistic, cultural, and religious—suggests the parallel interaction of different groups. It may include the demarcation of the notion of plurality from other related concepts such as syncretism, liminality, or singularity. Though these concepts will be discussed in different chapters that follow, it seems appropriate to outline the rationale of the idea of plurality in the context of its actual, historical, and contemporary, as well as reflected forms as it occurs in academic disciplines, and also becomes relevant in current politics. In fact, how carriers of multiple religious traditions can share social spaces creatively, rather than antagonistically, is among the most challenging of questions of our time.

Plurality does not lead necessarily to pluralism, for pluralism is differentiated from plurality by its active and reflexive perception of the other. Pluralism implies more than coexistence of two or more communities at the same time and in the same space. It presumes that the

---

[1] The topic of religious pluralism in comparison owes much to a joint initiative of the religious studies departments of the universities of Bremen and Erfurt for a collaborative research entitled 'religious pluralism in Europe'. Much of what follows is taken from Hans G. Kippenberg and Jamal Malik (speakers): 'Transregio-Sonderforschungsbereich 1907, »Religiöser Pluralismus in Europa«, Konzept', Universities of Erfurt and Bremen, November 2000, submitted to the German Science Foundation. See also Hans G. Kippenberg and Kocku von Stuckrad, 2003, 'Religionswissenschaftliche Überlegungen zum religiösen Pluralismus in Deutschland: eine Öffnung der Perspektiven', in Hartmut Lehmann (ed.), *Multireligiosität im vereinten Europa. Historische und juristische Aspekte.* Göttingen: Wallstein, pp. 145–62.

chronological and territorial coexistence was made into an issue either by those who were/are politically in charge, or/and by the concerned religious communities themselves. Such traditions can be considered self-reflexive, having been discussed and legitimized within the religious traditions as well as in academia.

The intention of this comparative volume is to explore religious history and the dynamic process through which people engage with one another in and through their deepest differences, as a history of plural systems of religions, in apparently two different universes: Europe and South Asia. In doing so, religion is understood in terms of cultural dynamics, being integrated in and affiliated to specific networks of change and exchange also with non-religion. In this process the actors are crucial, because they shape their cultures, religions, thereby being contextually dependent and exposed to perpetual change. Hence, religion is considered as a process of appropriation of a metaphysical world, a system through which human beings appropriate the world. Instead of establishing and fostering essentialized positions—which is often being done not only by, say, non-Muslims regarding Islam but also by Muslims themselves, when some of them claim that Islamic practice and confession are not subject to historical change—culture and religion can be grasped as a repertory of references that enables people to interpret their complex lifeworlds and hence make them meaningful. I doubt whether religion is the prime force for Muslim, Christian, or Hindu rationality. Rather, contextualization is most important, because it is here that mutuality of social entities can be traced.

THE ISSUE

First of all, the unquestioned presupposition that European identity and value-society was tightly knit to Christian religion, i.e. religious plurality and diversity had never been part of European history is interrogated. Similarly, in the South Asian context one needs to recognize as to how far religious pluralism was a sine qua non for the coexistence of different religious groups living or immigrating here, and in how far this idea was programmatically supported, and by whom and by what means.

The significance of Christianity for Europe on the one hand and of Hinduism for South Asia on the other cannot certainly be ignored. But this should not lead to the importance of other powerful or even not so powerful religious traditions being ignored. Certainly, tracing the religious path of both, Europe and South Asia, is not conceivable without recognizing the mediating role played by Muslims in transmitting the philosophy and science of other civilizations. The great store of their literature and philosophy is unthinkable without the profound influence from the Jewish religion and people. Their histories have by no means been the monolithic religio-cultural unity that some have made out of them, and their contemporary religious landscapes are certainly of increasing religious plurality. A change in perspective is particularly imperative when looking at both the academic as well as the current social, religious, and political discussion.

In the European context, it was more or less taken for granted that one individual could have one religion only. It was also anticipated that increasing secularization and 'demystification' would inevitably lead to religious indifference or to a restless search for 'substitute religions'. It was also thought that religious irrationalism would result in seductivity and political instrumentalization. Looking critically at the European and certainly South Asian religious histories one might, however, get the impression that religious pluralism was always inherent (t)here. However, because of theological and historiographical constructions this remained largely unrecognized and was pushed into the margin, or was rendered into some kind of political programmatic.

The preconditions of the rejection of pluralism and the idea of mutually exclusive religious options can be regarded as elements in the long-drawn-out processes of singularization and normatization of religious dynamics, in the course of which open—'polytheistic' or different or other—systems were marginalized in the public perception and legitimacy. The extensive establishment of monotheistically inclined theologies led to a process of *regularization*, in which alternative options were even hereticized by the respective 'meta narrative'.[2]

It will require a great effort before the academic study of religion frees itself from paradigms which either dramatize internal religious differences as heresies, ignore them as irrelevant, or render them innocuous in classifications such as mysticism, apocalypticism, viz., until the question of whether the German neighbour of a Turkish boy living in Germany will celebrate Eid ul-Fitr is widely answered in the affirmative. Similarly,

---

[2] With regard to the ethnological description of foreign religions, Mary Louise Pratt has coined the term of *normalising discourse*, which has the function 'to fix the Other in a timeless present' (Mary Louise Pratt, 'Scratches on the Face of the Country; or, What Mr. Barrow Saw in the Land of the Bushmen', in Henry Louis Gates Jr (ed.), *'Race', Writing, and Difference*, Chicago: University of Chicago Press, 1985, 135–62, here p. 139); cf also Mary Louise Pratt, *Imperial Eyes: Travel Writing and Transculturation*, London: Routledge, 1992; and Johannes Fabian, *Time and the Other: How Anthropology Makes Its Object*, New York: Columbia University Press, 1983.

the reactions of the leading decision-making bodies of a religion against such 'marginal' phenomena vary and range from stigmatization such as 'heretic' or 'heresy' to fundamental criticism, official condemnation, and active oppression.

Consequently, the complex network of different religious attitudes and unfolding reciprocal relationship cannot be characterized by singular closed systems, like Samuel Huntington's reductionist clash of civilizations suggests. Rather, it requires a different viewpoint: Replacing the dominant monocausal and monolinear concept of religious history through a 'polyfocal' analysis of an open, plural(ist) field. In doing so, a new perspective on history is possible, and more justice will be done to the historical as well as contemporary situation of incremental pluralization in a global framework, which, one might add, is most important for peaceful coexistence.

FIELD OF DISCOURSE

Bearing in mind the traditions which have been highly centralized by different epistemologies, one way to open up this closed view is to look at them from an un-centred angle, i.e. from the margin, and to recognize the interaction and reciprocities or even mutualities as operating in a floating discursive field, in which plural religious options strive for public acceptance or for a place in the respective master narrative. In other words, appreciate innate plurality and pluralism, and the view from the edge.

This is especially relevant when looked, for example, at the current context of an increasingly pluralizing Europe, when different religious traditions remind Europe that the way in which it lives and organizes itself is not the only possible way for it to do so. It is the way it has chosen for its development. The idea of alternative modernities or shared faith are cases in point.

The traditional viewpoint is the result of an approach to religions originating in the normative demands of highly organized monotheistic and univocal religions, including, I believe, reformed Hinduism. Even sociological investigations which have focused on the economic, moral, legal, political, or aesthetic functions of religion often took into account only a single long-term, transmitted, and usually organized, religious tradition in a particular geographical area, neglecting other contesting traditions. Based on the assumption that 'world religions' are religions which have become independent of all contexts—because they transcend their specific cultural traditions and also transcend their own original culture, and are constantly being made and reconstructed by religious actors—research into the history of religion did not pay enough attention to their mutual interrelations or to their local circumstances. Consequently, studies that would take local issues seriously, were at the most put into the dusty shelves of ethnography, and were termed the 'little tradition'.

The notorious lack of interest in religion might well be related to the conviction that until the 1970s, and partly beyond, scientists of all disciplines including the academic study of religion were convinced that religions would, in the near future, disappear from both history and the public sphere and become a purely private matter. Therefore, it was even more surprising that since the mid-1970s religion returned into the public domain and increasingly has been influencing the history since the last quarter of the twentieth century.[3]

Some sociologist studies, however, have been referring to the contemporary religious scenario in terms of pluralism. But they also claimed that, as a result of secularism, religions would be demonopolized. In an utilitarian turn this pluralism was rendered into a market metaphor: religions would have to be sold,[4] thereby losing authority, and eventually leading to the decline of religion per se.[5] This viewpoint proclaimed the dramatic loss in the plausibility of institutionalized religions, but the reality was different. Pluralism did force religions to compete, it did not lead to their decline, but rather stimulated growth.[6] This view perceived religious activity as an investment in the limited asset of 'salvation'. The 'rational choice theory of religion' provided the proven theoretical background to illuminate the plausibility of religion for one individual/group or the other.[7] While lot of this is true, its economistic and utilitarian background does not consider a conceptualization of religion in terms of interpretation of lifeworlds.

[3] Cf., Peter L. Berger (ed.), *The Desecularization of the World: Resurgent Religions and World Politics*, Washington: Michigan University Press, 1999; Martin Riesebrodt, *Die Rückkehr der Religionen. Fundamentalismus und der 'Kampf der Kulturen'*, München: C. H. Beck, 2000.

[4] Peter L. Berger, *Zur Dialektik von Religion und Gesellschaft*, (Engl. 1967), Frankfurt: Fischer, 1973.

[5] See Peter L. Berger, *Der Zwang zur Häresie: Religion in der pluralistischen Gesellschaft* (Engl. 1979), Freiburg: Herder, 1992, p. 9.

[6] Roger Finke and Rodney Stark, 'Religious Economies and Sacred Canopies: Religious Mobilization in American Cities, 1906', in *American Sociological Review* 53, 1988, pp. 41–9.

[7] Rodney Stark, 'How sane people talk to the gods: A rational theory of revelations', in Michael A. Williams, Collett Cox, and Martin S. Jaffee (eds), *Innovation in Religious Traditions: Essays in the Interpretation of Religious Change* (Religion and Society 31), Berlin and New York: Mouton de Gruyter, 1992, pp. 19–34.

We contend that pluralism was a feature of European and South Asian religious histories ever since. 'Paganism', Hinduism, Buddhism, Judaism, Christianity, Islam, Sikhism have developed and defined themselves by mutual reference. It seems as if the respective 'non-believers' were constantly near each other and floated around in the same cultural and spatial field. Conversions, religious violence, disputes, and violent usurpation of existing sacred traditions and places are only a few of its many symptoms, as much as the complex processes of reciprocity, of adaptation and adoption, of mutualities that produced al-Andalus and the Mughal empire. But, until now the structure of those mutual references as, for example, reflected by obvious synchronisms and connected or shared histories and faiths has hardly been examined, viz.the simultaneous appearance of Jewish, Christian, and Islamic messianism in different regions in the sixteenth century, or multiple modernities in the eighteenth centuries, or modern fundamentalism in the last quarter of the twentieth century.

This is even more remarkable, since the large religions were not only living locally in the same territory, but also societally and culturally. It was not the distance, but the proximity, which persuaded all religious communities to draw up boundaries—boundaries that were important for the construction of the self and of the other. Indeed, accepted borders are conducive to peace; recognized conflicts are in general the condition for tolerance to be identified as such. However, the blurring of these boundaries was a constant process that marked interaction and encounter all along.

Moreover, because Europe and South Asia both are highly value-bound constructions with problems of definition in terms of geography and content, one has to go beyond these two universes. From the very moment of their 'arrival' in and migration to, as well as their birth in Europe and South Asia respectively, the religions lived in the awareness of their respective differences. This diversity was connected with their cultural claims, such as exclusive claim of truth. Developments with the native cultures of the religions outside these two universes were an independent but powerful factor. The reference to a (often imaginary) centre like Jerusalem, Mecca, or Benares points precisely to this fact. Similarly, the construction of an alternative outline of European/South Asian self-understanding, which deliberately makes use of images of the non-self, has influenced, if not determined, historical and religious debates since early modernity. One might consider that it is from the perspective of the 'periphery', actually from the marginalized perspective, that the 'other', constructed as a counterfoil, has not only an invisible history of its own, but also refers to a substantial influence on the comparative study of religion.[8] These circumstances have to be considered by all means.

But without the inclusion of the religions located 'beyond' the European as well as South Asian borders, the migration, acculturation, and identity formation of immigrants to and into a region, especially in the twentieth century, cannot adequately be understood.[9] There are international linkages between different universes, involving co-religionists in other parts of the world, such as the tensions between Hindus and Sikhs following the storming of the Golden Temple in Amritsar and between Hindus and Muslims after the destruction of the mosque at Ayodhya. Both led to actual conflicts in Europe, with attacks taking place on individuals, organizations, and places of worship. This interrelatedness has become more intensive in modern society which has experienced what has been called 'the annihilation of distance'—and which has become a 'global village' of religions.[10] For migration is not a one-sided movement but often a dislocation in which the notion of home and away are shifting. In this context, all religions, or better their actors, have to relearn how to organize themselves and to interact with others.

All of this explains why problematizing of the definition of plurality and pluralism is an important task. The questioning of interpretative patterns and devices as well as the conceptions underlying them, leads systematically into the core of the problems of the book. Therefore, it seems advisable not to choose isolated investigations of single religions right from the beginning, but rather to examine the plural field in which they operate and go for their juxtaposition.

This becomes even more evident when religious testimonies are no more understood as an expression of perennial experience or as a peep into a strange and past world, but as a reflection of the thoughts of those who wrote them and passed them on. In fact, when a source is seen as an expression of a social construction, the academic study of religion itself is included in the social structural process of 'meaning', viz. as a producer of texts on a meta-level.[11] This, in turn, is connected to the

---

[8] *Compare* David Chidester, *Savage Systems: Colonialism and Comparative Religion in Southern Africa,* Charlottesville and London: University Press of Virginia, 1996.

[9] *See* Reinhold Viehoff and Rien T. Segers (eds), *Kultur—Identität—Europa. Über die Schwierigkeiten und Möglichkeiten einer Konstruktion,* Frankfurt/M.: Suhrkamp, 1999.

[10] *See* Paul Weller: Inaugural Lecture as Professor of Inter-Religious Relations on 'Insiders or Outsiders?: Religion(s), State(s) and Society: Propositions for Europe', at the University of Derby on 8 November 2000.

[11] Further to that: Tomoko Masuzawa, *In Search of Dreamtime: The Quest for the Origin of*

social discourses on power, because even the term religion is not only an instrument of knowledge, but also one of domination.[12]

Therefore, the interrelationship of religions with each other, in connection with the cultures of knowledge, has to be appreciated. Again, we encounter interaction between academic description and religious practice. As has been pointed out elsewhere, exponents of the academic study of religion persist in the naïve belief that they are only observers—but actually they are not.[13] In fact, the interrelationship of religion and academic study of religion is endemic. In most cases academic description originally created, or even established, religion. Hence, there is an interrelationship of religion on the one side and academic study of religion on the other, implying an interrelatedness between religio-historical knowledge and self-depictions of religion as well as the inter-dependent relationship between academia and popularized or public formation of opinion about religion. It might require quite some amount of hermeneutical struggle to consider the transition from religious-historical knowledge to self-depictions of religions and the reciprocity of academic and popular opinion on religion.

THE PLURALISM OF CONTRIBUTIONS

Similar issues and core values are raised in the contributions informed by different academic disciplines, such as history, philosophy, social anthropology, theology, literature, communication, sociology, and political sciences. The contributions are arranged in a way that it is hoped the chapters speak to each other. Hence they are clustered around three sections, viz. legitimation of plurality; individual, church, and community; and living plurality. This intra-textual communication between the chapters might reify divisions between the classifications but it is hoped that

---

Religion, Chicago: University of Chicago Press, 1993; *See also* James Clifford and George E. Marcus (eds), *Writing Culture: The Poetics and Politics of Ethnography*, Berkeley: University of California Press, 1986; Allison James, Jenny Hockey and Andrew Dawon (eds), *After Writing Culture: Epistemology and Praxis in Contemporary Anthropology* (ASA Monographs 34), London and New York: Routledge, 1997.

[12] Cf. David Chidester, 1996, *Savage Systems: Colonialism and Comparative Religion in Southern Africa*, Charlottesville and London: University Press of Virginia, especially p. 266.

[13] Friedrich H. Tenbruck, 'Die Religion im Maelstrom der Reflexion', in J. Bergmann, A. Hahn and Th. Luckmann (Hrsg.), *Religion und Kultur*, Opladen: Westdeutscher Verlag, 1993, S. 31–67. *See also* Karl (Robert) Hoheisel, 'Rückwirkungen abendländischer Religionsforschung auf neuere Entwicklungen in den Weltreligionen', in Gunther Stephenson (Hrsg.), *Der Religionswandel unserer Zeit im Spiegel der Religionswissenschaft*, Darmstadt: Wissenschaftliche Buchgesellschaft, 1976, pp. 262–75.

they speak within the categories as well as across them. They can briefly be classified as follows:

Legitimation of Plurality

Legitimation of plurality can be found in a pluralist field only if the political society developed rules and instruments for the coexistence of several, even contesting religious communities, and the world views of the participating religious communities recognize and accept the plural situation.

In order to show these developments, processes of singularization and normatization of religious dynamics of the church, such as the politics of confessionalization in the sixteenth and seventeenth century, and the edicts of tolerance are considered as much as the pertinent issue of secularization which seemed to have had changed the role of religion in society. Mark Häberlein, in his essay about the historical roots of plurality in Europe, outlines these issues, relating them to the agents and channels of these processes—the state, scholars, common people, and institutions. 'The transition from a unified Latin Christian tradition to a modern Europe of secularized, multi-confessional state' he argues, 'was not synonymous with the rise of tolerance and the triumph of pluralism.' While secularization in Europe can be explained by tendencies of rationalization and modernization, plurality cannot be considered a result of mainstream development. Rather, it was marked by ambivalence of tolerance and intolerance, of conformity and plurality, such as the break of the Latin Christian church, the reformation, and the institutionalization of Christian churches. First thoughts of European scholars about tolerance and acceptance of different religious groups in the sixteenth and seventeenth centuries, adoption of tolerance to maintain political and economic power, and ideas of a modern state all questioned the role of religion and its legitimization through the church. Radical demands for a strict separation of church and state and the existence of a confessionally neutral state in the nineteenth century were factors that painfully influenced the emergence of plurality and tolerance in Europe. Outlining these versatile factors and demonstrating that plurality and tolerance did not only appear between, but also within religions, Häberlein poses the central question: whether plurality is and has always been a contested tradition in Europe.

India, on the other hand, offers a versatile picture of demographic structures right from the beginning. With a population of more than a billion people it covers nearly one-fifth of the world population. It also offers a wide field of different religions, such as Hinduism, Buddhism,

Jainism, Sikhism, which originated in India and Christianity and Islam, which came from outside. T.N. Madan, with his deep and sensitive anthropological insight, looks at all these religions from two different points of view, a global one, distinguishing one religion from the other, and from an intra-religious level, describing the different movements within a religion. The history, the organization, and the plurality of these major traditions are focused, dealing with two major questions: has plurality generated pluralism and, can religious pluralism become an ideology for India? 'It is obvious that, whenever a religious community comprises many regional cultural groups, and also has considerable numbers, running into millions, internal plurality becomes inescapable', Madan opines.

Addressing the question of pluralism is closely linked to the issue of religious freedom and religious tolerance, as pointed out by Christian Troll. From both a Christian and an Islamic point of view he approaches the issue of freedom of religion in India. A major question is: how does a convinced believer organize the fact that different religions exist—a matter that could represent a mystery for him. Part I of this chapter provides insights about Christian ideas of encountering non-Christians in terms of an inter-religious dialogue as well as the claim to universality and religious freedom, thereby remembering both sides of the story, the core message of the Gospel of peace and reconciliation, but also the responsibility for wars. Part II refers to the ideas of five Muslim thinkers as to how they arrange the plurality of religions, especially in the context of a minority status. This specific minoritarian aspect might put into question the idea that Islam is the only possibility to 'encompass all aspects of individual and social life.' Indeed, the ideas presented hardly consider religion or culture as a closed independent system. Instead of a literalist interpretation of the divine sources, Quran and Sunna, they tend to interpret them in text and context, trying to maintain their fluid identity. Against the background of the latest political development, therefore, Troll postulates that we need 'to defend and promote uncondi-tional respect of the free decision of any person regarding matters of faith and membership to a religious community (religious allegiance), if only such a decision has been made freely, i.e. according to the demands of conscience.'

The role of the state and its use of power stand out when religion becomes a nationalized monopoly, or when normative criteria to create religion and non-religion are fixed,[14] when the state looks after the

---

[14] *Laïcisme* in France. In Germany, the ecclesiastical authority over territories was given

equilibrium between the competing claims of truth, and when it tries to prevent a politics based on religious communalism, such as in the case of France. 'It is clear in the expression of religious conviction in public arenas, through religious processions, display of religious symbols, or the allowed absence of officials on holy days, that jurisprudence grants priority to religious freedom over neutrality of the public domain and institutions, as long as the concerned persons are "users" (i.e. pupils, students) of the public institutions and not employees of the institution (i.e. teachers, university professors, doctors)' as Claire de Galembert puts it. Indeed, French laïcity represents a compromise resulting from the conflict between church and state based on Catholic values, human rights, and republic demands—liberty, equality, and fraternity. Accordingly one can presume that religious freedom is granted to every single religious group. But in fact the strict separation of state and religion entails many questions and problems such as how religious plurality can be accommodated, how cult and culture be distinguished, and to what extent religion be practised publicly? Even though religious minorities are advantaged by the withdrawal of the Catholic church, one has to go beyond the representation of laïcity in order to recognize how ambivalent or even contradictory it is in reality. Indeed, the example of the relationships between state and Muslims and Catholics demonstrates the still implicit predominance of Catholicism within France. The question posed by de Galembert then is, whether French laïcity has failed, or whether it can handle new emerging problems.

But the state is not the exclusive guardian of the achievement of toleration of other communities. Religious communities themselves have also developed criteria for legitimacy of the plurality of truthclaims. As far as the three monotheistic religions are concerned, they perceived the other as the non-believer, and they conceptualized history as a time of trial.[15] How far, then, do state law and religious beliefs, both participate and compete in preservation or restriction of the diversity of religious options?

These crucial issues can, however, be dealt with only against the background of the—necessary—construction of religious history, because it is here that the plural structures of competitive religious systems can be appreciated. Hence, the ingenious processes of the construction and

up but the churches assured of an institutional existence, acknowledging a few religious communities as public bodies.

[15] ... at whose end the Messiah, the Son of God, the Mahdi will bring longed-for salvation—a concept also adopted by reformed Hinduism, I believe.

establishment of *master narratives* of a dominant normative history has to be interrogated as against divergent 'sect histories' or in relation to historical constructs of other religions or traditions. Similarly, the role of memory and of the *narration of the history* as a conscious and non-innocent process has to be valued, because scientists get involved in a multilayered process of making sense of synchronous and diachronous issues in which the narrative inevitably becomes rhetorical and the representation of the past gets involved in a discourse of power. This again depends on non-academic discourses. And if the historical narrative becomes feeble, another term, equally important for religious legitimacy, has to be interrogated: *tradition*. Instead of regarding tradition as a firm and authoritative part of religious and cultural identity, one may emphasize the cultural and discursive limitations of what is negotiated as tradition, as is evident in the following chapter.

'For the controversy between the multiculturalist and the liberal to be meaningful, we have to single out those aspects of culture into which the liberal democratic state cannot avoid getting involved', argues Michael Dusche. In his theoretical approach towards multiculturalism and liberal pluralism he demonstrates how religious pluralism can be discussed from these viewpoints. Referring to the problems of dismissing and of recognizing a culture, the question arises as to what extent liberalism and multiculturalism and their repertory of dealing with a group or an individual, really offer possibilities to handle these problems, where they fail, and where they have to find compromises. Certainly, these problems entail questions of identity, legal and moral aspects as well as minority and majority issues linked to culture and its representation. Crucial questions are: where does identity have its roots, how can it be defined, and where do identities overlap? Who actually, in a pluralist society, is in charge of setting moral and legal standards, and how can reasonableness be justified? While public reason can be an explanation, one has to question how culture expresses itself in terms of minority or majority status. What are the factors that express culture or cultural identity? These issues are throughout the chapter informed by the question of what deserves more importance: the group or the individual?

Connected with these questions, as also the construction of history, is the issue of negotiation of identity of members of different, but also of same religious traditions, a major issue raised in part II.

Individual, Church, and Community

As it stands, it is not enough to understand the construction of the self or the other with reference to the scriptures alone. Context is crucial for determining present identities, because it is here that mutual dialogue plays a creative role, and the polyfocality of actors' religious identities emerges. In reality, culture and religion are produced by different fields of discourse in which realities meet and are contested, rather than by a singular essentialist discourse. The respective repertories of different religious groups differ according to context and time, but they also come to share spaces. Their very overlapping proves to be most crucial. The perspective of plural or multiple identities enables us to argue for social constructions of self and other that lie beyond assumptions of primordialism. Plural identities imply, rather presuppose, ambivalence. Hence, the other is perceived in some ways to be part of the self. These ambivalences and interdependencies replace rigid dichotomies because pluralized group identities are entangled at several points of conjuncture.[16] Hence, identity is understood as a procedural event in the argument between self-reference and reference of the other, which can be changed without problems according to context. It can be described as situational, corporate or multiple, and it is open rather than a 'religious closure'. Identity matters in context, especially when it comes to cultural and religious encounter: reciprocity, dialogue, and oscillation between what is perceived as self and as other necessarily lead to cultural multi-dimensionality which can, indeed must, extend predetermined boundaries. Normative and hegemonic identity constructions are being shifted and displaced exactly at these points of friction, at the margins of the lived realities of collectives. Multiple affiliations and loyalties, code- and identity-switching processes are cases in point. The processes of shifting or oscillating are even more obvious between minority and majority who mutually conceptualize each other and form a complex cultural ensemble. 'Different social contexts certainly ask for the foregrounding of different identities: But at the same time, these identities are constantly changing according to their position within the universe of possible alternatives, defining and re-defining each other: identity is not a fixed, but a relational category', writes Margrit Pernau, suggesting that

[16] *Compare also* Ayse S. Caglar, 'Hyphenated Identities and the Limits of "Culture", in Tariq Modood and Pnina Werbner (eds), *The Politics of Multiculturalism,* 1997, pp. 169–85; Kingsley Purdam, 'Settler Political Participation: Muslim Local Councillors', in Wasif Shadid and Sjoerd van Koningsveld (eds), *Political Participation and Identities of Muslims in Non-Muslim States,* Kampen: Kok Pharos, 1996, pp. 129–43; also Wasif Shadid and Sjoerd van Koningsveld, 'Loyalty to a non-Muslim Government: An Analysis of Islamic Normative Discussions and of the Views of some Contemporary Islamicists', in Wasif Shadid and Sjoerd van Koningsveld (eds), *Political Participation and Identities of Muslims in Non-Muslim States,* 1996, pp. 84–114, who address the issue of the legal debate of Muslims in non-Muslim states.

multiple identities are linked with a multiple membership to different communities. How an individual (or a community) handles multiple identity on a social and personal level, especially in terms of integration and identity, is exemplified with Mirza Ghalib (1797–1869), Delhi's most famous poet. Questions are raised as to what do multiple identities contribute to religious pluralism, when can problems of mutual misunderstanding arise. Even though multiple identities do not offer an explanation or a solution, they go beyond the simple perception of regarding existing religions merely side by side or next to each other. They are overlapping and, though not possessing fixed boundaries, they can claim exclusiveness. Can religion then be considered an identity-subsuming factor?

A different but nevertheless related issue is that of the invisibility of religion in a plural context. '[...] under conditions of religious plurality, when religions with different appearances in public life come together, the norm of privatization and individualization may be used as a means of distinction towards those religions that do not (and for the moment cannot) adapt to this form. Individualization and privatization of religion then, paradoxically, may become an element of "cultural defence"', opines Monika-Wohlrab-Sahr. Religious privatization and individualization as a Luckmannian process result from a close link between religion and personal identity. Considering the increasing religious and cultural pluralization within European countries, individualization and privatization in the sense of 'discrete religion' can be seen as part of 'cultural defence'. This cultural defence becomes evident when considering the passionate debate about the headscarf in Germany and France. All of a sudden, the question arose as to how to manage visible signs of expressing religion or whether such a public expression of religiosity and its symbol represent a threat to secular European culture. How does this reaction relate to religious individualization, since religion has been simply seen in the process of secularization as a cultural heritage whence religion became invisible. Thus, religion intermingles with culturalization and may react in terms of cultural defence. However, invisibility of religion seems hardly possible in the South Asian context where the discourses are highly confessionalized.

As far as religious identity with reference to the individual and/or collective is concerned, the religious foundation of the individual identity may also be related to the concept of church and community when a national identity is constructed on the basis of religion. Sacred nationalism might negate the transcendental aspects but at the same time endows the nation with a transcendental quality. On the other hand, religious fundamentalism or political religion hegemonizes one religion, which also includes the denial to other religious traditions and their integration as 'sects' within the all-encompassing framework of one religion. Denial of plurality shows the negative construction of a singular approach, forced conversion being one channel. Seen from a theological angle, the need for conversion can be perceived as postulating the superiority of one religion over the other and hence denying plurality. But it can also be seen as a process of reconciliation between different religious traditions if the painful process of inter-religious dialogue is taken seriously. From the angle of the individual, the freedom to change one's religion forms an essential element of the freedom of religion, hence a core area of pluralism. It is in this context that Sudhir Chandra looks at Gandhi: 'Only involuntarily, in the manner of a rose, could one's life pave the way for another's conversion. In no way would Gandhi countenance a conversion consciously inspired by someone other than the proselyte. A true conversion had to be entirely voluntary.' The central question of Chandra's contribution then is whether denial of plurality can be seen in the denial of conversion, traced in the examination of Gandhi's position throughout his statements, speeches, and reactions especially towards Christian missionaries. Although it is argued that he considered conversion to be 'the deadliest poison that ever sapped the fountain of truth', he concedes to every individual the freedom 'to choose/change their religion'. Contradictions and vagueness emerge, however, when he still disapproves of Hindus becoming Christians, or vice versa, even though they are convinced of the other religion and its faith. Accordingly, one might conclude that Gandhi feared denationalization and cultural alienation through conversion. Viewed from this angle it is virtually impossible to consider conversion as denial of plurality.

These questions are intrinsically connected with part III.

Living Plurality

As far as this is concerned (in a plural and pluralist culture), it is positively received but also threatened. This is especially true for world religions, which cannot be reduced to one region or cultural tradition. The thesis of enculturation of 'great traditions' into local context underlines this presupposition. Thus the Chishti tradition, analysed by Zaheer Jafri. Tracing the history of the khanaqah at Salon he shows that several factors aided in its initial establishment, thus endowing the institution with pluralistic foundations. The khanaqah in Awadh, which stands in the Chishti-Nizami tradition goes back to Shaikh Pir Muhammad (AD 1585–1687). Concentrating on the development of the khanaqah and its rituals and ceremonies which certainly display a pluralistic character, Jafri shows how this centre of spread arranged its existence with its environment, not only with local officials, but also with the government, and what kind of status the institution acquired and how its status gradually changed. The rituals practised demonstrate 'adoption of local customs and accommodation of prevalent Sufi institutions'. This 'innovative flexibility' offers an eclectic position to the extent that the khanaqah transcends orthopraxy by developing a 'fine sensitivity to local norms'. But then again, this 'pluralist' practice may have owed something to its particular location, away from major political centres, apart from its (rather ambiguous) Chishti legacy. Eventually, the Chishti tradition faced primarily the main problems from other (Muslim) Sufi orders, such as the Qadiris and the puritanic Naqshbandis. Hence, structural topics such as resemblance between communities as well as folk religion are exemplifications for pluralism.

By the same token, localization and symbolic representation are crucial issues, because they ask as to what it is that places and spaces narrate, and how places are transformed into narration or even semiotic representation? Monica Juneja in her chapter discusses certain aspects of architecture in pre-colonial north India. 'A look at the mechanisms through which architectural form intervenes to make identities recognizable, to exhibit relationships, status, rank, to signify the coherence of a community, the force of an individual or the permanence of a power, would take us to the heart of issues clustering around the workings of architecture and the experience of plurality.' Indeed, buildings, their plans, and designs represent important elements of a high culture, mostly supported by authorities such as the state or social and political elites. But does a building stand only for an autonomous culture, or has it to be seen in a heterogeneous context, which includes cultures of non-elites, their beliefs, practices, traditions, relations between different communities and their intermingling, as well as their encounters? Juneja looks beyond the narratives and discourses on architecture which are often fixed and unchanging as it has been the case with 'Hindu' and 'Muslim' as constructed categories. The example of the Jama Masjid in Delhi illustrates that there has not been a specific or alleged plan for constructing a mosque in Islamic tradition. On the contrary, it demonstrates that its architecture evolved as incorporating factors depending on technology, climate, and regional tradition.[17]

---

[17] *Compare also* M. Bonine, 'The Morphogenesis of Iranian Cities', in *Annals of the Association of American Geographers*, 69, 1979, pp. 208–24; M. Bonine, 'The Sacred Direction

Furthermore, movement in a space, say during migration, through rituals or transmission of religious ideas and objects connected to it, seem to be fertile ground to elaborate on. Localization of religion can only occur if there are movements—through physical or normative changes—in a public space, in which prestige and power are constantly negotiated. Contested space is explored when looking at the definition and creation of boundaries—local and trans-local—since by implication all religions inevitably 'territorialize' themselves—even in the virtual space of World Wide Web. Multi-localization and polyfocality establish a very complex, multi-centred sacred geography. But the opposite is also possible: decentralized religious groups characterised by placelessness, virtuality or loose networks integrated by the charisma of spiritual leaders, often existent virtually, create and intensify but also shift loyalties and obligations through the power of imagination. Salil Misra's chapter on the world of Hindi and Urdu can be seen in this context when elaborating on language: 'Language emerges as a powerful vehicle of identity formation, promoting group solidarity. Language, under modern conditions (defined by, among other things, ideas of perpetual growth, literacy, mobility, and egalitarianism), acquires a power that it did not possess before. Along with culture and religion it emerges as a serious candidate for being a motivator of group formation and solidarity.' Hindi and Urdu, two distinct languages today, share a composite syncretic linguistic tradition. But how did a former common language develop into two linguistic branches? What did it entail in a social, political, and literary context and what factors influenced this division? Misra offers a survey focusing on the nineteenth and twentieth centuries, the modern influences, the development of the terms 'Hindi' and 'Urdu', problems of identification, linguistic purification and implications for creating a new nation, thereby considering language not 'only as a component of culture but as something that shaped and determined culture'. Keeping in mind that Urdu is not spoken exclusively by Muslims, neither is Hindi spoken by Hindus inclusively, language is used as the mere factor of identity. It is demonstrated that plurality is not only to be seen in terms of religion, often equated with syncretism. Language provides a pattern of syncretism and plurality as different aspects not necessarily shaping a unified pattern, as it is the case with Hindi and Urdu. This is polyfocality, multi-centredness, and placelessness in the best sense of the word.

---

and City Structure: A Preliminary Analysis of the Islamic Cities of Morocco', in *Muqarnas: An Annual on Islamic Art and Architecture*, 7, 1990, pp. 50–72.

To be sure, encounter, interaction, and pluralism, all go along with conflict, the major actor of the denial. Competitive or conflicting situations between different religions or between groups of the same religion can be distinguished and described, from a legal perspective, especially when it comes to violation of legal boundaries. But these conflicts do not necessarily end in violence. Accepted boundaries are conducive to peace, and recognized conflicts are in general the condition for tolerance.

Basically, a religious conflict can be answered from different perspectives: based on intra-religious pluralization it can lead to stigmatization and official oppression; a conflict based on inter-religious pluralization such as processes induced from outside a system; and a conflict based on extra-religious pluralization, such as religious fundamentalism competing with secular systems. A conflict can also be transformed into conflict management and conflict resolution, turning conflicts into creative channels of interaction and contributions, into the stability and cohesion of incremental societies, rather than pathological social diseases, or deviations.[18] Ashis Nandy tells the story of communal conflict in South Asia: 'These organizing myths or apocryphal stories work in two ways. Sometimes they supply a shorthand description of the primary concerns of the new theory; at other times they tell the story of the discovery in a way that hints at the latter's social relations and status in popular culture. In either case, they do what a physical or social theory by itself can never do; they ground it in the shared culture of a community; they humanize and socialize the theory.' To understand communal conflicts in South Asia different stories with different characters and qualities, represented by the candidates of the communal myth, tell their handling of traumas, relive fear of a communal conflict and reaction in these situations. Furthermore, it is shown what the heroes of the story can affect, whether they give confidence and trust, whether they are signals of solidarity or whether they act contradictorily or reflect experiences of political life. Nandy's intention is not to present these stories as explaining factor for violence. The idea is to go beyond the research of religious violence as 'an unrelieved catalogue of what human beings can do to each other', without falling into a 'backward-looking romanticism' that only refers to ordinary citizens.

Needless to say that socialization and transmission of knowledge epitomize all these issues raised and through a most complex procedure of dissemination render them into a normative discourse.

---

[18] It is therefore important to make the idea of 'religious war' a theme, in order to show what makes a war *religious* or what effect it has on the plural situation of a specific region.

PERSPECTIVE

To sum up, religious pluralism is more than mere diversity; it implies active engagement with plurality. It is not a given, but has to be created. It requires participation; and it is more than mere tolerance, because of its inherent active attempt to understand each other. And, it does not displace or eliminate deep religious commitments, but it is the encounter of commitments. The aim of the book is precisely to work towards these issues, towards mutuality as well as differences, hence towards po-lyphony of the histories of religion. Mere invocation of the concepts of multiculturalism and incantations of the mantras of pluralism will not achieve the vision that might lie behind such a volume. In the given situation, there is, beyond the historicization of the themes, a need to address how, in terms of concrete organizational and institutional ar-rangements, structures might be evolved that enable people who live by different and sometimes radically conflicting values and expressions of ultimate concern, to coexist and, if possible, not only to coexist, but also to cooperate, and to produce what may be called a theology of pluralism.[19]

This is even more important when it comes to minorities and majori-ties. I contend that in a situation where interactive mutualities exist between actors who perceive themselves in some way as equals, any kind of paternalism is bound to fail. Given that minority and majority form a very complex cultural ensemble, positions constantly have to be negoti-ated anew. In this process the rules of majority societies seem to be less binding and minority issues can unleash systemic debates, such as the one on religious education and dual citizenship in Germany, or the issue of laïcity in France. In the medium term such accommodations may be able to reconcile apparently intractable differences, so that eventually the (marginal) other will come to be situated in the midst of structures that are meaningful to him or her, that is, in European respective South Asian society. The religious repertory is without doubt flexible and adaptable enough to provide for this development, as several of the contributors to this volume make clear.

To reach towards an understanding of these evolving negotiations and discourses, an inter-cultural hermeneutic that interprets the encounter between different social realities is necessary. It can help to create space for comparison and critical evaluation. The marginal, i.e., the other, can help to set up a creative discourse, develop an aesthetic of liberation, and

[19] Cf. Diana L. Eck, 'The Christian Churches and the Plurality of religious Communi-ties', lecture delivered at Holy Cross Seminary Brooklin, MA, 5 October 2002.

demythologize stereotypical thought patterns. It seems paramount, though, not to approach the problematic of religious minorities and majorities merely from a normative standpoint; that is, it is important not to refer back to the scriptures alone. A normative approach on its own does not contribute to an understanding of the negotiation between majorities with minorities. Instead, the need is to accept the fact of discursive interdependency which actually leaves little room for ethnocentric universalism or a hermeneutic monologue that conceptualizes the other as a mere Non-Me. If we recognize that religious group-building processes respond to the wider cultural and political context, it becomes clear that religiosity is a symbolic expression of this process of negotiation, an interpretative context for describing and explaining social reality. Our task, then, is to contextualize historical and contemporary religious culture(s) and identit(ies) through a sensitive translation of locally given social and cultural codes.

I
LEGITIMIZATION OF PLURALITY

Historical Roots of Plurality in Europe

MARK HÄBERLEIN

INTRODUCTION

In the current debate on the admission of new countries to the European Union, the case of Turkey has received particular attention. Can an Islamic country, participants in the debate wonder, be regarded as part of Europe? Two eminent German historians, Hans-Ulrich Wehler and Heinrich August Winkler, do not think so. In an article published in the liberal weekly *Die Zeit*, Wehler made the case against Turkey for three reasons. First, contemporary Turkey does not qualify as a liberal democracy since the country had a strong Islamist movement, was still controlled by the military, and had a weak record on human rights. Second, Turkey's historical predecessor, the Ottoman empire, had been the foe of Christian Europe for centuries and did not share Europe's major historical achievements—the Graeco-Roman tradition, the Protestant Reformation, the Renaissance, the Enlightenment, and the Scientific Revolution. Third, Turks already constituted a weakly integrated 'foreign' element in many western European societies, and Wehler fears that after Turkey's admission into the European Union, millions of impoverished Anatolians would migrate to the European Union's commercial and industrial heartlands, thus exacerbating western Europe's already considerable social problems (Wehler 2002). Winkler concurs with Wehler's opinion that the political cultures of the European 'occident' and Turkey are fundamentally incompatible, since only western and central Europe have pursued a course towards the separation of church and state, pluralism and democracy in the medieval and modern periods (Winkler 2002).

While Wehler's and Winkler's assessment of contemporary Turkish politics and their construction of Islamic 'Otherness' with its xenophobic overtones are debatable in their own right, the most troubling aspect from the historian's point of view is their triumphalist historical narrative, which excludes Turkey from Europe's inexorable progress towards pluralism, human rights, and liberal democracy. Two of Germany's most distinguished senior historians have apparently never heard that the Ottoman empire until the late eighteenth century tolerated a much larger variety of religious beliefs than any Christian European country, and they fail to take notice of the myriad ways in which religion and politics remained intertwined in modern Europe.

My own reading of the historical literature suggests a more cautious interpretation of the historical roots of plurality in Europe. The transition from a unified Latin Christian tradition to a modern Europe of secularized, multi-confessional states, I argue, was not synonymous with the rise of tolerance and the triumph of pluralism. Instead, this transition, which mainly took place between the late fifteenth and the early nineteenth century, was more often than not accompanied by intolerance, persecution, and religious wars. The ambivalent dialectics of tolerance and intolerance, conformity and plurality become especially evident when we focus on what historians call the early modern period, that is the three centuries from the Protestant Reformation of the early sixteenth to the French Revolution of the late eighteenth century. At the beginning of the early modern era, a hitherto unified Latin Christian church broke apart, and the sixteenth and seventeenth centuries were characterized by the institutionalization of rivalling Christian churches in a process that has been labeled 'confessionalization'. While most Europeans clung to the idea of a confessionally homogeneous Christian state, some individuals began to propagate the concept of toleration, i.e. the acceptance of the existence of religious groups whose creed differed from that of the majority. Some early modern rulers adopted policies of toleration for economic and political reasons. Finally, from the late seventeenth century onwards there was a growing sense among politicians, jurists, and philosophical writers that the emerging modern state did not need religion and the church to legitimize its existence and secure its power. Radical thinkers began to argue for a separation of church and state and conceptualized religious liberty as an individual right. In the late eighteenth and nineteenth centuries, most European governments passed legislation which put the notion of a secular, confessionally neutral state into practice. This paper will examine these developments, focusing on central and western Europe, especially Britain, France, the Netherlands, and the German-speaking lands.[1]

THE MIDDLE AGES, THE REFORMATION,
AND CONFESSIONALIZATION

From the eleventh to the early sixteenth century, secular and ecclesiastical authorities in Europe asserted the unity of the Latin Christian church and used the powers at their disposal to subdue heretical groups like the Cathars and Albigensians in southern France, the Lollards in England, and the Hussites in Bohemia. There was a general agreement among late medieval theologians and jurists that heresy—the abandonment of the church's teachings—constituted a worse crime than heathenism, for religious dissent was constructed as rebellion against the political and social order. The establishment of the inquisition in the early thirteenth century was the strongest manifestation of the church's determination to enforce religious conformity.[2] While many churchmen and laypeople agreed that a reform of the late medieval church was necessary, there was also agreement that such a reform had to come from within the church. The great, but eventually unsuccessful reform councils of the fifteenth century had precisely this purpose. Attempts to revive Christian spirituality in the thirteenth to fifteenth centuries also reduced tolerance for unbelievers. Toleration of the largest non-Christian diaspora in Europe, the Jews, had traditionally been justified by Christian charity, the Augustinian notion that the Jews were witnesses to God's working in ancient times, and the belief that conversion of the Jews would usher in the Christian Millennium. Always confined to the margins of Christian society, the Jews had to confront increasing intellectual and popular anti-Judaism, epitomized in accusations of having murdered Christ, poisoning wells, and ritually killing Christians. Repeated waves of persecution and

[1] A full treatment of traditions of plurality in Europe, of course, would have to include Eastern Europe and the Mediterranean where Christians, Jews, and Muslims lived side by side for centuries. Henry Kamen, however, has recently emphasized the crucial difference between early modern northern Europe and its Atlantic colonies, 'where plurality of belief had slowly and painfully come to be accepted since the middle of the sixteenth century', and the Mediterranean, 'where plurality also existed but had never been officially accepted' (Kamen 2000: 251). By focusing on central and north-western Europe, therefore, I am dealing with those areas of the continent where concepts of toleration *and* practices of coexistence developed since the late Middle Ages.

[2] These developments are examined in Moore (1987); Nirenberg (1996); Waugh/Diehl (1996).

expulsion throughout western and central Europe during the later Middle Ages culminated in their expulsion from the kingdom of Spain in 1492.[3]

While the unity of Latin Christianity remained the overarching goal of most medieval rulers, writers, and churchmen, encounters with heretics and non-Christian groups forced intellectuals to cope with religious differences. As Cary J. Nederman (2000) has recently shown, a significant number of medieval writers voiced doubts about the efficacy of religious persecution and counselled policies of forbearance and toleration. Thus, writers like Peter Abelard in the twelfth century and Ramon Llull in the thirteenth century composed inter-religious dialogues advocating reasoned debate and free expression of sentiments. The twelfth-century English 'humanist' churchman John of Salisbury adopted a sceptical stance. According to him, the limitations of the human mind made the discovery of absolute truth very difficult if not impossible and therefore required freedom of expression and criticism. Medieval travellers like Wilhelm von Rubruck, who acquired first-hand knowledge of the Mongol empire, encountered a far greater variety of ethnic and religious groups than in any European society and learned to come to terms with adherents of other faiths. The fourteenth-century jurist and political thinker Marsiglio of Padua advocated a separation between 'public' political life and 'private' religious belief that opened the doors for the participation of non-believers in civic life. The fifteenth-century bishop and church reformer Nicholas of Cusa, finally, argued that a 'variety of rites', i.e. differing regional and national expressions of faith, were permissible within a broad, latitudinarian Christianity which agreed on a few basic teachings like monotheism or the Holy Trinity. A common trait of all these writers, according to Nederman, was:

Their recognition that by God's own ordination, the human world is composed of difference.... Tolerance is required because intolerant practices are not and cannot be efficacious in light of some significant and irremovable dimension of human existence. Toleration is, therefore, not a good or and end in itself, but a course of action or inaction sanctioned, ultimately, by God himself inasmuch as He created and endowed humanity with certain capacities and frailties (Nederman 2000: 4–5).[4]

Like earlier reform movements, Martin Luther's challenge to the Roman Catholic church in the early sixteenth century initially came from within

---

[3] On the Jews in medieval society, see J. Cohen (1982); Stow (1992); M.R. Cohen (1994).

[4] On medieval concepts of tolerance see also the contributions of Cary J. Nederman, Stephen Lahey, and Kate Langdon Forhan in Laursen/Nederman (1996) and the essays in Patschovsky/Zimmermann (1998).

the church. Despite the animosity of pope and emperor, however, the quick dissemination of Luther's new doctrines through the recently invented printing press and the protection the reformer received from powerful princes resulted in the establishment of a second Christian faith, which took hold in large parts of Germany, Scandinavia, and Poland. Several decades after Luther, John Calvin of Geneva initiated a second reformation in parts of Switzerland, France, the Netherlands, Scotland, and Germany. By the latter half of the sixteenth century, the unity of Latin Christianity had been irrevocably shattered. The now fragmented religious landscape of Europe was made up of three large confessional groups—Catholicism, Lutheranism, and Calvinism—and a host of smaller Protestant groups such as the anabaptists and spiritualists (Brady/Oberman/Tracy 1995).

What is important to stress here is that the new Protestant churches— like the old Roman Catholic church—were fundamentally intolerant. Luther, Calvin, and their followers initially demanded toleration for themselves, but their belief in the absolute authority of the Bible, their conviction that their interpretation of the Scripture was the correct one, and their self-perception as instruments and executors of divine will led them to advocate the persecution of 'heretics' like the anabaptists or anti-trinitarians, i.e. persons who did not believe in the trinity of the Christian god (Guggisberg 1984: 62; Schreiner 1990: 476–8). The attitude of Protestant reformers towards the Jews also hardened once they realized that the Jews were unwilling to accept the Gospel message, which the Reformation had now restored to its original purity and true meaning (Oberman 1984). In many parts of Europe, Catholics and Protestants engaged in massive violence against one another. France and the Netherlands experienced lengthy religious wars in the late sixteenth century and much of central Europe was ravaged by the Thirty Years' War between 1618 and 1648. Like Luther (who introduced the word 'tolerance' into the German language), most sixteenth-century writers thought that 'religious diversity was nothing positive in itself and was only to be tolerated in the short run, in order that true faith might eventually be victorious.' (Grell/Scribner 1996: 6; cf. Oberman 1996).

The few writers in Reformation Europe who advocated religious toleration on principle mainly came from a Christian humanist background. The great Dutch humanist Erasmus of Rotterdam (1466–1536) tried to promote Christian peace and 'concord' and rally the emerging religious camps around an undogmatic, latitudinarian Christianity. Most theological disputes of his time, Erasmus thought, were about minor, non-essential points that should properly be left to everyone's own judgement. Erasmus's reputation as a champion of religious toleration, however, is tarnished by his irrational hatred of the Jews (Guggisberg 1984: 69–76; Schreiner 1990: 474–6; Oberman 1996: 26). The mystic spiritualist Sebastian Franck (1499–1542) argued that God's will was only imperfectly reflected in the Bible; for Franck the true church was not an external institution but the invisible community of devout souls. The Savoyard humanist and biblical scholar Sebastian Castellio (1515–63) wrote several elaborate defences of religious toleration which stressed the importance of human reason in discovering the divine will and insisted that only God could know the heretics and punish them on the day of the last judgement. Therefore, it was wrong for humans to anticipate divine judgement and kill alleged heretics. Castellio's ideas were later adopted by champions of religious toleration in the Netherlands and England.[5] But these advocates of toleration, who emphasized the limitations of human knowledge of the divine will, characteristically were religious outsiders and spent most of their lives in exile. 'The development of a modern liberal society,' historian Andrew Pettegree has written, 'has taught us to admire tolerance above almost any other principle of social interaction. But in the early modern period it was only ever a loser's creed; and one which ... could easily be abandoned when yesterday's persecuted minority became the day's dominant elite' (Pettegree 1996: 198).

The new religious diversity of post-Reformation Europe thus did not usher in an age of tolerance, but an era of confessionalization. This term, which has been adopted by many historians of the early modern period, implies that the development of the three major Christian churches shows a number of parallels. In each case, the process of confessionalization began with the adoption of confessions in the original sense of the term: statements of faith and doctrinal creed like the Lutheran *Confessio Augustana* of 1530, the Reformed *Confessio Helvetica* (posterior) of 1566, and the Catholic 'Professio Fidei', issued by Pope Pius IV after the conclusion of the reform council of Trent in 1564. These confessional statements had the dual function of internally defining the true church and delineating the external boundaries of the community of believers. Whereas the term 'confession' originally signified the personal act of believing, it came to acquire a social significance and eventually encompassed the organized totality of believers.

Moreover, Catholic, Lutheran, and Calvinist European rulers took a number of measures to implement the newly defined creeds in their

[5] See Guggisberg (1984): 80–102; Guggisberg (1996); Furcha (1996); Schreiner (1990): 483–4.

respective countries and territories: they instituted new religious bodies like provincial councils, synods, and consistories; controlled clergymen and laypeople through visitations; founded new seminaries and universities to improve the education of the clergy; engaged in religious propaganda and censorship; promoted the printing and distribution of religious works like catechisms, sermons, and hymn books; and encouraged specific confessional rituals like the Catholic processions and pilgrimages. All these measures were designed to ensure that believers internalized confessional norms and values. Catholic and Protestant authorities shared the basic goal of creating a confessionally homogeneous citizenry. Minorities like the Austrian Protestants, Dutch Calvinists, French Huguenots and Mennonites were persecuted and often expelled. During the confessional period, the state essentially retained its sacral character and harnessed the resources and disciplinary mechanisms of the church to his own.[6] The notion of the sacred, Christian state manifested itself in a generally repressive attitude towards various forms of deviance—whether religious, sexual, or social—because toleration of the sins of individuals was thought to bring divine wrath down on whole communities. Thus, it is no coincidence that the confessional age was also an era of intensified persecution of 'sodomites' (a term for sexual deviants), gypsies, and witches (Oberman 1996; Scribner 1996).

Confessional competition and the religious wars of the sixteenth and seventeenth centuries, however, seldom ended in a clear victory for one side or the other. Therefore, religious peace settlements became necessary to prevent religious struggles from becoming completely dysfunctional and establish a working relationship between Catholics and Protestants. In the Holy Roman empire, the religious peace of Augsburg (1555) recognized the Lutheran faith in the imperial constitution and affirmed the princes' right to determine the faith of their subjects. The Peace of Westphalia, which ended the Thirty Years' War in 1648, also included Calvinism among the confessions sanctioned under the imperial constitution and took elaborate measures to guarantee the confessional status quo. In France, King Henry IV sought to end the religious wars by issuing the Edict of Nantes in 1598. The royal edict granted Protestants quite extensive legal rights but limited their worship to a number of specified places (Christin 1997; cf. Benedict 1996).

Moreover, in Germany, France, and the Netherlands, Catholics and Protestants continued to live side by side in a number of cities and towns

---

[6] My account of confessionalization relies particularly on Reinhard (1981, 1989) and Schilling (1995). For a concise summary of the concept and its evolution, see Ehrenpreis/Lotz-Heumann (2002: 62–79).

throughout the period of confessionalization and religious strife. Recent scholarship has shown that actual relationships between the two groups were often remarkably peaceful and cooperative. The peace settlements of Augsburg and Westphalia officially recognized the bi-confessional nature of several German imperial cities and instituted mechanisms for power-sharing. They also affirmed an individual's right to emigrate from a territory in which he could not practise his religious belief.[7] While Jews were denied equal rights of citizenship virtually everywhere, several case studies have revealed more regular and intimate economic interactions and social contacts between Jews and Christians than scholars have long assumed (cf. Häberlein/Schmölz-Häberlein 2002). Studies of religious coexistence suggest, in short, that toleration was not merely a matter of philosophical ideas, but evolved as a social practice in numerous early modern communities.

Still, it can hardly be denied that the religious peace settlements of the sixteenth and seventeenth centuries were documents of intolerance rather than statements of tolerance. They regarded religious plurality as a necessary evil eventually to be overcome by the restoration of a unified church. Thus, the religious peace of Augsburg could not prevent the Thirty Years' War, and the Edict of Nantes was revoked by King Louis XIV in 1685. This revocation, which sent several hundred thousand French Protestants into exile,[8] also highlights the fact that the absolutist European monarchies were fundamentally intolerant and continued to regard confessional unity as an important foundation of state power (Schreiner 1990: 485–9). Generally speaking, religious plurality usually prevailed in states and territories with a weak central authority (like the Netherlands) or where noble estates formed a strong counterweight to princely government (like Poland and Bohemia before the Thirty Years' War).

In England, the civil war between royal and parliamentary factions of the 1640s and the subsequent republican period of the 1650s were accompanied by a massive output of tracts and pamphlets advocating religious freedom and toleration for dissenters. New religious groups

---

[7] Case studies of confessional coexistence in early modern France and Germany include Hanlon (1993), Warmbrunn (1983) and François (1991). Benjamin Kaplan (2002) has recently demonstrated how the Dutch *schuilkerken* (house chapels) and their counterparts elsewhere in Europe served to contain religious dissenters 'within spaces demarcated as private' while at the same time they helped to preserve 'the monopoly of a community's official church in the public sphere. By maintaining a semblance of religious unity, they neutralized the threat posed by dissent to the identity and thus to the very integrity of communities' (1036).

[8] See Duchhardt (1985); von Thadden/Magdelaine (1985).

like the Quakers emerged from this hotbed of religious debate, but as Andrew Murphy has recently demonstrated, it was not the force of new ideas but the victory of the New Model Army that decisively advanced tolerationist ideas in mid-seventeenth-century England. In his *Instrument of Government* (1653), the Puritan army leader and Lord Protector Oliver Cromwell declared:

That such as profess faith in God by Jesus Christ (though differing in judgement from the doctrine, worship or discipline publicly held forth) shall not be restrained from, but shall be protected in the profession of the faith and exercise of their religion; so as they abuse not this liberty to the civil injury of others and to the actual disturbance of the public peace on their parts: provided this liberty be not extended to Popery or Prelacy, nor to such as, under the profession of Christ, hold forth and practice licentiousness (Murphy 2001: 119).

The restoration of the Stuart monarchy in 1660, however, annulled most of these gains for religious liberty, and the English Parliament re-established the public monopoly of the Anglican church as well as legal restrictions on religious dissenters. After the Glorious Revolution had toppled the regime of the Catholicizing Stuart monarch James II the *Act of Toleration* (1689) eventually struck a compromise between Anglicanism, which remained the established church, and Protestant dissenters, who could now obtain licences for their own houses of worship. Catholic worship, however, remained excluded from the public sphere (Coffey 2000; Murphy 2001). Despite the actual shortcomings of this religious settlement, eighteenth-century European writers often praised religious liberty in England as the model to be emulated. 'If there were only one religion in England,' the Frenchman Voltaire wrote, 'there would be danger of despotism, if there were two they would cut each other's throats, but there are thirty, and they live in peace' (quoted in Fitzpatrick, 2000: 42).

TOLERATION, REASON OF STATE, AND THE ENLIGHTENMENT

By the later part of the seventeenth century, a number of jurists and political theorists, taking their clue from the Italian Renaissance thinker Niccolò Machiavelli, argued that the policies of a state should not be guided by transcendent religious goals and purposes but rather by the state's own political interests. The new political doctrine of the 'reason of state' saw the preservation and improvement of the country through prudent politics and strategic government planning as an end in itself and partially emancipated the political from the religious realm. Even though proponents of 'reason of state' rarely advocated religious liberty,[9] they advanced a number of arguments for the limited toleration of dissenters and religious minorities (Weber 2000).

First, jurists, politicians, and philosophers now argued that the acceptance of religious diversity was necessary for the internal pacification of countries torn by religious strife, since the experience of countries like France during the religious wars had proven that enforced religious conformity divided the populace and threatened to destroy the nation. Second, advocates of 'reason of state' discussed economic motives for granting religious toleration. In their view, religious dissenters could be useful subjects, especially if they possessed valuable professional skills, capital, and trade connections. A plurality of religions might lead to beneficial competition, since all religious groups would strive to prove they were loyal and productive subjects. Advocates of toleration frequently cited the example of the unparalleled economic prosperity of the Netherlands, a small country in which the Calvinist authorities tolerated Catholics, Mennonites, and Jews (Schreiner 1990: 537).[10] This

[9] A special case is that of the French philosopher Jean Bodin (1530–96). In his political treatise *Six livres de la république* (1576), Bodin, like most of his contemporaries, argued that 'a single established religion is to be preferred since religious uniformity strengthens the state'. Limited toleration of different religions should only be granted where they already existed (as in France during Bodin's time). In his later *Colloquium heptaplomeres* (1588), however, a fictional discussion between seven representatives of different religions, Bodin took a more positive view of inter-religius dialogue 'as a possible peaceful means of confirming one's own religious beliefs'. For Bodin, Gary Remer argues, 'religious differences should not be retained for the sake of any single religion but because they, collectively in their opposition to each other, contain the whole truth' (Remer 1996; quotes on 122f., 127; cf. Schreiner 1990: 489–91).

[10] The perception of the Dutch republic as a haven of toleration by many foreign observers coincided with the self-perception of many seventeenth-century Dutchmen and has become a standard feature of the historical literature on the Dutch 'golden age'. Recent research clearly demonstrates, however, that Dutch ruling elites adopted policies of toleration out of pragmatism and expediency rather than principled commitment. While the Reformed church enjoyed the status of a privileged 'public church', Catholics were officially prohibited from engaging in religious activities but found ways to practise their faith in private or semi-public spaces. Relations between members of different confessions were characterized by both cooperation and conflict. In addition, recent scholarship stresses the multiplicity of local and regional variations in the politically decentralized Dutch Republic, with some communities taking a liberal attitude towards dissident religious practices and others engaging in at least sporadic persecution of dissent. 'It was not religious diversity itself that marked out the United Provinces in Europe', Willem Frijhoff has noted, 'for it could also be found in England or in Switzerland, nor official toleration, because it was better organized in France (with the Edict of Nantes 1598), in confessionalised Germany, or even in Poland. It is the combination of both these characteristics that made the United Provinces unique: a tacit toleration of religious diversity that was allowed to

economic line of reasoning presented religious toleration as a pragmatic necessity, not as a human right.

Third, overseas expansion, colonization, and maritime trade had multiplied European contacts with other peoples and civilizations, and there was a growing awareness among informed Europeans that some societies—the Ottoman empire, Mughal India, imperial China—allowed their subjects far more extensive religious freedom than was known anywhere in Christian Europe. To the surprise of European observers, religious toleration seemed to promote rather than endanger the internal peace and stability of these empires. Several eighteenth-century authors used the literary technique of portraying religious conditions in Europe through the eyes of fictive non-European observers. In his *Persian Letters* of 1721, the French philosopher Montesquieu let his learned Persian traveller remark that no other religion experienced as many civil wars as Christianity because everybody who came up with a new idea was automatically denounced as a heretic and persecuted. Montesquieu's countryman Voltaire claimed that '[t]he Turkish empire is filled with Jacobins, Nestorians, Christians of St John, Jews, Gebers, Banyans and various others; and yet their annals make no mention of any revolt excited by the toleration of all these different religions. Go to India, Persia or Tartary,' he continued, 'and you will find the same religious toleration and civil tranquility' (quoted in Grell/Porter 2000: 90).

These observations led some writers to propose the dissociation of religious questions from public life. While the public monopoly of the state church was to be maintained, private beliefs of individuals should be tolerated. Finally, a few writers like the German philosopher Gottfried Wilhelm Leibniz (1646–1716) continued to search for ways to bridge the gulf that separated the Christian confessions by emphasizing the fundamental convictions that all Christians held in common.[11] Late seventeenth-century thinkers like the German jurist Samuel Pufendorf (1632–94) and the English philosopher John Locke (1632–1704) conceptualized churches as essentially voluntary associations situated between the public and the private sphere. For Locke, liberty of conscience was

---

flourish as long as the necessary concord between believers did not endanger the unity of the body politic and the civic community'. See Bergsma (1995); Berkvens-Stevelinck et al. (1997); Hsia/van Nierop (2002); Frijhoff quote on 32.

[11] 'For Leibniz', Sally Jenkinson (1999: 177) argues, 'toleration is about negotiating unity, not accommodating diversity. Accordingly, he reformulates for Germany a revised, neo-Platonic foundation for a reunited empire. For that reason he expects the elite minds of the age to demonstrate their political support by compromising on details of religious doctrine'.

'every man's natural right', while the power of the state was limited to external affairs and government existed essentially to guarantee security, peace, and the rule of law, thus enabling individual citizens to realize their personal rights. This included liberty of conscience and free exercise of religion, as long as this liberty did not endanger the rights of others. While Locke's concept of toleration extended to Jews, Muslims, and other non-Christian religions, it explicitly excluded atheists because for Locke religion remained the foundation of civil society, and everybody had a duty before God to care for his own soul. In this respect, the French philosopher Pierre Bayle (1647–1706) went further than his English contemporary. For Bayle, the human conscience was exclusively a matter of personal, inner spirituality; religious truths were always subjective and could never be proven rationally. The differences among human beings therefore were the natural source of a plurality that included atheists and unbelievers. The radical freethinker Baruch Spinoza, finally, who had been expelled from Amsterdam's Jewish community for his heterodox theological views, argued for the widest possible freedom of thought and expression and wished to see 'state religion' reduced to a few basic, non-dogmatic (and even non-Christian) moral principles. While they developed different arguments for toleration, Locke, Bayle, and Spinoza shared the notion that liberty of conscience was an individual human right and religion essentially a private matter (Guggisberg 1984: 177–87, 199–206, 215–25; Dreitzel 1995; Laursen 1996; Israel 2000).

The essential arguments for religious tolerance and liberty of conscience had thus been advanced by 1700, and the eighteenth-century enlightenment thinkers contributed to the debate mainly in two ways. First, they linked the arguments for toleration to an increasingly strident anti-clericalism, as evident in Voltaire's *Traité sur la tolérance* (1763). From the nature of its teachings, Voltaire claimed, Christianity should be the most tolerant of religions; in practice, however, it was the most intolerant. For many enlightenment thinkers, religion was no more than a system of rational norms and moral laws, while miracles, supernatural events, and theological speculations were denounced as mere superstitions. A few radical French *philosophes* openly embraced atheism, but the enlightenment as a whole was not a purely secular movement. Most English and virtually all German enlightenment thinkers, for example, continued to argue within a fundamentally Christian context. 'What the vast majority of eighteenth-century writers were utterly unwilling to countenance,' according to Jonathan Israel, 'was a toleration of ideas which deviate from the core tenets of revealed religion' (2000: 102; cf. Schreiner 1990: 500–1; Fitzpatrick 2000: 40–43, 46–56).

Second, the enlightenment heightened public awareness for arguments in favour of toleration, which increasingly became the common stock of opinion among an educated European public. Religious toleration and liberty of conscience were now widely discussed in journals, magazines, public speeches, clubs, and coffee houses and became linked in public debate to other individual rights such as free speech and freedom of the press (Grell/Porter 2000). In the late eighteenth century, these arguments found their way into public law as well. Early in the century, only the Netherlands, England, Prussia, and some other German states had granted limited toleration to religious minorities, and in all these states a single church continued to hold a monopoly of public worship. 'Early-modern toleration edicts in the German lands,' Joachim Whaley has argued, 'were almost invariably granted from above for largely pragmatic reasons.' In the Prussia of King Frederick II (1740–86) as in other eighteenth-century German territories, 'religious toleration was for the most part still a political regime of licences or decrees granted by royal fiat to communities or groups' (2000: 184–5). In 1781–82, Austria, long a stronghold of Catholic confessionalism, extended toleration to Protestants, Greek Orthodox, and Jews in Emperor Joseph II's famous religious patents. Whereas Catholicism remained the dominant public religion in Austria, the Prussian religious edict of 1788 went a step further and granted Lutherans, Catholics, and Calvinists full legal equality, while smaller sects and religious groups like the Mennonites, Moravians, and Jews were also tolerated. In its common law code of 1794, Prussia then proclaimed complete freedom of worship and religious choice for all subjects. Most other German states followed this example in the early nineteenth century (Schreiner 1990: 506–8, 540–7).

In France, the Protestant Huguenots obtained religious toleration once more in 1787, after more than a century of exile and persecution. After the French Revolution, the constitutional assembly proclaimed complete religious freedom in 1791 (Fitzpatrick 2000: 34, 55; Linton 2000: 171–2). Even before the French Revolution, the independent United States of America had adopted the principle of religious liberty. Here, the Virginians Thomas Jefferson and James Madison took the lead by drafting the *Virginia Declaration of Religious Freedom* (1786) and the First Amendment to the Constitution (1791) (Peterson/Vaughan 1988). The American example had considerable impact in European intellectual circles. In Great Britain, which still conceived of itself as a Protestant nation throughout the eighteenth century, Catholics obtained full legal rights only in 1828.

All these legal measures reflected two fundamental insights: the first was that the state's responsibility did not extend to the defence of universal religious truths or the promotion of the eternal welfare of its subjects' souls. Instead, the state's purposes were limited to temporal affairs, especially the guarantee of internal peace, public order, and the rule of law. Second, the search for divine truth was now conceived a personal, private matter that should be left to each person's individual conscience. Liberty of conscience ceased to be a privilege granted by a ruler at his own pleasure and became an inalienable natural right. Consequently, the liberal constitutional movements of ninteenth-century Europe made toleration one of their guiding principles and included liberty of conscience and the legal equality of religious groups in virtually every catalogue of civic and religious liberties. The postulate of toleration was now extended to all areas of public life in which different world views and movements coexisted and competed with one another, such as parties and political movements. In this way, toleration and pluralism became fundamental principles of the modern constitutional state in Europe (Schreiner 1990: 564–70).

PLURALISM AND SECULARIZATION

The emergence of pluralism is often linked to the process of secularization, broadly conceived as the abandonment of transcendent religious orientations by individuals, social groups, and whole societies. For Max Weber, secularization meant the 'disenchantment of the world', the replacement of religious dogma and metaphysical world views by non-confessional rational principles. According to modern sociological definitions, the concept of secularization implies that religion as a fundamental, all-encompassing world view for most people has been replaced by other primary identifications (such as nationalism), while the churches have become specific functional institutions or 'sub-systems' in modern societies. In this strict sense, secularization and the growth of plurality were indeed intimately linked. Only when modern states ceased to define themselves as confessional, when the state's purposes were separated from transcendent religious purposes did religious toleration and pluralism become possible. If the concept of secularization is broadened into a general explanatory concept for all the major rationalizing and modernizing tendencies in Europe over the past three centuries, as in some philosophies of history, however, its relationship to the growth of pluralism appears less clear-cut. First, we have seen that the major arguments for religious toleration and liberty of conscience were developed in the early modern period within an essentially

Christian context, and leading advocates of toleration in the sixteenth and seventeenth centuries argued on biblical grounds. They quoted Christ's commandment to love one's neighbour and pointed out that God had reserved the final judgement on all human beings to himself. Second, Hartmut Lehmann has recently emphasized that the secularization of modern Europe was hardly a linear process. Instead, a number of Protestant and Catholic religious movements have sought to counter the secularizing and rationalizing tendencies in modern European societies. Since the eighteenth century, Europe experienced numerous religious revivals, awakenings, and reform movements, beginning with central European pietism and the evangelical awakening in Great Britain associated with the names of George Whitefield and John Wesley (Ward 1992). The study of these movements has led Lehmann to suggest that the concept of secularization should be supplemented by the notion of 're-christianization', which may well be an ongoing process (Lehmann 1997). Parts of Eastern Europe experienced a period of 're-christianization' following the collapse of the Communist regimes in 1989–91, and after the terrorist attacks on New York City and Washington D.C. on 11 September 2001, the Christian churches in Europe were suddenly reported to be filled with people again. While there is reason to doubt that this was more than a short-lived phenomenon, it nevertheless indicates that the Christian faith continues to remain an important orientation for a great number of Europeans—if only in times of crisis.

Finally, the experience of the Jews in modern Europe clearly shows that secularization was not synonymous with rationalization in Max Weber's sense of the term. From the late eighteenth century, Jews were included in the enlightened demand for religious toleration, and they gained full legal equality in most central and western European states until 1870. Legal emancipation did not preclude continuing social discrimination, however, and the late nineteenth century saw the rise of modern anti-semitism, which integrated older religious anti-Jewish stereotypes into a new racial ideology (Schreiner 1990: 575). The rise of National Socialism in Germany and the European Holocaust of 1939–45, of course, were the great denial of toleration and plurality in twentieth-century European history. Civil wars and 'ethnic cleansing' in Yugoslavia during the 1990s as well as the recent emergence of right-wing populist leaders on the political stage, who try to capitalize on irrational anti-foreign and anti-Semitic sentiments in their respective countries, also show that modern, secularized societies continue to retain profoundly irrational elements. Plurality thus remains a contested tradition in contemporary Europe.

BIBLIOGRAPHY

Benedict, Philip, Un roi, une loi, deux fois: Parameters for the History of Catholic-Reformed Co-existence in France, 1555–1685, in Ole Peter Grell and Bob Scribner (eds), *Tolerance and Intolerance in the European Reformation*, Cambridge: Cambridge University Press, 1996, 65–93.

Bergsma, Wiebe, 'Church, State and People', in Karel Davids and Jan Lucassen (eds), A *Miracle Mirrored: The Dutch Republic in European Perspective*, Cambridge: Cambridge University Press, 1995, 195–207.

Berkvens-Stevelinck, C., Jonathan I. Israel, G.H.M. Meyjes (Posthumous) (eds), *The Emergence of Tolerance in the Dutch Republic*, Leiden/New York/Cologne: Brill, 1997.

Brady, Thomas A., Heiko A. Oberman, and James D. Tracy (eds), *Handbook of European History 1400–1600. Late Middle Ages, Renaissance and Reformation*, 2 vols, Leiden: Brill, 1995.

Christin, Olivier, *La paix de religion. L'autonomisation de la raison politique au XVIe siècle*, Paris: Seuil, 1997.

Coffey, John, *Persecution and Toleration in Protestant England, 1558–1689*, Harlow, England: Pearson, 2000.

Cohen, Jeremy, *The Friars and the Jews: The Evolution of Medieval Anti-Judaism*, Ithaca: Cornell University Press, 1982.

Cohen, Mark R., *Under Crescent and Cross: The Jews in the Middle Ages*, Princeton: Princeton University Press, 1994.

Creppell, Ingrid, 'Locke on Toleration: The Transformation of Constraint', *Political Theory*, 24 (1996), 200–29.

Dreitzel, Horst, 'Gewissensfreiheit und soziale Ordnung. Religionstoleranz als Problem der politischen Theorie am Ausgang des 17. Jahrhunderts', *Politische Vierteljahresschrift*, 36 (1995), 3–34.

Duchhardt, Heinz (ed.), *Der Exodus der Hugenotten. Die Aufhebung des Edikts von Nantes 1685 als europäisches Ereignis*, Cologne et al.: Böhlau, 1985.

Ehrenpreis, Stefan and Ute Lotz-Heumann, *Reformation und konfessionelles Zeitalter*, Darmstadt: WBG, 2002.

Fitzpatrick, Martin, 'Toleration and the Enlightenment Movement', in Ole Peter Grell and Roy Porter (eds), *Toleration in Enlightenment Europe*, Cambridge: Cambridge University Press, 2000, 23–68.

François, Etienne, *Die unsichtbare Grenze. Protestanten und Katholiken in Augsburg, 1648–1806*, Sigmaringen: Thorbecke, 1991.

Furcha, E.J., ' "Turks and Heathen Are Our Kin": The Notion of Tolerance in the Works of Hans Denck and Sebastian Franck', in Cary J. Nederman and John Christian Laursen (eds), *Difference and Dissent: Theories of Toleration in Medieval and Early Modern Europe*, Lanham, Maryland. et al.: Rowman & Littlefield, 1996, 83–97.

Grell, Ole Peter and Bob Scribner (eds), *Tolerance and Intolerance in the European Reformation*, Cambridge: Cambridge University Press, 1996.

Grell, Ole Peter and Roy Porter (eds), *Toleration in Enlightenment Europe,* Cambridge: Cambridge University Press, 2000.

Guggisberg, Hans R., *Religiöse Toleranz. Dokumente zur Geschichte einer Forderung,* Stuttgart-Bad Cannstatt: Frommann-Holzboog, 1984.

Guggisberg, Hans R., 'Tolerance and intolerance in sixteenth-century Basle', in Ole Petre Grell and Bob Scribner (eds), *Tolerance and Intolerance in the European Reformation,* Cambridge: Cambridge University Press, 1996, 145–63.

Hanlon, Gregory, *Confession and Community in Seventeenth-Century France. Catholic and Protestant Coexistence in Aquitaine,* Philadelphia: University of Pennsylvania Press, 1993.

Häberlein, Mark and Michaela Schmölz-Häberlein, 'Competition and Cooperation: The Ambivalent Relationship between Jews and Christians in Early Modern Germany and Pennsylvania', in *The Pennsylvania Magazine of History and Biography,* 126, 3 (2002), 409–36.

Hsia, Ronnie Po-Chia and Henk van Nierop (eds), *Calvinism and Religious Toleration in the Dutch Golden Age,* Cambridge: Cambridge University Press, 2002.

Israel, Jonathan I., 'Spinoza, Locke and the Enlightenment Battle for Toleration', in Ole Peter Grell and Roy Porter (eds), *Toleration and Enlightenment Europe,* Cambridge: Cambridge University Press, 2000, 102–13.

Jenkinson, Sally L., Bayle, and Leibniz: Two Paradigms of Tolerance and Some Reflections on Goodness without God', in John Christian Laursen (ed.), *Religious Toleration: 'The Variety of Rites' from Cyrus to Defoe,* New York: St. Martin's Press, 1999, 176–89.

Kamen, Henry, 'Inquisition, Tolerance and Liberty in Eighteenth-century Spain', in Ole Peter Grell and Roy Porter (eds), *Toleration and Enlightenment Europe,* Cambridge: Cambridge University Press, 2000, 250–8.

Kaplan, Benjamin J., 'Fictions of Privacy: House Chapels and the Spatial Accommodation of Religious Dissent in Early Modern Europe', *American Historical Review,* 107, 4 (2002), 1031–64.

Kautz, Stephen, 'Liberalism and the Idea of Toleration', *American Journal of Political Science,* 37 (1993), 610–32.

Laursen, John Christian, 'Spinoza on Toleration: Arming the State and Reining in the Magistrate', in Cary J. Nederman and John Christian Laursen (eds), *Difference and Dissent: Theories of Toleration in Medieval and Early Modern Europe,* Lanham, Maryland. et al.: Rowman & Littlefield, 1996, 185–204.

Lehmann, Hartmut (ed.), *Säkularisierung, Dechristianisierung, Rechristianisierung im neuzeitlichen Europa,* Göttingen: Vandenhoeck & Ruprecht, 1997.

Linton, Marisa, 'Citizenship and Religious Toleration in France', in Ole Peter Grell and Roy Porter (eds), *Toleration and Enlightenment Europe,* Cambridge: Cambridge University Press, 2000, 157–74.

Moore, Robert I., *The Formation of a Persecuting Society: Power and Deviance in Western Europe, 950–1250,* Oxford: Blackwell, 1987.

Murphy, Andrew R., *Conscience and Community: Revisiting Toleration and Dissent in*

Seventeenth-Century Europe and America, University Park, Pennsylvania: Pennsylvania State University Press, 2001.

Nederman, Cary J., *Worlds of Difference. European Discourses of Toleration, c. 1100– c. 1550,* University Park, Pennsylvania: Pennsylvania State University Press, 2000.

Nederman, Cary J. and John Christian Laursen (eds), *Difference and Dissent: Theories of Toleration in Medieval and Early Modern Europe,* Lanham, Maryland et al.: Rowman & Littlefield, 1996.

Nirenberg, David, *Communities of Violence: Persecution of Minorities in the Middle Ages,* Princeton: Princeton University Press, 1996.

Oberman, Heiko A., *The Roots of Anti-Semitism in the Age of the Renaissance and Reformation,* Philadelphia: Fortress Press, 1984.

Oberman, Heiko A., 'The Travail of Tolerance: Containing Chaos in Early Modern Europe', in Ole Peter Grell and Bob Scribner (eds), *Tolerance and Intolerance in the European Reformation,* Cambridge: Cambridge University Press, 1996, 13–31.

Patschovsky, Alexander and Harald Zimmermann (eds), *Toleranz im Mittelalter,* Sigmaringen: Thorbecke, 1998.

Peterson, Merrill D. and Robert C. Vaughan (eds), *The Virginia Statute for Religious Freedom, its Evolution and Consequences in American History,* Cambridge: Cambridge University Press, 1988.

Pettegree, Andrew, 'The politics of toleration in the Free Netherlands, 1572– 1620', in Ole Peter Grell and Bob Scribner (eds), *Tolerance and Intolerance in the European Reformation,* Cambridge: Cambridge University Press, 1996, 182–98.

Reinhard, Wolfgang, 'Konfession und Konfessionalisierung in Europa', in Wolfgang Reinhard (ed.), *Bekenntnis und Geschichte Die Confessio Augustana im historischen Zusammenhang,* Munich, 1981, 165–89.

Reinhard, Wolfgang, 'Reformation, Counterreformation, and the Early Modern State: A Reassessment', in *The Catholic Historical Review,* 75, 3 (1989), 383– 404.

Remer, Gary, 'Bodin's Pluralistic Theory of Toleration', in Cary J. Nederman and John Christian Laursen (eds), *Difference and Dissent: Theories of Tolerance in Medieval and Early Modern Europe,* Lanham, Maryland et al.: Rowman & Littlefield, 1996, 119–37.

Schilling, Heinz, 'Confessional Europe', in Thomas A. Brady, Heiko A. Oberman, and James D. Tracy (eds), *Handbook of European History 1400–1600, Late Middle Ages, Renaissance and Reformation,* vol. 2, Leiden: Brill, 1995, 641–81.

Schreiner, Klaus, 'Toleranz', in Otto Brunner, Werner Conze, and Reinhart Koselleck, (eds), *Geschichtliche Grundbegriffe,* vol. 6, Stuttgart: Klett 1990, 445–605.

Scribner, Bob, 'Preconditions of Tolerance in sixteenth-century Germany', in Ole Peter Grell and Bob Scribner (eds), *Tolerance and Intolerance in the European Reformation,* Cambridge: Cambridge University Press, 1996, 32– 47.

Stow, Kenneth R., *Alienated Minority: The Jews in Medieval Latin Europe*, Cambridge, Mass.: Harvard University Press, 1992.

Thadden, Rudolf von and Marie Magdelaine, (eds), *Die Hugenotten*, Munich: Beck, 1985.

Ward, W.R., *The Protestant Evangelical Awakenings*, Cambridge: Cambridge University Press, 1992.

Warmbrunn, Paul, *Zwei Konfessionen in einer Stadt. Das zusammenleben von Katholiken und Protestanten in den paritätischen Reichsstädten Augsburg, Biberach, Ravensburg und Dinkelsbühl von 1548 bis 1648*, Wiesbaden, 1983.

Waugh, Scott L. and Peter D. Diehl (eds), *Christendom and its Discontents: Exclusion, Persecution, and Rebellion, 1000–1500*, Cambridge: Cambridge University Press, 1997.

Weber, Wolfgang E.J., 'Staatsräson und konfessionelle Toleranz. Bemerkungen zum Beitrag des politischen Denkens zur Friedensstiftung 1648', in Johannes Burkhardt and Stephanie Haberer (eds), *Das Friedensfest. Augsburg und die Entwicklung einer Neuzeitlichen Tolerauz-, Friedens-und Festkultur*, Berlin: Akademie Verlag, 2000, 165–205.

Wehler, Hans-Ulrich, 'Das Türkenproblem', *Die Zeit*, No. 38, 2002.

Whaley, Joachim, 'A Tolerant Society? Religious Toleration in the Holy Roman Empire, 1648–1806', in Ole Peter Grell and Roy Porter (eds), *Toleration and Enlightenment Europe*, Cambridge: Cambridge University Press, 2000, 175–95.

Winkler, Heinrich August, 'Wir erweitern uns zu Tode', *Die Zeit*, No. 46, 2002.

Religions of India

Plurality and Pluralism

T.N. MADAN

INTRODUCTION: DISTRIBUTIONAL PATTERNS

If the term 'religion' is used to refer to particular aspects of India's cultural traditions (see below), the country can be said to have long been the home of all religions that today have a worldwide presence. Hinduism, Buddhism, Jainism, and Sikhism—called the Indic religions—were born here. Christianity, Judaism, Islam, Zoroastrianism, and the Bahai faith arrived here from abroad at different points of time during the last two millennia.

The plurality of religions in India is often obscured by the fact that Hinduism is generally regarded as both the demographically dominant and the culturally characteristic—even hegemonic—religion of the country, not only in popular imagination but also by official reckoning. According to the census, four out of five Indians are Hindus, and they inhabit the length and breadth of the land. From the cultural perspective, anthropologists and sociologists have provided details of the many components of culture and aspects of social structure of the non-Hindu communities that have either been borrowed from the Hindus, or are residues from their pre-conversion Hindu past, with or without significant alterations.

The foregoing popular view of the cultural scene in India, buttressed by official statistics, needs to be qualified in several respects. Unlike the other religions of India, Hinduism is a federation of faiths with a horizontal as well as vertical distribution rather than a single homogeneous religion. Not only do the religious beliefs and practices of Hindus vary from one cultural region of the country to another, Hindu castes in different areas are also characterized by differences of status and lifestyle even when similarly named. Details of such internal plurality among the Hindus will be dealt with later in the paper.

Suffice it to note here that, first, Hinduism has a long and eventful history, which has resulted in much internal diversity, and, second, there are communities today that are considered Hindu by others but who themselves no longer concur in this judgement. Most notably, the scheduled castes of official literature, including the Constitution of the Republic, who have traditionally comprised the bottom rungs of the caste hierarchy, and were called Harijan ('the Children of God') by Mahatma Gandhi (1869–1948), are today by self-description the Dalit ('the Oppressed'). If their claim that they are not Hindu (Ilaiah 1996) is accepted, the proportion of Hindus in the total population will come down significantly from four-fifths to two-thirds.

Further, clarification regarding the use of the term religion in the Indian context, anticipated at the very beginning of this essay, may now be offered. Whether we have the Indic faiths in mind, or the major religions of non-Indian origin, notably Islam, religion in India is not a discrete element of everyday life that stands wholly apart from the economic or political concerns of the people. To assume so would amount to yielding to the temptation of words. The point is not that the religious domain is not distinguished from the secular, but rather that the secular is regarded as being encompassed by the religious, even when the former is apparently inimical to the latter. The relationship is hierarchical. In other words, religion in the Indian cultural setting traditionally permeates most aspects of life, not through mechanical diffusion, but in an integrated, holistic perspective (Radhakrishnan 1927). The processes of secularization are, however, gradually circumscribing the scope of the religious domain, particularly in urban areas.

A second clarification concerns the conception of divinity. The monotheism of the Abrahamic religions (much more uncompromisingly in Judaism and Islam than in Christianity) is either absent in the Indic religions (as in the case of Buddhism and Jainism), or we find in its place other conceptions, notably an abstract notion of 'Essence' or 'Being' as the source of all that truly exists (the Brahman of Vedantic Hinduism), or polytheism (as in Puranic Hinduism), or the exuberant 'spiritism' of folk Hinduism.

The non-theism of orthodox Buddhism and Jainism, which was a major scandal in the eyes of the Vedic metaphysicians two thousand years ago, persuaded a modern European scholar of comparative religion, Emile Durkheim (1858-1917), himself born into the Jewish faith, to abandon belief in divine beings as an essential element in the constitution (or recognition) of religion anywhere. Instead, he focused on the conception of 'sacred things', i.e. 'things set apart or forbidden' that contribute significantly to the constitution of society as a 'moral community'. The notion of sacredness is itself problematic in several respects, however, but we will not go into that issue here (Durkheim 1995).

Finally, it may be noted here by way of clarification, that the notion and word most widely used in India as a synonym for religion, namely the Sanskrit *dharma* (from the root *dhri*), or its Pali equivalent *dhamma*, denotes the ideas of maintenance, sustenance or upholding, steadfastness, and moral virtue. It is a different idea than the dependent bonding of the human being with supernatural powers conveyed by the term religion, which is of Latin derivation (*religio*, obligation, bond); it also denotes reverence, but in Lucretius it means, 'fear of gods'. While a conception of self-sustaining cosmo-moral order is found in all Indic religions—subtle differences of nuance notwithstanding—Islam literally stands for submission to the will of God, conveyed through his Word as recorded in the Quran, which is to be read repeatedly as an essential act of piety.

Keeping the foregoing observations in mind, we will now use the word religion here without further elucidation or qualification. Let us begin with the demographic picture (on the basis of the 1991 census). The Hindus (including most of the scheduled castes, who account for 16.48 per cent of the total population) number 688 million, constituting 82 per cent of the total population of about 839 million. (The estimated population at the time of writing in 2002 is well above one billion, but the religion-wise proportions are believed to be about the same as in 1991.) Next to the Hindus are the 102 million Muslims (12 per cent), and they are followed by the Christians (20 million, 2.32 per cent) and the Sikhs (16 million, 1.99 per cent). Buddhists (0.77 per cent), Jains (0.41 per cent) and others account for the remaining nearly 2 per cent of the population. Among the 'others' mention may be made of those tribal peoples who adhere to their own traditional faiths—which used to be earlier grouped together arbitrarily as animism under colonial rule—and of the Zoroastrians and the Jews. The total population of the scheduled tribes is about 68 million, or 8 per cent of the total population. Although their religion-wise distribution is not available, it is generally known that most of them either follow Hinduism of the folk type or are Christians; only a minority still adhere to their ancestral faiths. As for the Zoroastrians and the Jews, they are counted in thousands only; both are threatened by declining birth rates and assimilation among other religious communities through intermarriage. Some Jews have migrated to Israel.

State-wise distribution of the religious communities provides a picture of regional dispersal and variation. The Hindus, spread over virtually the entire country, outnumber all the others in the states of Himachal Pradesh (96 per cent), Orissa (95 per cent), Madhya Pradesh (93 per cent), Andhra Pradesh (89 per cent), Gujarat (89 per cent), Haryana (89 per cent), Rajasthan (89 per cent), Tamil Nadu (89 per cent), Pondicherry (86 per cent), Tripura (86 per cent), Karnataka (85 per cent), Delhi (84 per cent), Bihar (82 per cent), Uttar Pradesh (82 per cent), Maharashtra (81 per cent), West Bengal (75 per cent), Sikkim (68 per cent), Assam (67 per cent), Goa, Daman and Diu (65 per cent), Manipur (58 per cent), and Kerala (57 per cent). Similarly, Hindus outnumber all the others in the Union Territories of Dadra and Nagar Haveli (95 per cent), Chandigarh (76 per cent), and Andaman and Nicobar Islands (68 per cent). They are the principal minority community in the states of Arunachal Pradesh (37 per cent), Punjab (34 per cent), Meghalaya (15 per cent), Nagaland (10 per cent), and Mizoram (5 per cent), and in the Union Territory of Lakshadweep (5 per cent).

The only other religious community with a perceptible countrywide distribution are the Muslims. They are the majority community in the state of Jammu and Kashmir (64 per cent according to 1981 census) in the extreme north and in the Union Territory of Lakshadweep (94 per cent) in the south. They are the principal minority in the states of Assam (28 per cent) in the north-east, West Bengal (23 per cent) and Bihar (15 per cent) in the east, Uttar Pradesh (17 per cent), Delhi (9 per cent), Rajasthan (8 per cent), and Haryana (5 per cent) in the north, Maharashtra (10 per cent) and Gujarat (9 per cent) in the west, and Kerala (23 per cent), Karnataka (12 per cent), and Andhra Pradesh (9 per cent) in the south.

Christians are the majority community in three north-eastern states, namely Nagaland (88 per cent), Mizoram (86 per cent), and Meghalaya (65 per cent). They are the principal minority in the states of Manipur (34 per cent), also in the north-east, and Goa, Daman and Diu (30 per cent) in the west, and in the Union Territory of Andaman and Nicobar Islands (24 per cent) in the south. Sikhs account for 63 per cent of the population in Punjab and are the principal minority in the adjacent state of Haryana (6 per cent) and the Union Territory of Chandigarh (20 per cent).

The state of Arunachal Pradesh in the north-east presents an interesting variation of the general pattern: the followers of traditional (tribal) religions at 36 per cent are about as numerous as Hindus (37 per cent). Buddhists (13 per cent) and Christians (10 per cent) are in the third and fourth positions. The only other places in the country where the Buddhists are a presence in demographic terms are the district of Ladakh (in Jammu and Kashmir), where they account for four-fifths of the population, and the states of Sikkim and Mizoram where their share in the population is 27 per cent and 8 per cent respectively. Jains are concentrated in Rajasthan, Delhi, and states along the west coast. Zoroastrians, more generally known as Parsis, four-fifths of whose estimated world population of 120,000 lives in India, are concentrated in the urban areas of Gujarat and Maharashtra. Far fewer than the Parsis are the Jews, who are, however, divided into three distinct groups, namely the Baghdadi Jews of Kolkata, the Cochin Jews, and the Bene Israeli of Mumbai. Only the last named group may be called a community; the other two are really clusters of families.

We may parenthetically observe here that among the countries of South Asia, Sri Lanka shares with India the contemporary plurality of religions more than the other countries. Although predominantly Buddhist, it harbours sizeable religious minorities, including Hindus, Christians, and Muslims. Nepal is more predominantly Hindu, but Buddhists and Muslims also are present, the latter in very small numbers. Bangladesh is predominantly Muslim (85 per cent), with Hindus and Buddhists as notable religious minorities. Pakistan and the Maldives are almost exclusively Muslim and Bhutan is primarily Buddhist.

In what follows in this paper, the focus is on the historical and organizational aspects of the religions of India. We are not concerned with their cognitive and ritual dimensions. The plurality of the major traditions is briefly outlined in 'Indic Religions' and 'Christianity and Islam'. 'Religious Pluralism as Ideology' examines, again briefly, the elements of pluralism in the traditions earlier described. Limitations of space have precluded any discussion of the so-called tribal religions and of Judaism and Zoroastrianism. Also excluded, regrettably, is an exploration of the interaction of the religious traditions and of the peaceful coexistence of religious communities (Gottschalk 2001).

INDIC RELIGIONS

Vedism and Hinduism

The beginnings of religious diversity in India go back to the country's proto-historic past. Arguably, there is material evidence of the existence of religious activity in the urban centres associated with the Indus Valley or Harappan civilization of about five thousand years ago, spread over vast areas in north-western, northern, and western parts of the Indo-Pakistan subcontinent. It is reasonable to infer that religious beliefs and rituals of a somewhat different kind (e.g. shamanism) may have been present in the rural hinterlands. The mature Harappan religion was perhaps characterized by internal diversities reflecting social and theological divisions. Some scholars have written about a public religion, centred in temples, comprising ritual bathing (there is a 'great bath' in the citadel of Mohenjo-Daro), worship of gods and goddesses, fertility rituals, and perhaps animal sacrifice. The current consensus, however, denies the existence of temples. Apart from the public (state) and private (domestic) rituals, differences reflecting clan-based cleavages also seem to have existed (Ratnagar 2000: 69–77, Thapar 2002: 83–6).

The city cultures, it is generally believed, were overridden by nomadic Aryan-speaking peoples of central or west Asian origin around 1500 BC. They brought in their own religious beliefs and practices, and these focused on the creative and destructive powers of nature. According to this generally accepted view, the Aryans owed little in their religious life to the presumably Dravidian-speaking people they displaced from their homelands. Scholars who do not accept the general view, but consider the Harappan culture a continuing rather than a closed phenomenon, whether wholly internal or aided by a limited migration, maintain that the old and the new cultures coexisted, and the latter absorbed elements, both religious and linguistic, from the former (Parpola 1994).

Vedic religion and Sanskrit took several centuries to acquire the forms in which they are known to us. The major source of our knowledge about the religious life of the Aryans, besides the numerous archaeological sites, is the body of sacred literature called the Veda ('knowledge', 'wisdom'), which is believed to be ever-existent (*sanatana*) and therefore lacking any human author (*apaurusheya*), and stretches over almost a thousand years. The earliest of the Vedic texts is the *Rig*, which has been dated no later than 1200 BC (but is perhaps older). Its ten books of hymns in praise of divinities presumably represent ten family traditions among the Brahmans (rituals specialists) and took several centuries to compose. The *Sama* and *Yajur* Veda extend the scope of the *Rig* into music and ritual respectively. Finally, the *Atharva Veda* is believed to represent the absorption of folk religions into the vedic corpus, resulting in significant changes in it. These religions were encountered by the Aryans as they moved east into the Gangetic valley and adopted more settled ways. Indeed, the valley came to be called the home of the Aryas, *Aryavrata*. Thus, vedic divinities lost their supremacy and magical spells, and rites became ascendant (Flood 1996 and Brockington 1992).

The Vedas became the basis for an immense textual efflorescence, comprising manuals of ritual performances (*Brahmanas*, *Aranyakas*), and later discursive speculative treatises (Upanishads), also called Vedanta (the culmination of the Veda) (Olivelle 1998), all of which brings us close to 300 BC. Schools of Vedic learning and ritual, called 'branches' (*shakha*), flourished, producing a cultural ambience of at times bewildering plurality within the Vedic framework.

But that is not all; Vedic philosophy gradually made way for the emergence of what is generally called Hinduism on a subcontinental scale, which brought more texts on more varied subjects into existence, notably the *Grihya Sutras*, which are guides to the performance of domestic rituals, and the *Dharma Sutras* (Olivelle 2000), which have social ethics and law as their subject matter. Besides, there are the *Shrauta Sutras*, which are technical treatises on the correct procedures for the performance of Vedic rituals of public significance. The *Grihya Sutras* have a regional character: a text followed in one part of the country may be unknown in another. The Vedic corpus, considered revealed, is said to be based on *shruti* (that which has been heard, by the inner ear, as it were), and constitutes the first source of dharma understood as both the law and righteous conduct. After the sutras we come to the second source, namely *Smriti* (that which is remembered), and these texts are credited to human authors.

Later still than the *sutras* are the *Dharma Shastras* which continue with the same themes but in much greater detail. The best known of these texts today is the *Manav Dharma Shastra*, attributed to a seer called Manu, and therefore also known as the *Manu Smriti* (Doniger 1991). It is believed to have been composed between 200 BC and AD 300, which rules out single authorship. What stands out in this and other similar texts is the institutional framework for the conduct of both domestic life and public affairs.

In domestic life the key principles of *varna* (social class) and *ashrama* (stage of life) are adumbrated for the definition of appropriate rituals and worldly affairs. While universal norms (*sarva sadharna dharma*) are not wholly eliminated, but retained as the foundation of all righteous conduct, it is the varna- and ashrama-specific rules that emerge as preponderant. It is thus that Hinduism has been defined as varna-ashrama-dharma, or a context-sensitive morality. Not only the householder, but the kings too, are bound by their respective duties defined in terms of varna and ashrama (Lingat 1973). As for those who repudiated such divisions, notably the renouncers (*sannyasis*), even they have been grouped into sects (*sampradayas*) since at least the time of the composition of the *Mahabharata* (c. 400 BC–AD 400), and are guided by their own (*yati*) dharma. It is obvious that when variant regional, *varna* (including occupation), and ashrama identities defined the appropriateness of behaviour in particular situations, Hinduism could have been only a family of faiths and the behaviours that went with them, and the Hindu society, a confederation of communities.

The speculative or philosophical concerns of the Brahmanical tradition were formulated as different systems of orthodox thought (*jnan*) and termed *darshana*, or 'visions', or 'views' (in both senses of the word 'view' as something seen and also as a philosophical position) of life based on the Veda. Each of these darshanas, six in number, has its own authoritative texts. The thought (or reflections) that follows from each position is not exclusive in the manner of the various guides to ritual performance and social behaviour. The 'root' text of each darshana is concerned with extra-referential (*paramarthika*) knowledge, and transactive (*vyavaharika*) knowledge is built or grafted on it. Together they constitute what can only be called a complex totality aimed at deliverance from ignorance through true knowledge. The soteriological character of the darshanas is undeniable as are their theistic tendencies.

The six schools are: (i) Samkhya ('enumeration') which asserts the ontological duality of matter (*prakrti*) and the 'self' (*purusha*); (ii) *Yoga* ('joining', 'mixing') which constitutes a pair with Samkhya in terms of its metaphysics; (iii) *Mimamsa* (vedic exegesis) which takes a pluralist view of reality; (iv) *Vedanta* ('culmination of Veda'), grouped with Mimamsa, which denies the reality of the many; (v) *Nyaya* (logic); and (vi) *Vaisheshika* (dialectics), considered a pair, which deal with logical, ontological, and dialectical issues within an empiricist, pluralist (more precisely atomist) framework (Hiriyana 1993). The primacy which the monism of Vedanta has enjoyed in contemporary literature on India does little justice to the internal diversities of Brahmanical thought even when dealing with the same issues, or with its method of dealing with them to preclude mutual incomprehensibility.

The foregoing pluralities of scripture, metaphysics, and social organization that are the background to Hinduism and indeed partly constitute it, are characteristic of Brahmanical orthodoxy. This orthodoxy has not remained unchallenged. Indeed, the challenges came from within long before any major external threat materialized. The followers of public Vedic ritual, called the *Shrautas* (*shruti*, 'revelation'), first yielded space to those who gave precedence to domestic rituals, whether the *Smartas* (followers of the *Smritis* or *Dharma Shastras*) or the *Pauranikas* (those who organize their religious life on the basis of the Puranas, which are legendary accounts of the acts of gods, goddesses, and other supernatural beings as well as human beings like kings and ascetics). The latter two categories of Hinduism remain within the Vedic fold.

It is the Tantras, texts that are claimed by their followers, the Tantrikas, to be revealed, are non-Vedic. Traced to folk cults of Assam and Bengal, the eastern frontier of Vedic (Aryan) northern India, tantrism is characterized by enormous internal diversity including within its fold magical fertility rites as well as arcane metaphysics. The human body is the key site of tantrik practice; it reveals considerable variety, but is generally characterized by secret rituals, performed often at special sites, such as cremation grounds, and frequently at night. Thus, tantrik rituals that invoke the power of Shakti, the Supreme Goddess are performed at night in the famous temple of Puri (Orissa), where worship of the god Jagannatha (an incarnation of Vishnu, the patron deity of Vaishnavas) and his divine consort, is performed publicly during the day (Marglin 1985). The celebrated, yearly 'car festival' (*ratha yatra*) is dedicated to him.

We must pause here to mention two other important bodies of sacred texts, namely the epics of Mahabharata and Ramayana (c. AD 200), and the Puranas, which are post-vedic and fall into the category of the *Smriti*. They mark the transformation of the Vedic Brahmanical religion into what has come to be known as Hinduism. Shiva and Vishnu, somewhat vague figures in the Vedic pantheon, now emerge as the supreme gods not always at peace with each other. Moreover, the notion of incarnation (*avatar*) is formulated within the Vaishnava tradition—Krishna (of the *Bhagvata Purana*) and Rama (of the Ramayana) being the most notable among the nine or ten avatars generally recognized. The Puranas describe in great detail the deeds of the Hindu trinity (Brahma the creator, Vishnu the preserver, and Shiva the destroyer) and other mythological personages. The Puranas were composed between the sixth and sixteenth centuries (Dimmit and van Buitenen 1978).

While the worship of Vishnu is combined in the Smarta-Pauranika traditions with that of Shiva, Shakti or Devi, Surya (the sun god), and Ganapati (the lord of auspiciousness), in some parts of the country, particularly in the south, mutually exclusive and often hostile sects have emerged centred on the cults of the first two gods. These five deities together represent a syncretic movement in Hinduism, dating back to the ninth century, which sought to overcome sectarian and other divisions within Hinduism. Surya and also Vishnu and Shiva are of Vedic origin; Shakti represents the folk religious cults (Bhattacharji 1988).

From as early as the fifth century, the Vaishnavas were divided into the sects of Pancharatras and Vaikhanasas. Similarly, the Pashupata,

Kapalika, and Kalamukha sects were prominent among the Shaivas (Bhattacharji 1988, Brockington 1992, Lorenzen 1972). Starting in the seventh century, the Vaishnavas and the Shaivas began to generate distinctive liturgical texts called the *samhitas* and *agamas* respectively. Each sect claimed the supremacy of its own deity on the latter's own authority. In the development of these theistic traditions, from around the closing centuries of the last millennium BC, a number of elements from various sources, including the high Sanskritic and folk religious traditions, fused. Personal devotion (*bhakti*) to one's chosen deity (*ishta*), whether Vishnu in his various incarnations including most notably those of Rama and Krishna-Vasudeva, or Shiva, is a striking characteristic of these cults, and originated in the south and then spread to the north. This devotionalism found expression in emotionally surcharged poetry particularly among the Vaishnavas from the sixth century onward, and later also among the Shaivites, though the latter's devotion tended to be more austere (Ramanujan 1973 and 1981).

Expectedly, the relationship of the devotee to the deity, whether expressed in human (anthropomorphic) terms or through abstract formulations, constitutes the core of the speculative thought of these religious traditions, ranging from absolute monism (*advaita*), associated with the name of Shankara (c. 788–820), to qualified non-dualism (*vishishitadvaita*) of Ramanuja (c.1017–1137), and dualism (*dvaita*) elucidated by Madhva in the thirteenth century. The teachings of the latter two saints combine the metaphysics of the Upanishads with the theism of Vaishnava and Shaiva cults.

Associated with these both is a third tradition, namely the worship of the great goddess, Devi, which emerged virtually independently as the Shakta (from shakti, 'power') tradition. Here also the roots go far back in time, perhaps to the Harappan culture, and later developments entail the amalgamation of Puranic, tantrik, and folk goddesses and ideas. As Lakshmi, the divine consort of Vishnu, the great goddesses is presented as a benign bearer of auspiciousness; as Uma-Parvati, she is the divine consort of Shiva, mother of the universe; and as Durga or Kali, the highest manifestation of divine power, she is the fearsome destroyer of evil and greater than all the male gods through the pooling of whose powers she comes into being. At the village level she appears as the goddess who brings and removes illness and misfortune, such as Shitala, the goddess whose visitations were held responsible for smallpox (Hawley and Wulff 1996).

The Hindu religious tradition, we have seen, is characterized by strong pluralistic tendencies emanating from various sources and inspirations. Syncretistic tendencies have also been in evidence as that, for instance, of the smarta worship mentioned above, believed to have been instituted by Shankara. Remarkably for his time and short life (he died at the age of thirty–two), he is believed to have travelled from his native place in Kerala to the banks of the Narmada river and then on to Varanasi, to Badrinath near the source of the Ganga in the Himalayas, and finally to Kashmir. Wherever he went, he engaged in disputations wilth rival seers, expounded his non-dualist philosophy (*advaita*) and promoted non-sectarianism. His travels, deemed by his followers to have been successful, are remembered by them as his widespread victory (*digvijay*).

Hinduism has tended to absorb non-Hindu religious ideas and practices, including, in medieval times, elements of Sufi Islam (Mujeeb 1967). It has dealt with internal dissent through accommodation, sometimes carried to the furthest extremes. Occasionally, this strategy has failed and resulted in breakaway sects that in course of time grew into independent religions, such as Buddhism and Jainism, adding a new dimension to the religious plurality of India.

Buddhism

The most widely spread religion in Asia today, namely Buddhism, has adherents in the West also, but it is a minority religion in India, the country of its origin. Named after the title *buddha*, ('the enlightened one') of its founder, Gautama (c. 563–483 BC), Buddhism began as a revolt against the vedic preoccupation with the supernatural, rejecting the beliefs as well as the rituals that went with them. The rejection entailed repudiation of the authority of the Brahmans on the part of the *Bauddhas*. Gautama himself belonged to the Kshatriya (warrior) caste and, indeed, he was the heir to a kingdom in the Bihar-Nepal area. Following his own awakening to knowledge and wisdom—his enlightenment—the Buddha attracted disciples whom he taught 'the four noble truths' that constitute the fundamentals of all schools of Buddhism (Harvey 1990).

The first truth of life, the Buddha said, is sorrow (suffering); the second, the source of sorrow is ignorance and desire; the third, sorrow can be ended if desire is overcome; and the fourth, the way to the 'blowing out' (*nibanna*) of both desire and sorrow lies through 'the noble eightfold path'. This path, which is the path of righteousness (dharma, dhamma) consists of the right views, resolve, speech, conduct, livelihood, effort, mindfulness, and concentration.

The Buddha adopted a stance of silence on the issue of the existence of the divinity but denied the Vedic gods any significance in human affairs, and concentrated on human agency. He did, however, retain the root paradigm of karma understood as the doctrine of agency and retribution. It is doubtful that the Buddha thought of himself as anything more than a reformer within the tradition, and his teachings as 'a new expansion, not against, but within Brahmanism'. Nevertheless, his teachings were said by the establishment to be negatory (*nastika*), repudiating Vedic revelation and the notion of divinity, and attacked as unforgivably heterodox. The Buddha's rejection of the varna system, ritualism, and techniques of self-mortification could not but have been aberrations in the judgement of the Brahmans.

Nevertheless, it is not unreasonable to believe that Gautama's concerns and dissatisfactions must have been shared by some other reflective persons. They chose, however, to work from within the tradition. The fact that the early Upanishads (c. 600–400 BC) are more or less contemporaneous with the beginnings of Buddhism would seem to support such a conclusion. Thus, the Upanishadic notion of an abstract Brahman (with which the self, atman, is identical) appears to stand midway between Vedic polytheism and Buddhist atheism. With the passage of time, Brahmanism and Buddhism came closer together.

The Buddha originated the idea of the monastic community of monks and nuns (*sangha*), subject to a rigorous regime (*vinaya*), as the ideal arrangement for the pursuit of true knowledge. An easier way of life was envisaged for the lay community, with the sangha as their exemplar and refuge. Such was his confidence in this institution that the Buddha did not name a successor nor formalize or codify his teachings. He advised resolution of doubts on matters of common concern through discussion and consensus; in the event of failure to reach a consensus the majority view was to be respected. It was thus that the seeds of a plurality of belief and practice among the Buddhists were sown by Gautama himself.

The first great split is believed to have occurred a century after the Buddha's passing at a council of sanghas convened at Vaishali (Bihar) to settle contentious issues concerning monastic discipline and the character of the Buddha's personality. The opposing factions, namely the orthodox Sthaviras (Elders) and the Mahasanghikas (upholders of the 'Great Community'), reached a temporary truce, but split formally four decades later. While the former held the Buddha to have been an enlightened human preceptor, the latter claimed for him the status of a transcendent being.

The foregoing and other issues continued to cause disagreements. In

the process, as many as eighteen viewpoints were formalized and collectively referred to as the Hinayana, or the little (or lesser) vehicle (or
approach). One of them, the school of Sthaviras emerged as Theravada
(the Way of the Elders) in the second century BC in Sri Lanka, where it
is now the state religion (see Gombrich 1988). It later spread to Myanmar,
Thailand, Cambodia, and Laos. As for the Mahasanghikas, they were
the progenitors of the adherents of Mahayana (great vehicle or approach) Buddhism that is today a major religion in the Far East (China,
Japan) and elsewhere. Mahayana arose between 150 BC and AD 250.
Apart from moving in the direction of theism (the Buddha as a glorified,
transcendent being), it also developed a new philosophical perspective,
Shunyatavada, emphasizing the 'emptiness' of phenomena. The great
teacher of this doctrine was Nagarjuna, who was born a Brahman,
became a Buddhist, and founded the Madhyamika (the Middle Path)
school of Buddhism.

Mention may also be made of a later development (seventh century)
in north India where a convergence of Buddhism and tantrism occurred,
resulting in what came to be called the Vajrayana (thunderbolt vehicle).
This in turn spread north into Ladakh (Jammu and Kashmir) and the
kingdom of Bhutan (three-fourths of the people there are Buddhists) and
Tibet where it absorbed further extraneous elements from Shamanism.
In the north-eastern states of Tripura, Mizoram, and Arunachal Pradesh
in India there are close to 200,000 Buddhists of the Theravada school.

The presence of the Dalai Lama and settlements of refugees in India,
since their exile from Tibet in 1959, has enhanced general awareness
about Buddhism in its different expressions of doctrine and practice in
India. The conversion of large numbers of low-caste Hindus, who call
themselves Dalits and are generally referred to as Neo-Buddhists, in
1956 under the charismatic leadership of B.R. Ambedkar (1891–1956)
and thereafter, has contributed significantly to the same process. The
population figures for all of India were under 200,000 in 1951 and about
three-quarters of a million in 1991. Conversion has, however, explicitly
politicized Buddhist identity (see Zelliot 1996).

The virtual disappearance of Buddhism as a distinct religion from the
country of its origin calls for comment. The early hostility of Brahmans
has already been mentioned. Since Buddhism was finally driven out of
India in the twelfth and thirteenth centuries, it would seem that, by itself,
this hostility alone is an insufficient explanation. The emergence of
Mahayana in, fact, opened the way for the incorporation of the Buddha
within the Vaishnava tradition as an incarnation of Vishnu and the
selective absorption of Buddhist ethics, metaphysics, and logic into it.

This process continued into the Gupta and post-Gupta periods. There is ample evidence that the brahmanization of Bengal was at the cost of Buddhism which was transformed. There was much mutual borrowing and the two religions came very close to each other, particularly in the eyes of the common people (Chakrabarti 2001: 109–64).

In addition to the complex Brahman-Buddhist relationship, there is a consensus among historians that the moral decline of the monastic communities, the withdrawal of royal patronage, and the decline of the support of the laity were also major causes. The final blow was the Muslim invasions: these were widespread (all the way from Kashmir to Bengal) and brutal (the destruction of Buddhist universities, notably Nalanda, and the accompanying massacres of monks were staggering events). The devastated Buddhist communities escaped to Myanmar and further east, and the Muslims occupied the cultural, religious, and political spaces that they vacated (Thapar 1966: 263–4, Kosambi 1970: 176–82).

Jainism

Jainism too arose around the same time as Buddhism, in the same area (Bihar), for broadly the same reasons, and in a similar manner. But there are significant differences between the Buddhist and Jain visions of life. The terms Jainism and Jain (*Jaina*, follower of the religion) are derived from *jina*, 'the conqueror' (of one's physical self and thus of karmic action). This title was bestowed on prince Vardhamana (c. 599–527 BC)—also called Mahavira, 'the great hero' —to whom are attributed the basic teachings of the faith in their final form. Actually, he is regarded as the last of a line of teachers called *tirthankara* ('ford maker'), who reiterated time and again the perennial 'three jewels' of right faith, right knowledge, and right action. They also founded the Jain community comprising ascetics (monks and nuns) and the laity (householders). It is their community that is considered by the Jains a spiritual ford (*tirtha*) to help all seekers to wash off karma and terminate the cycle of birth-death-rebirth (Dundas 1992).

Sentiments such as desire, anger, greed, and attachment are the human failings that generate karma (fruit-bearing action). Karma is visualized as material: it contaminates the inner self and is the cause of suffering in one's own life and of injury to other living beings. The Jain ideal therefore is to be forever engaged in self-purification (through the suppression of all bodily appetites) and to assiduously refrain from injury to others (this is the ideal of ahimsa, 'non-injury'). Renunciation is highly valued and the final worldly goal for the ascetic is to end one's life through abstinence from food and drink. For laymen, the house-holder's life, guarded by numerous rules and regulations, is the ideal.

Paradoxical as it may seem, the Jains in actual practice are also very successful merchants and visible in urban centres (Laidlaw 1995). Although fewer in number than Buddhists, the Jains are the more visible religious community in India. They share many religious practices, including fasts and festivals with the upper-caste Hindus, and are often regarded by the latter as a sect of Hindu society, rather than a separate religious community. Their original atheism and repudiation of Vedic revelation had of course earned them, alongside the Buddhists, the opprobrium of being heterodox in the judgement of the Brahmans.

Among the Jains themselves, heresies and sectarian schisms began to make their appearance even while the Mahavira was alive. According to the mainstream Jain tradition, eight such deviations (*nihnava*, 'conceal-ment' of the true teaching) occurred over a period of six centuries. The last of these resulted in the emergence of a heretical sect. Accounts of this schism are shrouded in rival legends of the so-called mainstream and the breakaway groups, the Shvetambaras (clad in white cloth) and the Digambaras ('clothed by the sky', naked).

The mode of clothing refers to the practices of the ascetics rather than the lay householders, but Digambara nuns do wear clothes; only men remain naked. The Shvetambaras use a bowl to receive food given to them, from which they also eat. Food is important because even those monks who have attained full omniscience (*kevalin*) must eat to survive. The Digambaras do not use a bowl but their cupped hands to receive alms, and it is from the hands so held together that they eat. They insist on absolute non-possession: no clothes and no alms bowls. In their judgement true omniscience means, among other things, that one does not need to eat food any more. Women are deemed unequal to the demands of total conquest of the passions leading to omniscience and deliverance from the fruits of karma.

The two sects are also separated by the scriptures that each acknowl-edges. On the fundamentals of Jain faith and knowledge, however, there is no serious difference. Sectarian differences seem to have taken very long to acquire their present rigidity, and regional distribution— Shvetambaras in the north and the west and Digambaras in the south— seems to have contributed to it. The differences notwithstanding, the high value that all Jains place on non-violence has prevented the two sects from adopting aggressive measures to settle scores. Currently, sectarian conflict among the Jains seems to focus on the issues of ownership of and access to places of worship rather than on matters of doctrine and practice. Regrettably, the same cannot be said about other communities.

Sikhism

The beginnings of Sikhism (*sikha*, disciple) early in the sixteenth century followed a major development in the history of religions in India over the previous eight hundred years, namely the arrival and growth of Islam. This development is described in the next section, but is mentioned here because it contributed significantly to the making of the new faith. Like Vardhamana and Gautama before him, Nanak Dev (1469–1539), the founder of Sikhism, was an upper-caste Hindu (of the Khatri jati of traders, originally Kshatriyas). From his experience and reflections, he developed an acute dissatisfaction with the ritualism, idol worship, magic, and miracles of the faith into which he was born, and with the stranglehold of the Brahmans over it (McLeod 1968 and Grewal 1990).

Nanak also took a positive view of worldly existence generally and of the householder's life and productive labour in particular. He rejected caste distinctions and the traditional ideal of renunciation. Above all, he extolled the virtue of the life of religious obedience and devotion focused on an abstract conception of the divinity and affirming the same through 'name remembrance' (*nam simran*), i.e. recitation and singing of hymns. Declaring that there were no true Hindus or Muslims to be found anywhere, he called for a third path comprising moral duty (*dharm*), human effort (*karm*), spiritual knowledge, truth, and divine benevolence.

In all this, Nanak was carrying forward the medieval Sant tradition of syncretic religious devotionalism, which had given rise to many 'paths' (*panth*) or sects. The disciples who gathered around him and carried forward his teachings after his death came to be called the Nanak Panthi or, later, Sikhs. Some of his followers did not follow all of his core teachings and, like his son who became a renouncer, founded other sects. Other changes and dilutions of dogma and practice, particularly the latter, occurred over the next two centuries, blurring the distinction between Sikhism and caste Hinduism, and rendering the Sikh identity rather 'misty'. Simultaneously, changing historical circumstances—which brought the Jats into the Sikh fold in large numbers, and also created suspicions in the minds of the Muslim rulers about the loyalty of the Sikhs—radically altered the pacifist character of the Sikh community.

The tenth guru of the Sikhs, Gobind Rai (1666–1708), intervened effectively on all fronts—theological, practical, social, and political—and created a sharpened sense of identity among the Sikhs by instituting (in 1699) a ritual of initiation (called *pahul*), and laying down norms of conduct including, most visibly, the injunction to retain bodily hair unshorn. He also asked all Sikh men to uniformly substitute Singh ('lion', the caste name of Rajputs) for their various last names; the women were to call themselves 'Kaur' (lioness').

The institution of these requirements also created unintended divisions among the Sikhs between (i) those who went through pahul and came to be called Amritdhari ('bearers of nectar', the baptismal water); (ii) those who kept their hair and beard and were called Keshdhari (bearers of hair); and (iii) those who affirmed Sikh identity but did not immediately follow the new injunctions, called the Sahajdhari (bearers of the spontaneous, inner light). The first category also called themselves the Khalsa, or the 'pure' and 'the chosen of God', and were to play a hegemonistic role in the second half of the nineteenth century in defining Sikh identity.

A hundred years after Guru Gobind established the Khalsa, a Jat Sikh chieftain, Ranjit Singh (1780–1839) established the kingdom of Lahore, which did not, however, last long after his death. In the aftermath of the defeat of the Sikhs at the hands of the British in 1846, several reformist movements emerged among the Sikhs.

Of these, the most notable were the Nirankari and Namdhari (or Kuka) movements. Both were sectarian in character and acknowledged gurus subsequent to Gobind Singh, who had proclaimed closure of the line of personal gurus. The beliefs of these sects were therefore considered violative of the true Khalsa faith by orthodox Sikhs. The Nirankaris called for a return to the teachings of Guru Nanak who had characterized the divinity as 'formless' (*nirankar*). The Namdharis focused their attention on regenerating the Khalsa as instituted by Guru Gobind. A modernist version of the same effort (namely Khalsa rejuvenation) was the agenda of the so-called Singh Sabhas which also had a considerable agenda of secular goals. Currently, the Namdharis are not very much in the news, but conflicts between the Nirankaris and the orthodox Khalsa or Akali Sikhs have resulted in violence and loss of life. The fundamentalist preacher Jarnail Singh Bhindranwale, who later came into conflict with the government on the issue of Sikh grievances, originally appeared in public (in 1978) as a fierce opponent of the Nirankaris (Kapur 1986).

From the account of developments in the long history of Indic religions, it is clear that pluralistic tendencies characterize them all, particularly Hinduism, which lacks a founder or a set of fundamentals of belief and practice or a 'church'. And yet they share a concern with unity in diversity, or the Absolute transcending its myriad expressions. The notions of dharma and karma are key ideas in the metaphysical foundations of each, but the manner in which they are developed and articulated differs from tradition to tradition. While the relations of Buddhism, Jainism, and Sikhism to Hinduism are too complex to be discussed in a few pages, it is noteworthy that each of the new religions began as reformist movements. Their founders were aiming at the correction of corruptions rather than self-consciously founding new religions. Otherwise, why should the Buddha, for instance, have been concerned about the definition of a true Brahman (*Dhampadda,* Chapter 26)? Broadly speaking, each reformist movement began as a loosening of bonds and moved towards a rupture. Consolidation is the next phase and, then, begins the process of internal fission within each tradition. Such pluralism is not, however, without its critics, the best recent example being the emergence of fundamentalism among the Sikhs in the 1970s (Oberoi 1994, Madan 1997: Chapter 3).

CHRISTIANITY AND ISLAM

Christianity

Of the religions that originated outside India but found a home here, Christianity is the oldest. If tradition is to be believed, it was brought to Kerala by the Apostle St Thomas. Written records testify to the presence of Christians in Malabar from the fourth century onward. There is evidence that the persecution of Persian Christians through most of the fourth century led to the exodus of East Syrian refugees to south India in enough numbers to constitute a viable community. They do not seem to have undertaken missionary work immediately: this began in noticeable form from the sixth century and was mostly confined among the ritually clean castes. Further migrations of East Syrians occurred in the eighth and ninth centuries under the leadership of Nestorian prelates. Apparently, they did not face any serious opposition from the Malabar rulers and people. Indeed, it is believed that they were accorded a high social status alongside the Hindu upper castes. They themselves were divided into two major endogamous groups on the basis of ancestry and domicile (Atiya 1968: 359–66 et passim). The Thomas Christians are also known as Syrian Christians for, apart from their origins, their liturgy was in Syriac, and they acknowledged the jurisdiction of the Syrian Patriarch of the East in Damascus (Syria). The community has remained confined to Kerala. It subscribes to various fundamentals of the Christian faith—

such as Immaculate Conception, the divinity of Jesus, and the status of the Bible as revealed scripture—and practice (for example, celebration of the Eucharist) (see Visvanathan 1993).

It was only in the middle of the sixteenth century that Franciscan missionaries made Goa their base, after it had become a part of the Portuguese colonial empire. They spread out to other parts of south India and Sri Lanka and even ventured north. The Franciscans were followed by other Catholic groups, including the Dominicans, the Augustinians, and the Jesuits. Jesuit missionaries participated in the religious debates in Agra in the presence of the emperor Akbar (ruled 1556–1605). When they encountered the Thomas Christians, they asked them to sever ties with the Nestorian Church and come under the jurisdiction of Rome. This led to a series of splits among the Syrians: while about one-half of the community complied, the rest resisted, and reaffirmed their loyalty to the Syrian Patriarch of Antioch. When some of those who had relented recanted and returned to Nestorianism, they suffered inhuman torture at the hands of the Inquisition, which had been extended to India on the advice of none other than St Francis Xavier (arrived in Goa in 1542), who is considered one of greatest and gentlest evangelists to have come to Asia (Atiya ibid.: 367). A long-lasting dissension among the Thomas Christians and the Jesuits was whether missionary activity was to be confined among the upper castes, and whether caste was to be deemed a religious institution and abolished, or only a secular social arrangement and therefore tolerated.

During the high noon of Portuguese power in Asia, the Vatican had played second fiddle but came into its own as the former declined. The area of missionary activity was expanded and Indian priests were trained to participate in it. A major event was the arrival of the Italian Jesuit Roberto de Nobili in the city of Madurai in Tamil Nadu in 1606. He focused his attention on the Brahmans, among whom conversions had been rather uncommon, presenting himself as a Roman Brahman who respected their high status, dressed like they did, and even wore the sacred thread. His success as a missionary was considerable and the 'saved souls' were counted in tens of thousands. Others followed, including, in about a hundred years the Protestants, who began their evangelical work in 1705. The range of activities also expanded. Bartholomew Zigenbalg, a Danish missionary, established the first printing press in India (at Tranquebar, Tamil Nadu) in 1712. He published from there a Tamil translation of Martin Luther's *Catechism*. In course of time (eighteenth and nineteenth centuries), other Protestant groups, such as the Baptists and the Presbytarians also came to India to evangelize Indians.

The arrival of the British in India in the mid-eighteenth century had at first no impact on the spread of Christianity as the East India Company, in deference to the wishes of the home government, did not allow missionary activity. It was only in the early nineteenth century that the British Parliament removed the restriction and chaplains of the Company began to make converts. The Anglican diocese of Calcutta was founded in 1814. To begin with, Anglican chaplains administered to the spiritual needs of only the British in India, but an Indian Church also had come into existence by the end of the nineteenth century. A close association of the Church with the state (under the colonial dispensation) was a liability and came to be loosened by the 1930s (Gibbs 1972). Meanwhile, Anglicans, Protestants, and non-conformist societies had sent out missions, producing a plurality of churches and an interflow between congregations. Thus, some Thomas Christians became Protestants and established the Mar Thoma (Syriac for St Thomas) Church. The majority, however, remained loyal to the Syrian Patriarch, nominally acknowledging his spiritual authority, but otherwise independent. They are known as the members of the Jacobite or Orthodox Church (Mathew and Thomas 1967).

In 1947, the year of India's independence, the Anglican, Methodist, and other Protestant churches came together to establish the Church of South India. Similar efforts in the north resulted in the establishment of a united Protestant Church in 1970. The predominance of Roman Catholics (nearly 60 per cent) is a noteworthy feature of the Christian communities of India. Also noteworthy has been the search for Indian idioms of expression.

Christians of all denominations have retained many of their pre-conversion beliefs, social attitudes, and liturgical practices incorporating them into Christianity (Bayly 1989, Robinson 1998). Diversities of pre-conversion origin (from among tribes, castes of varying social status, and different religious and speech communities) are responsible for much internal heterogeneity among them. But evangelicalism also has remained alive and is indeed a cherished goal. The fundamental right to propagate one's religion, and not merely to profess and practise it, was written into the Indian Constitution (Art. 30) to accommodate Christian sentiment on the subject. Whether propagation is for the edification of others or in fact implies the right to convert has been a matter of disagreement. The consensus of opinion is that propagation ithout conversion is an empty right. Conversions are therefore considered legitimate so long as force and fraud are not employed (Madan 2002).

Islam

The Third and the yongest member of the family of Abrahamic religions, Islam ('submission to the will of God') is dated back to AD 622, when its promulgator, the Prophet Muhammad (571–632) migrated from his native city of Makkah (in Arabia), where he did not receive the support he desired, to Madinah. In the latter city he established the first ever Islamic state. He accommodated resident Jews and Christians in it, since they too were judged to be in possession of books of divinely revealed knowledge and, therefore, entitled to protection.

The fundamentals of religious faith and practice among Muslims ('the submitters') are explicit and universally binding. They must affirm the oneness of God and the status of the Quran ('the text to be read and recited') as the word of God. Besides, they must believe in God's angels and messengers (of whom Muhammad was the most perfect and therefore the last), and in the Last Day, when God will judge the actions of one and all, and despatch the pious to heaven and the sinners to hell (Rahman 1979).

Moreover, every true Muslim must recite the creed (kalimah, 'the word'), which affirms the oneness of God and the finality of Muhammad's prophethood; say daily prayers (namaz) at the appointed times; observe the yearly month of fasting by day (rozah) to burn away sins; give alms (zakat); and, if circumstances allow it, go in pilgrimage to Makkah (hajj) so as to be there on Fidul-Azha. (This day, it is generally believed, commemorates the willingness of Ibrahim (Abraham) to sacrifice his son Ismail (Ishmael) on God's command). It is noteworthy that Indian Muslims do not include the waging of war (jihad) for the extermination of unbelief and the propagation of Islam among the obligations of a Muslim, as is done in many Muslim countries.

Islam is, however, more than what is stated above and similar other fundamentals. Everywhere it incorporates much that is local and pre-Islamic, whether this be in the Arab heartlands or in distant places such as India. Students of Islam have commented on this internal tension owing to its character as a world religion that admits of no variation (e.g. the daily prayers are everywhere said in Arabic), and its regional, country or national characteristics, like, for example, the worship of saints and relics, which is common in India (see Khan 1994). It is arguable that the Quran itself recognizes implicitly the possibility of some degree of internal diversity within the universal umma (community of true believers). Chapter 5, verse 3, of the Holy Book, addressed to 'true believers' informs them that Allah has in his mercy perfected their religion, Islam, for them to follow. There is, on the one hand, a paradigm of perfection that obviously admits of no variation. On the other hand, there are the believers who obviously come from diverse geographical, ethnic, linguistic, socio-cultural, and religious backgrounds. It is obviously impossible to wipe out these differences completely.

It is widely believed among South Asian Muslims that the Prophet Muhammad had himself wanted to bring the people of India into the universal Islamic community. Since Arab traders already had contacts with the western seaboard of India from pre-Islamic days (the Mapillas of Kerala were born of mixed marriages of Arab men and Malayali women), they must have been the first carriers of the new faith to the subcontinent. Islam arrived here as a political force in AD 712, when Sind was conquered on behalf of the Umayyad caliphate and incorporated in it. With the new rulers came the ulama, their advisers on matters concerning Muslim holy law, the shariah (Ahmad 1964, Mujeeb 1967).

The numbers of the immigrants were naturally not large, and they were strangers who knew neither the culture, language, and religions (both Buddhism and Hinduism were present) of Sind, nor the prevailing system of governance. In the circumstances, native support was necessary, but this in turn entailed a conciliatory attitude towards Indians, which included the assurance that, by and large, there would be few restrictions on non-Islamic religions. In terms of strict Islamic orthodoxy, however, these religions could only be called ignorance (*jahalat*, incorrect belief). The long-term consequence of this initial compromise made for reasons of the state was twofold: firstly, it laid the foundations of multi-religious polities in which Islam and the Indic religions would coexist, much to the chagrin of the guardians of orthodoxy; secondly, it sowed the seeds of an Indian Islam, accommodating Indian culture traits and forms of social organization (notably caste).

From the time of major incursions of political Islam into India, beginning with the invasions of Mahmud, king of Ghazni, in the early years of the eleventh century, two kinds of religious specialists became prominent. These were the ulama, doctors of shariah, and the Sufi, mystics in search of direct religious experience. The ulama urged the kings to uphold shariah and to be vigilant on behalf of their own religion rather than tolerant of other misguided faiths. One such outstanding medieval scholar, Zia ud-din Barani (c. 1280–1360), was of the opinion that the Muslim kings could not be the refuge of Islam unless they completely destroyed unbelief, polytheism, and idolatory. If the kings cannot actually exterminate the unbelievers (because they are so many), they surely should deny them authority and honour, he advised (de Bary

1959: 479–81 et passim). Such extremist opinions, however, never became general among the ulama or ascendant in the ruling circles. The ulama actually split into two categories: while some of them confined themselves to their specialized duties and kept aloof from statecraft, others opted for a close relationship with the kings. They supported the actions of the rulers even when these were grounded in statecraft rather than true faith as interpreted by those qualified to do so.

Islam spread throughout the length and breadth of India, less by the episodic coercion and violence of the kings, and more by the generally peaceful efforts of the ulama and the Sufis. In areas of mass conversion, notably East Bengal (or what is today Bangladesh) and the Kashmir valley, other factors also, including the ecological and the economic, contributed (directly or indirectly) to the phenomenon (Eaton 1993). It is noteworthy, however, that at the time of partition in 1947, after 800 years of Muslim rule, no more than a quarter of all the people of India (400 million) were Muslims. In the Gangetic valley, where Muslims provided enormous support to the demand for Pakistan, fewer than two out of every ten Indians professed Islam.

When Islam reached India, it was already marked by divisions of various kinds. According to Muslim tradition, Muhammad himself had prophesied that there would be more sects (firqah) in Islam than among the children of Israel, but that they would all be sent to hell by God. Only those who followed the revelation and his words and deeds, and of his closest companions, would be the ones to be saved (najiyah). They came to be called the Sunni (from sunnah, customary way of life) or traditionalists, and account for the great majority of Indian Muslims. Their opponents are the Shiahs ('followers'), who came into being following Muhammad's death as the partisans of Ali, the Prophet's cousin and son-in-law, whom they considered the legitimate successor (khalifah) and leader (imam). It was not Ali, however, but Muhammad's father-in-law, Abu Bakr, who was chosen, resulting in the Sunni-Shiah split which even today leads to violence in both India and Pakistan.

Besides the Shiahs, it is the Sufis who are excoriated by the traditionalists. A connection has been sought to be established between the two heterodoxies by claiming Ali as one of the founders of Sufism (tasawwuf). According to another view, the Arabian philosophy derived from the teaching of al-Ghazali (1058–1111) was absorbed into Islam in the form of a mystical theology, but this locates Sufism late in the fifth century of Islam.

Some scholars, including the renowned early medieval historian al-Biruni (973–1048), found similarities between some key ideas of Sufism and the Brahmanical philosophy of Yoga or the magical tantra. Indeed, it has been suggested that Abu Yazid Tayfur of Iran (d. 874), a key figure in the development of Sufism, may have learned the principles of Brahmanical and Buddhist mysticism from Abu Ali of Sind who himself may have been a convert to Islam. Be that as it may, two general observations can be made. First, a considerable number of Indic elements are recognizable in Sufism in India, but only some of these are pure borrowings, the others being adaptations of classical Islamic Sufi ideas in the Indian cultural environment. Second, Sunni orthodoxy has always frowned upon both Shiahs and Sufis (see Rizvi 1978, 1982).

Four major worldwide Sufi orders—namely Chishti, Naqshbandi, Qadiri, and Suhrawardi—are present in India. Besides, there are numerous local orders of seekers, faqirs, and darveshs: while some of them are seriously devout, the devotion to higher spiritual goals is highly suspect among others, who are often given to excesses of various kinds, including drug abuse. Among the former, mention may be made of the Rishi order of the Kashmir valley (Khan 1994).

Islam was brought to Kashmir, it is generally believed, by the Kubrawi Sufi Sayyid Ali Hamadani late in the fourteenth century, but his efforts seem to have been confined to a small group of neo-converts including the sultan in the city of Srinagar. It was Shaikh Nuruddin (AD 1379–1442), the founder of the Rishi order, who carried the new faith to the masses. His success owed much, not only to his amiable disposition and peaceful methods of preaching, but also to his familiarity with and adaptation of prevailing Brahmanical religious ideas and practices (Kashmir Shaivism). His choice of the name Rishi (a Sanskrit word meaning 'seer') for his order is itself revelatory. He adopted vegetarianism for himself and his followers out of his compassion for animals, and thus abjured the universal Muslim practice of animal sacrifice.

While some historians have written of two types of Sufism in Kashmir, the immigrant and the native, or the classical and the folk, others have denied the existence of this dichotomy, pointing out that Sufis of the Suhrawardi order, and even the Kubrawis, befriended and eulogized the Rishis. According to the latter, the very rootedness of the Rishis in Kashmir's old religious traditions, combined with their exposure to the ideas of classical Sufism, made them the ideal agents of the Islamization of Kashmiri masses. It is noteworthy that Nuruddin claimed the Prophet of Islam himself as the real founder of his order, locating himself in shariah, the 'highway' of Islam.

It is not the Sufis alone who have contributed to the culture of religious diversity in Indian Islam. The reputedly more stringent ulama also have done so. Thus, in the late nineteenth century three groups of these doctors of the holy law of Islam led sectarian movements differentiated from one another by big issues (such as matters of belief and law) as well as small (including minutiae of everyday life). The most influential of these were the ulama of a famous seminary called the Darul Uloom at Deoband in north India (founded in 1867) (Metcalf 1982). Their educational programme too was grounded in the traditional curriculum and thus opposed to the innovations and accommodations of western science that characterized the efforts of the modernists at the Mohammadan Anglo-Oriental College in Aligarh (founded in 1874).

Besides the Deobandis, the two other prominent reformist groups were the Ahl-i Hadis ('people of the tradition') and the ulama of Bareilly, popularly known as the Barelwis, who were opposed to both the other groups. In their disputations, one or the other of the four recognized schools of Islamic Law (Hanafi, Maliki, Shafii, Hanbali) were invoked, but the Hanafi school has always been the dominant one in India (Fyzee 1955).

Finally, mention must be made of the Ahmadiyah sect which was formally proclaimed to be heretical, and therefore a non-Muslim minority, in Pakistan in 1974. Its founder, Mirza Ghulam Ahmad (1839–1908) was born in Qadiyan a village in north Punjab. Not trained as a Sufi, he was a law clerk by occupation. He also claimed to be the recipient of divine revelation and therefore the messiah (*mahdi*) promised to the Muslims. Although Ahmad did not dispute the Islamic belief in the closure of prophecy with Muhammad, he asserted that he belonged to a line of secondary prophets. Provoked and influenced by the work of Christian missionaries and the activities of the Hindu revivalist Arya Samaj movement, he organized his response on similar lines, and gathered a considerable following. The sect called Ahmadiyah, or Qadiyani, continues to be recognized as Muslim in India, reflecting a general attitude of tolerance rather than stern disapproval of diversity within the Islamic faith as well as among different faiths (Friedman 2002).

RELIGIOUS PLURALISM AS IDEOLOGY

In the previous three sections we described the diversity or plurality of religions in India at two levels. These were, first, the global level, at which the major religions of India were in focus, and, second, the intra-religious level at which sectarian or quasi-sectarian movements operate. We have seen that a naive distinction between pluralist Indic religions and homogeneous (fundamentalist) Indian religions of foreign origin is wholly misleading. It is obvious that internal plurality becomes inescapable whenever a religious community comprises many regional cultural groups, and also has considerable numbers, running into millions. But whatever is present empirically may yet be denied or deprecated ideologically. The question then is: has the long history of religious diversity in India produced serious arguments supporting and justifying the phenomenon? In other words, has plurality generated pluralism (see Coward 1987)?

Contemporary ideologues of secularism, understood as religious pluralism, speaking on behalf of or within the Hindu tradition, often claim that pluralism is as old as the oldest Veda. It is recalled that the *Rig Veda* (1.164.46) proclaims that 'the Absolute is one, although the sages have given it different names'. The oneness of the Absolute is the primary assertion here, but the fact that the wise sages choose to state it variously must imply worthiness of pluralism. This pluralism is, however, internal to the Vedic tradition. It is silent on inter-religious pluralism. Similarly, it is pointed out that the *Manu Smriti* (II.14) resolved the problem of conflict between contradictory revelations by laying down that they are all valid and must therefore be respected. Although revelation (shruti) enshrined in the Vedas and other sacred texts is respected, it does not follow that it is widely known among Hindus, like, perhaps, the Bible is among the Christians or the Quran among the Muslims. In the absence of a single core text—the Bhagavad Gita has come to acquire such a position in relatively modern times—or a single founder, or a set of irrefutable fundamentals, or the practice of conversion from other religions, it is not surprising that the Hindu religious tradition has from its earliest beginnings been marked by pluralist tendencies. These have been in consonance with the cellular social organization based on the institution of caste and are essentially hierarchical in character (Madan 1997).

A further observation is in order. The making of the so-called Hindu tradition has been a gradual process of fusion. It has been documented by historians how the carriers of the Brahmanical tradition, as they travelled east and south, established their hegemonic position through give and take (propagation and accommodation) (Chakrabarti 2001). Cultural anthropologists engaged in fieldwork in the 1950s wrote about the processes of parochialization (the downward flow and spread of elements of the Great Sanskritic Tradition) and universalization (the upward rise and spread of elements of the Little Folk Traditions) (Marriott 1955). The homogenizing tendencies never had free rein and diversities have remained resilient and a distinguishing feature of later

Hinduism (Marriott 1976). In short, pluralism is said to be inherent in Hinduism in respect of its internal structure.

Such pluralism as is present operates within the Hindu tradition and is only derivatively applied to other religious traditions. Hinduism tolerates difference by incorporating and hierarchizing it: Buddhism, Jainism, and Sikhism are all considered inferior varieties of Hinduism. Moreover, conflict has not been altogether absent, as the record of the persecution of Buddhists and Jains by various Hindu groups, or of inter-sectarian conflicts between, say, the Shaivas and the Vaishnavas, shows. One can say, however, that the traditional Brahmanical notion of the legitimacy of the right of a group to its own way of life (*svadharma*; *adhikara bheda*), without conceding that the different ways are of equal merit, is a form of pluralism.

In modern times, the Bengali mystic, Ramakrishna (1836–86) and his renowned disciple Vivekananda (1863–1902) are credited with promoting the ideology of religious pluralism by word and deed. Ramakrishna was no intellectual, but in his quest for spiritual experience he practised a simplified Islamic life for sometime, withdrawing completely from his Brahmanical observances. He also disregarded sectarian differences among the Hindus (Sarkar 1993). Vivekananda formulated an ideology of pluralism, but it was based on tolerance of other religions rather than their acceptance as being equal to Hinduism. In fact, within Hinduism itself, he raised Vedanta above all other creeds, calling it the mother of all religions and truer than any other religion. He was explicitly critical of Buddhism and Christianity. The ultimate goal of the Ramakrishna Mission, which he established, was the spiritual conquest of humanity (Basu 2002). Often referred to as neo-Hinduism, this late nineteenth-century development was a reversal of traditional internal pluralism, which was wide in range, and accompanied by such a diversity of belief and practice that some Western scholars, writing from the perspective of biblical religiosity, doubted if Hinduism could be called a religion at all (Weber 1958: 23). In its place, an inter-religious pluralism, but within a hierarchical framework, was sought to be put in place. Both innovations had clear political implications: the forging of a national consciousness in the context of colonial subjugation, on the one hand, and the projection of Hinduism as a tolerant, universal religion, ready to provide spiritual leadership to the followers of all faiths, on the other.

While Bengal witnessed these developments, Punjab was the scene for the flowering of the Arya Samaj movement, founded by Dayananda (1824–83) in Bombay in 1874. He not only rejected post-Vedic forms of Hinduism as erroneous, and condemned what he called 'blind faith' (e.g.

idol worship) and 'harmful customs' (e.g. practice of caste and gender discrimination), but also denied that Christianity and Islam could be considered divinely inspired religions. He made derogatory observations about them as well as Buddhism, Jainism, and Sikhism. The teachings of Arya Samaj represent the exclusivist strand of vedic Hinduism, anticipate later explicitly fundamentalist developments (notably the thesis of Hindutva, or Hindu identity), and militate against pluralism as an ideology.

In the twentieth century, Mahatma Gandhi (1869–1948) put forward the most explicit formulation of religious pluralism when he announced on 30 May 1913 that, in his opinion, 'the world as a whole will never have, *and need not have* a single religion' (emphasis added). By acknowledging his indebtedness to Christianity and Islam, Gandhi implied that Hinduism could be enriched by incorporating in it some of the truths discovered by other religions. While he maintained that all religions were equally true, he added that, because of the limitations of human intellect, they were also equally imperfect. He refused to hierarchize the relationship between different religions, and thus moved in the direction of a genuine religious pluralism.

Writing in *Young India* in 1920 (11 August), Gandhi conceded that his critics were often right from their perspective in considering his ideas and actions wrong, while he was from his own point of view sure that he was right. Expressing his admiration for the Jain doctrine of 'many-sidedness' (*anekantavad*), he wrote: 'It is this doctrine that taught me to judge a Mussalman from his own standpoint and a Christian from his.'

According to Jain ontology, whatever exists has three aspects: substance (*dravya*), quality (*guna*), and mode of expression (*paryaya*). Substance is not matter, for even the soul is considered a substance. *Dravya* is the means through which qualities exist. These qualities are numerous and their modes are infinite. Therefore, no ordinary person can perceive the existent in its entirely or 'many-sidedness' (Jaini 1979: 90–1). Hence the epistemology of *anekantavad* or manifold aspects of reality. This doctrine has certain consequences, a notable one being conditional assertion (*syadavada*). Absolute, that is unqualified, statements about existential reality cannot be made. Four specifications are required. These are: the specific being (*sva-dravya*), location (*sva-kshetra*), time (*sva-kala*), and state of being (*sva-bhava*) of the reality under reference (ibid.: 94ff.).

Buddhist pluralism is even wider in its scope, and nothing is expressed in unities. The four noble truths are at the very core of the Buddha's teaching. The first of these truths, namely the universality of suffering has many causes, notably worldly attachments (the second truth). The way to the ending of both (suffering, attachment) lies through the eightfold noble path (the fourth truth), which brings release (*nibanna*) (the third truth), of which there are at least two modes. For the laity, there are three refuges: the Buddha, the Law (dhamma), and the community (sangha). According to Mahayana metaphysics, even the Buddhas are many.

Doctrines of ontological and epistemological pluralism within Jainism and Buddhism do not, however, translate into inter-sectarian toleration. The original teaching of the Buddha came to be regarded, as already noted above, as the lesser vehicle (Hinayana) by the later Mahayanists who virtually drove it out to Sri Lanka. Jain sects too are characterized by mutual exclusiveness.

Islam is, as we have seen, the second major religion of India. Except in Indonesia and Bangladesh, there are more Muslims in India today than in any other country. The attitudes of Muslims to the phenomenon of religious plurality are, therefore, of great importance for the future of the ideology of pluralism. Given the fundamental Muslim belief that Islam is the most perfect of all divinely revealed religions, and that the Quran is the Word of God, any attempt to project pluralism has to honour these beliefs. A careful reader of the holy book of Islam will find many passages on which an ideology of religious pluralism can be based. To give but one example: 'To you your religion and to me mine' (109.3), although this is often said to be applicable only to the peoples with a revealed book.

In the mid-seventeenth century, Dara Shikoh, heir to the Mughal throne, disciple of a Sufi master and a Sanskrit scholar, made a close study of the Upanishads and even translated some of them into Persian. He concluded that they were revealed scriptures, anticipating the divine message of monotheism elaborated in the Quran. He described Vedantic Hinduism and Islam as 'twin brothers': for this he was declared a heretic by the ulama, and beheaded on the orders of his brother, the emperor Aurangzeb, who had usurped the succession.

In the twentieth century, the most elaborate effort to argue for religious pluralism on the basis of the Quran itself was made by Maulana Abul Kalam Azad (1888–1958), profound scholar of religion and distinguished political leader. His many-stranded argument focused on, among other issues, the attributes of God and the true nature of divine revelation. He maintained that the manner in which 'divine providence' (*rububiyat*), 'divine benevolence' (*rahmat*), and 'divine justice' (*adalat*) are defined in the Quran, makes it obvious that Allah is God of all creation, and that the oneness of humanity is derived from the oneness of God. As for divine revelation, for it to be itself, it must provide guidance to everyone without distinction. Like Dara Shikoh, he detected significant common truths and insights in Islam and Vedantic Hinduism on the foregoing and other key issues. His effort, in the form of an exegesis of the Quran, ran into difficulties with the ulama who detected in it many serious flaws, including an alleged devaluation of the intermediary role of the Prophet and of the importance of formal prayer. In the event, Azad never brought his monumental undertaking to its conclusion (Azad 1962).

Pluralism as an ideological stance within the Hindu and Indian Muslim religious traditions recognizes and respects plurality, but stresses the oneness of the ultimate goal of different expressions of the religious quest. It is an invitation to coexistence, dialogue, and even syncretism. Religious devotionalism (*bhakti*) of the medieval period in northern India, expressed through 'the voice of the seekers of the truth' (*sant vani*), was echoed by the ecstatic mysticism of the Sufis. Nanak, the first Sikh guru, was a unique representative of the *sant* tradition. He sought emancipation from all external formalisms (rituals, customs, social distinctions) through a valorization of the inner spiritual quest. He dismissed the meaningfulness of the prevailing religious distinctions. More than a reconciliation or synthesis, his teaching presented a transcendent third path. The last of the Sikh personal gurus, Gobind, also declared that the true Sikhs or the Khalsa ('the pure' or 'the chosen') would have to be different from both Hindus and Muslims in physical appearance (unshorn and uncircumcized) as well as moral fibre (expressed through a code of conduct beginning with formal initiation or pahul). He too pointed to a higher path transcending not only the divide between Hinduism and Islam, but also the inner polarities of the former (e.g. domesticity versus renunciation). Like the Hindu and Indian Muslim perspectives on religious pluralism, the Sikh vision also is hierarchical. Moreover, as we move from Guru Nanak to the tenth and last personal guru, Gobind, there is an explicit tightening of the definition of Sikh identity, differentiating it from the Hindu identity and homogenizing it internally. In this context, the drawing up of the codes of conduct, *rahitnamas*, (McLeod 1989) for the Khalsa is a significant development. For the Sikhs generally, the only true source of spiritual knowledge is the *gurubani*, the word of the Guru, as present above all in the Guru Granth Sahab. Those born to other religious traditions are welcome to embrace the Sikh faith and identity (hence the *gora* Sikhs of North America), but a Sikh who is lax in the observance of the Sikh way of life or, worse, follows the practices of other traditions is a lapsed or fallen (*patit*) individual. In short, the Sikh faith in its Khalsa version is exclusivist, not pluralist. The Bhindranwale phenomenon showed that a fundamentalist turn too was possible (Madan 1997: Chapter 3).

The task of developing a well-argued ideology of religious pluralism on the basis of the religions of India awaits serious and competent attention. The emergence of state-sponsored religious pluralism, summed up in the slogan *sarva dharma samabhava* (equal respect for all religions), and presented as Indian (in contrast to Western) secularism, does not go very far in strengthening inter-religious understanding and appreciation (Smith 1963, Madan 1997). These values are more profound than a working strategy of passive tolerance, and will have to be promoted by men and women of faith themselves. As Gandhi pointed out, the task of the secular state is to leave matters of religion to the people.

Contrary to the assumption of many modernists that religious faith is necessarily exclusive and therefore results in communal conflict, there is considerable historical and ethnographical evidence that the common people of India, irrespective of individual religious identity, have long been comfortable with religious plurality. They acknowledge religious difference as the experienced reality: they do not consider it good or bad. In other words, social harmony, or agreement, is built on the basis of difference.

The traditional elite of the nineteenth century were familiar with this folk pluralism, but considered it as no more than the ignorance of unlettered masses. Today's modernist intelligentsia have opted for the ideology of secularism. In its extreme version, it seeks to drive religion into the privacy of people's lives, if not altogether eliminate it. More generally and eclectically, secularism in India stands for mutual respect among the followers of different religions and a non-discriminatory state. This ideology envisages a pluralism that is a concomitant of structural differentiation in society. Needless to emphasize, the two pluralisms—the people's and the intellectual's—are different in several crucial respects. For example, and most notably, the former is wholly spontaneous—the lived social reality—but the latter is ideological and in that sense self-conscious or constructed; the former is based on a positive attitude towards religion, but the latter is sceptical. Indeed, there is a hiatus between the two pluralisms, but this has not been so far examined with the seriousness it deserves (Madan 1997).

BIBLIOGRAPHY

Ahmad, Aziz, *Studies in Islamic culture in the Indian environment*, Oxford: Clarendon Press, 1964.

Atiya, Aziz S., *A History of Eastern Christianity*, London: Methuen, 1968.

Azad, Abul Kalam, *The Tarjuman al-Quran*, Vol.1. Ed. and tr. by Syed Abdul Latif, Bombay: Asia, 1962.

Babb, Lawrence A., *Absent Lord: Ascetics and Kings in Jain Ritual Culture,* Berkeley: University of California Press, 1996.

Baird, Robert D. (ed.), *Religion in Modern India*, New Delhi: Manohar, 1995.

Basu, Shamita, *Religious Revivalism as Nationalist Discourse*, New Delhi: Oxford University Press, 2002.

Bayly, Susan, *Saints, Goddesses and Kings: Muslims and Christians in South Indian Society*. Cambridge: Cambridge University Press, 1989.

Brockington, J.L., *The Sacred Thread: A Short History of Hinduism*, Delhi: Oxford University Press, 1992.

Bhattacharji, Sukumari, *The Indian Theogony*, Delhi: Motilal Banarsidass., 1988.

Census of India, *Census of India 1991*, Series I, India Paper 1 of 1995: Religion, New Delhi: Government of India, 1995.

Chakrabarti, Kunal, *Religious Process: The Puranas and the Making of a Religious Tradition*, New Delhi: Oxford University Press, 2001.

Coward, Howard G., (ed.), *Modern India's Responses to Religious Pluralism*, Albany: State University of New York Press, 1987.

de Bary, Wm. T. (Gen. ed.), *Sources of Indian Tradition*, New York: Columbia University Press, 1958.

Dimmit, Cornelia, and J.A.B. van Buitenen, (eds & trans.), *Classical Hindu Mythology*, Philadelphia: Temple University Press, 1978.

Doniger, Wendy (with Brian K. Smith), trans., *The Laws of Manu*, New Delhi: Penguin Books, 1991.

Dundas, Paul, *The Jains*, London: Routledge, 1992.

Durkheim, Emile, *The Elementary Forms of Religious Life,* (trans.) Karen E. Fields, New York: The Free Press, 1995.

Eaton, Richard, *The Rise of Islam and the Bengal Frontier, 1204-1760*, Berkeley: University of California Press, 1993.

Flood, Gavin, *An Introduction to Hinduism*, Cambridge: Cambridge University Press, 1996.

Friedman, Yohannes, *Aspects of Ahmadi Religious Thought and Its Medieval Background*, New Delhi: Oxford University Press, 2002.

Fuller, C.J., *The Camphor Flame: Popular Hinduism and Society in India*, Princeton, N.J.: Princeton University Press, 1992.

Fyzee, A.A.A., *Outlines of Mohammedan Law*, Bombay: Oxford University Press, 1956.

Gibbs, M.E., *The Anglican Church in India, 1600-1970,* Delhi: ISPCK, 1972.

Gold, Ann Grodzins, *Fruitful Journeys: The Ways of Rajasthani Pilgrims,* Berkeley: University of California Press, 1988.

Gombridge, Richard, *Theravada Buddhism*, London: Routledge, 1988.

Gottschalk, Peter, *Beyond Hindu and Muslim: Multiple Identity in Narratives from Village India,* New Delhi: Oxford University Press, 2001.

Grewal, J.S., *The Sikhs of the Punjab,* Cambridge: Cambridge University Press, 1990.

Halbfass, Wilhelm, *India and Europe: An Essay in Understanding,* Albany: State University of New York Press, 1988.

Harvey, Peter, *An Introduction to Buddhism: Teaching, History and Practices,* Cambridge: Cambridge University Press, 1990.

Hawley, John Stratton, and Donna Marie Wulff (eds), *Devi: Goddesses of India,* Berkeley: University of California Press, 1996.

Hiriyana, M., *Outlines of Indian Philosophy*, Delhi: Motilal Banarsidass, 1993.

Ilaiah, Kancha, *Why I am Not a Hindu*, Calcutta: Samya, 1996.

Jaini, Padmanabh S., *The Jain Path of Purification*, Delhi: Motilal Banarsidass, 1976.

Jones, Kenneth, W., *Socio-religious Reform Movements in British India,* Cambridge: Cambridge University Press, 1989.

Kapur, Rajiv, *Sikh Separatism: The Politics of Faith,* London: Allen and Unwin, 1986.

Khan, Muhammad Ishaq, *Kashmir's Transition to Islam: The Role of Muslim Rishis,* New Delhi: Manohar, 1994.

Kosambi, D.D., *The Culture and Civilization of Ancient India in Historical Outline,* New Delhi: Vikas, 1970.

Laidlaw, James, *Riches and Renunciation: Religion, Economy and Society among the Jains,* Oxford: Clarendon Press, 1995.

Larson, Gerald James, *India's Agony over Religion,* Albany: State University of New York Press, 1995.

Lingat, Robert, *The Classical Law of India*, Berkeley: The University of California Press, 1973.

Lorenzen, D.N., *The Kapalikas and Kalamukhas: Two Lost Shaivite Sects,* New Delhi: Manohar, 1972.

Madan, T.N., *Modern Myths, Locked Minds: Secularism and Fundamentalism in India,* Delhi: Oxford University Press, 1997.

——, *Freedom of Religion*, Typescript, 2002.

Marglin, Frederique Apffel, *Wives of the God-king: The Rituals of the Devadasis of Puri,* Delhi: Oxford University Press, 1985.

Marriott, McKim, 'Little Communities in an Indigenous Civilization', in M. Marriott (ed.), *Village India*, Chicago: University of Chicago Pres, 1955.

——, 'Hindu Transactions: Diversity without Dualism', in B. Kapferer (ed.), *Transaction and Meaning*, Philadelphia: Institute for the Study of Human Issues, 1976.

Mathew, C.P. and M.M. Thomas, *The Indian Churches of Saint Thomas*, Delhi: ISPCK., 1967.

Metcalf, Barbara Daly, *Islamic Revival in British India: Deoband 1860-1900*, Princeton, N.J.: Princeton University Press, 1982.

McLeod, W.H., *Guru Nanak and the Sikh Religion*, Delhi: Oxford University Press, 1968.

——, *Who is a Sikh?*, Oxford: Clarendon Press, 1989.

Mujeeb, Muhammad, *The Indian Muslims*, London: Allen and Unwin, 1967.

Oberoi, Harjot S., *The Construction of Religious Boundaries: Culture, Identity and Diversity in the Sikh Tradition*, New Delhi: Oxford University Press, 1994.

Olivelle, Patrick, *The Early Upanisads*, New York: Oxford University Press, 1998.

——, *Dharmasutras: The Law Codes of Apastamba, Gautama, Baudhayana, and Vasishtha*, Delhi: Motilal Banarsidass, 2000.

Parpola, A., *Deciphering the Indus Script*, Cambridge: Cambridge University Press, 1994.

Possehl, Gregory L., (ed.), *Harappan Civilization*, New Delhi: Oxford and IBH., 1982.

Roy, Asim, *The Islamic Syncretistic Tradition in Bengal*, Princeton N.J.: Princeton University Press, 1983.

Radhakrishnan, S., *The Hindu View of Life*, London: Allen and Unwin, 1927.

Rahman, Fazlur, *Islam*, Second edition, Chicago: The University of Chicago Press, 1979.

Ramanujan, A.K., *Speaking of Siva*, Baltimore, Penguin Press, 1973.

——, *Hymns for the Drowning: Poems for Visnu by Nammalvar*, Princeton N.J.: Princeton University Press, 1981.

Ratnagar, Shereen, *The End of the Great Harappan Tradition*, New Delhi: Manohar, 2000.

Rizvi, Saiyid Athar Abbas, *A History of Sufism in India*, Vols 1 & 2, Delhi: Munshiram Manoharlal, 1978, 1982.

Robinson, Rowena, *Conversion, Continuity and Change: Lived Christianity in Southern Goa*, New Delhi: Sage, 1998.

Sarkar, Sumit, *An Exploration of the Ramakrishna-Vivekananda Tradition*, Shimla: Indian Institute of Advance Study, 1993.

Smith, Donald Engene, *India as a Secular State*, Bombay: Oxford University Press, 1963.

Thapar, Romila, *A History of India*, Vol. One, Harmondsworth: Penguin, 1966.

Thapar, Romila, *Early India: From the Origins to AD 1300,* London: Allen Lane, 2002.

Uberoi, J.P.S., *Religion, Civil Society and the State: A Study of Sikhism,* Delhi: Oxford University Press, 1996.

Visvanathan, Susan, *The Christians of Kerala: History, Belief and Ritual among the Yakoba,* Delhi: Oxford University Press, 1993.

Weber, Max, *The Religion of India: The Sociology of Hinduism and Buddhism,* Glencoe, Illinois.: The Free Press, 1958.

Zelliot, Eleanor, *From Untouchable to Dalit,* New Delhi: Manohar, 1996.

Plurality of Religion and Plurality in Religion
Christianity and Islam

CHRISTIAN W. TROLL

CHRISTIANITY

A Few Basic Aspects of the Christian Vision

The 'Good News' as it was proclaimed and lived by Jesus of Nazareth, consists in the revelation of God as Father of all human beings, of God as all-embracing, unconditional love, with a predilection for the 'down-trodden' and 'marginalized', 'the sinners'. In this love of God, Jesus wishes to gather the women and men of his people and all human beings. All women and men—in the first place the 'poor'—are called into the 'kingdom of God', i.e. into the reign of the love of God.

In the New Testament, which bears witness to the faith of the earliest apostolic Church, Jesus Christ is the Word of God, the highest, last and definite revelation of God. God in and through Jesus the Christ turns to all human beings; Christianity is essentially universal. History shows that the Church from its first beginnings has understood its mission as universal. It knew herself to be called into the service of the universal, all-reconciling love of God (cf. 2 Cor 5:18–21; Eph 2:11–12).

Historically speaking, Christianity generated and developed because of the dynamic faith of the apostles and the first Christian generations. Their witness and proclamation was effective, in spite of, even because of, the persecutions. After the Edict of Milan (AD 313), which guaranteed to the Church full religious freedom and led to the Church becoming soon afterwards under emperor Theodosius I, in AD 380, the official religion of the empire, Christianity got entangled and allowed itself to be embroiled in various bellicose clashes. Having accepted the privileged status of religion of the state, it promoted or tolerated state precautions of dissidents and exertion of social pressure upon them. Thus Christianity became co-responsible for corresponding law enactment and policies. Although these were political undertakings, not infrequently they were justified in religious terms, in order to add to their impact. The question of the crusades seems to belong to a slightly different category, in so far as here religious motivation (e.g. the question of the liberation of the Sacred Tomb) without doubt constituted an important, if not the primary, motive. The relationship between colonialism and mission(s) must not be conceived on the lines of a unified, regular scheme. At times the missionaries accompanied or followed the colonialists (often, if not normally in the case of the Portuguese and Spaniards during the fifteenth and the sixteenth centuries). At other times they arrived first and independently (e.g. in Central Africa, China); and at yet other times the missionaries opposed colonization (cf. Las Casas in Latin America, French Africa).

With regard to the question as to the place the non-Christian religions occupy in the view of the Christian faith, Christian thought has gone through a long development, from Justin (d. 165), who speaks of spiritual seeds, which wait in all humans beings for the Word of God, in order to bear fruit, via the views of Augustine of Hippo (AD 354–430), who, in the context of our discussion here, in rhetorical exaggeration considered even the virtues of the pagans as vices, to the theories of those who concede to the unbelievers that they are in good faith (bona fide) and hence not to be condemned. In more recent times there existed the theory of the pièrres d'attente among the non-Christians (i.e. the Christian-theological teaching of the elements of the faith and the morals of the peoples and cultures which, as it were, are waiting for their fulfilment and clarification in the light of the incarnation of God in Jesus Christ), which eventually led to the presently prevailing positions.

Among the more recent efforts to develop an adequate theology of the non-Christian religions, two merit special mention here. The second of the two in the meantime has found a wide echo.

- *Accent on the distinction between faith and religion:* This theory was first exposed by the Protestant theologians Karl Barth (1886–1968) and Dietrich Bonhoeffer (1906–1945) and later, with modifications, taken over and adapted by Catholic thinkers like Jean Daniélou

(1905–1974). Religion is the natural movement of the human crea-ture towards God—collective manifestations, translated into rites, expressions, and forms of piety. In the conception of Barth, at least during the early phase of his thought, religions are seen as mere products of human will and power and are judged negatively as standing in contrast with faith in the word of revelation. Daniélou assigns to them a much higher position: each human group, each circle of civilization has its own religion. Thus one can speak duly of a Celtic, Germanic, Mediterranean, African, and Indian religion. In the Christian religion, too, one detects traits and comes across elements that are comparable to the other religions. On the other hand, faith is the human response to the Word of God, to God who takes the initiative to encounter his creatures and put them, literally speaking, 'in question', i.e. challenges and allows them to respond by way of religious and cultural choices to this call. If religion is the movement of the human soul towards God, faith is the answer of the human person to the Word of God, which reaches him in revelations. Faith in Jesus Christ has to incarnate itself in each religion; by entering in contextual, relevant ways into the cultures it transforms these and provides their rites, laws, and traditions with new meaning and importance. Daniélou's conclusion is that the human person by adopting the Christian faith 'does not move from one religion to another', but rather that the person's religion is being newly formed and transformed in this encounter.

Distinction between common and special revelation: A new approach was developed by Karl Rahner (1904–1984) and subsequently, in essential aspects, by many other Christian theologians. From the beginning of human life on earth, God has never ceased to commu-nicate Himself to the human being. This 'general' revelation is witnessed to by the Bible, with Adam, Noah, the book of Wisdom, the Letter of Paul to the Romans (1:19ff). The great non-Christian religions are the higher manifestations of the general revelation. Then, however, the Word of God appeared in a 'special' way, in the history of the people of God, beginning with Abraham, through the patriarchs and the prophets, and finally, 'in these last days', through Jesus Christ—the Word of God made human who constitutes the fullness of revelation. In the 'special' revelation the self-communica-tion of God, which happens also in the 'general' revelation, becomes, as it were, historically palpable; it receives a human face: Jesus of Nazareth. 'Who has seen me, has seen the Father' (Jo 15:9). From here, light is also thrown upon the presence of God in all religions.

But the revelation of God in Jesus Christ, too, will be unveiled in its full meaning only at the time of the *parùsia*, i.e. God's 'coming' at the end of time. Understood in this way, the recognition of Jesus Christ as fullness of revelation, far from devaluating the other religions and demeaning them, denying the true relation to God and true veneration of God, is to be understood as an invitation to recognize the other revelations as various, different contributions to unveiling the full meaning of revelation. Thus, the dialogue of religions can be viewed as a process in and by which both Christians and non-Christians are purified and enriched.

Christianity can be true to the Gospel only as message of peace and reconciliation. Jesus clearly and definitively refused being the—or a—political Messiah. He decided to die rather than to revolt politically; to forgive and not to seek political power and revenge. Later, as the result of the support that was granted from Emperor Constantine the Great (reigned 306–337 ce), the Church entered into such a close relationship with the state, that at times it even proclaimed wars, and blessed and justified them. For decades now it is the effort of the Catholic Church under the leadership of the pope as it is also the effort of the World Council of Churches, on all possible occasions to further peace and justice. Certainly, the Church recognizes the right of individuals and peoples to self-defence and also the right—in given cases even the duty—to resist political regimes that are evidently unjust. A Christian should however—where and whenever possible—prefer non-violent actions (which are far from futile) and do what is in her or his might to overcome the narrowness of theocratic, nationalistic, religious-fanatic ideologies and their potential for violence.

Faith is a true gift from God. It is either accepted freely by the human person or rejected. History knows of 'conversions' which came about through compulsion or under duress (e.g. the pagan Saxons compelled by Charlemagne reigned 771–814 to accept baptism under penalty of death), or of cases, where conversion came about because of, or was to some extent collaterally influenced by, purely human motives and social factors. For a long time it had been the prevalent opinion in the Church that the best system of relations between Church and State is the one where Christianity is proclaimed and accepted as the religion of the state and where 'error has no right whatsoever'. It is also true that the Church has repeatedly asked for the freedom to be able to accept the Christian faith without having to accept disadvantages for doing so; however it has been much more reluctant to accept—in principle—the freedom of a Christian to interpret the faith independently and in his or her own ways or even to give up one's Christian faith or 'to change to another religion' (e.g. the inquisition). The knowledge about the long and painful process of the development of the idea of religious freedom in Christian history can help Christians to understand better certain attitudes, reactions, and difficulties of other religious groups with regard to subscribing totally to the principle of religious freedom.

At least from the time of the Second Vatican Council (1962–5) and its 'Declaration on Religious Freedom' (*Dignitatis Humanae*) onwards the attitude of the Church in this matter however is, at least on the normative level, unmistakably clear: religious freedom is to be respected and promoted as one of the basic and absolute rights of the human person as such. The way of religion and of its presentation in the private and public sphere, the way of mission and proclamation must be shaped by the respect of the dignity and convictions of 'the other'. Thus, it becomes clear that what we are talking about is witness in and through dialogical relations. Faith is, from its essence, to be presented in the way of a kind of begging and inviting (cf. 2 Cor 5, 20). It must never be imposed (*faith always is to be proposed not imposed*). Each single person remains free and responsible for her or his personal option, in the light of one's own conscience and in the face of God.

A Few Further Considerations

The Multiplicity of Religions

The multiplicity of religions is a fact and at the same time, for the believer, a mystery. Religiously speaking, it may well have to do something with God's respect for the freedom of the human person, whereas, empirically speaking, it has to do with the natural conditions of the religious and cultural development of humanity. For thousands of years the greater groups of humanity lived in relative isolation from one another. Today, the world is marked by multiple networks and the consciousness of mutual dependence. Various tensions and even wars between human groups continue. In this age, which one might characterize as the age of the birth pangs towards a truly global world, religions have to play a significant role and are thus responsible for the realization of greater justice and harmony in the relations between nations, economic blocks, and cultural groupings of our world. Any conflict (polemics, tactless proselytizing between religions) has to be banned. Only dialogue, and the process of mutual learning that goes with it, can open religions one to the other so that men and women find one another in their diversity and get to know and understand one another better. This does not mean denying differences but rather comprehending them and understanding where they exist, and in what, more exactly, they truly consist. Also, dialogue does not exclude in any way the witnessing to one's own faith nor inviting others to join it. In any case, however, different religions should, wherever common ground can be honestly made out, give a shared witness of faith, which includes a true search for unity, in humble submission to the will of God as best as one has come to know it.

The Multiplicity of 'Universal' Religions

It is a fact that both Islam and Christianity make the claim to universality. There seems to be no reason why they should give up this claim. All depends on which methods and mental attitudes are advocated and adopted on the path towards reaching the realization of this universality. Today, on the way to evermore interconnectedness on a global level, one would plead that those methods should be given up which seem to base themselves on priming individual or collective egoism or egocentrism: the willing acceptance of support on the part of political powers, violence, war, compulsion in all its—including the more subtle—forms and manifestations. The only path acceptable before God and humankind would seem to be universal respect for the values one holds to be true, valid and, therefore, of benefit to all. The testimony of a living faith and of a sincere striving for inter-cultural and inter-religious dialogue and collaboration in justice flows directly from catholic Christian teaching as it articulates itself in our days. This implies the necessary respect for the free decision of persons and consciences.

Religions Responsible for Wars

We have to concede that religions—not least among them catholic Christianity—have been in the past responsible, or at least co-responsible, for wars. Even today, tensions, where religions constitute in one way or other a contributing factor, exist Universal history seems to be marked in this respect, too, by light and shadow. The fact is that religion has on more than one occasion hindered the use of violence or mitigated it. We may think here, of the institution of the 'Landfrieden Gottes' (i.e. the religiously prescribed prohibition or restriction of feuds) during the Christian Middle Ages or of the strict conditions which Islamic Law stipulates for a 'just' war; or of the care for prisoners of war and innocent victims of wars etc. Furthermore, the main reason for religious wars appear to have been not so much animosity between the religions themselves but rather the obsession with, or the thirst for, power on the part of individuals and human groups (realms, dynasties, and nations) where religion has been used in order to satisfy personal and collective ambition. With regard, finally, to contemporary conflicts, information must be checked carefully and critically, before it is simply ascribed to religious motivations. To describe the conflicts in Lebanon, Northern Ireland, the Balkans, the Philippines, and Afghanistan, among others, as religious conflict would merely be an oversimplification. In many, if not most, of these cases certain religious groups and authorities, far from having fostered these religious conflicts, have on the contrary repeatedly intervened for peace and reconciliation.

Freedom of Religion

Religious freedom constitutes one of the sacrosanct rights of each human being. To suppress it or even to chain it is equal to mocking God and the human being. It is the linking of religion and state (or also, today, the linking of nationalism and state or practical atheism—of the capitalist or communist sort—within a given state system) which, not only in the past but right up to our days, has been largely responsible for considerable violations in this area. All religions have the right to work towards being freed from such systems and towards breaking their resistance against the effective putting into practice of religious freedom.

Each person lives for and is committed to promote solidarity, peace, and well-being of one's own religious community or group, be it umma, Church or khalsa and so on. However, today, more than ever before, we need to go beyond this: to defend and promote unconditional respect of the free decision of any person regarding matters of faith and membership to a religious community (religious allegiance), if only such a decision has been made freely, i.e. according to the demands of conscience. The only binding law in this area is the following of the voice of conscience, a conscience that honestly seeks the truth. Only God can probe the heart. For the sake of authenticity of faith and religion decisions in this area should be made in total freedom. In this matter ultimately religion asks of persons only this: to remain constantly in the search for the Will of God. Obviously, though, the freedom mentioned here has its limits in allowing for the right to the same freedom of fellow persons.

ISLAM

Introduction

In this essay we shall evoke a handful of contemporary Islamic voices addressing the question of social, cultural, and religious pluralism. I deliberately name them Islamic and not Muslim voices, because they expressly situate themselves in the context and parameters of the great, living religious tradition of Islam, that is, of the normative sources feeding it and of the religious-legal sciences that developed in it. Hence, these voices for me are Islamic and not only Muslim ones.

It will be wise right at the start to avoid the danger of overestimating the significance of these voices as to their representative quality. The voices are single ones and furthermore they are few, selected from among many other, equally relevant ones. They do not speak in the name of great parties and movements. They articulate—often coura- geously and farsightedly—sentiments, thoughts, and concerns which certainly are shared by many other Muslims, however not by the major- ity and the religious and/or political establishment. All the five thinkers whose ideas we present here are intellectuals who try to face questions that in their view arise from the encounter of Islamic civilization, and its long tradition of religious thought, with the pluralistic, secular 'West' in various regional variations. At the same time, they intend constructively as well as critically to articulate the positive contribution which, in their view, Muslims and hence Islam, could and should make to a peaceful coexistence of all persons in pluralistic societies, ultimately in the one global as well as pluralistic world of our day.

The Reassertion of Islam and Islamism

In choosing the persons presented here I have given preference to those who consciously and decidedly view, and reflect upon, society as some- thing to be shaped by all citizens together. Roughly speaking, one may be allowed to say that for more or less three decades now, that is to say, since the turn from the fourteenth to the fifteenth Hijri century (I am thinking in this context of two eminent events marking this turn: the Islamic Festival in London of 1976 and the Islamic Revolution in Iran under the guidance of Imam Khomeini in 1979) the Muslim world in both its Sunnite and its Shiite variant has been largely shaped by a vision which divided the world into two camps: that of the programmatically godless Marxist dictatorships, and that of the not programmatically but actually godless liberal-capitalistic states. In such Islamic thought one views

Islam as an alternative and complete and independent system, as a comprehensive *nizâm-i mustafâ*, as a 'Third Way', with its own comprehensive ideology and way of life.

The protagonists of such a vision are bound together by the consciousness of the growing power of the umma reasserting itself. The latter—in the sense of an alternative system meant to encompass all aspects of individual and social life—is called to replace the other ideologies and social systems. It will reach this goal in the foreseeable future. The clear formulation of Sayyid Qutb (1906–66) in his work *Ma'âlim fî t-tarîq* (Milestones) has become classical by now:

Islam knows only two categories of society, the Islamic and the pagan one. The Islamic society (*al-mujtama' al-islâmî*) is the one, in which Islam is put into practice in all its dimensions: in doctrine of faith, cult, *sharî'a*, political system, morals and ethical behaviour. The pagan society (*al-mujtama' al-jâhilî*) is the one, where Islam is not practised, i.e., a society ruled neither by its doctrines of faith, nor by its principles, its values and criteria, its political order and laws nor by its moral and ethical standards.

This pagan society finds expression not only in the social system that denies the existence of God and interprets history according to the principles of dialectical materialism and which applies so-called 'scientific socialism' as a political-societal system; it is equally represented by a society which, not denying the existence of God, 'assigns' to him the dominion of the skies, in order to remove him from ruling over the earth. This so-called 'secular', 'laicist' society, does not practise his divine law (*sharî'a*), neither in the ordering of human lives nor in respecting the values which God has ordered as the unchangeable basis for social life ... Hence, this society does not live the religion of God, which he in his own words defines thus: '*The decision is due to God alone. He has commanded that you should serve none but Him. This is the true religion*' (Sure 12, 39–40). This society therefore is a pagan society, even if it does recognize the existence of God and permit man to practice the religious rites in synagogues, churches and mosques.[1]

Such thinking is marked by a remarkable 'simplification' as to the analysis of the West and such realities (and terms) as secular society, secularization, and secularism, including their intellectual and moral bases. The West and secularism are projected as total negation of what Islam stands for. 'In fact, the secular world view is the total negation of the Islamic faith,' 'Abdullah Naseef, the general secretary of the Islamic World League, wrote in 1989. He considers it to be the foremost task

[1] Quoted in Andreas Meier, *Der politische Auftrag des Islam*, Wuppertal, 1994, pp. 203f.

of the Islamic thinker, whom he qualifies as *dâ'i* ('inviter', missionary), to destroy

...the world view of secularism and its intellectual bases. This task includes not only the philosophical refutation of the basic position of secularism but the detailed analysis of all its manifestations, in the Islamic societies as elsewhere. The struggle of Islamic thought with modern secularism is part of the eternal warfare of Islam against *kufr*, against the powers of atheism, lie and evil'.[2]

However, soon, in fact already from the middle of the 1980s onwards, there came into prominence among Muslim intellectuals a disillusion-ment, linked with the premonition that the expectation one had invested in the cogency of the Islamic vision would hardly be fulfilled. At the end of a critical analysis of the Islamic resurgence, the Pakistani juridical scholar Kemal A. Faruqi wrote, in 1985:

The Islamic Resurgence can well turn out to be an anachronistic and false spring, although it may also turn out to be the beginning of an inspiring and positive chapter in the history of humanity in this world of an evermore narrowing mutual dependence.

Let us listen now to the voices of some Muslim thinkers, who consider Islam, at least potentially, a positive force in the effort of forming a pluralistic and just society. However, all of them put critical questions to their fellow Muslims as well as to their non-Muslim partners. They all have been rethinking Islam in terms of its potential for pluralis-tic living in secular democratic societies.

Islam in a Worldwide Community of Communities

Mohamed Talbi, besides being a well-known and outstanding historian of the Maghreb, can well be regarded as the pioneer Muslim thinker and protagonist of inter-cultural dialogue. He is especially conscious of the cultural and religious problems which shape the contemporary Islamic world, especially of its attempts to respond to the challenges of the modern world.

Born in 1921 in Tunis, Talbi taught many years in the 'Institut d'État d'Études Supérieures' in Tunis and obtained his doctorate at the Sorbonne in Paris. The study of the medieval history of North African-Islamic history, linked with a clear analysis of the cultural and political dynamics in the wider context of the technological and cultural developments in

---

[2] 'Muslim Intellectuals and the Future of the Ummah: An Agenda for Thought' in, Ziauddin Sardar (ed.), *An Early Crescent: The Future of Knowledge and the Environment in Islam,* London: 1989, p. 224.

modern societies, led him as early as the late 1960s, to dedicate himself to the task of inter-cultural dialogue and to research its conditions, demands and essential features. Dialogue for Talbi became a form of life. It led him to a protracted participation in systematically promoted initiatives in this field—especially among Muslims and Christians of the Mediterranean, as, for instance, in the *Groupe de Recherche Islamo-Chrétien* (GRIC).

The whole of Talbi's thought is based on a conviction which he had gained not least as an eminent historian of medieval Maghreb: no culture or religion must be regarded as a system totally closed within itself or as an independent reality for that matter. On the contrary, openness linked with critical discernment has been and will be today the condition for the vital development of cultures and religions. In this sense dialogue between them is absolutely necessary.

Globalization, i.e. that rapidly intensifying experience of worldwide pluralistic living together in our day, compels, as it were, all to reflect anew about the content and the function of what community means.

Today, the barriers disappear ... On a probably not to too distant day the features which determined the physiognomy of certain cultures, will hardly be more than the local colors and the folklore of a lovingly and nostalgically kept-alive province. Has the believer in this situation not to reflect critically about the direction, the content and the function of community, which after all occupies a central place in all expressions of religious faith and especially in Islam?[3]

Contemporary women and men must not be content with merely harmonizing their loyalties within a culture, comfortably furnished by the contributions of previous generations whose product and heir they are. Men and women today no longer enjoy such comfort. In the context of the astounding acceleration which marks the historical movement carrying us, alert women and men have to learn in all seriousness to situate themselves within this new universal field of forces, without however losing their own identity in the process of doing so. 'Hence we must muster the courage,' Talbi exhorts his fellow Muslims, 'to transcend the categories that merely protect us and provide us with security within the customary parameters. Each faith and faith community today has to ask as to what is its place and task within the new universal order, and it has to search for the resources within its own tradition that can be of positive help on the way ahead.'[4]

---

[3] Mohamed Talbi, 'Une communauté de communautés. Le droit de la différence et les voies de l'harmonie', in *Islamochristiana* 4 (1978), p. 11.

[4] Ibid., p. 12.

In all this Talbi distinguishes between 'Islam-culture' which provides the Muslim with roots and authenticity and 'Islam-conviction', which consists of living faith, metaphysical engagement, conviction, and cultic observance.

'One fact today is certain and irreversible: the frontiers of the *umma* no longer run along geographical-political lines, from now onwards they exist exclusively in the hearts of those who pray—whether these hearts live in Sweden, China or Cairo. The German and the Malay can belong to it; the Tunisian and the Egyptian can be excluded from it by their free and conscious decision ... this is not to say, that *Islam-communauté* has to renounce playing its role within the state, however this role has to be constantly projected, invented and adapted to all the facts and needs of the historical moment. ... *Islam-conviction* is not a nation; rather it is engaged in the nation ... It is a community of the faith, that is to say, of the heart, in one geo-political community.'[5]

Which positive traits then characterize the umma, the Islamic community? Islam will always remain *dîn wa dunyà* (heaven and earth). It exists definitely in this world, but it is not of this world. The difference between the temporal and the spiritual sphere cannot and must not be overlooked; rather, we have to do with two faces, as it were, distinct yet intimately linked, of one and the same reality.

Caesar does not stand above God, nor does he command a private domain, of which he would be the sole and independent Lord. From the perspective of the believers he is—as all creatures are—subject to God and his Law. Islam is and remains essentially indivisible. It organizes both, the balance of the individual and that of the community. However, whereas the *sharî'a* in the past regulated the life of a community exclusively ruled by Islam, the Islamic community today has to make the effort to build up not only the Islamic community proper but also to build together with others the shared plural community, struggling for greater justice for all women and men. Is this contrary to the spirit of Islam? In no way! Islam certainly is an integrated whole in itself, but it is also open. It accepts and respects diversity.[6]

In the centre of the thinking of Talbi we find the human person and his or her freedom. The latter finds expression in modern times—and here Talbi has no room for any doubt whatsoever—in fully accepting and furthering human rights. Among these the freedom of conscience for Talbi is basic, because it is precisely the condition which allows man to be conscious of their freedom and to live according to their free choice.[7]

[5] Ibid., p. 14.
[6] Ibid., p. 15.
[7] Mohamed Talbi, *Plaidoyer pour un Islam moderne* (Casablanca 1996), p. 25.

Since this position in the modern Muslim world is shared only by a few, and since the freedom of conscience and religion is limited and even at times prohibited, Talbi has returned again and again to this point which is so central to his entire thinking. He has backed up his position by means of a renewed or even new exegesis of the Koran and has asked for the translation of this new understanding into social and political reality. The Koran, Talbi says, clearly teaches—if only it is taught correctly—that freedom is the basis of human nature. A correct interpretation consists in a—as he puts it—'lecture finaliste' of the Koran, which tries to make explicit the finality, the ultimate, overriding maqâsid (objectives) of the lawgiver by basing itself on the undeniable fact of historical evolution. In other words, Talbi takes the Koran as the basis for the modern principle of the freedom of religion.

About four years ago Talbi spoke of 'cultural identity and the problem of a world culture' at the Vienna Conference 'One World for All'. His central concern he formulated in the following way: the right to difference and identity of a given culture must not serve as a pretext or even justification for simply rejecting openness, integration, and pluralism. The culture of Islam and that of the West have lived from the beginning in a tension, separating from one another and at the same time enriching one another. Today it is our task to counter the temptation to closed worlds, against an anti-humanism, which lives from the contempt of the other.[8]

The Voice of the Muslims Living as Minorities: Missionary Instead of Political Islam

Here, we shall draw attention to the voices of two Muslim Indians—Syed Zaiunul Abedin (1928–93) and Maulana Wahiduddin Khan (b.1925)—whose thought was first shaped in the Republic of India, the home to the numerically largest Muslim minority in the world, a minority which, however, comprises not more than 12 per cent of the overall Indian population.

Both, Dr Syed Z. Abedin and Maulana Wahiduddin Khan grew up in undivided India. In their college and university days they experienced the passionate ideological and political disputes the fight for independence and India and for and against, respectively, the creation of a decidedly Muslim, and later Islamic, state of Pakistan. The development

---

[8] We can observe here, ion Talbi's thought, the creative coming together of malekite thought with the evolution thinking of Henri Bergson (1859–1941) and Teilhard de Chardin (1881–1955).

of the thinking of these two scholars was shaped by such far-reaching and decisive question as the relationship of Islam to the modern national state—from the point of view of culture and of religion plurally composed and secularly constituted. Also influencing the development of their thinking were the questions as to how Muslims could thrive as a minority within a democracy that, by definition, is largely ruled by majorities; how Muslims would relate to the caste system (perceived as structurally cemented and religiously justified injustice).

During his studies at the Aligarh Muslim University and later in the United States, which he adopted as his country during his student years in Philadelphia, Abedin was close to the *Jamā'at-i Islāmi-i Hind.* In the early 1980s he became a councillor of the *"Rābitat al-'Ālam al-Islāmī"* at Mecca. He established the Institute for Muslim Minority Affairs in Jeddah with a branch in London and founded and directed for many years its important organ, the *Journal of the Institute of Muslim Minority Affairs.* Abedin's thought merits to be kept alive, because he emphasized with prophetical foresight the fundamental fact that today at least every fifth citizen of the world is Muslim and a third of the total number of Muslims live in non-Islamic states. Abedin was concerned with bringing the problems of this growing third of the Muslims that by now lives worldwide in minority situations, into the forefront of the consciousness not only of the Muslims but of all those who today and in future reflect about Islam.

The most important element for Muslims living in a nation where they are in a minority is that they have to live under non-Muslim jurisdiction, in a society in which Islam is not the predominant religion or culture and in which, therefore, there does not exist positive incentives for the growth and strengthening of Islamic values and norms, and also, in which Islamic identity is in danger of being lost if the Muslim community as a whole fails to make a constant and intelligent effort to the contrary. Ultimately, Abedin is convinced, only an effective revival of the original Koranic umma-consciousness will be able to secure the long-term well-being of Muslims in this new worldwide situation; this is in explicit contrast to the vision and the basic aims of the pan-Islamic movement, which ultimately aims for an worldwide Islamic state.

In contrast to such Islamic-state thinking, today, Abedin argues, a Koranically informed umma consciousness is demanded of the believers, together with the full recognition of the identities of the existing nation states 'to exhort one another to truth and to exhort one another to endurance' in the words of Sura 103 (al-'Asr). The material side of the inner-ummatic solidarity—the propagation of the Koran and help in building mosques and Islamic centres, of seminaries and the formation of Imams—is being put into practice by Muslims on a worldwide level to a certain extent. 'What, however, is likely *not* (emphasis added) to be forthcoming easily, is the perspicacity, the judgement and the will to engage in this venture within the framework of the Koran-derived concept of umma consciousness, and to monitor such consciousness from deteriorating into pan-Islamic consciousness, preventing the particular from determining the universal, the political from subverting the religious.'[9]

It does not come as a surprise that Abedin again and again takes position against an Islamistically oriented Islam that accentuates one-sided political power. Yet in our context it would seem of major interest to know, how he relates to the Meccan and Medinan phase of Koranic revelation and of the career of the Prophet and how he estimates their relative importance, not least with regard to the minority situation of so many Muslims in single states as well as in the umma, globally considered.

It has to be clearly understood that the role of the Prophet at Makkah and his role at Madinah are amenable to quite a legitimate distinction. In Makkah the Prophet was a Messenger of God. In Madinah the turn of events had given him an additional role—he was now a head of state as well. Whereas in Makkah all his actions were determined by his role as messenger, a *dâ'i*, in Madinah, besides this, he had the staggering responsibility that had been entrusted to him by the inhabitants' choice. It also happened that this state being the only one of its kind became identified with the survival and dissemination of the message as well. This again is a historical event. Even quite learned Muslims get confused here.[10]

Later generations cannot leave aside Mecca as a moral category, because Mecca is a moral category. Medina, in contrast, is an option that may or may not come the Muslims' way. *Istikhlâf* (i.e. the nomination of a caliph [as happened first in Medina]) is a gift; in modern terminology you would say it is a bonus. Mekka is a necessity. There is no escaping Mekka.

Now, when a generation has passed its inevitable Maccah and if God in his wisdom decides to bestow on it a Madinah, it doesn't have to look upwards to Heavens: Now what? The Prophet's Madinah is there in history, *hâdha min fadl rabbi*, such are the blessings of my Lord.[11]

Then the surrendered people (Muslims) who have been bestowed the grace of

[9] *Islamochristiana*, vol. 16 (1990), p.7.

[10] Syed Z. Abedin, 'Islamic Fundamentalism, Islamic Ummah and the World Conference on Muslim Minorities' in *Encounter* (Roma), no. 204–205, April–May 1994, p. 11.

[11] Ibid., p. 11.

Madinah come forward and with Makkah at their side, acting as their vision, they set out to re-enact a Madinah in their own spatial and temporal contexts.[12]

Abedin asks his fellow Muslims, 'Who can claim the mantle of Madinah: Where is your Makkah? Where is the sacrifice, the suffering, the absolute sincerity of commitment to the pleasure of the Lord and subjugation of His will?, a commitment in other words to the uplift, the reform, the redemption of all God's creatures, of giving peace and tranquility to humanity at large, comfort and solace to all mankind?[13] And he adds significantly: There is a small historical fact that we all tend to neglect. The first, the original Medina, was not attained by conquest. The Prophet was invited to Yathrib/Medina by its inhabitants.[14]

At this point the behaviour of the believer towards unbelief and the unbeliever is relevant. Depending on whether the Muslims in a given country constitute the majority or the minority, quite different goals and objectives result for them from this constellation.

Naturally in Madina, i.e. in the situation of a formally organized Islamic state, rights and duties have to be defined and prescribed. Distinctions have to be made. There exist juridical and administrative imperatives for the structure and the smooth functioning of the machinery of the state. However, in situations where this does not apply, the Muslims have to continue to determine their thought and behaviour from the presupposition that *kufr* (arab. unbelief) is not a once and for all determined category. The deniers of today can be the believers of tomorrow. This applied in Mecca, the historical Mecca, on a daily basis. Why should it be different in today's Mecca, i.e. in contemporary situations where Muslims frequently are a persecuted and despised minority.[15]

In other words, as long as a person is alive, the Muslims should see in him the potential believer. In the Koran condemned are only 'those who disbelieve, and who die in the state of disbelief; on them is the curse of Allah and of Angels and of men combined Sura (2, 161)'.

Also, from this point of view the duty to *da'wa*, to invitation, to mission in the Islamic sense, is not a time-bound but rather an enduring duty. Nothing can free a person from it or can replace it. 'Whatever may be the answer of the one invited, however discouraging, frustrating or apparently hopeless the situation may be, there can be no giving up.'[16]

---

[12] Ibid.
[13] Ibid., p.11f.
[14] Ibid., p.12.
[15] Ibid., pp. 12–13.
[16] Ibid., p.13.

The voice of Maulana Wahiduddin Khan is significant, far beyond the borders of his homeland India. He received his theological-juridical formation in the madrasa system of South Asian Islam and hence writes throughout in Urdu, the literary language of the Muslims of northern India, of Pakistan, and even of many religiously educated Muslims in central and south India and even Bangladesh. Right into his mature years Wahiduddin was a committed adherent of the influential Islamist thinker and leader Maulana Abul A'la Maududi (d. 1979) and member of the Jamâ'at-i Islâmi-i Hind. First, he was shaped by and actively propagated the kind of thinking we find in Syed Qutb and the Muslim Brotherhood (*Al-Ikhwân al-Muslimùn*, in short the *Ikhwân*) in Egypt. However, by the beginning of the 1970s he disengaged himself from the movement of Maududi. Arguing from the Koran, he first demonstrated how in his view Maududi and his followers depart from the ethos and spirit of Koranic revelation.

Wahiduddin does not in any way put into question the traditional faith of Muslims in the Koran and sunna as divinely revealed sources of Islam. In this respect he also develops no new ideas. He does not believe that the post-medieval, globally effective developments in thought, put into question the central traditional Muslim vision of God, history, revelation, and eschatology. Other religions, corrupted with regard to the text of their Holy Scripture and its interpretation, may indeed need such a radical reformulation; not so Islam as it is the religion that alone has been preserved from error and that is final.

However, Wahiduddin, like Abedin, takes very seriously the minority situation of Islam in India as well as in many other parts of the world. He draws from this fact far-reaching, drastic conclusions, which for him result from the essential nature of Islam and the central task entrusted to the Muslims by God. Islam has to be studied in the spirit of *ijtihâd*, that is to say, of a creative, original thought, without being dependent upon the modern world. He advocates, in other words, openness for the chances that offer themselves to Islam in the modern world. Thus, Islam will be seen and lived once again as the religion of the witness for the truth (*shahâdat al-haqq*) and as invitation (*da'wa*) to a life in conformity with the will of God on the path to unrestricted encounter with him, the Creator and Judge.

From the basic task to 'invitation' (*da'wa*) result the following empha-ses of his thought, which, by the way, has found expression in a compre-hensive, stylistically appealing body of writing in Urdu and in manifold translations: priority to the inner dimension of the Muslim life of faith, the right to religion accruing to all men, non-violence as a condition for the free invitation of women and men and their free decision in matters of faith and, last but not the least, the separation of religion and politics according to the model of the Constitution of the Indian republic. Wahiduddin tries to demonstrate in his writings that all these doctrines and principles of religio-political action correspond to the original message of the Koran and the Sunna. No doubt, because of the limitations and the failures of Muslim believers and their community, for centuries they have been obscured or/and not fully developed in Muslim societies.

At the same time Wahiduddin is firmly convinced that the Muslims' duty to practise *da'wa* (i.e., Islamic mission) in the past has never been as powerful, urgent, and promising as it is in our day. The Koranic verse *'Remind them, for thou art but a remembrance!'* (Sura 88, 21f.) is of basic importance. Invitation excludes any kind of violent confrontation. Rather the effort should be to win over by argument and convince in liberty: hence his sharp criticism of the Islamic idiom and the political activism of the Islamist movements. The Islamic message is directed towards the free decision of men and women and, on the basis of its own essence, is to be communicated in peaceful ways. Violent efforts to erect Islam are utterly mistaken.

Islam as a political system may be introduced in legal ways sanctioned by the Koran by way of the free decision of people but never through imposition from above. Jihâd, the effort in the way of God, of which mention is made in verse 78 in Sura 22 (*al-Hajj*), signifies the quality and intensity of the giving of witness (*shahâda*). So, for Wahiduddin, jihâd moves clearly with the limits of witnessing and invitation. It excludes any kind of use of force and political oppression.

It is revealing and significant how Wahiduddin tries to prove on the basis of the Koran and the *sîra* (biography of Muhammad) the principle of the separation of religion and politics. In a lecture on the theme 'A policy for peace in Islam' delivered in August 1995 in Jerusalem, he clearly took position against the fatwa of the Al-Azhar University dated 19 May of the same year. This fatwa stated: As long as the Al-Aqsà mosque and the city of Jerusalem are subjected to foreign, i.e. non-Islamic domination the Muslims shall not be allowed to go there even if it is only in order to pray there as pilgrims. Doing so, they would ratify the occupation of the temple and of the city.

Wahiduddin explains why in his view this decision is totally mistaken. On the one hand, from the beginning of Islam it has been the natural desire of every Muslim to pray there; on the other hand, the Muslims share the holy place with other, non-Muslim, believers, for whom the place is holy in the same way—holy as the essential element of their very ancient rites of worship. Now, according to the rules of logic, one and the same place cannot at the same time be under the political control of communities belonging to three faiths.

Here, Wahiduddin argues, the life of the Prophet taken as sunna for all Muslim believers, offers a solution: choose in such cases the *'ibâdatî* aspect and put the political aspect in second place. Follow the principle—contained in the sunna—of *al-fasl bayn al-qadiyyatayn:* the separation of religion (more precisely, of *'ibâda,* or worship, in other words, issues related to the cultic-moral dimension of religion) and politics (*siyâsa*). In this important issue, three events in the life of the Prophet have to be interpreted as deliberate options. They have normative character:

i)   Until the end of the year 623 (i.e. up to one and a half years after the Hijra) Muhammad and his umma continued to pray in the direction of Jerusalem. Then, in the beginning of the year 624, Muhammad received the divine order to pray in the direction of the Ka'ba, which—and this is significant—remained full of idols until the conquest of Mecca. From this we learn about a basic principle of Islam: 'the separation between the two things (areas)'. The Ka'ba and the idols are certainly two quite different things. Practice patience (cf. Sura 2,153) with regard the idols in the Ka'ba, and simply continue to pray in the direction of the Ka'ba.

ii) The night journey (*isrâ'*) and the ascension (*mi''râj*), too, support this principle. Muhammad entered Jerusalem, performed the prescribed ritual prayer in the Al-Aqsà mosque at a time when Jerusalem was still ruled by the pagan Persians. Here, again, the prophet separated ritual-moral and political issues.

iii) Finally, the Prophet performs the *'umra* (small pilgrimage) when Mecca is still heathen. This again he did on the basis of his separation of religious and political affairs.

From all these, Wahiduddin draws this conclusion: the principle of holding apart religion (understood as *'ibâda*) and politics is of a generally valid nature. Disregarding it has caused damage to Islam and the witness for Islam and has hindered *da'wa,* the 'invitation' to it. Viewed strictly from the perspective of faith, Islam indeed comprises religion and politics. However, with regard to the planning of action in the world of today, we should by all means take account of the prevailing situation. Any rebellion, whether in the name of Islam or not, against an established non-Islamic or Islamic government is forbidden, because rebellion leads to common disorder and turmoil (*fitna o fasâd*).

Wahiduddin explicitly rejects in this connection political-military activism, as it is practised by Islamist groups in the name of Islam, for example in places like Kashmir, Chechnia, Bosnia, Burma, the Philippines, and Egypt. Also, in his opinion the forced introduction (implementation) of the *sharî'a* equals the spread of disorder and revolt (*fasâd*). It is not legitimate anywhere to impose the Islamic order in the form of the *sharî'a* anywhere (Pakistan, Afghanistan, Iran, Nigeria) without the overwhelming majority of the population wanting this definitely. The necessity of separating religion and politics concerns all Islamic prescriptions. If the Muslims keep to this principle, no door in the contemporary world to life and hence the witness to the truth of Islam, will remain closed.'[17]

FOR A KORANIC PERSPECTIVE OF INTERRELIGIOUS SOLIDARITY AGAINST SUPPRESSION

Farid Esack (b. 1958) belongs to the category of socially and politically committed researchers and teachers. His writings are scientifically solid, thoroughly researched, and, at the same time, informed by a passionate search for social justice. Very probably his past is partly responsible for this. He was born in a suburb of coloured people in Cape Town and began to be active in the anti-apartheid movement even while he was in school. Thus, from early on he was active for solidarity beyond the limits of the Muslim community, which in South Africa forms a small yet not unimportant minority. There followed years of Islamic-theological formation in one of the big madrasas in Karachi. There, Esack, together with Pakistani Christians, fought for the poorest, the marginalized, and the excluded.

After his return to South Africa he co-founded the 'Call to Islam', the most active and firm Muslim movement against apartheid. All this led to the 'search for a South African Koranic hermeneutic of pluralism for liberation', rooted in the fusion of the nation's crucible and in his own commitment to comprehensive justice.[18] On this search he came in the middle of the 1980s to the 'Centre for the Study of Islam and Christian-Muslim Relations' (CSIC) in Birmingham, U.K. His main endeavour was to define from the bases of the Koran, the Sunna, and classical

[17] Christian W. Troll, 'A significant voice of Indian Islam: Maulana Wahiduddin Khan' in *Encounter* (Rome), nr. 254, April 1999, p. 19.

[18] Farid Esack, *Qur'ân, Liberation and Pluralism: An Islamic Perspective of Interreligious Solidarity against Oppression*, Oxford: Oneworld, 1997, p. 9.

Islamic thought the position of the Muslim community in the new, independent Republic of South Africa. From this emerged the book *Qur'an, Liberation and Pluralism: An Islamic Perspective of Interreligious Solidarity against Oppression* (Oxford 1997). We propose to point out here a few salient points of the work.

Esack first analyses the context, i.e. the economic and social situation of the Muslims of South Africa, past in present. Then he discusses the relationship between text and context with regard to the interpretation of the Koran. In this he is especially interested in understanding and in making understood the Koran as a living document. The addressee of the Koran not only has the liberty but also the duty, to ponder anew the meanings and statements of Holy Scripture, in order to promote liberation and the cause of justice: 'I argue for the freedom to rethink the meanings and use of scripture in a radically divided, economically exploitative and patriarchal society and to forge hermeneutical keys that will enable us to read the text in such a way as to advance the liberation of all people.'[19]

Central keys for the interpretation of the Koran are *taqwa*: the integrity of the relationship to God; *tawhîd*: divine fullness and unity; *'adl wa qist*: balance and justice; *jihâd wa 'amal*: struggle and praxis. These keys are applied within the framework of a Koranic theology of liberation. Such a theology of liberation is developed and formulated through and in solidarity with those, whose personal liberation becomes real through participation in this process.

Liberation theology takes on a specifically Islamic character when it takes the measure of the Koran and of the struggle of all the prophets. To practise Koranic hermeneutics in a situation of injustice means to indulge in theology and to experience faith as solidarity with the oppressed and the marginalized, in a battle for their liberation. The implicit message of Islamic liberation theology is: Islam can be experienced only as what it really is, if it is lived as a liberative praxis of solidarity.

Is there a shift in understanding when it is taken seriously that according to the Koran (as also according to the Bible) there does not exist faith without works, whereas one can certainly imagine a faith without an explicit assent to dogmatic formulations? Such questions are not of a mere theoretical nature; they are in fact linked closely to attitudes towards the South African apartheid regime. At the time of apartheid there were Muslims who fitted flawlessly into the thoroughly unjust regime, whereas some non-Muslims gave preference to prison and

[19] Ibid., p. 78.

contempt over military service. This shows, how misleading it is to conceive of Islam first and primarily as a reified religion or system.

Islam proclaims God as the ever greater—greater than any conception or institutional service of it can ever be or be conceived. Islam calls to ever new submission to the ever greater God.[20] If for a committed interpreter truth can never be absolute, it has to do with this. Whereas the methods of interpretation constantly develop, the interpreter is guided in the direction of ever-growing authentic truth, a truth that leads on to evermore intensive praxis of liberation. 'There is no point at which God has disclosed the truth to the interpreter, but it continues to be disclosed, for there is no end to *jihâd* and thus no end to His promise to disclose.'[21]

Another emphasis of the theological approach of Esack is the new theological definition of the other. How does the Koran view the other? One cannot reproach Esack for avoiding difficult issues in trying to answer this question. So he asks: 'How does the universality of the Qur'an relate to the exclusivism and virulent denunciation of the other?[22]. The answer to this question, Esack argues, has to recognize that the Koranic teaching with regard to the religiously other has developed gradually and within a specific context or contexts. In other words, there does not exist a final Koranic position towards the other; rather, the Koran merely offers indications that have to be interpreted in and from the respective context.[23]

According to Esack the 'people of the Book'—a group of people, the Koran privileges — today are 'of questionable relevance'. Instead, he demands the elaboration of 'a qur'anic hermeneutic concerned with interreligious solidarity against in justice ... [that] would rather opt for more inclusive categories which would, for example, embrace the dispossessed of the Fourth World.'[24]

Esack wishes to distance himself clearly from a purely liberal theological position, which holds coexistence and freedom to be identical with absolute equality of all. In his view, the Koran claims the ideological leadership of the community of the Muslim faithful. But how does this go together with pluralism and justice? The eminent importance of 'the just' does not mean that Islamic society can claim a permanent position of socio-religious superiority. The Koran does not place the

---

[20] Cf. Ibid., p. 134.
[21] Ibid., p.111.
[22] Ibid., p. 146.
[23] Cf. Ibid., p. 147.
[24] Ibid., p. 153.

Muslims as a social group above the others. Were this the case, the criticism which the Koran directs towards the Jews of his time—accusing them of arrogance, of a faith in election understood in exclusivist terms, and of the attempt to instrumentalize God for their own particularist (exclusivistic) objectives—would apply to the Muslims. The Koran clearly states (Sura 2, 134) that there does not, and must not exist any superiority on the basis of the merits of one's ancestors.

The Koran teaches an inclusive understanding of the faith in election and presupposes the teaching that the idea of inclusiveness is superior to that of exclusivity. 'In this sense the advocates of pluralism had to be "above" those who insisted that the religious expressions of others counted for nothing and that theirs was the only way to attain salvation. The relationship between the inclusivist form of religion and the exclusivist form can be compared to that of a democratic state and fascist political parties.'[25]

Inclusiveness, however, does not mean that we can leave any idea and practice whatsoever untouched. Rather, it wishes to include the excluded, the marginalized, the suppressed, i.e. it wishes to struggle for their liberation, so that they can adore and serve God integrally and freely. The Koran teaches that the Muslim, the Muslim community, on the basis of their responsibility before God, have to oppose actively any unjust conceptions of faith and morality that exclude or marginalize the poor. In other words, it must not attribute to such ideologies, in false liberalism or tolerance, a position of equality.

The responsibility of calling humankind to God and to the path of God will thus remain. The task of the present-day Muslim is to discern what this means in every age and every society. Which is to be invited? Who is to be taken as allies in this calling? How does one define the path of God? These are particularly pertinent questions in society, where definitions of Self and Other are determined by justice and injustice, oppression and liberation and where the test of one's integrity as a human being dignified by God is determined by the extent of one's commitment to defend that dignity.[26]

Who then are the allies of the Muslims in this commitment in the struggle for integral justice? Do we have to define our allies and enemies anew? The Koranic prohibition of *wilâya* (pact) with Jews and Christians (Sura 5,51) has to be interpreted in context. It prohibits 'collaboration' in the negative sense of the term, but certainly not true (i.e. interreligious) solidarity. In the South-African context this means, for

[25] Ibid., p. 175.
[26] Ibid.

instance: There was a number of Muslims ready to collaborate with the apartheid regime, yet in contrast to these there existed white Christians who were not deterred by prison and discrimination from struggling for race equality and justice.

The exodus paradigm as the Koran propounds it, insists on solidarity prior to preaching and proclamation and, further, on the rejection of any (foul) compromise with the oppressor. In other words, it demands an ecumenism of liberative praxis.

Humankind, especially the marginalized and oppressed, need each other to confront these dangers and challenges of liberation. Let us hope, that, because of, and not despite, our different creeds and worldviews, we are going to walk this road side by side. Let us hope that we will be able to sort out some of the theological issues whilst we walk this road side by side. Let us hope that we will be able to sort out some of the theological issues whilst we walk this road. If not, then at least we will get another opportunity after we have ensured our survival and that of our home, the earth.[27]

From 'Muslim in Europe' to 'European Muslim'

Tariq Ramadan (b. 1962 in Geneva) is on his mother's side the grandson of the founder of the Moslem Brotherhood, Hasan al-Banna (1906–49) and the son of the Egyptian diplomat and jurisprudent Said Ramadan. He took his doctorate in Islamic Studies in Fribourg/Switzerland and today teaches philosophy in the universities of Fribourg and Geneva. However, as the president of the Association des Musulmans, Musulmanes de Suisse he is intimately acquainted with the life and problems of the younger generation of Muslims in the mosque organizations and communities of French-speaking Switzerland and France.

Ramadan concentrates above all on two issues: 1) the place of the Muslims in the West and 2) the reawakening and resurgence of Islam in the context of the encounter of the Western and the Islamic civilizations. The titles of Ramadan's numerous publications demonstrate the emphases of his thinking: e.g. *Les musulmans dans la laïcité* (1994); *Islam, le face-à-face des civilizations: Quel project pour quelle modernité?* (1995); and *To be a European Muslim* (1998).

Here we shall deal only very succinctly with the development of Ramadan's ideas as to a European-Muslim identity. Ramadan is one of the first, if not the first, among the Muslims born in contemporary Europe who decidedly tries to set into motion a process of mutual

---

[27] Ibid., p. 261.

questioning and common searching for genuine and realistic juridical solutions for the new generations of Muslims in Europe. In this he is essentially concerned with the question, as to which specific contribution could and should Islamic life and thought make to contemporary Europe.

Ramadan's basic conviction is this: 'Islam is an affirmative faith which carries within itself a global understanding of creation, death, and humanity. This understanding is, or should be, the source of Islamic rules of thinking and behaviour.'[28] Muslims living in Europe have the task to make this understanding and its immediate consequences for human life 'understandable in the light of our new context within European society.'[29]

One presupposition for this is that the Muslims really accept Europe as their new home. Of late there exists, says Ramadan, a growing number, if not a majority of Muslims in Europe, who are conscious that their own future, and especially that of the young generation, will be European, that they will be European citizens—European and Muslim at the same time. After an early phase which was shaped by fear, even panic and reaction vis-à-vis the new, secular environment, a period of quiet and creative development has now begun.

Ramadan observes changes in the basic tenor of the sermons and legal decisions of the ulamâ. Formerly, everywhere in the forefront there stood the appeal to keep a distance from the surrounding society, by no means to accept the citizenship of a western state, not forgetting ever that soon one would return to the homeland. In contrast, now the conviction has gained general acceptance everywhere that for Muslims there does not exist a real alternative to conceiving and shaping their future in Europe. Because for millions of young Muslims Europe has already become the first and only homeland.

Until now the Muslims—not least also because of the rejection they experienced on the part of the long-established Europeans—have concentrated on the solution of certain legal problems and in doing so they have almost forgotten the preservation of their deeper identity through change. They are in danger of becoming discretely invisible, in other words, to be Muslims without Islam.

Today, however, especially with the growth of the second and third generation, there has begun a kind of counter movement, marked by the desire to detect anew the Islamic identity and to live according to Islam.

[28] Tariq Ramadan, *To be a European Muslim,* Leicester: The Islamic Foundation, 1999, p.3.
[29] Ibid.

A new consciousness of themselves arises which is based on Islam. This has to do with an Islamic identity which breaks of from the identification with the respective homeland and is based rather on Koran and sunna.

For Ramadan it is an urgent task to help the European Muslims—together with the ulamâ who guide them in religious matters—to respond to the new reality in Europe with a decidedly constructive thought. They have to develop a clear mental outlook. Part of this will be to think and act from an essential basic core of Islamic prescriptions allowing them to develop a balanced Muslim-European identity which—free from false and unfounded fears—understands itself as part and parcel of the European societies.

A special problem that Ramadan encounters is that the young Muslims in Europe conceive of Islam in Europe almost exclusively in the categories of 'permitted' (halâl) and 'forbidden' (harâm). They are hardly aware, Ramadan observes, that their own European experience has a positive contribution to make in the elaboration of a properly Muslim and yet also genuinely Muslim identity. The elaboration of a juridical framework, which allows Muslims in Europe to be European without having to give up their Muslim identity, should lead to a dialectical process of mutually challenging exchange between the mosque communities and the competent and at the same time creatively thinking scholars of law (mujtahidîn). Only in this way will it be possible, Ramadan argues, to find adequate juridical answers. A genuinely Muslim-European identity is defined not only by the mere number of legal prescriptions, it is an ensemble of emotions, lifestyles, manners and morals, touching also food and dress and forming, last but not the least, a mentality.

In order to understand the true nature of identity it is necessary to live it, to live in it, to be part of it. Hence, every 'âlim, who has to deduce and formulate specific legal prescriptions for those Muslims who live in the West, should make use of the problems, experiences, and questions of all the Muslims who live there. For Ramadan, the participation of the young in this process of a European-Muslim search for identity is of central importance. With their specific experience and their understanding of the European context the young should formulate the questions that emerge from their life situation in order to thus enable the ulamâ to arrive at adequate answers. This younger generation therefore has the task, in dialogue with the ulamâ and their expert knowledge to find in the area of religious education and formation adequate legal answers and to put the emphasis on contents that fit the situation.

Ramadan is not a naïve, unrealistic dreamer. He knows that a debate between the Muslim communities in the West and the ulamâ for the time being remains hardly more than a hope. However, there are clear pointers that in this area too things have begun to move in the right direction. What are, according to Ramadan, the special chances that result for the Muslims from the encounter with their European context?

i) The neutral space that exists inside secular societies has often been—mistakenly, Ramadan argues—identified with the total abstinence form religiosity. However, it is precisely in this 'space' that those aspects of Islamic life which emphasize religious experience and that are alive in Sufism, find a new echo, especially among the young Muslims. In other words, a new consciousness of the importance of spirituality is being born.

ii) An enormous chance consists in the fact that the new context forces, as it were, the Muslims and their ulamâ to return to the Koran and the Sunna and to consider seriously in this a two-fold distinction. First, that between Islamic doctrine as such and its historical realizations. Because the latter are based on an analysis which responded to specific past historical contexts, which have become irrelevant now. Second, the opportunity now offers itself to remove the Islamic legal system as such from its culturally conditioned traditional interpretations. In other words, the new situation makes it almost inevitable to return to the essential core message of Islam.

iii) In this new, contemporary context the venerable concepts of *dâr al-islâm* (space of Islam) and *dâr al-harb* (Raum des Krieges) are being discussed with new intensity. These concepts are found neither in the Koran nor in the Sunna, and they do not fit into our contemporary reality which is marked not least by the process of the globalization of ideologies and religions, and by pluralist? coexistence almost everywhere in the world. Ramadan proposes to designate instead the whole of the globe as 'spaces of the witness for Islam' (*dâr shahâdat al-Islâm*).

iv) The massive pressure of modernity in fully industrialized societies and especially the power of the ideology of modernism impose on Muslims the task, to contribute from an Islamic perspective to the contemporary debates about values, morals, and ethics, within the framework of secular pluralist societies. Suffice it here, to mention the questions which recent biotechnical and medical development pose in modern societies and in fact everywhere in the world.

v) Furthermore, the European context makes it indispensable to define anew content and method of Islamic education. Islamic education does not only concern the transmission of knowledge about the Koran and the Hadith, but also that of the religiously relevant results of modern natural science and humanities. The all-pervasive ideology of modernism—which according to Ramadan is composed of individualism, unbridled capitalism, and consumerism—renders difficult the keeping alive of the religious dimension and of the basic values in the life of the individual as well as of the communities. Here, Ramadan asks the Muslims to recognize plurality within a secular society at least as a fact and to understand that not only Islam but in fact all the other religions and religious groups are equally put into question by them. The family and the question of how to conceive of, and organize, the teaching of religion, the establishment and financing of Islamic schools and further related questions, are other core issues. Finally, it will be of decisive importance for the younger generation of Muslims in Europe, whether they succeed in developing in the modern secular social contexts genuinely modern, Islam-inspired forms of cultural life.

However, with regard to the success of a shared future of Europe, Ramadan argues, the non-Muslim population, too, has to allow itself to be critically questioned:

i) Are the old established populations in Europe capable and willing to recognize the contribution which Islam has made to its civilization? Can they conceive of their identity as one co-shaped by Islam (besides the formative influence of Greek-Roman and Judeo-Christian elements) so that Islam will no longer be seen as a cultural-religious tradition that is alien to Europe's identity?

ii) Islam primarily and essentially is a faith, a religion, a way of life and not primarily a problem. The massive presence of the Muslims in Europe in our day raises the fundamental question: can one practise in this Europe a religious conviction (and this includes socially effective practice), without immediately being labelled individually or corporately as representative of fundamentalism, fanaticism, and extremism? Linked with this is the question of whether Muslims can be so-called Europeans, without having to submit to the 'ideology of modernism'. Can one regard a practising Muslim as an authentic European or are doubts inevitable and automatically justified with regard to the practicing Muslim and Islam?

OUTLOOK: COMMON TASKS IN SHAPING THE FUTURE

We have been able to present here only a few Islamic voices. Among many other voices in our context, I think the following would be of particular interest: Professor Dr Hüsein Atay from the Faculty of Theology of Ankara University and Professor Nuri Öztürk of the Faculty of Theology of the University of Istanbul (both accept, as Islamic thinkers, the secular order of modern Turkey and each one in his own way stands for a radical return to the Koran; from Iran, especially Abdol Karim Soroush (mediation between religion and true, plural democracy) and the U.S. American Shiite scholar Abdulaziz Sachedina (Islam and democratic pluralism); from Indonesia, the former Prime Minister Abdurrahman Wahid (Islam as supporting non-violence and national transformation towards pluralism and social justice). Also important are voices from the Arab world, e.g. the Tunisian Ahmuda an-Naifar (secularization in Islam as religious reform) and the Egyptian Nasr Hamid Abu Zaid, living in exile in Leyden/Holland (God's word as the word of men—a new approach to the Koran) and, finally, the Lebanese scholar Ahmad S. Moussalli (the seeds of the notions of democracy, pluralism, and human rights are embedded in harmony in many notions of government and politics found in Islamic religious thought).

Even if each of these thinkers departs from quite different experiences and perspectives and takes quite different paths in trying to come closer to a realization of their objectives, all of them are mainly concerned with making the message of the Koran in its historical and at the same time trans-historical dimension an answer to contemporary challenges to Muslims, in the diverse regions of the world.

BIBLIOGRAPHY

Abedin, Syed Z., 'Islamic Fundamentalism, Islamic Ummah and the World Conference on Muslim Minorities', in *CSIC Papers*, No.7, June 1992. Birmingham, UK: Centre for the Study of Islam and Christian-Muslim Relations.

——, 'Muslim Minority Communities in the World Today', *Islamochristiana*, 16, 1990, 1–14.

Catholic Bishops' Conference of India, *Commission for Dialogue and Ecumenism, Guidelines for Inter-Religious Dialogue*, Second revised edition, New Delhi: CBCI, 1989.

——, *The Commission for Ecumenism and Dialogue, Guidelines for Ecumenism. Towards an Ecumenical Life-Style*, New Delhi: CBCI Centre [1, Ashok Place], 2000.

Esack, Farid, *Qur'an, Liberation & Pluralism. An Islamic Perspective of Interreligious Solidarity against Oppression*, Oxford: Oneworld, 1997.

——, *On Being a Muslim. Finding a Religious Path in the World Today*, Oxford: Oneworld, 1999.

Gauhar, Altaf (ed.), *The Challenge of Islam*, London: Islamic Council of Europe, 1978.

John Paul II, *The Pope speaks to India. (All the addresses and homilies of the Holy Father during his ten-day Visit to India)*, Bandra, Bombay St. Paul Press, 1986.

Pontifical Council for Interreligious Dialogue, *Interreligious Dialogue. The official teaching of the Catholic Church (1963–1995)*, Francesco Gioia (ed.), Boston: Pauline Books and Media, 1997.

Ramadan, Tariq, *Les Musulmans dans la laïcité. Responsabilités et droits des musulmans dans les sociétés occidentales*, Lyon: Ed. Tawhid, 1994.

——, *Islam, le face à face des civilisations. Quel projet pour quelle modernité?*, Lyon, Collection deux rives, 1995.

——, *Muslims in France. The Way towards Coexistence*, Leicester: The Islamic Foundation, 1999.

——, *To be a European Muslim*, Leicester: The Islamic Foundation, 1999.

Talbi, Mohamed, 'Islam and dialogue', *Encounter, Documents for Muslim-Christian Understanding* (Rome), nos. 11–12, 1975, 1–19.

——, 'Une, communauté de communautés. Le droit de la différence et les voies de l'harmonie', *Islamochristiana*, 4, 1978, 11–25.

——, 'Islam et Occident au-delà des affrontements, des ambiguités et des complexes', *Islamochristiana*, 7, 1981, 56–77.

——, 'Religious Liberty: A Muslim's Perspective', *Islamochristiana*, 11, 1985, 99–113.

——, *Plaidoyer pour un Islam moderne*, Tunis: Ceres Editions, 1996.

——, 'Cultural Identity and the Problem of a World Culture' in Andreas Bsteh (ed.), *One World for All. Foundations of a Socio-political and Cultural Pluralism from Christian and Muslim Perspectives,*. New Delhi: Vikas, 2000, 283–309

Troll, Christian, 'A Significant voice of Contemporary Islam in India, Maulana Wahiduddin Khan', *Encounter, Documents for Muslim-Christian Understanding* (Rome) No. 254, April 1999. Also in A.Th. Khoury and G. Vanoni (eds), '*Geglaubt habe ich, deshalb habe ich geredet' Festschrift für Andreas Bsteh zum 65. Geburtstag*. Würzburg: Echter, 1998, 491–510.

Sardar, Ziauddin, *Islamic Futures. The Shape of Ideas to Come*, London/New York: Continuum International Publishing Group, Inc., 1986.

French Laïcity

Representations and Realities

CLAIRE DE GALEMBERT

My paper is about the discrepancy between the common and ideologically dominant representation of the French laicity and its practice. According to the dominant representation or, as Benedict Anderson puts it, how French 'laicity' is imagined, the French laical system would be a radical separation of state and religious institutions and a system in which religion and religious groups or institutions have no legitimacy in the public domain. It would be as if the public domain was a space whereby only the political identity had relevance. Logically, according to this representation, the question of religious plurality would be neutralized, being a sort of non-question for political figures, whose aim would be to unify the nation through a common republican culture, rather than to accommodate religious diversity. However, observation of actual practice in the field demonstrates that the dominant representation does not correspond to the reality.

French laicity does not exist as univocal, but rather as a contradictory reality. Various debates in the 1990s provide very good examples of the controversial dynamic of the French laicity. One can recall the huge controversy surrounding the baptism of King Clovis which took place in 1996. Clovis was a middle-aged king whose conversion to Catholicism was supposed to have unified the French nation through religion. Debate ensued over whether this event should be an 'official' ceremony, and whether it was legitimate for President Chirac to attend the religious commemoration with Pope John Paul II in the same audience. One can also recall the 'headscarf controversy' or the so-called 'affaire du foulard' which divided French opinion and politics in two: those who argued that carrying the scarf in public schools represented a danger for the Republic; and those who argued that the laical school is compatible with the indirect expression of one's religious identity, such as distinctive dress. These different debates represent the discrepancy between the representation of the French laicity and actual laicity in action. Laicity exists fundamentally due to the conflict and debate among various concepts, definitions, and understandings of its nature.

IDEOLOGICALLY DOMINANT REPRESENTATION OF THE FRENCH LAICITY

France is often presented as a model of a state in which religion and politics are radically separated. It should be (is?) an exception not only throughout Europe, but also globally. To a certain extent, the difficulty we face when translating the term 'laicite' into other languages (resulting in neologisms such as 'Laizität' in German, 'laicity' in English, the content of which is more or less understood), is a significant sign of singularity of the French model.

The French Model Among other Models

The following chart presents in a very synthetic way the various ideal types of relationships between religion and state, contained in a nation state configuration. It allows a positioning of the French model of relations between state and religious groups or institutions among the various ideal-types, which have more of an analytical versus descriptive quality and never perfectly reflect reality.

The chart displays the distinguishing character of the French case as being least open to religion. Religion is not recognized as having public relevance. Therefore, it is reserved for an individual's private occupation and has no legitimacy in the public forum.

As is implied in the chart, there is a strong correlation between the way the state relates to religion, on the one hand, and the way the state and civil society articulate that relationship. It shows as well that religious configuration is a central variable of how the state deals with religion. As we can see, the French case is representative of a model of relationships between a strong state and a weakly organized civil society; it is typical of a state that allows no intermediary to the citizenry and which attempts to shape the society according to a unifying political culture founded on the abstract universal values derived from the principles

Models of Relationships State/Religion within the Modern Nation State[1]

	Republican Separatist Model	Liberal Separatist Model	Corporatist Model	Communautarist Model
Main characteristics	• neutrality of the state	•. neutrality of the state	• neutrality of the state	• more or less neutral state
	• non-recognition of religious institutions; no subsides	• Recognition without funding of religious institutions	• Recognition of Religious + subsides	• Recognition of public relevance of religion
	• negative religious freedom	• positive religious freedom	• positive religious freedom	• Recognition of public relevance of religion
	• no cooperation	• possible cooperation	• Cooperation with recognized religious institutions	
State/Society	• State + Society –	• State – Society +	• State –/+ Society –/+	• State – Society +
Citizenship/ Religion	Republican citizenship (closed to religion identities/ laïcity as civil religion)	Liberal citizenship (open to religious identities)	Ethno-cultural citizenship (more or less integrating religious identity)	Multi-religious citizenship
Society religious configuration	Mono-confessional Catholicism	Religious pluralism Protestantism	Pluri-confessional Protestantism	Religious segmented society
Process of political secularization	Conflictual	Harmonious	Harmonious	
Examples	France	United States	Germany	Great Britain

[1] This chart is partly inspired by Stein Rokkan, 'Dimensions of State-formation and Nation-building' in Charles Tilly (ed.), *The Formation of National-States in Western Europe*, Princeton: Princeton University Press 1978.

of human rights. To a certain extent, the laicity which represents this state sacralization as a political philosophy, can be considered as a civil religion. The French laical system as it stands is the result of a very conflictual process of state secularization. It is well known that this conflictual configuration of separation is paradigmatical of catholic Europe, especially in countries where Catholicism predominates. In contrast, predominantly protestant or pluri-confessional countries, e.g. Germany, are more typical of an harmonious process of religious and political separation.

The Conflictual Dynamic of the French Way of Laicization of the State

I do not intend to get into a detailed description of the historical process of the separation of religion and politics, in other words, the separation of the state and the Church. Nevertheless, two important sequences of this story of the secularization of the state should be recalled in order to understand the spirit of the French laicity.

The French Revolution as the Inaugural Sequence of Separation

The first sequence, which could be considered the opening sequence, is the revolutionary sequence. This sequence is divided into two parts. The first part corresponds to the bourgeoise Revolution (1789–91). During this phase, the revolutionary factions opposed Catholicism as the religion of the kingdom and the Catholic Church as a supranational power. In this regard, the subordination of the Church by the power of the sovereign people was at stake. The revolutionaries imagined that Catholicism could become a sort of 'national religion' and the church a national institution, whose clergy would be chosen (elected) by representatives. But this project collapsed as a result of the opposition of Rome and a part of the French Clergy, the so-called 'refractors' who refused to swear loyalty to the nation.

This resistance was paired with the radicalization of the Revolution (1792). As a result of these two factors, the revolutionaries became more repressive and intended to eradicate the influence of the church on society. The tension turned very violent. It was not only violent at the symbolic level; e.g. the Contantinian calendar was replaced. Also, a revolutionary cult, which was a combination of French enlightened philosophy and the idea of civil religion according to Jean-Jacques Rousseau, was created. Notre Dame de Paris became the Temple of the Etre Supreme, meaning that registries (where birth, wedding, and death were consigned) were transferred from parish records to community records. It was also violent at a physical level; about 3000 priests were sent to 'Guillotines'. It is true that this radical phase did not last long, since Bonaparte (1798), who came a few years before Napoleon (1801), softened and balanced the revolutionary vestiges. Although Catholicism was not the state religion, it was recognized as being the religion of the majority of the French. Besides this majority religion, Napoleon recognized three other cults: Judaism (the so-called 'culte israelite'), Protestantism, and Calvinism. These were, like Catholicism, funded by the state. With the recognition of these four cults, known as 'concordat ire regime', institutionized religious pluralism began, whereas Catholicism had long been the official and exclusive religion.

The Third Republic Phase: 'La guerre des deux France'[2]

There was an appeasement phase and a rebalancing of the revolutionary vestiges, which were prolonged through the return of the monarchy (1815–48) and the second Empire (1850–70). Beginning with the third Republic, a new phase of turbulence arose. This phase, called the War between two Frances comprised the confrontation of two universalisms, i.e. the Franco-catholic one (identified as the 'anticléricaux') and the Franco-republican one which was founded on the 1789 Principles ('our Evangel' according to Jules Ferry).

This second phase began with the foundation of the Third Republic (1870) and ended with the 1905 law, the so-called Law of Separation of the Church and the State, which is still in vogue. This law is still the major symbolic and legal reference informing the relationship between state and religious institutions or groups. The republicans had two aims as they came to power. The first was the laicization of schools;[3] the second, the institutionalization of the separation of the state and the religion. It is easy to understand why the laicization of schools was paramount; schools are arenas of future citizens' socialization. And with the establishment of universal suffrage, it was particularly important to bring the citizenry away from the influence of the Catholic Church (which was supporting the anti-republican front of reactionary social and political forces). Yet, the influence of the Catholic Church was still of critical import in public schools. First, 'free, laical, and compulsory' school was established (instituted) between 1879 and 1883.

---

[2] Cf Emile Poulat, *Liberté, Laïcité. La guerre des deux France et le principe de Modernité*, Paris: Cerf/Cujas, 1987.

[3] Yves Déloye, *Ecole et citoyenneté L'individualisme républicaine de Jules Ferry à Vichy*, Paris: Presse de la FNSP, 1995.

Jules Ferry, the minister of public instruction, was the driving force behind the laicization of schools. He went on to organize the institutional transformation. Parallel to this transformation, the moral and civic aspects[4] to religious instruction has been substitute to the traditional religious instruction, which till now was delivered outside the school.

The second axis of the laicization policy of the Republican platform during the third Republic was the institutionalization of the separation of church and state.[5] The state was constitutionally neutral but there were still recognised cults, funded by the state. This, then, is what is salient in the Law of Separation, whose main proponent was Emile Combes and Aristide Briand. The law itself was a bone of contention within the republican camp between radicals and liberals. The result of internal debate was to suppress the recognized cults and their subsidies. As such, the 1905 law ended the phase begun by the revolutionary sequence which was subsequently softened by Napoleonic religious policy. As Article 2 of the 1905 law disposed, the Republic neither recognizes cults, nor funds them, nor provides them with subsidies whereas Article 28 declares the illegitimacy of religious symbols on public monuments. As the socio-historian of the French laicity put it: with the law of separation, France crossed a new threshold.[6] Not only was the institutional differentiation reasserted but also, the lack of public religious relevance was signified. Religion was not thought of as 'public good' in the sense that it was not considered as requiring support, real or symbolic, from the state and consequently had to privatize. Legally, there were no longer religious institutions as such, but rather, religious associations, which were governed by private law. Not only was the principle of incompetence of state as far as religion is concerned reasserted, but also the principle of indifference; indifference to individual beliefs, but also, indifference to confessional institutions. To a certain extent, this stance was strongly recalling a conception of citizenship not only as including symbolic space which transcends the religious, regional, and cultural differentiations, but also as an alternative ideology. As expressed in relation to Jews during the Revolution: we can give everything to the Jews as citizens, nothing as a people or a nation.

A few remarks concerning the impact of this conflictual history on accomodating religious plurality be made in conclusion First of all, it is

---

[4] Jean Baubérot, *La morale laïque contre l'ordre moral*, Paris: Le Seuil 1997.

[5] Jean-Marie Mayeur, *La séparation des Eglises et de l'Etat*, Paris: Editions ouvrières 1991.

[6] Jean Baubérot, *Histoire de la laïcité française*, Paris: Presse Universitaire de France 2000.

to be underlined that the opposition between republican universalism and the catholic one has functioned according to a dynamic of mimetical rivalry. That is to say, the French republican ideology is not to be thought of only as a counter-culture to the catholic hold over French society, but also a culture that is structured by the same monolithic dynamic.[7] As a result, the republican ideology is as unable to accept the expression of singularity as the catholic one. Nevertheless, religious minorities have benefited from this new political configuration. Because, germane to the republican forces was not religion as such but rather catholic clericalism and its pretension to govern the political city. One cannot deny the fact that the religious French minorities, such as protestants and Jews have drawn advantages from the withdrawal of the catholic influence as a dominant structuring factor in the French nation. Consequently, Jews and protestants comprised the driving force promoting laicization of French institutions and society, even if this laicization implied a minimalist conception of religious freedom.

LAICITY IN ACTION

One cannot deny that this republican conception, founded on the revolutionary principle of sacralization of the general will and consequently, sacralization of state as the main means to implement this general will, has and still has some political and social efficiency. I do not intend to argue that ideas do not matter. The law of separation shows us what could be called the performative dimension of this ideology and of this driving principle. And, as the Islamic headscarf controversy demonstrated, there remains a militant conception of laicity which rejects the public relevance of religion and sometimes expresses itself as being anti-religious.

Laicity as a Dynamic of Compromise

One must recognize that these principles and ideologies were completely consensual and that they were established through conflict, and resulted in compromise. This dynamic of compromise should all the more be taken into account when considering recent socio-historical works referencing French laicity.[8] This work tends to relativize this confrontational dynamic and loosen numerous arrangements not only between the two

---

[7] Marcel Gauchet, *La religion dans la démocratie. Parcours de la laïcité*, Paris: Gallimard, 1998.

[8] In particular the works of Jean Baubérot.

Frances, but also between principle and practice. The work of Jean Bauberot, who conceived laicity as a contract or pact rather than a struggle, is of noted importance. What socio-historians are also expressing is that, if republican forces created civil religion in France, this civil religion was less a pure political culture based on abstract principles of the French revolution, than it was a syncretism which associates and combines (more or less secularized) catholic values, symbols of and references to human rights, and republican values such as liberty, equality, and fraternity.

De jure Separation, de facto Recognition

Admitting the relevance of this interpretation of history, the 1905 law should then be seen not only as the result of a struggling dynamic, but also as a translation of a dynamic of compromise between the competing political and social forces. Actually, the evolution of the text of the law as such is the sign of these arrangements, since the original text was far more radical than its final version, as shown in Jean Bauberot's work. Reading the disposition of the 1905 law relative to property and use of cultural edifices brings evidence of the relativity of the conception of separation: even if the cults are no longer recognized by the state, they are still dependent on right public law. Moreover, the cultural edifices, which were built before the 1905 law and are still within the public domain, although remaining at the disposal of the ancient cults, actually implies de facto recognition.[9] In the same spirit, what the 1905 law disposes regarding state-funded chaplainship in prisons, hospitals, schools, and nursing homes is expressive of the respect for the principle of religious freedom which demands a relative flexibility of the separatist principle.

Parallel to this analysis of the construction and constraints of the law, it is advisable to avoid making a determinist lecture of it, as unilaterally structuring practices. In other words, the way the law is interpreted or even convoluted by officials may be as or more significant than what the law says and disposes. The role played by the courts is, in this logic, to be precisely analysed. It is clear in the expression of religious conviction in public arenas, through religious processions, display of religious symbols, or the allowed absence of officials on holy days, that jurisprudence grants priority to religious freedom over neutrality of the public domain and institutions, as long as the concerned persons are 'users' (i.e. pupils,

[9] Danièle Lochak, 'Les ambigüités du principe de séparation', Actes, Les religions face au droit. Cahiers d'action juridique, avril 1992. N° 79/80, pp. 9–13.

students) of the public institutions and not employees of the institutions (i.e. teachers, university professors, doctors).

There is another example of the flexibility of the law regarding the question of subsidies to religious associations. The law disposes that the state should not fund religious groups. Nevertheless, if the cults are not subsidized, that is an impactive difference from previous practice and it dramatically changes the position of the religious groups. However, they may still receive benefits from various financial concerns such as fiscal advantages or specific conditions supporting the building of new cultural edifices (e.g. free land). Sometimes, these indirect financial advantages are turned into direct funding. For example, ten years ago, a new catholic cathedral was built in a new town on the outskirts of Paris, la ville-nouvelle d'Evry. The culture ministry, which was at that moment under the responsibility of the socialist minister Jack Lang, not only attempted to 'sell' the project presented as a 'national' one (and which was partly financed through public subscription) but also offered to take as its charge a part of the cost (five million francs out of a total of sixty million francs). This financial participation of the French state in the building of the cathedral utilized rhetorical tricks like the French minister arguing that he was not giving subsidies to a cultural edifice but to a cultural, artistic masterpiece. No one was fooled by this political artifice, which appeared to respect the principle of separation and indifference of the state regarding religion. But this financial participation of the state seemed quite normal to French citizens, who showed no reluctance regarding explicit public financial support to the catholic cult.[10]

Proportional Recognition of Religious Groups

The example of Evry's cathedral is all the more interesting in that public figures not only gave support for the catholic cult but also supported the local Islamic community by helping them to build one of the very first mosque/cathedrals in France. Of course, the local Islamic figures did not receive direct financial support from the public authorities, which they (the Islamics) complained about as they discovered that the cathedral was partly funded by Jack Lang. However, they benefited from certain facilities, and in particular, with respect to the land upon which the mosque was built. Yet, the relationships to the Catholics and the Muslims were not identical, which is significant of laicity in action.

[10] Claire de Galembert, 'Cathédrale d'Etat, cathédrale catholique, cathédrale de la ville-nouvelle ? Les équivoques de la cathédrale d'Evry', Paru dans *Archives des Sciences sociales des Religions*, N° 107, 1999, pp. 109–37.

There are even good reasons to think that the officials originated the construction of the cathedral, although the local catholic community was rather reluctant to undertake such a project. They aim to give a centrality to the new town, whose previous centre had failed to structure the urban space. It seemed to the local planners that there could be nothing better than a church facing the mayor's office (or City Hall) symbolizing the centrality of the town. The minister of culture maintained the cathedral as a national symbol, irrespective of whether it was cult or culture. In comparison, the mosque, which was mostly funded through petrodollars was situated at the margin of the town and had no national relevance since Islam was a minority religion. In this regard, it can be argued that the degree of recognition and centrality of the various religious groups depends on the pro rata distribution of their historical and numerical representation. This example gives evidence to the fact that public action regarding religion is still more or less implicitly reflective of a paradigm of recognized cults, among which Catholicism is still considered as being predominant.

THE FRENCH ISLAMIC POLICY: CONTINUITY AND BREACH OF THE PUBLIC ACTION RELATIVE TO RELIGION

If one acknowledges that the French laical system de facto functions according to the paradigm of implicitly recognized cults, how the French state has dealt with the Islamic issue for a decade—characterized by visible and deliberate action to shape and 'organise' the Islamic presence—is less surprising and new. This policy reveals religion as an object of public policy, thought of as a new trend in the reinterpretation of laicity—sometimes called the 'positive laicity' or the 'open laicity'—in the sense of a more positive account of religion. From a historical perspective, if we consider practice rather than principle, it appears that the schema of state action relative to Islamic issues, reveals more continuity than breach. With growing awareness that the Muslim population was settling in French society, the question of integration and organization of Islam became the agenda. As a result, public and political figures lobbied for reconnaissance of the 'Islam of France', thereby designating Islam as a legitimate religion of France.[11] They advanced the structure of the Islamic reality present in France. Consequently, for nearly a decade, the interior ministry has been defining a representative central-

[11] Claire de Galembert, 'De l'inscription de l'islam dans l'espace urbain', *Annales de la Recherche Urbaine*, no. 68-9, septembre-décembre 1995, pp. 178–87.

ized instance of what is often designated as the 'Islamic community' (whose reality is doubtful, since the Islam in France is fragmented not only according to nationality differences, but also according to different versions, traditions, and trends). The constitutive policy which Jean-Pierre Chevènement inaugurated in 1999 is worthy of mention because of its national characteristic. In 1999, the ministry sent a letter to some of the most pre-eminent Islamic organizations, federations, associations, and proponents to announce the intention of consultation to organize the Islam of France as a 'cult'. To be more convincing, he mobilized the Arabic and Islamic concept of *Isticharat* (consensual decision) to define the initiative. As a result, the various Islamic luminaries involved in this consultation were regularly invited to the ministry of the interior to converse about future representation. The electoral way was chosen: the various associations, prayer rooms, or mosques were given votes in pro rata. On this basis, the various local units would vote for a regional delegate who would then vote for national representatives who would occupy seats in the future centralized structure. Without going into further detail, it should be emphasized that, in its modus operandi, this policy is nothing less than a policy of positive discrimination, if not of affirmative action in favour of Islam, which could actually seem paradoxical according to the usual conception of laicity. Moreover, in this top-down dynamic (the Central state imposing its conception of the integration of Islam, irrespective of what the Islamic proponents think about the opportunity of centrally organizing Islam), the policy implemented by the ministry of interior is not dissimilar to the Napoleonic policy that successfully attempted to transform the French Jewish communities into a centralized institution, the so-called 'Consistoire'. The policy aims to only control and regulate the French Islamic realities, but also to place Islam on the same level as the other religions. However, the interior minister clearly demonstrated that the 1905 law failed in its intent to privatise religion and withdrew it from the public arena.

THE POLICY OF INTEGRATION OF ISLAM TO THE STATE—THE INSTITUTIONAL DEREGULATION OF RELIGIOUS IDENTITIES

Since public policy regarding the Islamic issue in France reveals more continuity than breach in how the state deals with religious issues, the problems that confront the state with the institutionalization of Islam, meaning 'unifying' Islamic diversity into a cult in France, are, in my opinion, quite reflective of the current transformation of the relationship between religion and politics under the pressure of a radical religious pluralism.

It appears as if the state action to 'institutionalize' Islam in France would have the opposite effect from what was expected, i.e. this action has unified less and underlined more the fragmentation of the community. A few interpretations of this dynamic can be offered. First, it can be argued that these dynamics are due to the discrepancy in the way the proponents represent how religion should be organized and the reality of Islamic organization in practice. One cannot deny that French officials foster a central institution that is quite christiano-centric, that is more or less derived from the roman-catholic church model. To a certain extent, it reveals a total misunderstanding of the Islamic realities since Islam has no clerical institutions comparable to the roman catholic church. Secondly, it is clear that the French public initiative to organize' the Islam of France, is mortgaged by the high level of heterogeneity of the Islamic populations which are present in France (the various nationalities, trends, generations, nominal designations, etc.). But, more fundamentally, one may ask sociologically, whether the pattern of public policy which officials refer to as they approach Islamic realities is not simply in total discrepancy with the current deployment of religious identities. In other words, the difficulty the French state is facing with the institutionalization of Islam not only reveals a specific reluctance by the Islamic communities in France to be organized according a foreign pattern of organization but also highlights the general transformation of religion within the modern world.[12] In this sociological perspective, the difficulty the ministry of interior is currently facing with the organization of Islam should be analyzed with regard to the broader crisis of religious institutions, the rise of individualism, and the radicalization of religious pluralism. Actually what makes sociologists of religion salient, such as Daniele-Hervieu Leger in France, is the crisis of the institutionalized belief according to which the religious institutions should, in a top-down dynamic, shape and control the believers and consequently regulate the religious identity.[13] The decline of the Christian churches in Europe is evidential to this development. Parallel to the decline of institutions on the formation of religious identities various new modalities of belief are emerging. These are not institutionally regulated, but rather organized by inter-subjective relations which gives rise to new

[12] Claire de Galembert, 'Etat, Eglise et Religion musulmans : entre institutionalisation et désinstitutionnalisation', Cahiers du Centre Marc Bloch. Islam(s) en Europe, approches d'un nouveau pluralisme culturel européen. (Berlin: Centre Marc Bloch, 1998), pp. 67–79.
[13] Danièle Hervieu-Léger, Le pèlerin et le converti, Paris: Flammarion. 1999.

plasticity of religious identities. This is occurring in the Christian field as well as in the Judaic and Islamic fields. In other words, officials no longer encounter a well-regulated religious field where religious institutions, more or less, subordinate to the frame of the nation state and interface the political and social spheres. Rather, they now encounter the development of new forms of religious allegiances which not only fragment the religious field, applying pressure to the status quo, but also 'denationalize' the field. What this means is that the religious principals deploy themselves less in a 'national-society' boarded world and more in a 'world-society' as Luhmann put it.

The dynamic of deregulation of identities which is at work in the religious field is present in the political one as well. In other terms, the difficulty that the churches are facing to regulate the beliefs and the practices of their followers presents some evident common points with the difficulty the nation state is facing to regulate the civil society in which citizens less and less admit to be 'shaped' by the state. As a result, it could be argued that the French laicity is nowadays facing a big challenge, in the new forms of articulation between religion and politics.

Multiculturalism, Communitarianism, and Liberal Pluralism[1]

MICHAEL DUSCHE

INTRODUCTION

Hindu–Muslim relations in India as well as questions of religious pluralism in Europe and other parts of the West are often discussed from a
multiculturalist, communitarian or liberal perspective. This paper takes
a deeper look at some of the theoretical problems surrounding these
families of theories.

The first part of this paper approaches these problems from a
multiculturalist perspective, and starts by pointing to the main concerns
of multiculturalists and communitarians on the one hand, and liberals
on the other. The former are convinced of the importance, if not pre-
eminence, of the group for/over the individual whereas the latter are
primarily concerned with the well being of the individual. These concerns are expressed in the demand for group rights and individual rights
respectively. The individualism propagated by liberalism, I maintain, is
methodological, not descriptive. Therefore, I am focussing on methodological individualism as a critical point in the debate between
multiculturalists/communitarians and liberals. Multiculturalists, and
sometimes communitarians, claim the inadequacy of individualism as

[1] Sincere thanks to Helmut Reifeld and Jamal Malik, organizers of the conference on
Traditions of Religious Plurality in South Asia and Europe in Gajner, Rajasthan, 23–26 November 2002, for inviting me to the conference and allowing me to contribute a paper to this
volume. Heartfelt thanks also to Margrit Pernau for comments on an earlier draft of this
paper.

a methodological principle in liberalism. Liberals, on the other hand, maintain that methodological individualism is sufficient to account for even group-related needs of the individual. This is normally expressed in terms of individual rights to cultural or community membership. While multiculturalists tend to argue in favour of culture as an insuperable horizon for normative reflection, liberals warn of the trap of self-defeating normative relativism and favour some form of Universalist ethics. As a mediatory position, I propose internal universalism, which is a form of meta-ethical relativism. Internal universalism does not rule out the possibility of universal norms but insists that these are attained through a process of dialogue and negotiation approximating universal consensus.

Multiculturalism, I argue, can attack methodological individualism on two levels: on the normative level, and on the level of practical relevance. Two problems, I argue, are most salient in the debate between multiculturalists and liberals: (a) the problem of the abolition of unjust cultures and (b) the problem of adequate public recognition of cultures.

(a) The identity of any person depends on culture. Unlike voluntary associations, however, culture is not normally acquired; one is born into one's culture. Thus, if a culture is dismissed following consideration of justice, its members suffer disadvantage with regard to the members of the majority culture. This dilemma is particularly disturbing from a liberal point of view. Since the liberal perspective departs from method-ological individualism, the individuals of the dismissed culture count as much as the individuals of the majority culture. Liberalism, however, has nothing to offer them in compensation for the depreciation of their cultural anchorage.

(b) Critics of liberalism have pointed out that there is a limit to the cultural neutrality of the liberal state. I embrace this argument in a qualified way by asking, what the cultural aspects among which a liberal state cannot avoid favouring one culture over another are. I maintain that language is such an aspect. Language, at the same time, is particu-larly important in the identity formation of the individual. In this sensitive respect the liberal state cannot avoid setting the members of those cultures at a disadvantage whose language is not among the media of political debate, education, and other areas relevant for the realiza-tion of civil rights.

Both criticisms of liberalism, (a) and (b), are in principle valid. However, as I try to show, neither helps to establish the case of multi-culturalism for even multiculturalism cannot offer satisfactory solutions to the two dilemmas.

The second part gives an outline of an informed liberal conception of pluralism by taking Rawls' political liberalism to a more principled level. I take Rawls' concept of public reason and argue that, for good philosophical reasons, we are not to expect any conception of justice, liberal or otherwise culturally grounded, to be able to decide political matters in lieu of the members of a polity. At some stage, a collective decision which remains arbitrary to a certain extent cannot be avoided. From this fact of plurality follows the necessity, for the member of each culture, to take into account possible alternatives while construing their conception of justice. The labour of taking into account alternative conceptions of justice makes for the reasonableness of that conception of justice. The requirement of reasonableness in the public use of reason is a mutual one. A conception lacking reasonableness does not meet the criterion of mutuality and will be ignored. From this argument certain constraints of cultures can be inferred, allowing us to distinguish (negatively) just from unjust cultures. The argument also allows us to distinguish between politically irrelevant aspects of culture and those aspects that are politically relevant and can thus give rise to multiculturalist concerns over majoritarianism. As an approximate answer from a liberal perspective to problem (b), I discuss federalism, decentralization, and the principle of subsidiarity. As an answer to (a), it seems, only a pragmatic solution is available. From the liberal perspective, the dismissal of an unjust culture is permissible only if the harm done to its members by being uprooted is balanced by the advantage the dismissal has for those who would otherwise have suffered the injustices ascribed to that culture.

MULTICULTURALISM

Much of what is now couched in the terminology of multiculturalism[2] has a precursor in the communitarian critique[3] of liberal positions attributed to thinkers like Bruce Ackerman, Ronald Dworkin, and

---

[2] The following owes much to Axel Honneth, *Kommunitarismus.* Campus Verlag, Frankfurt am Main, 1993, pp. 7–17 and Rajeev Bhargava, 'Introducing Multiculturalism', In *Multiculturalism, Liberalism and Democracy* edited by Rajeev Bhargava, Amiya Kumar Bagchi and R. Sudarshan, New Delhi: Oxford University Press, 1999, pp. 1–57.

[3] Cf. Charles Taylor, *Hegel and Modern Society,* Cambridge: Cambridge University Press, 1979; Alasdair MacIntyre, *After Virtue: A Study in Moral Theory,* Notre Dame: University of Notre Dame Press, 1981; Michael Sandel, *Liberalism and the Limits of Justice,* Cambridge: Cambridge University Press, 1982; Michael Walzer, *Spheres of Justice,* New York: Basic Books.

particularly John Rawls.[4] Whereas liberals see first to the needs of the individual and justify social institutions such as families, communities, associations, societies, states, and ultimately trans- and supranational institutions by way of asking what they contribute to the well-being of the individual, communitarians take the needs of social institutions, particularly those of communities within the nation state, as equally or even more basic. The ensuing debate has been largely about how to place the emphasis right. Moderate liberals as well as reasonable communitarians largely agree on the basic features of the liberal democratic state with a firm place for individual rights which includes the right to form associations within the state, to practise one's religion and to maintain the relevant religious and cultural institutions under the protection of the state. The lines between communitarians and liberals have been drawn differently. I am not interested here in defining these terms or in accounting for all the subdivisions in each school. For the purpose of this paper, I shall focus on one major division, namely the question whether doing justice to the individual's need for cultural or community attachment requires us to depart from methodological individualism and to stipulate collective rights.

I shall call liberal the position that maintains that we can account for the individual needs for attachment and belonging within the limits of methodological individualism. The communitarian and the multiculturalist positions, on the other hand, claim the need for departure from that premise. Both advocate collective rights (i.e. 'human rights' for groups) on the same or even on a more fundamental level as individual human rights. Of course, intermediate positions exist. Bhargava for instance differentiates between republican and liberal individualism, political and cultural communitarian, democratic, authoritarian, liberal, and even 'boutique' multiculturalism.[5] All these distinctions are valid. However, as Habermas put it, 'Included in the set of human rights are rights to cultural membership. Everybody has the same right to develop and maintain her identity in just those intersubjectively shared forms of life and traditions from which she first emerged and has been formed during the course of childhood and

---

[4] Cf. John Rawls, *A Theory of Justice,* Oxford: Oxford University Press, 1971; Ronald Dworkin, *Taking Rights Seriously.* London: Duckworth, 1977; Bruce Ackermann, *Social Justice in the Liberal State,* New Haven: Yale University Press, 1980; on Rawls and some of his critics see also Thomas W. Pogge, *Realizing Rawls,* Ithaca, New York: Cornell University Press, 1989.

[5] *Introducing Multiculturalism,* pp. 48ff.

adolescence.'[6] From such membership rights follow almost all of the immunities, protections, subsidies, and policies which communitarians demand for cultural minorities in the liberal state. 'These rights need not be conceptualised in terms of collective rights.'[7] I am therefore not interested in those kinds of communitarianism or multiculturalism that do not challenge methodological individualism. In this paper, these positions will also be subsumed under liberal pluralism.

By the term 'methodological individualism', I mean any approach that uses the individual as the basic unit for normative considerations. On this level, lest it fall into the trap of the naturalist fallacy, liberalism does not make any claim as to how people really are, how they develop and what they need for a good life. This would be 'empirical' or 'anthropological individualism'. Methodological individualism grants that individuals, seen from an anthropological perspective, grow up in families and possibly in communities. It grants that much of the material normative input constituting any individual personality stems from these allegiances, and that families and communities are crucial in the maintenance of a healthy (empirical) individual. In isolating an individual for the purpose of moral reflection, the liberal does not pretend that the resulting abstraction is a realistic image of a human being in this anthropological sense. That is not the purpose. Moral thinking has to abstract from certain givens in order to reach out into the counterfactual realm of normativity. Thus, the question is not how realistic the concept of the individual would be after this abstraction but the reverse: How much anthropological 'flesh' do we have to add to an abstract individual in order for our counterfactual considerations to remain relevant for real-life purposes? The relationship between normative and empirical theory has been elucidated by Habermas in his discussion of Kohlberg's moral psychology.[8] While Kohlberg's six-stage model of moral development admittedly presupposes a normative theory whose direct justification has to rest on independent normative grounds to avoid natural fallacy, it nevertheless contributes indirectly to the justification of the normative theory by proving its usefulness and relevance to real-life matters. Thus, multiculturalism can attack methodological individualism for two reasons. It can call into question the normative validity of

---

[6] Cf. Juergen Habermas, 'Multiculturalism and the Liberal State' *Stanford Law Review* 47, May 1995.

[7] Ibid.

[8] Cf. Juergen Habermas, 'Rekonstruktive vs. verstehende Sozialwissenschaften', In *Moralbewusstsein und kommunikatives Handeln*, Frankfurt am Main: Suhrkamp Verlag, 1983, pp. 29–52.

methodological individualism or it can attack liberalism on the ground that methodological individualism renders it irrelevant to real-life affairs.

It is perhaps thanks to the communitarian critique that the importance of a grounding of liberal values in a lived political community has been brought home. Among the preconditions for the working of liberal institutions is a common horizon of values, a largely implicit background consensus, which is eminently social and subjective and cannot be captured by individualistic and objectivistic considerations alone. The abstract individual of the rational choice school was ruled out even for liberals like John Rawls who had started with an 'Outline of a Decision Procedure for Ethics'[9] in the early 1950s but who already stresses the 'subjective circumstances of justice'[10] in his *Theory of Justice*; i.e. it is not merely rational agents who assemble in the *original position* to deliberate over the basic structure of a future society' but persons with 'their own plans of life' and 'conceptions of the good'.[11] On another level, the justification of the original position itself involves 'us' not only as rational beings but in 'our' well-considered judgement regarding basic questions of value that may or may not be open to rational scrutiny.[12] Nowadays, differences between liberals and multiculturalists pertain to questions regarding the active involvement of the state in the protection of communities and their institutions and their legal status. Habermas notes a self-contradiction in any attempt to reproduce culturally engendered ways of life through the judicial machinery of the state:

The reproduction of traditions and cultural forms is an achievement which can be legally enabled, but by no means granted. Reproduction here requires the conscious appropriation and application of traditions by those native members who have become convinced of these traditions' intrinsic value. The members must first come to see that the inherited traditions are worth the existential effort of continuation. But new generations can acquire such a belief only on the condition that they are capable—and have the right—of saying yes or no. Legal

[9] John Rawls, 'Outline of a Decision Procedure for Ethics', *Philosophical Review* 60, 1951, pp. 177ff.

[10] *Theory of Justice*, § 22.

[11] Ibid., p. 127.

[12] Cf. my discussion of the subjective circumstances of justice in *Der Philosoph als Mediator: Anwendungsbedingungen globaler Gerechtigkeit*, Passagen Verlag, Vienna, 2000. My use of the term 'subjective circumstances of justices' differs from that of Rawls in that I am including in it all culturally dependent normative preconceptions that enter into the justification of the original position including the definition of the veil of ignorance. For a clarification on this point, I am grateful for a discussion with Thomas Pogge during a seminar on global justice in Halle in December 2002.

guarantees of survival would deprive members exactly of this freedom to break off from their own tradition—and would thereby destroy the very space for hermeneutical appropriation which provides the only way to maintain cultural forms.[13]

While the debates between liberals and communitarians centred on the status of the community as a source for belief formation of individuals, multiculturalism has defended culture as an irreducible horizon in the justification of moral and legal obligation. At this juncture, multiculturalism risks falling prey to normative relativism. We can distinguish three forms of relativism: descriptive, meta-ethical, and normative relativism.[14] Within descriptive relativism we can again distinguish between a fundamentalist and a non-fundamentalist sort. Descriptive relativism in its non-fundamentalist form makes the prima facie uncontroversial statement that individuals or groups adhere to conflicting values and norms. From here, fundamentalist relativism goes a step further to claim that the conflict among these norms is normally not resolved through ethical reflection or dialogue and that therefore the different groups either clash or coexist peacefully albeit separately. All this is still on the descriptive level. Normative relativism, now, takes the discussion to the level of ethical reflection and maintains that even on that theoretical level, the conflict cannot be resolved: two or more normative systems coexist separately and there is no independent ground to determine which one is right. From this, normative relativists draw the conclusion that we have to assume an attitude of equal respect for each of the normative systems, thereby contradicting its own assumption that there is no independent ground for upholding even the norm of equal respect for different normative systems. Normative relativism thereby defeats itself. The way out would be a meta-ethical position that grants to the relativist the fact of conflicting normative systems and the lack, as of yet, of any universalist common ground, but does not preclude the possibility of achieving such common ground through dialogue and negotiation. Norms, after all, are human-made and can be shaped and reshaped according to human need.[15]

For the multiculturalist, culture is an indispensable level of analysis when it comes to questions of identity and belonging. However, the moral and legal status of groups, defined as communities or cultures is

[13] Juergen Habermas, 'Multiculturalism and the Liberal State', in *Stanford Law Review* 47, 1995, no. 3.

[14] Cf. R. B. Brandt, 'Ethical Relativism', in P. Edwards (ed.), *The Encyclopedia of Philosophy*, Vol. III, New York: Macmillan, pp. 75–8.

[15] This is roughly my position in *Philosoph als Mediator*, cf. §5 on *Internal Universalism*.

problematic. A host of questions arises regarding the definability of cultural groups: what carries the moral or legal status of a group if the boundaries between groups cannot be drawn easily and groups within groups cannot be limited to a manageable number? Moreover, there is no easy one-to-one correspondence between individuals and groups. Each individual may belong to a number of different groups simultaneously and over time.[16] Thus, the group allegiances of any individual cannot easily be defined objectively but have to depend on the self-ascriptions and preferences of any individual at a given point of time. An individual can change its identity over time and / or have several identities simultaneously, depending on the context. Identities can overlap and mutually depend on each other in a variety of ways. Ultimately, only the individual person can inform us about her various allegiances and their preferential order. It seems that thereby, again, the individual gains central importance. From the point of view of the theorist and more so from the point of view of the policy maker, the individual cannot be bypassed in the definition of the community or culture in which it wishes to be included. All these problems set aside, in this paper I am asking whether multiculturalism did succeed in demonstrating a fundamental flaw in the liberal approach. I shall discuss two problems assuming that they could represent a real obstacle for methodological individualism: (a) the problem of abolition[17] of unjust communities or cultures and (b) the problem of public recognition of communities or cultures.

The identity of the individual person, so the multiculturalists claim, is rooted in something bigger than the individual, namely its culture. Therefore, the conclusion that, cultures need to feature somewhere in the normative account of just social institutions. The liberal answer to this would be swift. Cultures do feature in the liberal account of just institutions. They are part of what Rawls had called the basic structure of society and they are one among many institutions under scrutiny in a normative account of social justice. Thus, a culture that conforms to the basic principles of justice for the basic structure of any society would be called a just culture and would occupy its just place in the overall scheme of things in that particular society. Cultures that sanction violation of basic principles of justice would justly be dismissed as any association of individuals would have to be dismissed if it violates basic principles of

[16] Very instructive in this regard is Margrit Pernau's contribution to this volume.

[17] The allusion to the abolition of slavery in the US is deliberate. No one, I take it, would object to the abolition of slavery and yet the abolition of the 'culture' of the society of slave-owning masters will also have left them with a sense of uprootedness.

justice. Liberalism grants every individual a catalogue of basic rights including the right to form, or be part of, any association provided that this association respects the same basic rights of all the other members of society. Here, the multiculturalist will object that the analogy between cultures and associations in the liberal's account is flawed for the following reason: While individuals can join associations voluntary, people are not altogether free in choosing their culture. People cannot easily renounce their culture or assimilate to another culture. Born German, I cannot suddenly choose to become Indian in culture and vice versa. Thus, the multiculturalist will ask: How does the liberal go about a person who happens to be born into a culture deemed unjust by liberal principles of justice? The liberal will dismiss the person's culture. Will he dismiss the person along with it?

The liberal faces a problem at this juncture. On the one hand, by force of normative individualism, the liberal is committed to treat each person indiscriminately of any unchosen circumstance including culture; on the other hand, principles of justice compel her to deliberately set a group of individuals at a disadvantage since these principles mark a certain culture as unjust. An ideal society conforming to a given set of liberal principles of justice will not leave any room for unjust cultures. A less-than ideal society on its way to more justice will thus have to work towards the abolition of unjust cultures within its boundaries. However, abolishing the stipulated unjust culture, the non-ideal society cannot offer any compensation to those whose culture and thereby whose identity it has to tamper with. It cannot give them a new culture to make up for the loss in identity and belonging, if our assumption is correct that cultures in a certain deep sense cannot be voluntarily acquired. The individuals concerned, i.e. at least one or two generations from those who used to belong to the dismissed culture, will suffer the consequences of being uprooted until their offspring eventually grows up among equals in the majority culture.

I had called the problem just described the 'problem of abolishing unjust cultures' or simply the 'abolition problem' (a). I shall discuss this problem in the light of a Rawls-type liberal pluralism below. Even at this stage, however, the multiculturalist could raise the objection that the choice of examples has been particularly disadvantageous for her. Alternatively, let us look at a society that consists of people belonging to different cultures each of which would stand the test of basic principles of justice advanced by a liberal theory of justice. Still, the multiculturalist could maintain that the political culture of a given society usually reflects the preferences of those who form the majority culture. Their culture, being the standard culture, normally receives more public recognition than minority cultures. The people belonging to the majority culture are thus at a greater advantage in terms of public recognition of what forms their identity than people belonging to any minority culture. As multiculturalists like Kymlicka[18] and other critics of liberalism[19] have pointed out, there is a limit as to how neutral the liberal state can be with respect to culture. In many existing nationstates, the official language is a divisive factor. With a secondarily acquired language being the official language in the political forum, people belonging to a minority with a different first language are at a disadvantage with respect to others who have acquired the official language as a first language. This disadvantage can be practical (following and participating in political processes, standing for office); it can also be more subtle. Rajeev Bhargava, for instance, gives an account of how personal identity relates to culture and links it to intentionality (beliefs, desires ...) and thereby language.[20] The ascription of beliefs and desires involves propositional attitude sentences (that-clauses):

> To have an identity, a person must consciously be able to identify with some of his/her beliefs, desires and acts ... [O]n the assumption of the centrality of beliefs, desires, and acts to the whole issue of personal identity, the identity of persons is constituted in large measure by the language.... Identification with beliefs and desires is impossible without language because a person would not know what these beliefs and desires mean.... Since entry into a world of meaning is crucial for the formation of beliefs and desires; the identity of humans is related to a world of meanings ... a culture.

Thus, language becomes the central point for practical reasons as well as for the more subtle theoretical reasons in connection with personal identity. Language being an important expression of culture, multiculturalism has a point here. However, multiculturalism does not normally focus on language but speaks of culture in a very broad and often undefined sense.[21] The problem can thus be narrowed down from cultures to linguistic communities. This is what I had called the 'problem

---

[18] Cf. Will Kymlicka, Ibid.

[19] Cf. Christoph Menke, *Spiegelungen der Gleichheit*, Berlin: Akademie Verlag, 2000; 'Grenzen der Gleichheit', in *Deutsche Zeitschrift für Philosophie* 50, 2002, no. 6, pp. 897–906.

[20] Cf. Bhargava, op. cit., pp. 4–9.

[21] I have criticized this in my review of Kymlicka (op. cit.), *Ethical Perspectives* 5, 1998, no. 3, pp. 227–9. For a theory on propositional attitudes emphasizing individual autonomy in belief ascription see my 'Signification in Opaque Contexts', in Harjeet Singh Gill (ed.), *Signification in Language and Culture*, Indian Institute of Advanced Study, Shimla, 2002, pp. 161–94 as well as my 'Interpreted Logical Forms as Objects of the Attitudes', *Journal of Logic, Language, and Information* 4, 1995, no. 4: 301–15.

of equal political recognition of different linguistic communities' or simply the 'recognition problem' (b).

For these two problems, (a) and (b), to be decisive, the multiculturalist has to show that (i) the liberal approach for principled reasons does not solve them adequately and (ii) that the multiculturalist approach does. I shall argue that the multiculturalist achieves (i) but not (ii). To show that for principled reasons, liberalism cannot adequately cope with the two problems, the multiculturalist has to say how his approach differs from the liberal fundamentally. The fundamental difference between the multiculturalist and the liberal approach lies in the question whether individuals or groups should be the ultimate unit of the normative analysis. Liberal theories use methodological individualism; multiculturalists use groups as the most basic unit. Therefore, the multiculturalist has to show how methodological individualism fails to account for the two aforementioned problems.

Problem (a) calls into question the normative validity of methodological individualism for normative reasons. Liberalism has to dismiss unjust cultures. Equally for normative reasons, liberalism cannot afford to dismiss the individual carrier of that culture along with it.[22] Problem (b) rests on the assumption that cultures thrive better when they are officially recognized.[23] Particularly, cultures profit from being 'state cultures'. Conversely, cultures are said to wither away when they are pushed into the domain of the unofficial. (I am not saying 'private' because I believe that there is a third realm between the private and the official that is the public sphere.) The liberal could simply deny that these assumptions are correct. There are numerous examples of cultures that have failed to wither away in spite of never having been official in any way. A prime example is the Jewish Diaspora that has maintained its cultural and religious distinctness over centuries in spite of not only being not official but even officially suppressed. There are also examples of cultures that have disappeared in spite of being state cultures, and not only because their states have vanished. One may think of the polytheist Roman culture that has given way to a monotheist Christian culture even before the Roman Empire fell apart. However, the liberal cannot deny

---

[22] I have criticized this problem in connection with questions relating to global justice in a critical appreciation of Rawls Law of Peoples, Cf. *Philosoph als Mediator* §16; John Rawls, 'The Law of Peoples', in *Critical Inquiry* 20, 1993, pp. 36–68, and *The Law of Peoples with 'The Idea of Public Reason Revisited'*, Cambridge, Massachusetts: Harvard University Press, 1999.

[23] Cf. Will Kymlicka, *States, Nations, and Cultures*, Assen, The Netherlands: Van Gorcum Press.

that states do have to make a choice in some aspects of culture and that therefore even in the liberal state, absolute neutrality with respect to cultural matters is not conceivable. As a consequence, some groups of individuals have an advantage over others in that their access to political participation is facilitated by the fact that their culture is part of the official culture. Those whose cultures are marginal in the state find it more difficult to profit from the opportunities that a state offers to its citizens. This line of attack questions the relevance of methodological individualism for real-life matters. The conflict is between the liberal's proclaimed objective of providing the individual with equal opportunities by levelling privileges and impairments that are due to unchosen circumstances (culture being one example) and real-life constraints in the feasibility of state neutrality.

LIBERAL PLURALISM

What makes liberalism appear so indifferent towards community? In the archetypical social contract, people whose shared interest it is to be left in peace and carry on with their business come together. Who are these individuals? Historically speaking, the individual of the social contract is a self-sufficient entity. He (sic!) owns an estate to provide for his economical needs and a family or clan for his social requirements. What he needs from society as a whole is protection for his property. Such was, in crude terms, the member of the social contract that Locke and also Kant envisaged. For Kant, individuals without property (interestingly with the exception of state officials such as professors), dependent labourers, women, and children were not full-fledged citizens because they were lacking autarky. Since it was first conceived in this crude form, liberalism has evolved into various forms, some of which attempting to constructively deal with the democratic, socialist, and pluralist criticism to which it was exposed. A prime example of this sort is John Rawls's political liberalism.[24] I shall now briefly outline how Rawls's political liberalism deals with the problem of plurality of world views—secular as well as religious—coexisting in the setting of a modern liberal democracy. Rawls speaks of comprehensive doctrines pertaining to questions of good life and just social order. These comprehensive doctrines can be based on secular parameters or grounded in a religious or culturally engendered perspective. Their defining feature is that in their attempt to give a foundation to a set of norms and values they refer

---

[24] Cf. John Rawls, *Political Liberalism*, New York: Columbia University Press, 1993.

to concepts and truths which are not commonly shared among citizens outside this particular community. However, the society, in spite of being divided along such lines, is in need of a shared basis of basic norms forming a sort of background consensus upon which social institutions catering to all citizens alike can rest. Since Kant, the realm in which such a background consensus is sought is called the realm of public reason.[25]

In his various publications on *public reason*,[26] John Rawls has developed a normative theory of politics for a plural environment where reasonable citizens who follow diverse religious and non-religious belief systems equally demand that their worldview be respected and the pursuit of their religious practices protected by the state—provided that they are reasonable. This is an important constraint, which is meant to protect us from relativism. What are we to understand by the term 'reasonable' as applied to citizens and as applied to secular and religious doctrines? Do we have to assume that there is an objective moral order, which humans can appreciate through their faculty of reason? Under this assumption, a conception of justice would be true if it corresponds with this given moral order. According to this position, which is called 'rational intuitionism' in the philosophical literature,[27] there can be only one true moral theory. Reasonableness, according to rational intuitionism, is the insight into the inner necessity of this moral truth. Anyone lacking this insight would not be called reasonable. Political liberalism rejects this position. There can be a plurality of moral conceptions which can be true internally.[28] Ultimately, however, only a consensus can bridge the gap between possible incommensurable truths. Ultimately,

---

[25] Cf. Immanuel Kant, 'Was ist Aufklärung?' in *Biesters Berlinische Monatsschrift*, December 1784; Ak. VIII, pp. 33–42.

[26] Cf. John Rawls, 'The Idea of Public Reason Revisited', in *The Law of Peoples with 'The Idea of Public Reason Revisited'*, pp. 129–80 for his latest discussion of the topic. Earlier publications on the same include 'Justice as Fairness: Political Not Metaphysical', *Philosophy and Public Affairs* 14, 1985, pp. 223–51; 'The Domain of the Political and Overlapping Consensus', *New York University Law Review* 64, 1989, pp. 233–55; *Political Liberalism* (loc. cit.); the introduction to the paperback edition of *Political Liberalism*, New York: Columbia University Press, 1995, pp. xxxvii–lxii; 'Reply to Juergen Habermas', *Journal of Philosophy* 92, 1995, no. 3, 109–31; and (only in German) 'Das Ideal des oeffentlichen Vernunftgebrauchs [The Ideal of the Public Use of Reason]', in *Zur Idee des Politischen Liberalismu: John Rawls in der Diskussion*, edited by Wilfried Hinsch, Frankfurt am Main: Suhrkamp Verlag, 1997, pp. 116–41.

[27] John Rawls, 'Kantischer Konstruktivismus in der Moraltheorie', in Wilfried Hinsch (ed.), *John Rawls: Die Idee des politischen Liberalismus, Aufsaetze 1978-1989*, Frankfurt am Main: Suhrkamp Verlag, 1992, p. 137f.; English in *The Journal of Philosophy* 77, 1980, pp. 515–72.

[28] Cf. my use of the term *internal universalism* in *Philosoph als Mediator*, §5.

truth is not the decisive factor but a decision taken collectively by all concerned individuals. Political liberalism calls 'reasonable' a position that takes this fact of ethical diversity seriously. The reasonable individual develops her moral conception, which can be true internally, taking into account that others may have their moral conceptions which internally may be equally valid. After coming to terms with herself on ethical matters, she enters into negotiation with other individuals to explore the possibility of an overlapping consensus. Ultimately, a collective decision will be reached and one of the many equally suitable moral conceptions will be validated.

A person would be called not-reasonable if she does not accept the fact that there can be a plurality of equally suitable moral conceptions. The reasonable person will therefore try to anticipate possible dissent and attempt to couch her conception in terms that are, in principle, acceptable for all. Conceptions, which are, in principle, not acceptable to all citizens are called non-reasonable. Their legalization would have to rely on force and thus be perceived as arbitrary and illegitimate by those who do not share the reasons behind the conception. A public conception of justice is reasonable to the extent that it takes into consideration all reasonable positions (as defined above). Reasonableness in the defined sense thus involves a momentum of adequacy (appreciation of the fact of reasonable pluralism) and preparedness to cooperate in the bringing about of an overlapping consensus between several equally suitable conceptions of justice. The implied principle of compatibility of reasonable positions could be called the 'categorical imperative of political reason': Act as if the maxim of your action were to become through your will the maxim of all reasonable citizens in your polity.

Kant's law-assessing (*gesetzepruefend*) categorical imperative can be regarded as a direct ancestor of Rawls' concept of public reason. Kant, however, had underestimated the range of possible dissent within the reasonable. He had hoped for a moral law just as eternal as the starry heaven above him.[29]

To show that the stated fact of plurality of suitable moral conceptions is not just an empirical coincidence but relies on a firm philosophical basis, I would like to point out a parallel between Quine's indeterminacy thesis and Rawls's thesis of the incommensurability of different, yet equally suitable worldviews regarding just social

---

[29] For further discussion of Rawls' and Kant's conception of 'reasonableness' see my *Philosoph als Mediator*, §10.

institutions.[30] I shall maintain that a thesis of indeterminacy of normative theories can be formulated in analogy to Quine's thesis of the
indeterminacy of empirical theories. In *Political Liberalism*, Rawls holds
the view that the long-run outcome of the work of human reason under
free institutions is an ever-growing diversity of world views and value
orientations.[31] This diversification comprises practical philosophy and
especially political theory and theory of justice. In view of certain limits
of human reason, as we will see further down, it is no longer reasonable
to expect the existence of only one reasonable world view to account for
the justice and legitimacy of our social institutions. Many reasonable
and yet incommensurable conceptions of justice compete for acceptance
in the forum of public reason. Their reasonableness is evaluated in the
light of what Rawls calls the 'idea of public reason'.[32] Any theory of
justice that deserves to be called reasonable has to take into account the
mere fact that there may be other reasonable but incompatible theories
of justice and accept mediation from the point of view of public reason.
If theories of justice would yield only non-controversial results, no such
mediatory position would be needed. Then, normative questions would
be on a par with other matters of expertise and the public would delegate
them to their experts just as questions of technological nature are
delegated to expert committees and not debated in parliament or court.
Unfortunately, however, normative theories are indeterminate in a way
to be explained and therefore normative decisions remain within the
discretion of the public and its representatives. They are the domain
proper of the political and cannot be delegated to experts outside the
political process. To explicate the point of view of public reason, we
have to avoid any claim that is potentially controversial among different
reasonable theories of justice. Determining the limits of what we can
legitimately suggest from the point of view of public reason amounts to
determining the reasons for potential disagreement between different
comprehensive doctrines. In Rawls's own words: 'The idea of reasonable disagreement involves an account of the sources, or causes, of
disagreement between reasonable persons.'[33] This is what Rawls calls
'the burdens of judgement'.[34] I have tried to give an account of these
'burdens of judgement' in a principled way using Quine's concept of

---

[30] Cf. Willard van Orman Quine, *Word and Object*, Cambridge, Massachusetts: MIT Press, 1960, p. 27.
[31] Cf. *Political Liberalism*, pp. xvi f.
[32] Ibid., pp. 212f.
[33] Ibid., p. 55.
[34] Ibid., pp. 54ff.

indeterminacy as a model. According to Quine, it is always possible to devise two or more theories that account equally well for the same set of empirical data but which are mutually incompatible.

The reformulation of Quine's indeterminacy thesis in terms of normative theory would yield the following proposition: It is always possible to devise two or more normative theories that account equally well for the same set of basic normative assumptions but which are mutually incompatible.

From this it follows that for any given theory of justice there can be at least one other equally adequate theory of justice and thus no theory of justice can ever be expected to remain forever undisputed. Reasonable disagreement based on at least one alternative and equally suitable conception of justice is always possible. No conception of justice can therefore hold a permanent claim to the domain of public reason and to the realm of the political.[35]

We are used to thinking with Kant in a dichotomy of legal ethics and virtue ethics. Therein, Kant follows the classical liberal framework that differentiates between law and ethics. This framework rests historically upon the experience of thirty years of religious war in Europe that eventually gave way to the opinion that reasonable disagreement between religions as regards the pious life of their supporters is possible and legitimate. It became common sense that the role of the state is not to forcefully eliminate religious disagreement between its citizens. Religion thus became disentrenched from state affairs, its normative propositions binding only the community of its supporters. Legal affairs, by contrast were viewed as binding for every citizen regardless of their faith. In the legislative process, the *res publica* had to remain neutral in all matters exceeding the limits of legal ethics and transgressing the bounds of virtue ethics. Rawls as a self-proclaimed disciple of Kant differentiates accordingly. In his terms, we have to differentiate between the scopes of public reason as opposed to private reason. Public reason is a matter of politics, virtue ethics a matter of private reason. The concept of the political, of legal ethics or of *res publica* has traditionally been defined in terms of material propositions as if the difference between public and private matters would lie in the material norm itself. Rawls, now, suggests a Copernican turn in moral theory by formalizing the concept of the political. It is no longer implied in the norm itself whether it is to be subsumed under the domain of legal ethics or virtue ethics. The distinction between legal matters and ethical matters is

---

[35] For a fuller account see my *Philosoph als Mediator.*

carried out formally and dynamically by recourse to the criteria of reasonable disagreement. The realm of the political and the scope of legal ethics are defined by the scope of reasonable disagreement alone. The domain of politics corresponds to the domain of disagreement in ethical matters. Politics is about the peaceful settlement of conflicts regarding matters of justice. It has to mediate between divergent views on justice between groups of individuals.

How can the concepts of public reason and normative politics help us to tackle the two aforementioned puzzles of multiculturalism: the abolition problem and the recognition problem? A lot depends on how the multiculturalist defines the central term in her critique of liberal democratic pluralism. If culture is left undefined the liberal will object to the following observation: Culture matters for persons in a variety of domains; the state, however, is not meant to provide or substitute for whatever culture can give a person. This follows from the above delineation of the realm of the political and of *res publica*. A state that takes upon itself the guardianship for the full range of affairs usually associated with the term 'culture' would become authoritarian. It would not discriminate between the private affairs of its citizens—a domain where citizens have the freedom to make individual choices, to embrace or reject certain parts of their tradition—and the public affairs, the domain proper of the state where it can legitimately apply its right to enforce certain norms independently of the momentary choice of the person concerned. The liberal democratic state cannot take upon itself all the tasks that the various actors of civil society are to accomplish by themselves. The actors of civil society, unlike the state, are voluntary associations. The right of exit of the individual prevents them from infringing on their liberties and becoming authoritarian. Cultures, as we have noticed earlier, lack this particular feature. Their membership is not voluntary in the same way as in the case of associations. If the state were to add its might to the inescapable character of cultures, being part of a culture would become a fate. To prevent this, the state has to steer clear to a certain extent from the procreation of culture. Its job is to shield off the polity from external threats and prevent internal strife so that the polity can negotiate its internal affairs through peaceful and democratic means.[36]

For the controversy between the multiculturalist and the liberal to be

[36] Cf. my 'Human Rights, Autonomy, and Sovereignty', in *Ethical Perspectives* 7, 2000, no. 1: 24–36; and my 'Ethik in der internationalen Politik—zum "Recht auf nationale Souveraenitaet"', in Ulrich Arnswald and Jens Kertscher (eds), *Die Autonomie des Politischen und die Instrumentalisierung der Ethik*, Heidelberg: Manutius Verlag, 2002, pp. 77–99.

meaningful, we have to single out those aspects of culture into which the liberal democratic state cannot avoid getting involved. It is here that Rawls' concept of the realm of the political can be of help. It provides us with a formula for discerning which cultural aspects fall into the domain of politics and which do not. We have already mentioned one cultural aspect any political community or society cannot avoid getting involved in, and this is language. Any political community needs a medium through which it negotiates and by the help of which the democratic right to political participation becomes meaningful. Certain aspects of education may provide further examples since only adequately educated citizens can be expected to become active and fully cooperating members of a political community. There are other aspects of culture, however, which need not be carried into the realm of politics. A political community need not take a uniform stance on religion, science, architecture, literature, theatre, music etc. Those matters are not directly relevant as prerequisites for the process of political negotiation. The multiculturalist had pointed out that culture is a necessary condition for any individual to preserve a sense of identity and belonging. The communitarian had indicated that the belonging to a community was a prerequisite for any individual to form beliefs and opinions on matters of value and justice. The political community, in turn, depends on individuals who are rooted in their respective culture and who have a sense of justice and ethical value to strive for. This however does not imply the reverse. The political community, while depending on individuals generally being rooted in some culture, does not depend on any particular culture for their individual citizens. This is true from the perspective of the state: the state should not limit itself to the promotion of one culture; and from the perspective of the individual, the state should not limit the individual to any one culture. From the latter follows that the state should also not promote a variety of existing cultures because it would thereby limit the bearers of each culture to follow an official interpretation of that culture. Humans have always been able to bring about culture without the help of the state. Involving the state in the reproduction of culture is underestimating human creativity. The motivation behind this is often authoritarian in nature.

All this is true, as we have said, for aspects of culture other than language (and possibly education). Here, by contrast, majoritarianism to a certain extent seems inescapable. In the paradigmatic, largely monolingual nation states of Europe this does not pose much of a problem. A state can afford to have two or more working languages (four in the case of Switzerland). However, in larger states like India and in conglomerations of states like the European Union the number of autochthonous linguistic communities is simply too large to be accommodated through a multi-language formula. One solution already at hand for this problem and well within the boundaries of democratic liberalism is federalism, i.e. the establishment of intermediate levels of political deliberation. A communal or regional government deliberating on behalf of a linguistic community can mediate between the Central government and the citizens without infringing on the priority of individual rights over collective rights. Of course, federalism and decentralization cannot solve but only reduce the problem that people belonging to some linguistic communities have an advantage over individuals belonging to other linguistic communities because their language happens to be among the working languages of a local or Central government. But this is a problem faced by liberal pluralism and multiculturalism alike. The multiculturalist seeking greater autonomy for certain linguistic communities faces the same problem. Within the domain of that linguistic community there will again be minorities who would fall under the hegemony of the main language of that area. There can only be an approximate solution, never a principled one if one wants to avoid sovereign political entities to exceed the size of a village.

The idea coping best with this impasse is the principle of subsidiary government which is available to the liberal and the multiculturalist alike. The concept of subsidiary government has its roots in the German legal tradition meaning the prevalence of the local customary law over the imperial law. The former used to be Germanic; the latter emerged as an adoption of Roman law. Roman law was used to supplement Germanic law where it was not sufficiently specific. Today, of course, federal law breaks state law and state law prevails over communal customs; local law is used to supplement federal law where it is not specific enough. Thus, subsidiary government has come to mean almost the inverse. The idea is that matters should be decided as far as possible by the concerned people: local matters by local legislative bodies, regional matters by regional ones and so forth. Following its inherent logic, human rights, since they concern everyone, would fall into the domain of a global legislative body, which so far does not exist. Subsidiarity, in Germany today, is supported mainly by Catholics. The idea, however, has a republican aspect to it which makes it universally acceptable. Concerned people should be in a position to deliberate on their own affairs. The principle of subsidiary government tends to maximize the autonomy of local and regional institutions, thereby leaving a maximum of questions to be decided within the bounds of the respective linguistic community. Which matters can legitimately be decided on a supra-regional or Central level has to be negotiated between local political entities. I have argued elsewhere that a nation state consisting of a variety of linguistic communities should conceivably be the result of a hypothetical process of deliberate convergence of local political entities on a common ground of shared fundamental values.[37] Any multiethnic or multinational state where such deliberate union is inconceivable would be illegitimate.

CONCLUSION

In the preceding paragraphs we have dealt with the recognition problem (a) as it was raised by the multiculturalist. The multiculturalist had intended to show how in a principled way liberalism cannot adequately deal with the problem of cultural majoritarianism in a constitutional democracy. To make more sense of the multiculturalist objection to liberalism, we have replaced the term culture by language, arguing that it is mainly the linguistic aspect of culture that matters in the realm of the political. Moreover, we have seen earlier that language out of all aspects of culture features prominently in the quest of the individual for identity and belonging, a central concern of the multiculturalist. Reformulating the multicuturalist's objection to liberal majoritarianism as an objection to linguistic majoritarianism, we have granted that the problem was salient and found that a principled solution was not available, neither for the liberal nor for the multiculturalist. As the best approximation to an acceptable solution to the problem of linguistic majoritarianism for both liberals and multiculturalists, we proposed the conception of subsidiary government. In conclusion it may be said that the recognition problem that was raised by the multiculturalist to show how liberalism fails on principled grounds to accommodate different cultures in the scheme of a liberal democracy represents an obstacle not only for liberalism but for the multiculturalist approach itself. The recognition problem can therefore not be decisive in our choice between multiculturalism and liberal pluralism.

As another problem for the liberal approach, we have mentioned the abolition problem (b). We assume that the reasonable multiculturalist will grant us the existence of unjust cultures, that is, cultures that do not conform to even basic principles of justice. The reasonable multiculturalist rejects with us normative relativism, which was demonstrated

---

[37] Cf. my *Human Rights, Autonomy, and Sovereignty* (op. cit.).

to be self-defeating. She shares with us the point of view of internal universalism, which holds that from within each culture an attempt is made at proposing a conception of justice that is at least in principle acceptable also to non-members of that culture. This can be called the criterion of reasonableness between cultures. A culture, which does not permit its members to conform to this very basic criterion of reasonableness, would equally not be called reasonable. It would be a negative criterion of its injustice that all reasonable cultures converge on the fact of its unacceptability. Thus, even in the absence of any universally accepted conception of justice, the concept of an unjust culture is not vacuous. Now, suppose a pluralist society dismisses a culture on grounds that it seems inconceivable that the established practices of that culture could figure in any conception of justice by any reasonable culture whatsoever. What, the multiculturalist will ask, does liberalism offer to those individuals whose culture it dismisses as unjust? A variety of scenarios are conceivable and the liberal's answer depends on which scenario we select.

Scenario I:
The Dismissed Culture Belongs to
an Immigrant Group

In this case, the liberal could reply that immigrants generally have made a conscious decision to leave their home country and to adapt themselves to the conditions in a culturally alien environment where they are expected to exercise their right to cultural membership within the limits of the basic principles of justice obtaining in the host country. If this leads to shortcomings for the first and second generation of immigrants, the ensuing disadvantages can be compensated for, to a certain extent, but not to the extent that the immigrants would be exempted from the fundamental rules governing the host society.

Scenario II:
The Dismissed Culture Belongs to
an Autochthonous Community

Here, we have to distinguish between two further sub-scenarios:

(a) The autochthonous group occupies a distinct territory. The given group could demand. (i) Segregation from the mother country and (ii) Autonomy to various degrees.

(b) The autochthonous group is scattered over the territory of the country in question. The given group could demand cultural rights, for example, differentiated citizenship, separate laws pertaining to each cultural group etc.

From the liberal's side, various replies are conceivable. They would, however, share one common feature. The liberal will never agree to any solution where autonomy or segregation, separate laws or exemption from general rules and principles would lead to an infringement on individual rights for even some members of the group in question. The multiculturalist remarks that at this point the liberal is contradicting herself. If her primary concern is with the individuals of each cultural group alike, why should she be less concerned about the individual members of the dismissed cultural group who have to suffer uprooted-ness and a host of identity problems under the hegemony of the liberal majority culture? The reasonable liberal will counter by saying that a balance has to be struck between those who lose out because they suffer injustices from within the dismissed culture and those who suffer from uprootedness when their culture is dismissed. This sounds like a utilitar-ian argument of the greater sum of happiness sort. If the number of those benefiting from the demise of the culture in question outnumbers that of those who would benefit from not being uprooted, the demise of that culture is justifiable. Some liberals will not like this, others will accept it if it does not call into question the very idea of rights. For us, it is important to note, which alternative the multiculturalist can offer. She was able to break even with the liberal without, however, being able to offer any viable alternative.

For the argument to become critical, let us assume that people belong-ing to radically different cultures share a polity. Let us suppose that people belonging to these different cultures are unable to reach a consen-sus on even the most fundamental principles by which to organize their polity. Furthermore, let us suppose that at least some of the divergent cultures are born by autochthonous sections of the population, not immigrants. There can therefore be no question of forcing an immigrant minority community to subscribe to the shared political values of the autochthonous majority community. In addition, let us assume that people of at least two of the incommensurable segments of the society live equally scattered all across the territory of the nation state. Hence, there is no option of carving out a separate territory for one of the communities. The severe circumstances thus described make it extremely difficult to imagine the viability of any state at all, be it liberal or multicultural. The forum of public reason as outlined above would remain vacant. The public fora, the organs of the state are all in the hands of the dominating community that imposes its conception of justice upon the dominated minority communities. This, in broad lines, is the scenario that haunts the multiculturalist. It is an extreme example, however, and existing examples are hard to find. Most liberal states do not fulfil these criteria. In most existing liberal democratic states, an overlapping consensus regarding basic principles of justice has been achieved and is constantly maintained. Furthermore, most existing liberal states are faced with the demands of immigrant communities who can legitimately be expected to first subscribe to the background consensus that constitutes the polity of their choice before they become one of its citizens. And if the liberal state on its territory contains a disparate culture, people upholding this culture are typically sharing an ancestral territory to the effect that their claims can be accommodated to a large extent by granting them regional autonomy or even allowing them to segregate. Our extreme example is realized only by very few countries, if any at all. Moreover, if this example is to pose insurmountable difficulties for a liberal democratic state, it is not clear how it should not pose equally insuperable difficulties for a multicultural state. It seems to be a general condition of statehood that the citizens of a political community share at least the most fundamental principles of justice.

Let us assume, counterfactually, that India was an instance of such a torn state as has been outlined above. Let us assume that Hindus and Muslims formed two such incompatible cultures, both autochthonous and scattered all over the subcontinent. What use would it be to stipulate that the people of each culture were allowed to live by their alleged incommensurable norms if no common ground could be found to settle issues in the unavoidable interface between these communities? In a torn state like the described one where people belonging to different allegedly incompatible cultures can neither separate nor live together, citizens face a choice between permanent strife on the one hand and, on the other hand, the use of their creative potential in order to overcome the communal divide. In such an impasse, if violence is to be avoided, both communities would have to overcome—not preserve—certain aspects of their respective cultures and create space for common ground. This is not to say that members of particular religions would have to abandon their religion wholly in order to merge into a new, common culture. It would be unrealistic to expect that of any religious person and it would be authoritarian on the part of the state to enforce such a fusion. Cultural republicanism, for instance, has been criticized for this authoritarian aspect. Without dismissing it as a whole, however, it should be always possible to reinterpret a religion and to modify religious practice in such a way that they become minimally acceptable form the point of view of an internally universal conception of justice. Hinduism, it seems, has been able to cope with the abolition of sati, child marriage, temple prostitution, and the like without Hindus losing their identity. Other cultures are expected to cope with the abolition of female circumcision to no detriment of their members.[38] It would amount to essentializing a culture, or a religion for that matter, if it were to be perceived as an unalterable entity. Such changes are preferably to come from within the culture/religion but, upon failure, can also be imposed from outside. In the stipulated situation this would amount to a painful process for the members of both cultures. For some generations, persons would lose out a bit on their well-deserved sense of belonging without any hope for compensation. The way we have construed the situation, there is no solution for the citizens concerned to the abolition problem. But again, as in the previous example, the problem is not only with liberalism. It is a more general one pertaining to liberal and multicultural conceptions alike. It is the problem of the subjective circumstances of justice which require that a fair amount of normative orientation be shared by all concerned individuals lest a justification of any institution designed to enforce certain norms be inconceivable.[39]

Suppose then, the abolition problem is inescapable. Can we conceive of any way of sharing the burden of uprootedness for the individuals concerned? Does fairness prescribe that all individuals of all cultures take the same burden upon themselves? Would it be unfair for the members of one culture to be more, members of the other culture to be less subjected to change? I believe not. Since the burden of one individual can not be lessened or compensated for by subjecting another individual to the same degree of change there is no need to quantify and negotiate the amount of change and the resulting pain for the individuals concerned. However, if we conceive of a fair negotiation process between representatives of individuals potentially belonging to either of the two cultures who convene to set the foundation of a new political culture,[40] it is hard to imagine that these representatives will not deploy

---

[38] For the Muslim community in India, Partha Chatterjee encourages a process of internal, democratic reform to minimize such problems as gender inequality and other injustices; cf. Partha Chatterjee. 'Secularism and Tolerance', in Rajeev Bhargava, *Secularism and its Critics*, New Delhi: Oxford University Press, 1998, pp. 345–79.

[39] Cf. my *Philosoph als Mediator*, §12.

[40] The negotiation process can be conceived of along the lines of Rawls' original position where representatives meet behind a veil of ignorance that prevents them from

a tit-for-tat strategy: 'If x has to give up y then p will have to give up q.'[41] As a result, the degree of uprootedness would be nearly the same for members of both cultures.

---

knowing to which of the two cultures their clients will belong, cf. Rawls' *Theory of Justice* (op. cit.).

[41] x and p being cultures, y and q being controversial features of these cultures.

II
INDIVIDUAL, CHURCH, AND COMMUNITY

Multiple Identities and Communities
Re-contextualizing Religion

MARGRIT PERNAU

INTRODUCTION:
THE CONCEPTS OF COMMUNITY AND IDENTITY

In the postmodern world, identities have become questionable, in both meanings of the word: The sense of belonging to well-defined communities with stable self-perception and recognized codes of behaviour is eroding. This opens the field for investigating and questioning identities, not only in academia, but also in the public sphere. However, the very amplitude of the debate, while generating a wealth of new information and insight, tends to render the concepts less precise—what exactly do we mean, when we talk about identity and community? What is the relation between these two notions and how are social and individual identities linked up?

If we take Max Weber as a starting point, a community shall be defined as a social relationship based on the subjective feeling of the parties that they belong together.[1] This feeling will be based on the belief of the members of the community that they have certain relevant traits in common, that they share an identity. The commonality in itself, however, does not suffice for the constitution of a community, if it is not invested with meaning—the mere fact of sharing certain bodily traits like a large nose or curly hair would not usually lead to the feeling of a community; other traits, like colour, however, will be given a cultural

[1] Max Weber, *Economy and Society: An Outline of Interpretative Sociology*, edited by Guenther Roth and Claus Wittich, Berkeley, 1968, Second edition 1978, p. 40.

importance which then forms the basis for the constitution of a community.

All communities thus are 'felt communities'.[2] This feeling, real as it is, however, should not be considered as an antithesis to the imagination of a community or its cultural construction. There is no way back to an objective reality—biological or historical—which the feeling would do no more than reflect. On the other hand, talking of the necessary cultural mediation of commonality in the construction of a community does not imply that this community is imaginary in the sense of unreal or even 'wrong'. Nor does it imply that the members or the leaders of the community have a free choice in their construction. Rather, they are limited on the one hand by the available commonalities, on the other hand by previous decisions, which imprint and structure the field in which they can act.

If the felt commonality is the starting point, it has to be expressed by behaviour in order to transform the community into a social reality. This can be a group-specific code of conduct which encompasses all the walks of life, but it can also be restricted to a limited number of symbolic practices, which serve to enact the community's identity.

Multiple identities can be examined along two axes. The first relates to their interaction within the same category, i.e. Hindu–Muslim, male–female etc. Traditionally, communities—and specially religious communities—have been perceived by scholars as clearly defined, both with regard to their identity and also to their boundaries. As long as it was held possible to oppose cow-slaughtering Muslims to cow-venerating Hindus, monotheists to polytheists, believers in the equality of mankind to practitioners of the caste system, a person could unambiguously be classified as either Muslim or Hindu. However, the British colonial officers and ethnographers had already pointed to the existence of a zone of interaction between the two communities. This strand of thought has been taken up by Muhammad Mujeeb in his classic work on the Indian Muslims.[3] His aim was to prove that the Indian Muslims were no foreigners in the subcontinent, but had integrated socially and culturally, pointing out numerous and colourful instances of common belief and worship. Nevertheless, in his narrative these encounters remained limited to those uneducated and rural classes who were 'superstitious and disposed to running to dead and living saints ... dependent on miracles

[2] Rajat Kanta Ray, *The Felt Community: Commonalty and Mentality before the Emergence of Indian Nationalism*, Delhi: Oxford University Press, 2003.

[3] Muhammad Mujeeb, *The Indian Muslims*, Delhi: Munshiram Manoharlal, 1967.

and magic to a degree incompatible with genuine belief in an omnipotent God'.[4] Syncretism could blur the boundaries. As a concept it was not powerful enough to challenge the perception of the dichotomy of the two religions and the monopoly of the orthodoxy to decide about inclusion and exclusion—on the level not only of religious belief, but also of social sciences.

The renewed interest in identity and the construction of knowledge from the 1990s onwards has provoked a shift from considering communities as 'given' to investigating the power relations and discourses by which they are constantly defined and redefined.[5] Without denying the importance of a 'paradigm of perfection'[6] for the believers, this methodological evolution makes it conceptually possible to conceive of competing and overlapping ideals of perfection within the same religion. It thus replaces the binary and exclusive model, in which a person could be nothing but either a Hindu or a Muslim and never both at the same time, with a polycentric and inclusive one, which admits the possibility of more than one orthodoxy for each religion and a third space between the religions.

Multiple identities on this level, together with questions of boundaries and overlapping areas between the communities will form the topic of the first part of this paper.

This complexity along the first axis is further enhanced by the introduction of multiple categories of identities with the second axis. In the same way as for the religious community, the communities based on gender, profession, class, caste, nation, or language, too, will have to be taken not as given entities, but as the result of ongoing negotiations, resulting in contested definitions and blurred boundaries. Fortunately, much research in this area has been undertaken in this respect in the past years.[7] The picture, however, becomes even more complicated, if we start looking at the interdependence between these categories. Different

---

[4] Ibid., p. 10.

[5] Harjot Oberoi, *The Cosntruction of Religious Boundaries: Culture, Identity and Diversity in the Sikh Tradition*, Delhi: Oxford University Press, 1994; Shail Mayaram, *Resisting Regimes: Myth, Memory and the Shaping of a Muslim Identity*, Delhi: Oxford University Press, 1997.

[6] T.N. Madan, personal communication.

[7] Kumkum Sangari, *Politics of the Possible: Essays on Gender, History, Narratives, Colonial English*, Delhi: Tulika, 1999; Nonica Datta, *Forming an Identity: A Social History of the Jats*, Delhi: Oxford University Press, 1999; Sanjay Joshi, *Fractured Modernity: Making of a Middle Class in Colonial North India*, Delhi: Oxford University Press, 2001; Anshu Malhotra, *Gender, Caste and Religious Identities: Restructuring Class in Colonial Punjab*, Delhi: Oxford University Press, 2002; Malavika Kasturi, *Embattled Identities: Rajput Lineages and the Colonial State in nineteenth century North India*, Delhi: Oxford University Press, 2002.

social contexts certainly ask for the foregrounding of different identities. But at the same time, these identities are constantly changing according to their position within the universe of possible alternatives, defining and redefining each other: identity is not a fixed, but a relational category. Thus, if we for instance compare a male middle class Muslim from Delhi with a female, middle-class Muslim from Delhi, it is not only the gender which changes, but also what it means to belong to the middle class, to be a Muslim, and to come from Delhi—without precluding the possibility for felt communities of the middle class, of Muslims and of people from Delhi including both men and women. This interaction between different levels of social identities will be dealt with in the second part.

This plurality of identities leads to membership in different communities, which can be concentric (for instance religious groups sharing a territory and a language), but usually this is not the case. This, in turn, has two major consequences. At the social level, the fact that communities are only partially overlapping, that gender, to choose one category, includes a different set of people in a felt community than profession or religion, limits the possibility for one community to successfully claim the exclusive loyalty of its members and to control their social interaction with outsiders, thus interlinking even those communities which would otherwise tend to drift apart.

At the personal level, the individual is faced with the task of integrating the multiple identities that link him/her to different communities. The resulting problems depend, on the one hand, upon the relations between the identities (for instance on their competing for the same social space or conceding each other autonomy, on their claim for exclusivity or at least priority), on the other hand upon the extent of the cultural demand for working out a coherent individuality. This will constitute the focus of the third part.

CHANGING CONCEPTS OF BOUNDARIES

Modern concepts of identity focus on the importance of boundaries, drawing a sharp line between 'we' and 'they'.[8] The self and the other reflect and constitute each other; exclusion is central to the creation of 'felt communities'. It can be asked, however, whether this constitutes a universal model. Already before World War II, the German philosopher

---

[8] Bernhard Giesen, *Kollektive Identität: Die Intellektuellen und die Nation*, Frankfurt: Suhrkamp, 1999.

Martin Buber evolved the alternative idea of the dialogic principle as central for the constitution of self-identity: 'Saying Thou a person becomes I'('Der Mensch wird am Du zum Ich').[9] Neither the periphery, nor the community itself are the primary realities, but it is the commonality of the relation to the centre, which alone guarantees a real and continued existence of the community.[10]

How far, might one ask, did this emphasis not on boundaries but on (possibly plural) centres correspond to pre-colonial South Asian concepts? How far, and through which channels, did the experience of the colonial power change these perceptions of boundaries?

Much has been written on the importance of the census in the transition from 'fuzzy' to 'enumerated' communities.[11] Here, however, it shall be suggested that this transition had already started almost half a century earlier, and that its prime movers at this time were, on the one hand, the expansion of the territorial state, which involved the settlement of borders and the assessment of the land revenue, implying in turn the necessity of reliable maps at a local, regional, and imperial scale; and, on the other hand, the attempt to shift the economic basis of the elite from land grants to pensions and the concomitant need to define the categories of persons belonging to a 'family' and hence entitled to the consideration of the government. At this stage, the need for defining and counting the members of religious groups was of minor importance for the colonial power, at least in north India. Though the examples will be drawn exclusively from Delhi in the nineteenth century, it is hoped that the implication reaches beyond the specific region and time.

After the victory against the Marathas in 1803, which led to the establishment of colonial rule over Delhi and its surrounding areas, the British were interested for quite some time in maintaining their influence with as little cost as possible. Consequently, they refused to be drawn into either direct administration or the settlement of boundary disputes. This attitude changed only after the final settlement of the Anglo-French rivalry on the subcontinent and the demise of the Marathas as a force to be reckoned with. The following decade saw the settlement of the borders between the independent principalities (notably Alwar

[9] Martin Buber, 'Ich und Du', in *Werke*, München: Kösel, 1962, p. 97.

[10] Ibid., p. 156, my translation.

[11] Bernard Cohen, 'The Census, Social Structure and Objectification in South Asia', in *An Anthropologist among the Historians and Other Essays*, Delhi: Oxford University Press, 1987, pp. 224–55; Sudipta Kaviraj, 'The Imaginary Institution of India', in Partha Chatterjee, Gyanendra Pandey (eds), *Subaltern Studies VII: Writings on South Asian History and Society*, Delhi: Oxford University Press, 1992, pp. 1–40.

and Bharatpur) and between the princely and the British territories.[12] These settlements not only aimed at the resolution of conflicts at one specific moment of time, but changed the very nature of the boundaries by drawing them out on paper and conceptualizing them as lying outside the permanent fluctuation of power. State power, perceived in this way, no longer emanated from a centre and diffused towards the ever-contested border, but spread uniformly over the entire territory. The clamping down on cattle theft, one of the traditional ways of testing power relations in the border regions, and the assigning of responsibility to the sovereign state for whatever 'crimes' were perpetuated from its territory have to be read in this context.

On the other hand, the same epoch saw the drawing of detailed reports on the jagirs, listing not only the exact nature of their tenure, but also defining their extent and the rights which went with the grant.[13] Here again the fluency of boundaries and the fluctuation between centrifugal and centripetal tendencies, which had been characteristic for the patrimonial system gave way to the new bureaucratic urge for unambiguous definitions. These definitions, as distinguished from former decisions, no longer took into account either the status of the person to whom they applied, nor were they—at least in theory—open for unspoken shifts through time.

Again during this epoch, the British started the large-scale mapping of their Indian territory. Whereas the older maps had drawn mainly on the reports of travellers, thus proceeding from a centre (or several centres), in relation to which the information was organized, the new technique of the trigonometrical land survey permitted situating each location with reference to its longitude and latitude.[14] These points were no longer related to each other nor to a common centre—the only regrouping which took place was by means of the boundary. This becomes even more clear once the princely states and the British-Indian territory are visually juxtaposed by means of different colouring.

A similar movement occurred with reference to the definitions of the

[12] Board Collection, F/4/813 21729, Oriental and India Office Collection (OIOC), London.

[13] Foreign Political Proceedings, 7.11.1818 / 65–71, NAI; T. Fortescue, 'Report on the Revenue System of the Delhi Territory', 1820, in Government of India, *Delhi Residency and Agency Records, 1807–57*, Lahore 1915.

[14] Matthew H. Edney, *Mapping an Empire: The Geographical Construction of British India, 1765–1843*, Delhi: Oxford University Press, 1999 [1997]; Kapil Raj, 'Circulation and the Emergence of Modern Mapping: Great Britian and Early Colonial India, 1764–1820', in Claude Markovits, Jacques Pouchepadass, Sanjay Subramanyam (eds), *Society and Circulation: Mobile People and Itinerant Cultures in South Asia, 1750–1950*, Delhi: Permanent Black, 2003, pp. 23–55.

family group. In the wake of Lord Lake's campaigns, the British confirmed and distributed jagirs on a great scale. In this they pursued the twin aims to reward allies and hence stabilize their power, but also to be burdened as little as possible with administrative duties. The distribution of the revenue of the jagir within the family and among dependents lay entirely with the grantee. Within the first generation two developments came together: the rise of the British as the sole power on the Indian subcontinent and the further expansion towards the Punjab which made a greater involvement in the Delhi region both possible and desirable. On the other hand, the passing away of the first generation of grantees provided an opening for a deeper penetration of the colonial power into families, by claiming the right to decide with reference to the inheritance of the jagir and to settle conflicting claims among the different branches of the family. The transformation of rights on land into pensions further permitted a subdivision of monetary claims among the contending heirs and their dependents. Traditionally, the family, and specially the extended families of the nobility, had been a fluctuating concept, certainly based on consanguinity, but without hard and fast rules as to membership and entitlements. The extent of the group and the position of the individual might depend as much on the momentary economic situation—wealth always leading to an expansion of the number of dependents—as on the power play of the individuals and factions.[15] Recurring conflicts within families offered the possibility of arbitration and interference to the British, which in itself need not have changed the system, if they had limited themselves to ad hoc decisions. Instead, the decades before 1857 saw the growth of administrative and bureaucratic rules, which regulated not only inheritance and division of property and pensions, but, even more importantly, classified the members of the family according to criteria of legitimacy and consanguinity, transforming the former fluidity of the group into a rule-bound universe with clear boundaries towards the outside and equally clear hierarchies and entitlements on the inside.[16]

These new concepts of community, shifting the emphasis from the centre to the boundaries and from fluidity to clear definitions, probably would not have been so influential, if they had not met with another development, already well under way before the advent of the colonial

[15] Margrit Pernau, 'Family: A Gendering and Gendered Space', in Margrit Pernau, Imtiaz Ahmad, Helmut Reifeld (eds), *Family and Gender: Changing Values in Germany and India*, Delhi: Sage Publications, 2003, pp. 9–35.

[16] For the royal family, see Foreign Political Proceedings, 23.6.1849/13–14; 10.4.1852/ 46–8; 8.5.1857/16–20, National Archive of India (NAI), Delhi.

power: the Islamic reformist movement. Whereas these reformist movements are by now quite well studied for the later decades of the nineteenth and for the twentieth century, our knowledge of the time between
1750 and 1850 is still fragmentary, and it is difficult to offer more than
informed hypotheses at the present stage.

The decline of the worldly power of the Muslims, which was by no
means limited to India, shifted the onus of guaranteeing the Islamic
character of the polity from the state to the community of believers, and
ultimately to the individual. Even if the government had fallen in the
hand of non-Muslims (as it had in north India even before the advent of
the British), the community could still preserve its Islamic character, so
the argument ran, if the rulers did not forbid religious practices and if the
leaders of the community lived up to their task of guiding their fellow
believers.[17] However, under these conditions, the questions of who was a
Muslim and which was the correct Muslim way of life, gained a new
importance. To a larger extent, as ever before, the difference between
Muslim and non-Muslim became vital, and not only for the ruler and the
scholars, but for an increasingly large stratum of the population.

To this new importance of the boundaries corresponded an attempt at
an homogenization of the community by favouring, on the one hand,
the unique canonical text over the plurality of traditions and, on the
other, the universal and Arabic character of Islam over the local forms
which had developed over the centuries. This new emphasis on just one
possible orthodoxy did not, of course, in itself reduce the plurality of
answers to the question as to the right way of being a Muslim. What it
did challenge, however, was the legitimacy of this plurality.

The exact lines of communication and mutual influences between
British administrators and Islamic reformists still remain to be traced. It
was once the two streams of ideas, the bureaucratic and the religious,
joined that the new concept of community, unambiguous and defined by
its boundaries, gained momentum—well before the enumeration of the
first large-scale censuses.

INTERACTION BETWEEN SOCIAL IDENTITIES

Granted that multiple social identities do not exist in splendid isolation,
but constitute and reconstitute each other, is it possible to analyse these

[17] Shah Abdul Aziz, *Fatawa-e Azizi*, translated into Urdu and edited by Abdul Wajid
Shahjahanpuri, Kanpur: Majidi Press, 1905, pp. 27–30, pp. 52–3, pp. 226–8; Warren
Edward Fusfeld, *The Shaping of Sufi Leadership in Delhi: The Naqshbandiyya Mujaddidiyya,
1750–1920*, PhD thesis, University of Pennsylvania, 1981.

relations more precisely? This issue will be addressed in the following section by using first the notion of 'elective affinities', and second, the concept of transfer of capital from one category to the other.

The idea of 'elective affinities' was first developed by Johan Wolfgang v. Goethe in a novel with the same title. Drawing on contemporary chemical theories, the author explains how elements are endowed with a 'relationship of the spirit and the soul' (Geistes- und Seelenverwandtschaft) towards each other. 'Such natures as, when they come in contact, at once lay hold of each other, each mutually affecting the other, we speak of as having an affinity one for the other'—this relation can be so strong as to dissolve existing and creating new compounds.[18] In the novel this forms the introduction for a complicated interplay of love stories, which however need not interest us here. The term was then taken up by Max Weber to explain the relation between economic, social, and cultural structures 'whether they further or impede or exclude one another—whether they are 'adequate' or 'inadequate' in relation to each other'.[19] The most famous elective affinity Weber discussed, is, of course, the relation between the protestant ethic and the spirit of capitalism, which neither allows the reduction of culture to a superstructure of the economic, nor explains the rise of capitalism solely through cultural categories.

A person who furnishes us with a wealth of self-description, was Ghalib (1797–1869), Delhi's most famous poet. He enjoyed talking about himself, both through the medium of his poems and his letters. In a famous Qata' he said:

> Ghalib, we are from the sacred land of Turan,
> Undoubtedly we are of glorious lineage.
> We are of Turkish descent
> And the chiefs of the tribe were our forefathers.
> We are Aibeks, belonging to the tribe of Turks
> And in perfection we are ten times better than the moon.[20]

In this case, his identity was constituted by his family lineage and the social status of his ancestors, who are defined by their foreign origin, by their hereditary claim to rulership and their innate qualities. Thus, Ghalib situated himself not only in the category of the Ashraf, the

---

[18] Johan Wolfgang v. Goethe, *Elective Affinities*, New York: German Publication Society, 1914, p. 38.

[19] Weber, *Economy and Society*, p. 341.

[20] Ghalib, *Kulliyat-e Farsi*, ed. Amir Hasan Nurani, Lucknow: Munshi Naval Kishore, 1968, p. 237; translation from Natalia Prigarina, *Mirza Ghalib: A Creative Biography*, Karachi: Oxford University Press, 2000, p. 4.

Muslim immigrants considered 'noble', as opposed to the local converts, but even claimed a position of excellency within this group. This social honour would find its expression in the place Ghalib was accorded in the official darbars of the Mughal king and the British officials and the rank of the khil'at bestowed on him.[21] In turn, this self-description and position drew him nearer to a Hindu of corresponding status than to a low-class Muslim. It would be stretching the point too far to claim that for the elite of the late Mughal empire the religious affiliation of their members was a matter of indifference, but while shared faith certainly was the criterion for the constitution of *one* 'felt community' of varying importance, it was neither the only one nor in all circumstances the most important.

At other times, Ghalib might proudly point out that he was the best among the living poets, both in Persian and in Urdu, an statement which might be qualified as a mixture between linguistic identity and a professional pride:

And let me impress this upon you: you will find that what I have to say about the construction of Persian words and the flights of meaning in Persian verse is usually at variance with what the general run of people say; and *I* am in the right.[22]

or again:

> Ghalib, thou art not a
> The only master of Urdu
> They say in former times
> There was a man called Mir[23]

His identities as a noble and as a poet were not directly linked. Many nobles were but very mediocre poets and not all the poets were of high origin—the most notable exception being Shaikh Ibrahim Zauq, the poetical tutor of none less than Bahadur Shah.[24] Still, the poetical habitus was closely tied to what was perceived as the character of a nobleman, and the memorizing of verses of the classics and the moderns

[21] Daud Rahbar, (ed.), *Urdu Letters of Mirza Asad Ullah Khan* Ghalib, New York: State University of New York Press, 1987, pp. 131 and 292.

[22] Ralph Russell and Khurshid ul Islam, *Ghalib Life and Letters*, Delhi: Oxford University Press, 1969, pp. 358–9.

[23] Ghalib, *Divan-e Ghalib*, translated by Yusuf Husain, Delhi: Ghalib Institute, 1977, p. 66.

[24] On his family background, see Muhammad Husain Azad, *Shaping the Canon of Urdu Poetry*, Translated and edited by Frances Pritchett in association with Shamsur Rahman Faruqi, Delhi: Oxford University Press, 2001, pp. 339–40.

formed a central part of his education.[25] Hence, poetical talent would stand a much greater chance for development in a noble than in a water carrier, though we know of water carriers, who apparently were good enough poets to be admitted to the selected literary circles of Delhi.[26]

In a similar way, both as a noble and as a poet, it would have been improbable for Ghalib to feel drawn towards the forms of piety propagated by the Islamic reform movement of Delhi (though here too exceptions were known, for instance, the older Momin Khan 'Momin'). Usually, he kept a poetical and bantering distance from orthodoxy.

In Paradise, it is true that I shall drink at dawn the pure wine mentioned in the Quran, but where shall I find again the star of dawn I used to see on earth, and my crystal cup? Where in Paradise are the long walks of intoxicated friends in the night, or the drunken crowds shouting merrily? In that holy tavern, silent and still, how canst Thou introduce the sounds of the flute and the gay bustle of the taverns of this earth? Where shall I find, there, the intoxication of raining clouds? Where there is no autumn, how can spring exist? If the beautiful houris are eternally in one's heart, what of the sweet thought of them? Where will be the sadness of separation and the joy of union? ... Where shall we find there, a girl who flees away when we would kiss her? Where will be, there, one who betrays us with false oaths of love? The beauties of Paradise will obey us and their lips will never say anything bitter; they will give us pleasure, but with a heart forever closed to the desire for pleasure.[27]

The topic of praising the beloved by comparing (and preferring) her to the houris of paradise was conventional.[28] The same hyperbolic structure would require the poet in other instances to compare her face to the moon or a good doctor to Galen, if not to the life-restoring messiah. Ghalib however transformed the traditional imagery and placed at its centre no longer the beloved, but a lifestyle, whose worth is extolled even in the face of paradise—a shift which finds its echo in the new self-confidence the lover displays towards the (human or divine) beloved in his more traditional lyrics.[29]

[25] On the role of poetical contests as social spaces for the acquisition of social status, see Margrit Pernau, 'From a 'private' public to a 'public' private sphere: Old Delhi in comparative perspective', in Gurpreet Mahajan, Helmut Reifeld (eds), *The Public and the Private: Democratic Citizenship in a Comparative Perspective*, New Delhi: Sage, 2003, pp. 103–30.

[26] Mirza Qadir Bakhsh 'Sabir', *Gulistan-e Sukhan*, edited by Saiyyid Imtiaz Ali, Lahore: Majlis-e taraqqi-e adab, 1966, p. 326.

[27] Ghalib, *Kulliyat-e Farsi*, pp. 125–6, translation by A. Bausani, 'Ghalib's Persian Poetry', in Ralph Russell (ed.), *Ghalib: The Poet and his Age*, Delhi: Oxford University Press, 1997, pp. 70–104, translation p. 81.

[28] See for instance Azad, p. 288.

[29] Waris Kirmani, 'Tradition and Rationalism in Ghalib', in Bruce Lawrence (ed.), *The*

On the other hand, there were occasions when Ghalib would write religious poetry of profound beauty. It is not possible to decide whether this shift reflected divergent sides of his personality or whether it was due to a different social setting or simply the use of a different poetic genre, requiring composition in a different mood. We know that at least one of these poems was written on the request of Fazl-e Haq Khairabadi,[30] the leading scholar of the (Sunni) rationalist tradition of Lucknow in Delhi.[31] In his support and in opposition to the reformist school of Shah Wali Ullah (1703–62), Ghalib defended the veneration of the saints and notably of Ali as necessary intermediaries on the way towards God. As with the royal court and most of the nobility, Ghalib's religious outlook was strongly influenced by the Chishti tradition. Chishti Sufis had for several generations acted as religious advisors and spiritual guides to the Mughal emperors;[32] the shrine of Qutb ud Din in Mehrauli drew large crowds on the occasion of the yearly flower sellers' festival in the rainy season.[33] While nobility, poetry, and (Chishti) Sufism thus had a high elective affinity, the rising middle classes found it hard to find their place in this cultural universe. How did their economic or class identity interact with their identities at the other levels, like their religious outlook or their approach to poetry?

In most societies, the economic position of a community of people tends to influence its social prestige as well: a group acquiring wealth will, at least in the long run, also rise in social status. However, very often this transformation cannot be effected directly; wealth, specially newly acquired wealth, is rarely in itself considered a source of honour.[34] Rather, it has to be translated through the acquisition of a new mode of behaviour: a new habitus, which either conforms to the values of the old social elite, or challenges them successfully.[35]

Rose and the Rock: Mystical and Rational Elements in the Intellectual History of South Asian Islam, Durham: Duke University 1979, p.52.

[30] Altaf Husain Hali, *Yadgar-e Ghalib*, Delhi, Idarah-e bazm-e Khizr-e rah, 1996, quoted in Ralph Russell and Khurshid ul Islam, *Ghalib*, p. 33.

[31] 'Bayan-e namudari-e shan-e nabwat o wilayat', in Ghalib, *Kulliyat-e Farsi*, pp. 383–90.

[32] Foreign Political Proceedings, 9.11.1807 / 75–76; 30.1.1809 / 113, NAI.

[33] Mirza Farhat Ullah Beg, 'Bahadur Shah aur phulwalon ki sair', in *Mazamin-e Farhat*, edited by Hafiz Saiyyid Aziz Hasan, Delhi: no publisher, no date, vol. 2, pp. 5–49.

[34] For the German context, see Christina von Hodenberg, 'Der Fluch des Geldsacks: Der Aufstieg des Industriellen als Herausforderung bürgerlicher Werte', in Manfred Hettling, Stefan-Ludwig Hoffmann (eds), *Der bürgerliche Wertehimmel. Innenansichten des 19. Jahrhunderts*, Göttingen: Vandenhoeck Ruprecht, 2000, pp. 79–104.

[35] Pierre Bourdieu, *La distinction: Critique social du jugement*, Paris: Les editions de Minuit, 1979.

Since the second half of the eighteenth century, upwardly mobile groups attempted to move into the cultural universe of poetry and poetical contests. Disgusted by the intrusion of these newcomers, the poet Mir exclaims: 'In finer days, this respectable art was cultivated by those whose nature was subtle. They were just and distinguishing, and kept this area free of rubbish. The lower classes (*ajlaf*) had no say in this art, it was taught only to the respectable.'[36] He continues with the edifying example of the Persian poet Hilali, who had imagined it possible to write poetry without the training by a master of the art. Only after he was beaten up by the Wazir for his bad poetry, he repented, went in search of an ustad and finally reached excellence.[37] Ghalib, in turn, is well known for his barbed comments on the poet Qatil, whose literary shortcomings he ascribed to the lowly social origin of this 'Khatri of Faridabad'.[38]

Nevertheless, in the 1840s, the influx of newcomers into poetry seems to have reached such an extent that either the guild-like teaching from master to pupil was no longer able to cope with it, or that it began to include persons of such origins, that the poets of renown refused to teach them. In Agra, an entire journal could thrive by catering for the needs of those who did not have access to regular mushairahs and who struggled with the rules of poetics without being able to find a teacher who would guide them.[39] While the attempt at integration into the ruling social values of poets and nobles had proved difficult for newcomers from the beginning, this cultural universe itself came under attack after 1857 and was increasingly denounced as the symbol of a degenerated Nawabi culture.[40]

More successful for the transformation of wealth into social honour than acquiring cultural capital through the practise of poetry, was the patronizing of the Islamic reformist movement and the espousal of its

---

[36] Translated in C.M. Naim, *Zikr-e Mir—The Autobiography of the eighteenth century Mughal Poet: Mir Muhammad Taqi 'Mir'*, Delhi: Oxford University Press, 1999, p. 180.

[37] Mir Taqi Mir, 'Tanbih al Juhhal' and 'Hikayat' in *Kulliyat-e Mir*, ed. by Ramnarainlal Prahladdas, Allahabad: 1972, pp. 142–5.

[38] Russell, Islam, *Ghalib*, p. 47. For the reclaiming of Qatil as a prominent member of the community of the Panjabi traders, see Sultan Rafi (ed.), *Biradari ki marhumen ka tazkirah: Yadgar-e raftagan*, Karachi: Ilyas Press, 1996, pp. 58–60.

[39] The *Mayar ush Shora* was published since 1848 by Ghalib's friend Aran, poet and Persian teacher at the Agra Madrasa. See Imdad Sabri, *Urdu ke akhbar navis*, Delhi, Sabri Academy, 1973, p. 56; Muhammad Atiq Siddiqi, *Hindustani Akhbar Navisi*, Aligarh: Anjuman-e Taraqqi-e Urdu, 1957, pp. 287–8.

[40] Frances Pritchett, *Nets of Awareness: Urdu Poetry and Its Critics*, Berkeley: University of California Press, 1994.

teachings. Drawing attention to the social function of religion should not be taken as doubting the sincerity of the believers. There certainly was an elective affinity between values propagated by the reformers and the rising middle classes, notably as far as the emphasis on self-reliance, personal responsibility and independence from mediating powers, the rationalization of everyday life, the positive assessment of hard work, planning, and economy of time and money are concerned. Nevertheless, being associated with this movement also had social implications, and it is difficult to believe that the merchants and traders were not aware of these.

This connection can be shown in an exemplary fashion for the relations between the Madrasa Rahimiyya, the school of the reformer Shah Wali Ullah—particularly its latter-day radical successors—and the Qaum-e Panjabian, a community of Muslim traders in Delhi. Today, the origin of this brotherhood, as they call themselves, is described in almost mythical terms: a group of sixty-four Hindu families, hailing from different trading castes of the Punjab, wandered to Delhi in the seventeenth century in search of new sources of income. On their way, they were converted by the saint Shams ud Din, hence the present-day tendency to adopt Shamsi as a collective surname. In Delhi, the narration goes on, they were received by Shah Jahan with great joy and many marks of honour.[41] However, reading the text carefully, it seems more probable that the immigration of groups of converts from the trading communities of the Punjab was a long process, taking place over several centuries and that their amalgamation into a qaum or a 'felt community' is a fairly recent development.

The economic conditions of these converts seem to have been quite disparate. In the first decades of the nineteenth century, many of them apparently were peddlers and petty traders.[42] Others, however, appear to have maintained their trading relations even after their conversion and accumulated considerable wealth. As a group, the economic rise of the Punjabis most probably began after 1857, mainly in connection with the advent of the railway, which turned Delhi into an important centre on the route for long-distance trade from Calcutta to Lahore and from there to Central Asia.

Already, before 1857, certain indications point to a close relationship between the traders of Delhi and the school of Shah Wali Ullah. Though the queries introducing a fatwa usually are stylized in such a manner that

---

[41] Sultan Rafi, *Biradari*, pp. 19–21.

[42] Mirza Sangin Beg, *Sair ul Manazil*, edited by Sharif Husain Qasimi, Delhi: Ghalib Institute, 1982, passim.

they do not yield information on the social background of the person asking for advice, the number of topics related to economic questions, such as the permissibility of letters of credit (hundi), the income from land mortgage or slave trade, show that traders were not slow in availing themselves of the legal knowledge of Shah Abdul Aziz.[43] That they could expect a sympathetic consideration of their problems is borne out by the rulings on whether India still was a Dar ul Islam, an abode of Islam, or had become a Dar ul Harb, an abode of war, discussions which have as much to do with enabling the traders to charge interest as with the legitimacy of the British government.[44]

The leads become clearer for the following decades. Saiyyid Ahmad Shahid and Shah Ismail, the radical leaders from the next generation of the scholars of the Madrasa Rahimiyya who conducted the jihad at the north-western frontier, had among their supporters and financiers one Shaikh Husain Bakhsh, a rich Punjabi trader, hailing originally from Calcutta.[45] Most probably this person is the same as the Shaikh Husain Bakhsh, who later founded a mosque and madrasa in Delhi, which served as the centre for the radical Muslim reformers[46] and who also coordinated the communication between the Punjabi supporters in Delhi of the Mujahidin and the fighters in the border region.[47] After rising to new wealth in the wake of 1857, the Punjabi traders started funding mosques and madrasas in large numbers, ranging from small schools for the neighborhood[48] to the support of prestigious ventures like the famous Ahl-e hadith seminary of Nazir Husain in the last decades of the nineteenth century.[49] At the same time, titles like Haji, Hafiz, and notably Shaikh (used for a person of religious authority but also denoting

[43] Shah Abdul Aziz, *Fatawa-e Azizi*, pp. 62–5, pp. 75–8, pp. 80–90. A rough calculation based on the table of contents of the first volume indicated that roughly 10 per cent of the fatwa deal with economic matters.

[44] Muhammad Khalid Masud, 'The World of Shah Abd al-Aziz (1746–1824)' in Jamal Malik (ed.), *Perspectives of Mutual Encounters in South Asian History, 1760–1860*, Leiden: Brill, 2000, pp. 298–315.

[45] Abul Hasan Ali Nadwi, *Sirat-e Saiyyid Ahmad Shahid*, Lucknow: Dar ul Ulum Nadwat ul Ulama, 1977 [1939], pp. 195, 318–21.

[46] The local tradition that he built the mosque for Shah Ismail after the latter had been forbidden to preach in the Jama Masjid is probably apocryphal, as the chronogram for the mosque gives the date of 1851–52, and Shah Ismail died in 1831 already. Bashir ud Din Ahmad, *Waqayat dar ul hukumat Delhi*, Delhi: Urdu Academy 1995 [1919], Vol. 3, pp. 146–7.

[47] North Western Province, Political Proceedings, 14.9.1852 /10–13, Oriental and India Office Collection (OIOC), London.

[48] Sultan Rafi, *Biradari*, pp. 121–376.

[49] Hakim Saiyyid Abdul Hayy, *Dihli aur us ke atraf*, Delhi: Urdu Academy, 1988.

the status of an ashraf, a Muslim who claims foreign origin as opposed to the local converts from Hinduism) start to proliferate—by the time of the Khilafat movement, the Punjabi community could successfully claim to constitute the leaders of the Muslims of Delhi.[50] Religion had proved the road to social respectability and political leadership for an economically upward community.

INTEGRATION OF MULTIPLE IDENTITIES: INDIVIDUALIZATION AND BIOGRAPHY

In his theory of the social systems, Niklas Luhmann investigates how systems react to the increase in complexity, as it occurred notably in the modernization process. The social system, according to him, can only relate to its evermore complex environment by differentiation. The rapid increase in complexity since the eighteenth century, therefore, leads to a restructuring of the social system into subsystems, which provide for the diversifying functions in an increasingly autonomous way. The integration of the system thus no longer proceeds hierarchically, but by allocating different problems to different subsystems, which operate according to their own rules.[51]

This division into subsystems meant that the individual can only be present in the social systems by virtue of the different roles he takes up— as a professional, as a member of a family, as a voter etc.—but no longer in his entirety.[52] Hence, the integration of the multiple roles and their corresponding identities becomes more and more problematic, before this project is altogether renounced in favour of the *bricolage* of a fragmented identity in postmodernism.[53]

This theory has been evolved to explain certain transformation processes which resulted in the modern social system, and within these parameters it can be meaningfully applied not only to Europe, but also to South Asia.[54] Difficulties arise, however, once a closer look is taken at

---

[50] Mushirul Hasan, Margrit Pernau (eds), *Regionalizing Pan-Islamism. Documents on the Khilafat Movement*. Delhi: Manohar Publishers, forthcoming.

[51] Niklas Luhmann, *Soziale Systeme: Grundriß einer allgemeinen Theorie*, Frankfurt: Suhrkamp, 1984; Niklas Luhmann, *Funktion der Religion*, Frankfurt: Suhrkamp, 1999.

[52] Niklas Luhmann, 'Individuum, Individualität, Individualismus', in *Gesellschaftsstruktur und Semantik: Studien zur Wissenssoziologie der modernen Gesellschaft*, vol. 3, Frankfurt: Suhrkamp, 1989.

[53] Stuart Hall, 'The Question of Cultural Identity', in Stuart Hall et. al. (eds), *Modernity and Its Futures*, Cambridge: Polity Press, 1992, pp. 273–327.

[54] Margrit Pernau, 'Middle Class and Secularization: The Muslims of Delhi in the

those traditional societies, which otherwise only form the background out of which the modern universe evolves. Both the multiplicity of identities in a person like Ghalib and his ability to handle what from the outside would be perceived as contradictions, is certainly no less than that of an individual living in a society which had undergone functional differentiation. It also cannot be argued that these identities were either less elaborate or less institutionalized. Ghalib and his contemporaries extensively reflected on what it meant to be a poet, what behaviour was considered appropriate from him and towards him (rules which Ghalib took great pain to teach the British, however without much success). Poetical identity found its institutions in the poetical contests, which were conducted according to well-established rules and which can be read, as has been attempted above, not only as cultural events, but also as venues where cultural capital was awarded or withheld and where the claim to an identity as a poet could be won or lost.

In this social space, other identities would only be permitted a very limited access: a noble patron risked boycott by the poets, if he, presuming on his nobility, claimed a higher rank in the poetical gathering than was due to him.[55] In the same way, the religious identity considered appropriate for this venue would be quite different from the views the same persons could evoke in a different context. In a ghazal, therefore, making fun of the orthodox Shaikh was as imperative as the avoidance of religious argument. 'But indeed, if someone writes a book in support of his religious belief, then it is the place for argument and proof.'[56]

So how were these multiple identities integrated, how were the contradictions within identities and between different levels of identities resolved? If the different ego-texts someone like Ghalib wrote in the course of his lifetime are taken together and read as a single representation, what strikes the modern reader, is their lack of coherence—Ghalib obviously did not feel uncomfortable with making different and even conflicting statements on different occasions. Unlike what Luhmann and other theorists on modernity lead us to expect, his different identities remained contradictory and were by no means encompassed by a religious system which endowed them with meaning and placed them within an unambiguous hierarchy. The hypothesis has to be risked that the harmony and integration of the pre-modern world is little more than

---

nineteenth century', in Imtiaz Ahmad, Helmut Reifeld (eds), *Middle class values in India and Western Europe*, Delhi: Social Science Press, forthcoming.

[55] Ali Jawad Zaidi, *Tarikh-e mushairah*, Delhi: A 1 Offset Printers, 1989, p. 78.

[56] Azad, *Ab-e Hayat*, pp. 292–3.

one of the myths of modernity. In that case, the question itself of how personalities became integrated would make no sense, as it presupposes an urge to personal integration, which might well be unknown to a person like Ghalib.

Instead of integrating multiple identities into a coherent whole, which would then constitute the unique identity of the individual, it might be ventured that what was primarily important was to act adequately in each given situation. The essential integration took place between each identity and its corresponding situation; the poet (or for that matter the saint, the noble or the trader) aimed at conforming to the offers of identity implied in a certain genre and in certain circumstances rather than at the expression of his individuality. Therefore, the warning from literary scholars not to take the self-statements at their face value, is well taken.[57] However, where this warning does not go far enough is its implication that there might be a 'real' personality behind or above all these rule-bound roles, which would then form the subject for the social sciences. The very concept of a dualism between world and individual, which this presupposes and which permits differentiation between a 'constructed' and an 'authentic' individual, is already drawn from a modern concept of the individual transcending roles which would seem anachronistic when applied to other historical times.[58]

In this respect, Ghalib is all the more interesting because he bridges the epochs. On the one hand he was still wholly immersed in the world of traditional poetry and proud of this heritage; on the other hand he creatively played with this tradition and went beyond it, to the point of claiming uniqueness, even individuality. It is worthwhile, therefore, to have a closer look at the universe of the ghazal and Ghalib's poetry.

Ghazals are essentially love poems, the character of the beloved scintillating between the human and the divine. Compared to other genres, its topics and imagery are extremely reduced—it is within this reduced space that each poem becomes part of an ongoing dialogue with its precursors. It takes up an image or a turn of a phrase and by varying it slightly makes it appear in a new light. More than with other poems, appreciation of the ghazal therefore requires knowledge of the artistic

[57] Stefan Elit, "Ich" war einmal: Literaturwissenschaftliche Problemhorizonte bei Subjektivität von Texten', in *Zeitblicke* vol. 1, part 2 (2002), *http://www.historicum.net*, Frances Pritchett, 'Convention in the Classical Urdu Ghazal: The Case of Mir', in *Journal of South Asian and Middle Eastern Studies*, 1979, pp. 60–77.

[58] Martin Scheutz, Harald Tersch, 'Individualisierungsprozesse in der Frühen Neuzeit? Anmerkungen zu einem Konzept', in *Wiener Zeitschrift zur Geschichte der Neuzeit*, vol. 1, part 2 (2001), pp. 38–59.

tradition. The artistic quality of the poet comes to bear not in his originality, in saying things that have never been said before, but in his successful play with the traditional themes, in saying things that have never been said so well before. The line between the permitted, even required innovation and the prohibited breaking of the rules is extremely thin, as is shown by a discussion which took place in a poetical gathering after Zauq recited a verse:

The objector made the objection, 'A proof is needed for fire moving inside rock'. The Shaikh [Zauq] said, 'When the mountain moves forward, the fires inside it will also move accordingly.' The objector said, 'There should be a proof for fire moving inside stone.' The Shaikh said, 'Observation.' He said, 'Give an authority drawn from a book.' The Shaikh said, 'It is proven from history, that in the time of Hoshang fire came out (from stone).' He said, 'In poetry, the authority of a verse is required. History is of no use in poetry.'[59]

Ghalib loved to show that he was a master of these rules. He knew how to play with them in his own poetry, but also used them for some devastating critiques of the work of his adversaries, notably of Qatil and his pupils, who developed an Indian style in Persian poetry and hence tended to use some words and images in ways not sanctioned by the classical tradition.[60]

On the other hand, more than any other poet of his time, Ghalib voiced a new sensibility to the right of the individual in the face of tradition. On the road of poetry, he holds, it is his own grief, which is Khizr, the mythical guide who leads him along the right path. He need not be Nizami, or any other of the poets of old, to tune his melody so that it seems like a revelation come down from above; it was from himself and his afflicted heart that he drew the exquisite treasures.[61] No longer the tradition, but the poet's own feelings and his exclusive personality could thus be placed at the centre, not consistently and at all times, and certainly against much resistance from the proponents of the classical theory, but this first burgeoning of a new awareness is worth noting.

These personal feelings, once they had come to their right, could no longer be contained exclusively in traditional images. 'The narrow canvas of the ghazal', as Ghalib put it, no longer sufficed for his ideas,[62] and new modes of expression had to be sought:

[59] Azad, *Ab-e Hayat*, pp. 354–5.
[60] Ghalib, 'Bad-e mukhalif', in *Kulliyat-e Farsi*, pp. 373–82.
[61] Ghalib, 'Mughanni-nama', in *Kulliyat-e Farsi*, pp. 444–56, paraphrase from pp. 454–5.
[62] Ghalib, Diwan-e Ghalib, trans. Yusuf Husain, p.237.

> In the signs of the splendour of the morning they behold the evening
> In the sign of a bat, they already perceive the day.[63]

The use of a bat as a symbol for the evening, fitting though it is in this context, is without known precedent—the animal associated with the night being of course the nightingale. The revolutionary impact that even such slight changes in the conventional imagery had is hard to reconstruct from today's point of view. More even than in the explicit self-descriptions, genre-bound as they are, it might be in these transformations in aesthetics that the profound changes of the perception of the individual can be looked for, in literature as well as in music.[64]

Identity became an increasingly important issue for reflection in its parallel aspects of description and self-description, of identification and self-identification. This development can be dated back to the end of the eighteenth century. However, it gained new force with the advent of the colonial power in north India and especially with the cultural forward policy since the 1830s, through which the state actively promoted English language, English science, and English religion.

Even a process so personal and individual as self-reflection is embedded in social structures. What, then, were the genres socially provided and sanctioned for reflecting on, defining, and describing individuals? For Europe, Alois Hahn has pointed to the outstanding importance of individual confession, which since the early modern age drew from a concept of sin no longer centred on particular deeds, but on motivations and attitudes of mind. This soul-searching reflection on one's life was pushed further in the pietistic diary—the 'confession without a father confessor' as Hahn calls it—and later led to the first modern autobiographies.[65]

For Muslim South Asia the central biographical genre was the tazkirah, a compendium of biographies, first of saints, then of other elite groups, notably poets as well.[66] Historians have all too long echoed the complaints

---

[63] Ghalib, *Kulliyat-e Farsi.*

[64] For the development of the Khyal as a genre giving more space to the individuality of the artist, see Bonnie C. Wade, *Khyal: Creativity within North India's Classical Music Tradition,* Delhi: Munshiram Manoharlal, 1997 [1984].

[65] Alois Hahn, *Konstruktionen des Selbst, der Welt und der Geschichte,* Frankfurt, Suhrkamp 2000, specially the essay 'Zur Soziologie der Beichte und anderer Formen institutionalisierter Bekenntnisse: Selbstthematisierung und Zivilisationsprozeß'; quotation p. 231.

[66] Marcia K. Hermansen, Bruce Lawrence, 'Indo-Persian Tazkiras as Memorative Communications', in David Gilmartin, Bruce Lawrence (eds), *Beyond Turk and Hindu: Rethinking Religious Identities in Islamicate South Asia,* Delhi: India Research Press, 2002, pp. 149–76. For the development of the poetical tazkirah from anthologies of poems, see Francis Prichett, *Nets of Awareness,* pp. 63–77.

of Muhammad Husain Azad and others on the lack of 'authentic' data on the biographies in these tazkirahs.[67] However, even if the tazkiras before *Ab-e Hayat* rarely give a coherent life story, following the person through the major events of his life, they do permit the insight into what contemporaries deemed necessary to know about a person and what facts, for them, constituted his essential identity. This information, in the first part, was relational: life, in this perception began not with birth and ended with death, but was embedded in the lineage—biological, spiritual, and educational: forefathers, pirs, and ustads were as important in defining a person as were his offspring and followers. These lineages, very often, were held to account for the personal characteristics encountered in a person. At least for the contemporaries of the, writer of the tazkirah, these were described at great length. The colourful Persian hyperbole—claiming for instance that everyone taught by Azurda would 'kick the knowledge of Plato on the head' and 'bring Aristotle from the height of perfection to the dust of disgrace'[68]—not only served as panegyrics, but can again be read as relational, placing the individual in a world where learning was still defined by the standard of Plato and Aristotle, wisdom by Solomon, medical knowledge by Galen, and generosity by Faridun. However, even within this seemingly standardized descriptions, astonishing variety was achieved, both within the same tazkirah and between tazkirahs of different writers, notably if they belonged to different factions, poetical or otherwise.

The second category of writing, in which identity and biography played a central role, were the writings produced for the government, Mughal or British. To an extent probably still underestimated, the bureaucracy was based on daily accounts at all levels, ranging from the official diary of the local police stations,[69] to the newsletters produced at the Exalted Fort or the Residency.[70] Though originally highly formulaic and focused on recording the 'official' version of events, some of these diaries were continued as private writings during the siege of Delhi in

[67] Farman Fathepuri, *Urdu shoara ke tazkire aur tazkirah nigari*, Lahore: Majlis-e taraqqi-e adab, 1972.

[68] Mirza Qadir Bakhsh Sabir Dihlavi, *Gulistan-e Sukhan*, Lahore: Majlis-e taraqqi-e adab, 1966 (reprint), p. 209. I wish to thank my ustad, Dr Yunus Jaffry for his help in the translation.

[69] See for instance Diary of the Police Station of Chandni Chauk, NAI, Mutiny Papers, collection 61, file 64; or Diary of Thana Turkman, ibid., collection 61, file 96.

[70] For details on the courtly newsletters see Margrit Pernau, 'The Delhi Urdu Akhbar: Between Persian Akhbarat and English Newspapers', in *Annual of Urdu Studies*, 2003, pp. 1–27.

1857, now including references to the events touching the life of the news writer and his personal view of the facts he was recording.[71]

For sure, even these personalized diaries were still written for a public—the identity in the 'Mutiny Diaries' was constructed with an eye to the colonial authorities and their power to decide about the future of the author. Interpretation of the events during the siege, the voicing of despair and despondency at the way 'the city of Delhi was emptied of its rulers and peopled instead with creatures of the Lord who acknowledged no lord—as if it were a garden without a gardener, and full of fruitless trees'[72] have to be read in this context.

However, the line between the construction of an identity for public consumption and a self-identity, which would be 'authentic', should probably not be drawn too rigidly. Ghalib's *Dastanbu*, the diary he kept during the revolt, but reworked for publication in the months following the British victory, is a case in point.[73] Its prime motivation may be seen as an effort to distance himself from the Mughal court and to secure the restoration of his pension and honour by the British. He was quite outspoken—as well as ultimately successful—in that respect. At the same time, the text was an attempt to safeguard his own essential identities as a nobleman and as a poet under the changed circumstances. Written in a highly elaborate Persian language, the *Dastanbu* aims to bridge the disruptive events of 1857 by ascribing them to the recurring juncture of Saturn and Mars, and placing them in the continuity of historical events well known to the Indo-Muslim elite.[74] 1857 was a calamity, the message went, but not the end of the cultural world and its rules, which gave sense and meaning to life. Ghalib's identity and the entitlements, which proceeded from it, were the same as ever, and it was the duty of the British to restore them, and the universe for which they were the symbol, as soon as possible. For this, the British were entitled to poetic praise and encomiums as every ruler always had been. Autobiographical writing, thus, was at the same time an affirmation of individuality and of socially ascribed, but also personally felt identities, which could be more or less integrated according to circumstances.

[71] See for instance the diary of Jiwan Lal, the former Munshi of the Residency, published in Charles Theophilus Metcalfe (ed.), *Two Native Narratives of the Mutiny in Delhi: Translated from the originals*, Westminster, Archibald Constable & Co., 1898. In spite of its title, the *Memoirs of Hakim Ahsanullah Khan*, edited by S. Moinul Haq, Karachi, Pakistan Historical Society, 1958, too, is organized as a diary rather than as memoirs.

[72] Ghalib, *Dastanbuy*, translated and edited by Khawja Ahmad Faruqi, Delhi: University Press, 1970, p. 33.

[73] Saiyyid Moin ur Rahman, *Ghalib aur inqilab-e satavan*, Delhi: Ghalib Institute, 1988.

[74] Ghalib, *Dastanbuy*, pp. 24–6.

CONCLUSION

Religious pluralism, the fact that two or more religious communities coexist within the framework of a single state, has often been seen as a problem. The concept of multiple identities offers no solution, but challenges the perceptions behind the framing of the question on three levels. First: historically, in South Asia, Islam and Hinduism have not opposed each other as monolithic blocks with clearly defined boundaries and universally accepted norms of inclusion and exclusion. Rather, a concept of community based on the allegiance to one or multiple centres permitted plural identities both between the religions and within each one.

Second: each individual is a member of overlapping 'felt communities'. Persons belonging to the 'other' with regard to one of the criteria constituting a community, may well be a member of the 'self' with regard to another criterion. Hence, members of the same religion will very often have different interests stemming from their different gender, profession or social status, while these categories in turn regroup people from different religions.

Third: at one time or another, most identities build up the tendency to claim the exclusive loyalty of their members. This was intensified on the one hand by the trend towards a sharper definition of the boundaries; on the other hand by the challenge to individuals to work out a coherent and contradiction-free personality for themselves. However, even the hierarchization of identities is by no means stable, uniform, and unequivocal. Religion can at times attempt to subsume all other identities, but so can class-consciousness, or for that matter, feminism.

Invisible Religion between Individualization and Cultural Defense

MONIKA WOHLRAB-SAHR

INTRODUCTION

The term 'invisible religion', taken from the title of Thomas Luckmann's book (Luckmann 1967), became extremely successful among European and American scholars in sociology of religion. Even though the author himself had never explicitly used this term—it was an invention by his publisher—it seemed to catch not only a basic idea in Luckmann's work, but also an important development in the religious field of Western European societies since the 1960s: the growing independence of religious phenomena from their organizational representation by the churches (and also the growing awareness for such independence).

Also, in theoretical and methodological terms, Luckmann's approach to religion must be considered a milestone for European and American sociology of religion, inasmuch as he opposed the lack of theory and the empirical shortcomings of the church-centred research on religion during the 1950s, which was mainly interested in participation rates in church services and other church activities, without relating its findings to societal developments on a more general level (Luckmann 1960). Through his critique, Luckmann inspired a type of research in the field of sociology of religion that was interested in religious phenomena outside the churches and in phenomena that could be looked upon as functional equivalents for substantial religion or religious semantics.

Theoretically, Luckmann's approach to religion starts from an anthropologically based sociology of knowledge, as has been elaborated by

Alfred Schütz. Thereby, he not only refers to organized forms of religion, but also to a general form of religiosity, that (according to his theoretical perspective) was present *before* religion had taken an institutionalized form, as well as to diffused forms of religiosity that were expected to spread *after* religion had been institutionalized and which were thought to undermine the organizational form of religion. Luckmann relates this early, general form of religion to the mere fact that human beings transcend their biological nature by developing world views.

Even if his approach is mainly identified with the term 'invisible religion', Luckmann's ideas are obviously closely linked to the social and religious context of Europe, in which the organizational forms of church and sects play *the* important role in the religious field. It is from this background and starting point of organized religion that the idea of the 'invisible religion' is derived.

In accordance with classical sociological theory, especially the works of Weber and Durkheim, Luckmann takes up specific assumptions regarding the fate of religion in the process of modernization. But it is definitely *not* the idea of a necessary and general decline of religion in this process, that he refers to. In this respect, Luckmann raises an explicit objection against theories of secularization: He considers secularization a modern myth, used for the self-description of modern societies (Luckmann 1980). But, nevertheless his theory contains the idea of— what I would call—a secularization process without real secularization —an assumption that refers to the preservation of the religious heritage, of religious motives and motifs, while substantial or specific religion is losing ground. This assumption is also part of the sociological classics' theory of religion: inherent to Weber's concept of the Protestant ethic as well as to Durkheim's concept of the consciénce collective.

In this article I will first elaborate on the theoretical construction of Luckmann's work and the theories he refers to. Typical for those is a close intertwinement of religion and —either personal or collective— identity. Luckmann especially focuses on the connection between religion and personal identity, and therefore, interprets the process of religious evolution as a process of privatization and individualization.

Next, I will derive from Luckmann's theory and discuss the basic elements of a theory of religious individualization with reference to empirical findings about the religious situation in different European countries. These elements are: (a) the de-traditionalization of religion; (b) the individualized attribution of issues of 'ultimate concern'; (c) the pluralization of institutionalized belief; (d) the (still limited) pluralization of the religious and spiritual landscape outside the churches; and (e) the emergence of a norm of privacy related to personal religious practice.

Finally, I will argue that not only has religion, to a large degree, become an individualized and private issue, but—despite the culturally and sometimes also politically privileged position of the churches—the privacy of personal religious expression itself has become a norm in Western European societies. If religion is 'going public', this is restricted to special opportunities and organizational settings, and is highly channelled in its expression. The churches seem to be the only ones to legitimately represent a religious dimension in public, and that too only in a very specific framing (in case of war, catastrophes, urgent ethical or political questions, or for representational or 'cultural' matters).

But, under conditions of religious plurality, when religions with different appearances in public life come together, the norm of privatization and individualization may be used as a means of distinction towards those religions that do not (and for the moment cannot) adapt to this form. Individualization and privatization of religion then, paradoxically, may become an element of 'cultural defence'.[1]

This will be shown with reference to the 'headscarf debates' in Germany and France. Motivated by the fear of Islamic fundamentalism, the wearing of the headscarf in certain public places, especially in schools, has been interpreted as a 'signal' of fundamentalism per se, which is breaking the rule to practise religion in a privatized, 'discreet' way. But at the same time this interpretation neglects the possibility of Muslim women to interpret religious symbols in an individualized manner themselves, inasmuch as their personal use of symbols is immediately identified with the 'objective meaning' of those symbols. As opposed to that, in case of Christian crosses (e.g. on a necklace) and Jewish kipas, the meaning of symbols is considered dependant on personal behaviour rather than on some kind of inherent meaning.

This example is discussed with reference to the process of religious and cultural pluralization in European countries.

INVISIBLE RELIGION:
SECULARIZATION WITHOUT SECULARIZATION

The close connection between religion and identity is in different ways inherent to the theories Luckmann refers to. Regarding Weber's (Weber 2001) theory, the heritage of religion in a growingly secularized society

[1] The term 'cultural defence' is taken from Bruce 1999: 25–7

is a structural leftover of the Protestant Ethic: it is the professional habitus focusing on the problem of probation. To describe this in more recent terms, one could say, the religious heritage has entered into a specific shape of social—professional—identity.

Regarding the late Durkheim (Durkheim 2001), who also has left traces in Luckmann's approach, it is religion and religious symbols as the symbolic representation of society, and religious sentiment as the overwhelming experience of something powerful beyond the individual—the 'consciénce collective'—that will necessarily survive, even if churches and concrete religious manifestations vanish. In contrast to Weber, who describes the de facto, but not the necessary survival of a structurally religious motive in the professional habitus, Durkheim claims functional religiosity as a necessity for social integration. In this respect, Luckmann's approach is closer to Durkheim's than to Weber's: According to his concept neither society nor religion can be conceived without a general form of religion.

A third strand that plays into Luckmann's theory is a phenomenological and anthropological view on religion. The basic idea is that the very nature of human experience and knowledge is dependant on acts of transcendence on different levels. Before there were any specific religious institutions and specific theological constructions organizing the 'great transcendences', there were human beings transcending their biological nature and only through this constituting a self. Luckmann calls this process of becoming a self and developing world views (Weltansichten) a religious process on a very general level (Luckmann 1967). Irrespective of what happens to specific religious institutions, those very basic acts of transcendence will remain, and they are thought to be religious.

During the societal development which is usually called the secularization process, religion—as Luckmann states—undergoes a transformation, changes its form, and becomes diffuse again. And—one could add—for those who only look for its organized and specific manifestations, it becomes 'invisible'.

This newly emerging social form of religion, which is more and more detached from the claims and substantial ideas of church-based religion, finds its topics mainly in the private sphere, from which it also gets its inter-subjective affirmation. Whereas the churches gradually lose the monopoly of interpretation, and the 'official model of religion' as represented by them more and more loses its subjective plausibility, the individual and the private sphere become the place as well as the central topic of this new social form of religion. In this sense, individualization and privatization are two main features of Luckmann's notion of the new form of religion.

But it is not only individuality as a place and a topic that constitutes the new religious form. Beyond that it is the connection between religion and identity that seems indissoluble in Luckmann's theory. This new form of religion has its place in subjective systems of ultimate significance, which constitute the legitimatory level of the personal identity. Thereby, Luckmann not only presupposes a close link between religion and identity, but also a specific concept of identity—as a hierarchy of meaning—in which the process of individuation and conscience-building is founded.

As long as the churches offer a convincing model of interpretation to articulate issues of ultimate significance, individuals will often refer to that. But the further these specific models of interpretation turn away from individual biographies—and as models developed by religious experts in specific religious organizations they *necessarily* do—subjective systems of ultimate significance tend to be formulated independently from them. Consequently, there will be a growing gap between the official model of religion and the prevalent individual systems of ultimate significance.

But in the course of the process of secularization the contents of these systems of ultimate significance and the level of transcendence that they refer to, are changing. Luckmann stresses that people refer less to the great transcendences that have been formulated by specific religions—e.g. the belief in the hereafter—but more to middle and small transcendences. The sacralization of individual autonomy and of private life indicates this shift.

RELIGIOUS INDIVIDUALIZATION OR SECULARIZATION?

The notion of religious privatization as a *general* development in the religious field has been seriously questioned by the American sociologist José Casanova (Casanova 1994) not only with reference to the appearance of public religions, especially fundamentalist movements, throughout the 1980s, but also to other forms of public religious manifestation. Casanova did not put into question that privatization of religion was *one* option in the course of the modernization process, but that it was the only and general option.

Among German sociologists of religion, the debate—with implicit reference to Luckmann's theory—was mainly about the idea of religious individualization (Gabriel 1992; Pollack/ Pickel 1999; Wohlrab-Sahr/

Krüggeler 2000) and its relationship to processes of secularization. Researchers of the Luckmann school tend to principally question the secularization thesis, especially the notion of religious decline, and rather speak of religious individualization: in the sense that religion in modern society is changing its form, but not necessarily losing ground. Others refer to Luckmann's notion of religious individualization and privatization, without sharing his general concept of religion and without questioning the salience of secularization theories. On the other side, in this debate were those who principally questioned the idea of religious individualization with reference to processes of religious decline and to the fact that new religious movements and phenomena find only little support among the German population.

In general, it became clear that the different positions depended to a large degree on the definition of religion, but also on the different ways of approaching potential religious phenomena empirically. Quantitative researchers usually stressed the notion of secularization and religious decline and questioned the idea of religious individualization, since their questionnaires largely referred to church- or group-bound religiosity and substantial beliefs, which obviously *are* declining. But it was neither Luckmann's notion of a sacralization of the individual as a modern phenomenon in the religious field nor his notion of individualized constructs of 'systems of ultimate significance' that these researchers were able to test with their findings, since this would have required qualitative and reconstructive ways of inquiry.

Looking at the empirical findings that were discussed in this debate, the following conclusions can be drawn:

1. First of all, religion as some kind of explicit reference to 'great transcendences' (belief in God, some higher power, in afterlife) in Germany, but also in other European countries, still correlates very strongly with the membership in a Christian church (Jagodzinski/ Dobbelaere 1993; Engelhardt et al. 1997: 306) or—among a growing migrant population—with being Muslim (Wolf 2000). People who leave the church usually also question or negate such great transcendences.

2. Compared to other big organizations, like unions or political parties, the churches do quite well in terms of membership, which means that there is still only a moderate decline of membership in the churches. But nevertheless they are—for example in Germany— losing about one per cent of their members every year, either by death or by leaving (Kastning 2000: 414). About 32 per cent of the

overall German population today are not members of any church or religious group. The decline in membership is especially high among the younger generations. One reason for that obviously is that even for parents who are members of the church themselves, it is not a matter of course to socialize their children into the churches by baptism and religious education, especially among couples with only one person belonging to a church. Under these circumstances, it is not self-evident any more to hand one's own church bond over to the next generation.

3. Opposed to current ideas of a religious 'market' (see Iannacone/ Finke/Stark 1996), data show that those who leave the churches, only rarely become members of another religious community. In most of the cases, to quit church membership also implies to consider religious interpretations in general no longer plausible. People who are leaving the church have become indifferent to religion, or they were already indifferent before and now draw the consequences in terms of membership. Therefore, for Germany as well as for several other European countries, secularization theory—in the sense of an ongoing *decline of church affiliation*—remains a valid interpretation (Pollack 1996). Indifference towards religions, but also explicit atheism—especially, but not only in post-socialist countries—have become broadly accepted positions, which need to be taken seriously as such by sociologists of religion.

4. Therefore, if the term 'religious individualization' is used for the interpretation of recent religious developments, it must be able to integrate empirical findings of the decline of the church, and therefore cannot seriously be completely in opposition to the secularization thesis. Religious individualization, if used as a term that refers to empirical processes, does not imply that the losses of church-bound religion are *compensated* by explicitly religious engagements outside the churches. Religious indifference and atheism have become accepted positions in several European countries. Religious development obviously is not a zero-sum game only involving a shift in religious engagements from one organization to the other.

There are also only very few indicators supporting the idea that a pluralistic 'market of religions' is developing in Europe. In this respect, Germany and other European countries are distinctively different from the USA. For this reason attempts to explain the situation in Europe with reference to market theories (Iannacone/Finke/Stark 1996), which seem to work well in the American context, are only of limited use with reference to Europe.

But what docs religious individualization mean then? I suggest differentiating five levels of individualization:

1. A process of *de-traditionalization* of religion with the effect of the *privatization of decision making* (Luhmann 1977: 232) *in religious matters.* Church membership and religious affiliation in most of the Western European countries nowadays are less influenced by social convention, social control, and by the subordination to an institution (Jagodzinski/ Dobbelaere 1993). Consequently, the barriers against leaving the churches become weaker. This process has been very dramatic in the Netherlands, where church membership declined inasmuch as the institutional pillars that were organized around religion or around secular world views dissolved: including schools, universities, the press, political parties, and other associations. Consequently, in statistical terms the religious situation in the Netherlands (Becker/de Hart/Mens 1997) today is quite similar to East Germany, which is one of the most secularized regions in the world. In general one could say: Because social restrictions are less relevant as external reasons for maintaining church membership, it becomes more or less an issue of private decisions. A prominent example for that in Germany was the swearing-in ceremony of Chancellor Gerhard Schröder after the 1998 election, who, as the first chancellor in the Federal Republic of Germany, did not refer to God in his oath. This was well noticed in public, but it was not considered a problem really. Something like this could hardly be imagined in a context like the United States.

In West Germany, this tendency of de-traditionalization is more obvious with regard to those 22 per cent *without* church affiliation.[2] In East Germany, it is to be observed already *within* the churches, which include only about 26 per cent of the East German population. Almost half of the baptisms in East Germany[3] today are baptisms of small children, juveniles or adults, but not of babies, which is still the rule in West Germany (Kastning 1996: 422). This means that parents who have their children baptized, or juveniles and adults who get baptized, do not act in a traditional manner, but consciously decide for baptism. Just the opposite is the case with those who do not belong to any church. Not belonging has become a sort of tradition itself. With reference to the

[2] In West Germany 78 per cent of the population are church members; in East Germany – mostly because of the anti-church politics of the state of GDR–only 26 per cent are church members.

[3] This refers to the Protestant church which is he biggest church in East Germany, whereas the Catholic church gathers only 4 per cent of the population.

German sociologist Niklas Luhmann this tendency can be called the *privatization of decision making* (Luhmann 1977: 232) *in religious matters.*

As the example of Gerhard Schröder's swearing-in ceremony shows, this privatization of decision making goes along with a privatization of religion itself. It is mainly in exceptional situations, like big catastrophes, violent conflicts or urgent political and ethical questions, that church religion is asked for as public religion. Apart from those situations, there seems to be a broad consensus that religion is a private matter.

2. The second aspect of the individualization process refers to changing attitudes towards issues that up to now have been closely linked to the religious sphere: for example, the question for the meaning of life, but also—and maybe more important—the question for the intentional termination of life in case of incurable illness. That one needs to give meaning to life oneself instead of receiving such meaning as a gift is broadly accepted nowadays, and there is also broad support to the conviction that people should have the right to decide upon the termination of their own lives in case of terminal illness. The laws about medically assisted suicide in the Netherlands or in Belgium, which provoked huge public debates, find support from the majority of the population outside these countries also, and they hint to the fact that issues which usually were considered non-disposable and non-negotiable, tend to become matters of personal decision. I call this aspect the *individualized attribution of issues of 'ultimate concern'.* In Protestantism, this certainly has its own religious tradition. But it nevertheless collides with theological interpretations, according to which the meaning of life and life itself is something that is perceived as a gift.

3. A third dimension of the individualization process is that the contents of personal beliefs deviate more and more from the dogmatic positions of the churches. In this respect the change that is going on is certainly hard to prove, since we know only a little about the 'patchwork belief' of the past. Obviously, it has always been the case that people believed in many things that were not in line with the official teachings of the churches, and convictions, that were most important to theologians, were not shared by believers. This is especially true for Catholicism with its diverse religious folk traditions. Survey research has shown that since the 1960s central elements of Christian belief (e.g. belief in hell, in the devil, in the hereafter, but also in a personal God) have lost ground among church members (Jagodzinski/Dobbelaere 1993) as well as among theologians (Ebertz 1993), and that elements from other religious or philosophical traditions found their way into the belief systems of members of Christian churches (Dubach/Campiche 1993).

One striking example is the belief in reincarnation. I call this dimension the *pluralization of institutionalized belief.*

4. A fourth dimension is a certain process of pluralization of the religious landscape itself. Even if the path into indifference towards religion is more likely in Germany and other European countries than the path into alternative religiosity, there is certainly some kind of religiosity outside the churches, e.g. Buddhism or different esoteric and magic beliefs and practices. And of course, migrants, mainly Muslim migrants, bring new elements into the religious landscape and produce a pluralized religious field as an effect of the more diverse composition of the population. To a small degree they also stimulate conversions of native Germans to 'foreign' religions, like Islam. But the main factor of religious pluralization is the growing diversity in the population's composition through migration (Wolf 2000). As long as ethnic groups are more or less segregated from the native German population, this diversity does not create a 'market' for religions.

5. In addition, one needs to add a fifth dimension, that does not come into view in Luckmann's theory and the notion of 'invisible religion'. It is the emerging *norm* that religious practice is a private matter and has to be handled in a private, discreet way—a norm which has developed since the 1960s in line with the process of de-traditionalization. This starts with the decline in church attendance also among Catholics and their deviation from the Church's norms of behaviour, especially in matters of sexuality, marriage, and birth control. But in line with this emancipation of private life from the control of the Church, religion itself became a 'private' issue, neither to be controlled by religious or state institutions, nor to be handled by believers in a way that might be considered 'ostentatious' or 'intolerant' by others. Therefore public 'invisibility' is also characteristic for a specific religious habitus.

This norm of privacy may also be looked upon as the reverse side of the public task which the churches are expected to fulfil vicariously, as Grave Davie (Davie 2000) put it in order to differentiate between the dominant European religious pattern as opposed to the American one. This vicarious role of the churches becomes especially visible in situations of collective crises (like the war against Iraq), in case of other catastrophes of national importance (like big accidents with many victims, shootings in school etc.), or with reference to important ethical or political questions (e.g. political decisions about reproductive technologies or medically assisted suicide). But, irrespective of this public task of the churches, the religiosity of persons has become a 'private' matter in many European countries, which corresponds to the religious pattern described by Grace Davie (2000: 33), with high levels of nominal believing on the one side and low levels of active religiousness on the other side. I call this fifth dimension of the individualization process the emergence of a *norm of privacy related to personal religious practice.*

These five dimensions—the privatization of decision making; the individualized attribution of issues of 'ultimate concern'; the pluralization of beliefs in the field of institutionalized religion, the pluralization of the religious and spiritual landscape outside the churches, and the emergence of a norm of religious privacy—may be interpreted as a process of *religious individualization.*

One could interpret the broad attention that was paid to these debates in different European countries, and the similarity of the conflicts in Germany and France as an indicator for some kind of countermovement (Neidhardt 1986) against the movement of multiculturalism, which is usually emphasizing the positive chances of a ethnically and religiously pluralistic society, and at the same time playing down the difficulties of diverse cultural backgrounds coming together. Nevertheless, looking at this 'countermovement', it is striking to see the unquestioning reference to Christianity as part of the cultural heritage, being mixed with assumptions of how religious symbols and personal religiosity are to be presented in the public sphere. It is obvious, that the *discreet* presentation of symbols as opposed to their ostentatious presentation is immediately linked to the fact that some of these symbols are *culturally common* and well known, whereas others are not.

CONCLUSION

The conflicts about Muslim headscarves reveal certain basic characteristics:

1) Freedom of religion in its negative aspect takes priority over freedom of religion in its positive aspect. In case of doubt, being free from the exposure to a foreign religious symbol is considered superior to the freedom to use such a symbol. This may per se be looked upon as an indicator for this emerging norm of 'privacy' in religious matters. And it indicates that European countries with different histories and ways of structuring church-state relationships—like Germany and France—show (and develop) common features in their ways of dealing with the growing religious and cultural diversity of their populations.

2) In many Western European countries religion is considered first of all a private issue. When it goes public, this is expected to happen in

a discreet way. Regarding Islam, this implies the expectation that headscarves may be worn 'privately', but not publicly, especially not in the realm of the state. One could conclude: Only if religion is not visible as such in public, has it a legitimate place there.

3) Whereas the indigene, well-known religiosity and its symbols are assumed to get their meaning via subjective interpretations, and for that reason the actual behaviour of persons has to be assessed, the headscarf as an Islamic symbol is seen to be independent of personal interpretation and behaviour. This implies a double standard in the interpretation of religious phenomena: an individualized perspective on Christianity, and an a-personal, objectivistic perspective on Islam, which, by definition, then is in conflict with the norm of privacy.

What are the implications of the headscarf cases for the question of religious individualization? On the one side, religion comes into play in a way that often was thought to have become irrelevant in the course of secularization: as a cultural heritage. But the reference to Christianity happens in a way in which the privatized—invisible—use of religion is taken as a norm. Fulfilling, this norm, paradoxically, depends on the 'invisibility' of a religion that has already become culture: in Germany, as well as in France, on Christianity. So the privatization of religion meshes with its culturalization. By this, it becomes a means of 'cultural defence' (see Bruce 1999).

It seems that in the course of a growing plurality in European societies, Christian religion may get a new role. A role which is less defined by the churches, than by judges and politicians referring to Christianity as a cultural tradition, and enforced by 'counter-movements' among European populations against multiculturalism and the growing visibility of Islam.

BIBLIOGRAPHY

Bader, Johann, Darf eine muslimische Lehrerin in der Schule ein Kopftuch tragen?', *Verwaltungsblätter für Baden-Württemberg* 19, 10, 1998, 361–5.

Baubérot, Jean, 'L'affaire des foulards et la laïcité à la française', *L'Homme et la Société*, n° 120, avril-juin, 9–16 1996.

Becker, J.W, J. de Hart, and J. Mens, *Secularisatie en alternatieve zingeving in Nederland*, Rijswijk: VUGA, J., 1997.

Bruce, Steve, *Choice and Religion. A Critique of Rational Choice Theory*, Oxford: Oxford University Press, 1999.

Casanova, José, *Public Religions in the Modern World,* Chicago/London: University of Chicago Press, 1994.

Davie, Grace, *Religion in Modern Europe. A Memory Mutates,* Oxford et al.: Oxford University Press, 2000.

Dubach, Alfred and Roland J. Campiche (eds), *Jede(r) ein Sonderfall Religion in der Schweiz,* Zürich: NZN, 1993.

Durkheim, Émile, *The Elementary Forms of Religious Life,* Oxford and New York: Oxford University Press, 2001.

Ebertz, Michael N., 'Die Zivilisierung Gottes und die Deinstitutionalisierung der "Gnadenanstalt". Befunde einer Analyse von eschatologischen Predigten', in Jörg Bergmann et al. (eds), *Religion und Kultur,* Kölner Zeitschrift für Soziologie und Sozialpsychologie, Special Volume 33: Westdeutscher Verlag, 1993, 92–125.

Engelhardt, Klaus, Hermann von Loewenich, and Peter Steinacker (eds), *Fremde Heimat Kirche,* Gütersloh: Gütersloher Verlagshaus, 1997.

Gabriel, Karl, 'Einleitung', in K. Gabriel (ed.), *Biographie und Gruppe als Bezugspunkte moderner Religiosität,* Gütersloh: Gütersloher Verlagshaus, 1996, 9–13.

Hervieu-Léger, Danièle, 'Die Vergangenheit der Gegenwart: Die Neudefinition des "laizistischen Paktes" im multikulturellen Frankreich', in P.L. Berger,. (ed.), *Die Grenzen der Gemeinschaft. Konflikt und Vermittlung in pluralistischen Gesellschaften,* Gütersloh: Verlag Bertelsmann-Stiftung,1997, 85–153.

Iannacone, Laurence, Roger Finke, and Rodney, Stark, 'Deregulating Religion: The Economics of Church and State', in Rehberg Karl-Siegbert (ed.), *Differenz und Integration, 1996, 28. Kongress der Deutschen Gesellschaft für Soziologie – Dresden, Kongressband II,* Opladen: Westdeutscher Verlag, 462–6.

Jagodzinski, Wolfgang and Karel Dobbelaere, Der Wandel kirchlicher Religiosität in Westeuropa, in Jörg Bergmann et al. (eds), *Religion und Kultur. Kölner Zeitschrift für Soziologie und Sozialpsychologie,* Special Volume 33, Westdeutscher Verlag, 1993, 68–91.

Kastning, Karin, 'Kirchliche Statistik', in *Kirchliches Jahrbuch für die Evangelische Kirche in Deutschland 1996, Zahlen und Fakten zum kirchlichen Leben,* Gütersloh: Gütersloher Verlagshaus, 2000, 411–67.

Krüggeler, Michael and Peter Voll, 'Strukturelle Individualisierung—ein Leitfaden durchs Labyrinth der Empirie', in Alfred Dubach and Roland J. Campiche, (eds), *Jede(r) ein Sonderfall? Religion in der Schweiz.* Zürich: NZN, 1993, 17–49.

Luckmann, Thomas, 'Neuere Schriften zur Religionssoziologie, *Kölner Zeitschrift für Soziologie und Sozialpsychologie,* 1960, 12, 315–26.

Luckmann, Thomas, *The invisible religion. The problem of religion in modern society.* New York: MacMillan, 1967.

Luckmann, Thomas, 'Säkularisierung—ein moderner Mythos', in Thomas Luckmann (ed.), *Lebenswelt und Gesellschaft Grundstrukturen und geschichtliche Wandlungen.* Paderborn et al.: Ferdinand Schöningh, 1980, 161–72.

Luckmann, Thomas, 'Schrumpfende Transzendenzcn, expandierende Religion', in Thomas Luckmann (ed.), *Wissen und Gesellschaft. Ausgewählte Aufsätze 1981–2002*, Konstanz: UVK, 2002, 139–54.

Luhmann, Niklas *Funktion der Religion*. Frankfurt/M.: Suhrkamp, 1977.

Luhmann, Niklas, *Die Religion der Gesellschaft*. Frankfurt/M.: Suhrkamp, 2000.

Neidhardt, Friedhelm, '"Kultur und Gesellschaft". Einige Anmerkungen zum Sonderheft', in F. Neidhardt, M.R Lepsius, and J. Weiß (eds), *Kultur und Gesellschaft, Kölner Zeitschrift für Soziologie und Sozialpsychologie*, Special Volume 33, Opladen: Westdeutscher Verlag, 1986, 10–18.

Pollack, Detlef, 'Individualisierung statt Säkularisierung? Zur Diskussion eines neueren Paradigmas in der Religionssoziologie', in Karl Gabriel (ed.), *Biographie und Gruppe als Bezugspunkte moderner Religiosität*, Gütersloh: Gütersloher Verlagshaus, 1996, 57–85.

Pollack, Detlef, 'Der Zusammenhang zwischen kirchlicher und außerkirchlicher Religiosität in Ostdeutschland im Vergleich zu Westdeutschland', in Detlef Pollack and Gert Pickel (eds), *Religiöser und kirchlicher Wandel in Ostdeutschland 1989–1999*, Opladen: Leske+Budrich, 2000, 294–309.

Pollack, Detlef and Gert Pickel, 'Individualisierung und religiöser Wandel in der Bundesrepublik Deutschland', in *Zeitschrift für Soziologie* 28, 1999, 465–83.

Stark, Rodney and Laurence R. Iannacone, 'A Supply-Side Reinterpretation of the "Secularization" of Europe', *Journal for the Scientific Study of Religion*, 33, 1994, 230–52.

Weber, Max, *The Protestant Ethic and the Spirit of Capitalism*, Chicago/London: Fitzroy Dearborn, 2001.

Wohlrab-Sahr, Monika and Michael Krüggeler, 'Strukturelle Individualisierung vs. autonome Menschen oder: Wie individualisiert ist Religion?', *Zeitschrift für Soziologie* 29, 2000, 240–4.

Wohlrab-Sahr, Monika, 'Politik und Religion. "Diskretes" Kulturchristentum als Fluchtpunkt europäischer Gegenbewegungen gegen einen "ostentativen" Islam', in A. Nassehi and M. Schroer (eds), *Der Begriff des Politischen. Soziale Welt*, Special Volume, Opladen: 2003, 273–97.

Wolf, Christof, 'Religionszugehörigkeit im früheren Bundesgebiet 1939 bis 1987', *Statistisches Bundesamt, Wirtschaft und Statistik*, 3, 2000, 201–7.

Denial of Plurality

Thinking of Conversion through Gandhi

SUDHIR CHANDRA

'I am against conversion whether it is known as *shuddhi* by
Hindus, *tabligh* by Mussalmans or proselytizing by Christians.'

'It [religion] is a matter for every individual to decide for himself
to which faith he will belong.'

M.K. Gandhi

The theme of denial of plurality in conversion seems to take too categorical a position on a very complex issue. It ought to resound to its
opposite as well, so as also to suggest the possible denial of plurality in
the denial of conversion. With that end in view, I have taken the liberty
of adding a question mark to the theme. My strategy in discussing this
aporetic issue is to focus on Gandhi, whose constant grappling with the
question could never yield, his own belief to the contrary notwithstanding, a definitive position for or against conversion.

Gandhi has in recent years been enlisted by those who claim to
oppose religious conversion per se. They have, in order to attribute to
him a plain anti-conversion stance, exploited the ease with which his
numerous contradictory utterances on the subject can be selectively cited
either way.[1] However, seen in their nuances and contexts, and examined

---

[1] Typifying such attempts, Rameshwar Shukla 'Pankaj' and Kusumlata Kediya assert:
'It is clear that Gandhiji considered religious conversion to be in every way improper,
reprehensible and sinful.' *Gandhiji aur Isaiyat* (in Hindi), Dilli, 2000, p. 86. Understanding
little the letter of Gandhian position, and its spirit even less, they call for legislation against

in terms of their larger internal logic, these utterances constitute a position too complex to be described simply as either for or against conversion. Nor does it help to attempt a formulaic description of the position.[2]

Thus, what the first epigraph above asserts in the isolation of that solitary sentence—'I am against conversion'—is complicated by the two immediately following sentences which aver: 'Conversion is a heart-process known only to and by God. It must be left to itself.'[3] Seemingly unequivocal rejection of conversion is, thus, followed by, and must be seen in conjunction with, metaphysical acceptance of it. No matter what the depth of his resistance to conversion, and how difficult his conditions for accepting it, Gandhi cannot anathematize conversion. Indeed, as the other epigraph shows, he feels impelled to support *every* individual's right to choose her/his own faith.[4]

Compulsory adherence to one's ancestral religion is fundamentally un-Gandhian. It subordinates the supreme authority Gandhi assigned to the 'inner voice'—'the deepest in me'[5]—to the chance of birth. This ultimate authority is what had inspired his famous statement that, should untouchability be integral to Hinduism, he would rather leave Hinduism than accept untouchability. Following that cue, one could peremptorily argue that even if Gandhi entertained a 'distaste for conversion',[6] rejection of it militates against his basic principles. Not, of course, to reject Gandhi, in the unlikely event of his opposition to

---

blasphemy, and for the eradication of 'sinful Christianity': 'Resurgent Hindutva would force Christianity to be restrained and religious. Gandhiji is our guide in this matter.' Ibid. pp. 43, 89, 106. See also note 79 below.

[2] Even if one seeks to abstract, as R.K. Gupta has done, Gandhi's main theses on conversion, suggesting when, in specific situations, conversion is to be justified or opposed, Gandhi's own conduct does not conform to those theses. R.K. Gupta, 'Gandhi on Conversion', *Gandhi Marg*, April–June. 2000, pp. 69–75.

[3] Gandhi's statement for Shraddhananad Memorial, *The Collected Works of Mahatma Gandhi*, Ahmedabad: The Publications Division, 1969, vol. xxxii, p. 515.

[4] See Gandhi's statement in the *Harijan* of 21 March 1936 on Ambedkar's statement about renouncing Hinduism. Ibid. vol. lxii, 1975, p. 280. Given the virtual inversion of right as duty in Gandhi's moral economy, it may even be seen as making the choice incumbent for every individual.

[5] 'And the deepest in me tells me that I am right.' Gandhi's speech at YMCA, Colombo, 15 November 1927. Ibid. vol. xxxv, 1969, p. 249. Nine years later, on 24 November 1936, Basil Mathews asked Gandhi: 'Where do you find the seat of authority?' Gandhi pointed to his breast as he replied: 'It lies here.' Ibid. vol. lxiv, 1976, p. 75.

[6] Antony Copley, *Religions in Conflict: Ideology, Cultural Contact and Conversion in Late Colonial India*, Delhi: Oxford University Press, 1997, p. vii.

conversion being established, but to overrule that opposition in defence of his own principles.[7]

At the same time, if as a votary of ahimsa—of which he claimed to be the highest acharya—he wanted the entire humanity to embrace it, what kind of a stance vis-à-vis conversion—including religious conversion— did that connote?[8]

Let us not, however, presume that Gandhi was opposed to conversion, and hasten to hoist him with his own petard. Let us, rather, grapple with the relevant details. And, in the spirit of grappling, choose a starting point that confronts us with the complexity, almost elusiveness, of Gandhi's position. Early in 1929, in an interview with Dr John Mott— an American evangelist, a prominent YMCA leader and chairman of the International Missionary Council—on being plainly asked: 'Do you then disbelieve in all conversion?', Gandhi replied: 'I disbelieve in the conversion of one person by another.'[9]

Careful, as always, in his choice of words, and catching the insinuating resonance in Mott's question, Gandhi emphasized that he was not opposed to *all conversion*. Five years later he would reiterate it more felicitously as opposition to 'conversion by human agency'.[10] This is a striking position, pregnant with profound implications for the relationship of individual human beings and communities vis-à-vis religion and God. However, the way Gandhi further clarified his position to Mott leaves us no wiser. Explicating his opposition to the conversion of one person by another, he added:

My effort should never be to undermine another's faith but to make him a better

---

[7] The question, to settle which Gandhi's authority has been used by those claiming to oppose conversion, pertains to religious conversion. It would be moot, though, to ask if, in Gandhian terms, it is not superfluous to add 'religious' before 'conversion'. Religion for him pervaded life. Truth was religion. So was ahimsa. And politics. If as a Hindu—which he insisted he was—he saw no reason for non-Hindus to be of the same faith as him, was he, in principle, opposing conversion, or religious conversion?

[8] Conversion to ahimsa apart, the success of ahimsa in every specific instance implied an act of conversion. 'My method,' Gandhi remarked, 'is conversion'; the 'ultimate conversion of the wrong-doers'. Raghavan Iyer, *The Moral and Political Writings of Mahatma Gandhi: Non-Violent Resistance and Social Transformation*, Oxford, 1987, vol. III, pp. 255, 572. While the issue deserves more serious reflection than is possible for me at the moment, Gandhi seems to have in mind a deeper level of religion—of one's relationship with God— than is meant by him when he talks of, for example, ahimsa and its reliance on the conversion—change of heart—of the other. There are differing domains of conviction. See also footnote 12 below.

[9] *The Collected Works of Mahatma Gandhi*, vol. xl, 1970, p. 60.

[10] Gandhi's conversation of 18 April 1934 reported in *Harijan*, 4 May 1934. Ibid. vol. lvii, 1976, p. 406.

follower of his own faith. This implies belief in the truth of all religions, and therefore respect for them. It again implies humility, a recognition of the fact that the divine light having been vouchsafed to all religions through an imperfect medium of flesh, they must share in more or less degree the imperfection of the vehicle.[11]

The explication, with its stress on *never* undermining another person's faith, but to strengthen it, could have sounded like opposition to all conversion, not just conversion of one person by another. It was this understandable suspicion of wholesale opposition that had induced Mott to add that crucial 'then' as he flatly asked Gandhi: 'Do you *then* disbelieve in all conversion?' It appears that Mott's was a typical suspicion entertained about Gandhi's attitude towards conversion by those brought up to idealize proselytization. Thus, after listening to Gandhi at a conference of missionary societies in Great Britain and Ireland in London on 8 October 1931, Reverend C.E. Wilson of the Baptist Missionary Society felt chagrined to remark:

Mr Gandhi seems to me to deprecate, almost to condemn, religious teaching. We are to go and live among people but not try to make them disciples or instill new faith into them. That seems to me to confute Mr Gandhi's whole life ... Mr Gandhi has been preaching to us today. Does he really mean to exclude all preaching?[12]

The suspicion was more than a figment of feverish Christian missionary imagination. Gandhi did valorize the idea of silent service, one rendered without any expectation of reward, not even the satisfaction of doing what one considered a good spiritual turn. Not 'even secretly', he insisted, should one pray for the conversion of another. 'Conversion and service,' he held, 'go ill together.'[13] He saw a sharp contrast between his

[11] Ibid. vol. xl, p. 60.

[12] The following remark made by Gandhi at this very meeting, especially if read in the context of the idea of differing domains of conviction (footnote 8 above), could be an answer to Rev. Wilson: 'Though my conviction is strong enough in me for me to die for that conviction, that force does not carry me to the goal of believing that the same thing should be believed by my fellow men.' Ibid. vol. xlviii, 1971, p. 125. Gandhi's abstention from conversion, one can see, will apply to his convictions about Hinduism, but not to his convictions about, say, ahimsa.

[13] Raghavan Iyer, ed., *The Moral and Political Writings of Mahatma Gandhi: Civilization, Politics, and Religion*, vol. I, p. 537. Asked by Mott, speaking for the missionaries, 'But must we not serve them?', Gandhi replied: 'Of course you will, but not make conversion the price of your service.' Ibid. vol. lxiv, p. 36. Similarly, in a note to Dr Thornton, written on a day of silence, Gandhi observed: 'If the missionary friends will forget their mission, viz., of proselytizing Indians and of bringing Christ to them, they will do wonderfully good work.' bid. vol. xlv, 1971, p. 223.

own missionary work and that of the Christian proselytizers, and left no doubt as to which one he valued, as he told them: 'While I am strengthening the faith of the people, you are undermining it.'[14] A true conversion occurred after the adherents of a faith had done their best to persuade the potential convert not to join them!

A tension is discernible in Gandhi's attitude towards conversion. Instinctively, on the one hand, he shrank away from the 'idea of conversion', believing it to be 'the deadliest poison that ever sapped the fountain of truth'.[15] His usual critical alertness could occasionally weaken before his avidity for arguments against conversion, tending him to clutch to just about anything that seemed to serve the purpose. At times, however, his critique of conversion equalled the grandeur and profundity of a Kierkegaard. On the other hand, despite the attraction of a conversion-free world, Gandhi recognized the freedom of individual human beings—never human groups though—to choose/change their religion. As he did in 1936 when he said: 'If ... any Harijan wants to give up Hinduism, he should be entirely free to do so.' Even adding: 'The wonder is that many more Harijans than already have, have not left Hinduism.'[16]

II

Gandhi had become conscious of the importance of inter-religious relations—including conversion—from his student days in England. He further nurtured this consciousness in South Africa, and recalled at least one experience of this period as a kind of decisive argument against conversion. Once in India, given the way religious disputes impinged upon Indian politics, his earnestness about religious-spiritual matters was turned into a never-ending reflection. He felt obliged in the very first year of his Indian public life to specify his position vis-à-vis conversion. That is when we get an early glimpse of the tension that characterized his views on the question during the remaining thirty-two years of his life.

The occasion was a speech, on 14 February 1916, at a Christian Missionary Conference in Madras. Gandhi carried with him a written text, anxious lest he should falter in formulating his position on a 'very delicate and difficult' subject. He began by telling the missionaries that it

[14] Ibid. vol. xxxiv, 1969, p. 260
[15] Discussion with Krzenski, a Polish professor of philosophy, 2 Janary 1937. Ibid. vol. lxiv, p. 203.
[16] Ibid. vol. lxii, p. 280.

was not 'without much diffidence' that he had undertaken to speak to them. He did not have, he felt, 'that command of language which is necessary for giving adequate expression to my thoughts'. This was no ritual expression of modesty, the kind of polite prefacing expected on formal occasions. Gandhi wanted the address to express accurately his ideas on swadeshi and its bearing on the question of religion. It was no ordinary matter. If 'reduced to practice', he was convinced, swadeshi would 'lead to the millennium'.[17]

To facilitate the millennium, Gandhi wanted the world to follow swadeshi: 'that spirit in us which restricts us to the use and service of our immediate surroundings to the exclusion of the more remote'. It meant, in concrete terms, that people should practise their 'ancestral religion'. If they found it in any way defective, they should 'serve it by purging it of its defects'.[18]

Gandhi 'briefly' examined the above proposition by focusing on Hinduism, assuming that the examination would apply generally to all religions. Hinduism, he observed:

...has become a conservative religion and therefore a mighty force because of the swadeshi spirit underlying it. It is the most tolerant because it is non-proselytising, and it is as capable of expansion today as it has been found to be in the past.[19] ... By reason of the swadeshi spirit, a Hindu refuses to change his religion not necessarily because he considers it to be the best, but because he knows that he can complement it by introducing reforms.[20]

Although this valorization of conservatism, with its panacea of internal reform, was meant to be 'true of other great faiths of the world', Gandhi also added the rider: 'only it is held that it is specially so in the case of Hinduism'. Held by whom? We are not told. Nor is it important. What is important is that, while in various ways establishing the equality of all religions, deep down he believed Hinduism to be special. Equally importantly, what made it special was its non-proselytizing, and *therefore*

---

[17] In true Gandhian pursuit of an ideal, the missionaries were, however, reminded: 'And as we do not abandon our pursuit after the millennium because we do not expect quite to reach it within our time, so may we not abandon swadeshi even though it may not be fully attained for generations to come.' Ibid. vol. xiii, 1964, p. 219.

[18] Extending the criterion to other realms, Gandhi observed: 'In the domain of politics, I should make use of the indigenous institutions and serve them by curing them of their proved defects. In that of economics, I should use only things that are produced by my immediate neighbours and serve those industries by making them efficient and complete where they might be found wanting.' Ibid.

[19] Ibid. p. 220

[20] Here Gandhi considered it necessary to clarify about Hinduism: 'It has succeeded not in driving, as I think it has been erroneously held, but in absorbing Buddhism.' Ibid.

tolerant character. The causality seemed so self-evident as to block from his cognitive horizon the other side of the refusal to proselytize, viz., orthodox Hinduism's fierce refusal to take in outsiders, no matter how desirous of joining the Hindu fold. Like to most Hindus then and now, the sense of superiority and intolerance lurking behind the other refusal remained invisible to him.

Celebration of Hinduism's tolerance brought Gandhi, in his written speech, to the point he had been 'labouring to reach'. If there was 'any substance' in what he had said, Christian missionaries must drop 'the goal of proselytising' but continue 'their philanthropic work'. By way of confirming the universal validity of his analysis, he insisted that the course of action proposed by him would 'serve the spirit of Christianity better'.

Gandhi, then, invoked the experiential reality of conversion to expose, in three quick moves, the unethicality and futility of conversion. He said:

It will not be denied, I speak from experience, that many of the conversions are only so called. In some cases, the appeal has gone not to the heart but to the stomach. And in every case, a conversion leaves a sore behind it which, I venture to think, is avoidable.[21]

The shift here from 'many' in the first sentence, through 'some' in the second, to 'every' case in the third shows a predisposition against conversion. Insofar as a socio-culturally charged phenomenon like conversion can admit of unanimity of perception, not many would question Gandhi's 'experience'. If anything, the 'some' in his second sentence seems an understatement. There was, in all probability, a larger incidence of 'stomach' and other materially motivated conversions than could be suggested by 'some'. One may not share Gandhi's revulsion for such conversions. Nonetheless one has to appreciate Gandhi's sense of outrage against actions inspired by an instrumentalist view of religion. He had of moral necessity to oppugn all extraneous, in his words 'so-called', conversions.

But that moral necessity could not possibly justify the disapprobation of conversion on the undifferentiated ground of the resultant 'sores'. Many of the sores, all of which Gandhi condemned undiscriminatingly, had a tragic-heroic aspect. His own pursuit of truth having exposed him to isolation, persecution and separation from beloved ones, he should have valued the sores caused by one's uncompromising obedience to conscience. In any case, he knew that 'not many will invoke suffering

[21] Ibid.

from an impure motive'.[22] That he still lumped together all the 'sores' as 'avoidable' suggests a deep predilection against conversion.

History—life—is dense with sores of the tragic-heroic stamp. Because Gandhi's aversion to conversion was primarily a function of his experience of Christian missionaries and converts to Christianity in colonial India,[23] we may recall some of the illustrious converts to Christianity who willy-nilly invited sores upon themselves and their loved ones. Beginning in the 1830s with the likes of Mohesh Chandra Ghosh and Krishna Mohan Banerji in Bengal, Dhanjibhai Naoroji and Narayan Sheshadri in western India, and P. Rajahgopaul in the south—all pioneer converts to Christianity from among educated middle-class Indians—and moving on to subsequent generations of similar converts—Lal Behari De, Nilkantha Shastri Nehemiah Goreh, Baba Padmanji, Raghunath Navalkar, Pandita Ramabai, and Narayan Vaman Tilak—all had to suffer the dreaded punishment of excommunication and severance of intimate family and affective ties. Their poignant saga bears witness to the converts' heroic adherence to conviction. Gandhi, the man of truth, who only lamented those sores could as well have rejoiced in them.

He then proceeded to seal the futility of conversion, again on the strength of experience, with the argument that 'a new birth'—which is what conversion ideally means—'is perfectly possible in every one of the great faiths'. In presenting it as the ideal mode of conversion, Gandhi was making a bold attempt to take to its logical limit the idea of reform within every religion. Having made the leap, he, however, felt uncertain about confining conversion within one's faith. 'I know,' he admitted disarmingly, 'I am now treading upon thin ice.' Uncertainty about extending the argument, though, did not mean relenting on the issue of conversion. Instead, in yet another bold move, he sought to undermine the familiar Christian justification for proselytization. 'May it not be,' he proposed, 'that the "Go Ye unto All the World" message has been somewhat narrowly interpreted and the spirit of it missed?'

Despite his diffidence, Gandhi's was a fairly forthright and confident address to the Missionary Conference. Still, the painstakingly drafted text betrays internal irreconcilabilities which escaped its author's notice

---

[22] Raghavan Iyer, ed., op. cit., vol. I, p. 327.

[23] Barring a brief phase, when he admitted that the Christian missionaries had done some good to India, Gandhi took a progressively dim view of their presence. He would now maintain that if they did any good, it accrued in spite of them. This view was widely broadcast in the mid-1920s when he serialized his autobiography, *My Experiments With Truth.*

and reflects the tension between his aversion for and acceptance of conversion.

The address gets ensnared into an interlocked dual trap, following inadequate apprehension of two sets of difficulties. First, there were difficulties of a general nature caused by the extension of the concept of swadeshi to the religious realm. Gandhi's text assumed the validity of the extension, and treated swadeshi in religion as little different from swadeshi in politics and economics. Then, compounding the general difficulties, were the specific difficulties of defining a religious swadeshi for the multi-religious Indian scene, which was the universe chosen by Gandhi to demonstrate the universal validity of his idea.

Gandhi defined swadeshi, in keeping with his seed-text, the *Hind Swaraj*, as 'the use and service of our immediate surroundings to the exclusion of the more remote'. Small scale—*immediate* surroundings—being the defining feature of swadeshi, *prima facie* the incongruity of locating it within something so vast as Hinduism should have struck Gandhi. It did not. Obviously, and unexceptionably, a homogenized pan-Indian Hinduism appeared to him as the locus of religious swadeshi in India.

Scale apart, the search for religious swadeshi among the multi-religious Indian population—as well in Gandhi's time as now—must yield not one but numerous contiguous, overlapping, even shifting, immediate religious surroundings. These would comprise particular forms or/and permutations of, besides Hinduism, Islam and Christianity and other faiths. Gandhi's inability to conceive for India a multi-centred religious swadeshi indicates the powerful hold of a particular cultural geography, one that inclined him to naturally view Hinduism as its sole core.

Gandhi's, however, was a complex experiential universe. The Bible, too, existed in it 'as part of my scriptures', prompting the assertion before the missionaries:

The spirit of the Sermon on the Mount competes *almost* on equal terms with the *Bhagvad Gita* for the domination of my heart. I yield to no Christian in the strength of devotion with which I sing, 'Lead, kindly Light' and several other inspired hymns of a similar nature.[24] (Italics added.)

One may be inclined to interpret Gandhi's 'almost' as an admission that, in the final analysis, the Sermon on the Mount was, indeed, for him not equal to the Bhagvad Gita.[25] Indeed, it could not have been equal, given

---

[24] *The Collected Works of Mahatma Gandhi*, vol. xiii, p. 220.

[25] Cf. 'I find a solace in the *Bhagvad Gita* and Upanishads that I miss even in the Sermon on the Mount.' Address to missionaries at the Calcutta YMCA, 28 July 1925. Ibid. vol. xxvii, 1968, p. 435.

the hold of that cultural geography. The just-less-than-equal status of the Sermon on the Mount, as a Christian text, points to something deeper and larger. At an abstract plane, physical proximity and distance were for Gandhi irrelevant to what was experienced as immediate and remote in religion. Concretely, in the Indian context, only the autochthonous Hinduism formed the immediate. But there was no problem about accepting Buddhism as the religion of Tibet, China, Japan, Burma or Sri Lanka. Though he would deny between these adopting countries and Buddhism the kind of organic relationship that India had with Buddhism.[26] (Rather than propose a theory of the ultimate alienness of a religion outside the region of its birth, this stresses a special relationship between Buddhism and India.)

If, then, the objectively remote could be proximate to the spirit, the reverse could also be true. The objectively proximate could be spiritually remote. Also, what was true of individual human beings could hold for their collectivities as well. Hence the phenomenon, confirmed for Gandhi by 'the frightful outrage' of the ongoing war in 1916, that the message of 'Jesus of Nazareth, the Son of Peace' had been 'little understood in Europe'. The logic of this reversal led him to envision the possibility that the East might be obliged to teach Europe true Christianity.[27] That would be 'a new birth, a change of heart'. A change of heart brought about in European Christianity by non-Christian East.

Gandhi, thus, extended the idea of swadeshi to religion and offered an overly narrow version of it for India. At the same time, he problematized radically the notion of immediate surroundings—and therefore of swadeshi—in religion. After discovering in Hinduism a stable centre for religious swadeshi in India, he decentred, and rendered volatile, the very notion of swadeshi in the domain of religion. He did not detect the splintering within his text. Rather, to the extent he was conscious of the interplay of different forces—like the Sermon on the Mount and the *Bhagvad Gita* competing to dominate his heart—he felt he had perfectly reconciled them.

This reconciliation came about through a conservatism that—as postulated in religious swadeshi—posited an essential difference between

[26] This may seem a strange claim. But Gandhi had his own interpretation which rested on two premises. One, that 'Buddha never rejected Hinduism, but he broadened its base'. Two, that Hinduism assimilated Buddhism so well that 'what Hinduism did not assimilate of what passes as Buddhism today was not an essential part of Buddha's life and his teaching'. Speech in reply to Buddhists' address in Colombo, 15 November 1927. vol. xxxv, p. 245.

[27] Ibid. vol. xiii, pp. 220–21.

the indigenous and the alien only to negate it for all practical purposes. Hence a conception of internal reform in which even absorbing an alien faith wholesale only meant self-realization for the devouring faith. This, clearly, is an overdrawn picture of swadeshi in the domain of religion. But it serves to show how the text of the address had got out of its author's control.

There is little in the address to explain why it interdicts inter-religious conversion while permitting the incorporation of elements of another religion to the point of wholly absorbing it. But, contrary to its explicit intentions, it carries a powerful argument for conversion from one religion to another. If what is objectively remote can be spiritually proximate, and vice-versa, a new birth need not be confined within one's ancestral religion. It should be available, within a particular fold, even to those not born in it. If the East can bring true Christianity to Europe, it can as well bring itself to true Christianity.

It is surprising that Gandhi's critical faculty should have been so dodged in this text. Maybe he was too preoccupied with fashioning for his favourite swadeshi a neat and comprehensive schema to worry about what he might otherwise have detected as inconsistencies in his argument. Still, he remains free from narrowness of spirit. His heart, deeply attached to Hinduism, also reaches out to the Sermon on the Mount. Later on, however, he would show greater awareness of the implications of his own position. Though he would do it his way, not worrying about what others thought of him. Prompted by the deepest in him, he would not mind taking positions about which he could at best say, as he once did about his ideas on labour: 'It is a somewhat embarrassing position, I know,—but to others, not to me.'[28]

Gandhi saw nothing embarrassing about his avowed, often impassioned, resistance to conversion. It remained integral to his understanding of religion. But, while he found reasons to be confirmed in the resistance, which he kept refining, he also fashioned an acceptable mode of conversion.

Primarily, as in the somewhat simplistic statement of 1916, the resistance was grounded in the truth of all religions. With growing reflection on the mediatorial effect of human fallibility, as we earlier glimpsed in Gandhi's reply to Mott, the central idea of the truth of all religions began to be relativized as the imperfection of all religions. In a passage spanning the refinement in his position since 1916, Gandhi told yet another gathering of missionaries fifteen years later:

[28] Ibid. vol. xxxv, p. 255.

I believe that the great religions of the world are more or less true and that they have descended to us from God. Having come to us, however, through human media, they have become adulterated. Holding this belief, I hold also that no religion is absolutely perfect. In the bosom of God there is nothing imperfect, but immediately it comes through a human medium, it constantly suffers change and deterioration. The seeker after truth must humbly recognize this possibility.[29]

The inadvertent use of 'possibility' apart, Gandhi has in mind the inexorable law that no religion can ever be perfect. There is, as he would say six years later, 'no such thing as one true religion, every other being false'. They are, all of them without exception, 'equally perfect or more or less perfect'. [30] He would, with regard to this law, make no distinction between what he habitually described as the 'great religions' and those supposed to be primitive or savage. There was, 'from a spiritual stand- point', no reason to feel 'superior to the so-called savage'. In any case, spiritual superiority was 'a dangerous thing to feel'. One could only feel the truth of one's belief for oneself, not for the whole world.[31]

If all religions were only 'true more or less' and 'necessarily imper- fect' and none could claim 'spiritual superiority' over the others, no one could justifiably ask others to leave their own imperfect religion for another that, too, was imperfect. This was a profound case against 'the conversion of one person by another'—though it did not damage the case for voluntary conversion. Religion being a matter between every individual and their God, one could still feel personally inclined towards one imperfect religion rather than another, without having to tender a public account for the choice.

There was more to Gandhi's case against conversion by human agency. The distortion necessarily caused by human fallibility in the reception of God's truth was aggravated by its transmission through the imperfect medium of language. Gandhi suggested something of this in his 1931 address to the missionaries in London. He said:

I have found that the progress of truth is impeded by the spoken word which is the limitation of thought, for no man has been able to give the fullest expression in words to thought. The very nature of thought is limitless and boundless.[32]

[29] Gandhi's speech at a conference of the Missionary Societies in Great Britain and Ireland, 8 Oct. 1931, ibid. vol. xlviii, p. 121.

[30] Ibid., p. 397.

[31] Gandhi's response, in Young India of 22 March 1928, to a letter from F.W. Ireland of the Cambridge Mission. Ibid. vol. xxxvi, 1970, pp. 136–7.

[32] Ibid. vol. xlviii, p. 121.

Compared to the way it was formulated here as a general cognitive problem,[33] Gandhi's was a more radical difficulty about the function of words in the religious-spiritual realm. Words there were not simply inadequate. They were futile. Religion was 'no matter for words'. It lay beyond speech. The 'deepest spiritual truths' were 'always unutterable'. Silence alone was the way.[34]

For all its sophistication, Gandhi's insight about language and silence was, like most of his ideas, no mere abstract formulation. He had received intimations of it in reflections on the life around, and he had to realize its potential in his own life. Already in South Africa he had discovered 'the wonderful efficacy of silence'. He would recall later his visit to a Trappist monastery there. Enquiring about the inmates' vow of silence, he was told by a Father: 'We are frail human beings. We do not know very often what we say. If we want to listen to the still small voice that is always speaking within us, it will not be heard if we continually speak.'[35] The lesson resonated in his heart: 'a seeker after truth has to be silent'. His weekly day of silence, observed in the midst of a ceaseless public life, shows how acutely he wished to be alone with himself and his God. Further reflective of that acuteness is his poignant lament that his silence was but 'a fraud', 'interrupted' as it was by writing of notes and carrying on conversation through them.[36]

Realization of his own inadequacies only deepened Gandhi's faith in silence. He often illustrated the working of silence by likening it to a rose which sends out its 'fragrance without the intervention of a medium'. The truth received in the depths of one's inner experience, being by 'its very nature self-propelling', radiates itself through silence.[37] The phrase 'self-propelling' may in this context sound mystical, even obscurantist. Not that there is anything wrong with the mystical in relation to religion, but the point Gandhi is making is experiential, simple and profound. He

[33] Gandhi often made this point in a general context. But it seems that he used it primarily with regard to religious and spiritual matters. Gandhi uses as interchangeable terms like religious, spiritual, and God's matters.

[34]Ibid. vol. xl, p.60. Cf. the Grand Inquisitor's confrontation with Christ, who utters not a word, in Dostoyevsky's *The Brothers Karamazov*.

[35]*The Collected Works of Mahatma Gandhi*, vol. xxvii, pp. 437–38.

[36] When Mott, in November 1936, described Gandhi's Monday silence as 'the greatest thing' he had done, the latter replied: 'It is not the greatest thing I have done, but it certainly means a great thing to me. I am now taking silence almost every day. If I could impose on myself silence for more days in the week than one I should love it. In Yervada Jail I once observed a 15 days' silence. I was in the seventh heaven during that period.' Ibid. vol. lxiv, pp. 40-1.

[37] Interview to Mott in 1929, ibid. vol. xl, p. 60.

is positing truth lived against truth professed.[38] The power of Gandhi's position flashes across his response to Mott's reservations about the unutterability of spiritual truths. The latter's subdued remonstrance— 'But even God sometimes speaks through His prophets'—elicited the quick reply, 'Yes, but the prophets speak not through the tongue but through their lives.'[39]

This links up with what is perhaps Gandhi's most balanced statement on the question of conversion. It came at the Colombo YMCA in 1927 (not coincidentally, most of his major pronouncements on the subject, barring those dealing primarily with *shuddhi,* were made in the presence of Christians): '... we do not need to proselytize or do *shuddhi* or *tabligh* through our speech or writing. We can do it really with our lives.'[40] 'Faith,' he remarked on another occasion, 'does not admit of telling. It has to be lived and then it becomes self-propagating.'[41]

Though Gandhi put it simply, proselytizing with one's life was no simple matter. He would not have anyone expressly use their life's example to convert others. A life of truth was an end in itself. Employing it as a means for proselytization introduced an extraneous motivation and vitiated the pursuit of truth. Hence the injunction against even

---

[38] One may, however, feel sceptical about the sharp distinction between lived truth and professed truth. There may also be the power of the words of one who has lived a life of truth. This may be seen in Gandhi's own reference to his work in South Africa. Though rarely, Gandhi himself invoked his known commitment to truth to vouch for the veracity of what he said. After telling the missionaries that a Christian had little need to speak, he added: 'May I cite my own case? Speeches were *the least part* of my work in South Africa. Most of the 16,000 people who rose like one man and joined me had not even seen me, much less heard me speak.' (Italics added.) Ibid. vol. xxxiv, p. 262. Even if the least, speeches did form part of his work. However marginally, in his own reckoning, words did add to the efficacy of his life.

[39] Ibid. vol xl, p. 60. It must, however, be admitted that Gandhi could overstrain his impeccable formulation regarding silence and faith. For example, to the perfectly valid question—'But may not one in all humility say, "I know that my life falls far short of the ideal; let me explain the ideal I stand for"?'—Gandhi replied: 'No. You bid good bye to humility the moment you say that life is not adequate and that you must supplement it by speech.' Ibid. vol. lxiv, p. 100. This defence of preacher's need for words was made in December 1936. A month earlier, Mott had justified the need for words of one seeking light. Recalling his Cambridge days as a non-believer, Mott described how the air was cleared for him by J.E.K. Studd: 'His life and splendid example alone would not have answered my question and met my deepest need; but I listened to him and was converted.' Gandhi ignored this completely. Ibid. p. 37. In a similar context, however, he had said five years earlier: 'Argument has never convinced any man, but, on the contrary, conviction precedes argument.' Raghavan Iyer, ed., op. cit., vol. I, p. 327.

[40] *The Collected Works of Mahatma Gandhi,* vol. xxxv, p. 249.

[41] Raghavan Iyer, ed., op. cit., vol. I, p. 26.

secretly praying, let alone actively working, for the conversion of others. Only involuntarily, in the manner of a rose, could one's life pave the way for another's conversion. In no way would Gandhi countenance a conversion consciously inspired by someone other than the proselyte. A true conversion had to be entirely voluntary. Cases of such 'real honest conversion', Gandhi believed, were 'quite possible'.[42]

This was an unexceptionable position. It also had a Christian provenance. 'A true Christian has little need to speak,' he exhorted the missionaries tersely.[43] Gandhi, one would imagine, must have hoped to convince his Christian addressees the better by reiterating this exhortation. Ironically, so at least he complained to Mott, he found himself, in this matter, 'up against a solid wall of Christian opinion'.[44] Though Mott protested feebly that a growing school of Christian thought favoured individuals discovering 'the deepest truths of life' for themselves, Gandhi's complaint was justified. This is illustrated by a protracted argument he was engaged in with the Federation of International Fellowships.

It began in August 1935 against the background of what Gandhi described as 'the so-called mass conversion of a village predominantly or wholly composed of Harijans'. A.A. Paul of the Federation of International Fellowships, who was having a discussion on these conversions with Gandhi, asked the latter to publicly define his position on conversion. Gandhi, in turn, asked the Federation to state their own position, and promised to respond to it. Nine carefully prepared propositions were passed on to him a month later. Although the propositions were 'framed from the Christian point of view', the Federation expected them to 'apply equally well to other Missionary Religions which are engaged in conversion programme'. The purpose of the discussion, Gandhi immediately realized, was to test the validity of mass conversion. Christianity's self-definition as a missionary religion was at stake. And the argument was with one who had definitively rejected mass conversion.

The nine propositions did nothing to make him reconsider that rejection. There was nothing in them, he remarked after he had read the propositions 'several times', to justify mass conversion. They could 'be applied only to individual contacts, never to the mass of mankind'. That

[42]Ibid., p. 537.

[43] He told them on 29 July 1927: 'A true Christian has little need to speak. He goes about his Father's business.' *The Collected Works of Mahatma Gandhi*, vol. xxxiv, p. 262.

[44] Mott said: 'Oh, no, even among Christians there is a school of thought—and it is growing—which holds that the authoritarian method should not be employed but that each individual should be left to discover the deepest truths of life for himself.' Ibid. vol. xl, p. 60.

initial clarification done, he proceeded to respond to the specific propositions.

The very first proposition showed how tantalizingly close Gandhi came to a broadly orthodox Christian definition of conversion. 'Conversion,' it said, 'is a change of heart from sin to God. It is the work of God. Sin is separation from God.' Gandhi could not have agreed more. But the agreement only served to open a vast exegetical chasm. He interpreted the proposition in a way that would make Christianity practically a non-proselytizing religion. He did that from within Christianity, deferentially adhering to what he believed to be its essence, as he stated:

If conversion is the work of God, why should that work be taken away from Him? And who is man to take away anything from God? He may become a humble instrument in the hands of God. Even so he cannot be a judge of men's hearts. 'Man, know thyself' must have been wrung out of a desperate heart. And if we know so little of ourselves, how much less must we know of our neighbours and remote strangers who may differ from us in a multitude of things, some of which are of the highest moment?

The second proposition dealt with salvation. Taking the dominant orthodox Christian view that there could be no salvation except through Jesus, it said: 'The Christian believes that Jesus is the fulfilment of God's revelation to mankind, that He is our Saviour from sin, that He alone can bring the sinner to God and thus enable him to live.' Having read the Bible with the eyes of a Christian—just as he had read other religious books from the viewpoint of their respective followers—Gandhi assumed the truth of this proposition.[45] For him it was just right that generations upon generations of Christians should have imbibed the belief contained in the proposition, without having felt called upon to test its truth. Beliefs relating to the mysteries of religion were best left untested. But, he warned, it would be 'a dangerous thing' to present the

[45] Talking to R.R. Keithahn on 5 March 1937, Gandhi said: 'If you read the Koran, you must read it with the eye of the Muslim; if you read the Bible, you must read it with the eye of the Christian; if you read the *Gita*, you must read it with the eye of a Hindu. Where is the use of scanning details and then holding up a religion to ridicule? Take the very first chapter of *Genesis* or of *Matthew*. We read a long pedigree and then at the end we are told that Jesus was born of a virgin. You come up against a blind wall. But I must read it all with the eye of a Christian.' Ibid. vol. lxiv, p. 420. In another pithy statement around the same time, he remarked about his attitude towards religious texts: 'I don't approach them with a critical mind.' Ibid. p. 75. In keeping with this attitude, he declared: 'Religious controversy serves no purpose.' Ibid. vol.xxvii, p. 204. Also: 'Religion is a matter of feeling or the heart and, therefore, not a matter for argument, and I would hold everybody's feeling as dear as my own, because I expect him to do so with reference to my feeling.' Raghavan Iyer, ed., op. cit., vol. I, p. 541.

Christian belief about salvation to those who had received different religious beliefs. It was for the adherents of every faith to realize that, for aught they knew, the untested beliefs of other religions might be as true as theirs. Giving the argument his favourite turn, Gandhi added: 'It is highly likely that mine may be good enough for me and his for him.'

The third proposition carried forward the logic of the second. Because Jesus alone could bring the sinner to God, it was the 'privilege and duty' of every Christian 'to speak about Jesus and proclaim the free offer which He came on earth to make'. In that this proposition, too, rested on an untested belief, Gandhi reiterated the point about the internality of beliefs: 'They work well enough among people living in the traditional faith. They will repel those who have been brought up to believe something else.'

The first three propositions were meant to provide the justification for conversion. Gandhi accepted the principles formulated therein. But he found nothing in them to justify conversion. He, consequently, dismissed the next five propositions, which dealt with the missionaries' conduct among prospective proselytes. His logic was simple: 'The start being wrong, all that follows must be necessarily so.' He pronounced the five propositions, laying down conditions for testing the sincerity of both the proselyte and the proselytizer, [46] 'to be almost impossible of application in practice':

Thus how is the Christian to sound the sincerity of the conviction of his hearers? By a show of hands? By personal conversation? By a temporary trial? Any test that can be conceived will fail even to be reasonably conclusive. No one but God knows a man's heart. Is the Christian so sure of his being so right in body, mind and soul as to feel comfortably 'right in accepting as his duty the care of the sincere convert—body, soul and mind'?

This brought Gandhi to the last proposition which, unlike the preceding ones, moved away from abstract formulation of principles to demand: 'It shall not be maintained against the Christian that he is using material inducements, when certain facts in Hindu social theory, out of his control, are in themselves an inducement to the Harijans.' Here, at the very end, was an attempt to repel the charge that the missionaries were luring the poor and helpless untouchables into the Church. Gandhi, who

[46] Especially propositions 5 and 6: 'The Christian shall do all in his power to sound the sincerity of conviction in all such cases and shall point out, as he can, the consequences of such a step, stressing the duty a man owes to his family.' 'The Christian shall do everything in his power to prevent any motives of self-seeking on his part and of material considerations on the part of the convert.' *The Collected Works of Mahatma Gandhi*, vol. lxi, 1975, p. 455.

had begun by specifying the actual circumstances of the exchange, could at this point have countered the brave propositions with the actual proselytization practice of the generality of Christian missionaries.[47] But he chose to remain on the high plane of principles, and returned once again to the cardinal formulation about conversion as change of heart from sin to God. Remarking that this formulation had not 'ceased to puzzle the brains of some of the most intellectual and philosophical persons even in the present generation', he probed:

Who knows the nature of original sin? What is the meaning of separation from God? What are the signs of him who is united to God? Are all who dare to preach the message of Jesus the Christ sure of their union with God? If they are not, who will test the Harijans' knowledge of these deep things?[48]

The questions actually related to the larger Gandhian position on language, silence, and conversion through life's example. The inadequacy of language for comprehending religious truths was matched by the difficulty of communicating them through the same means. Never absent, the difficulty was insurmountable in the case of ignorant masses of people, like the Harijans in India. 'Would you, Dr Mott, preach the Gospel to a cow?'[49] The fierceness of the question, which would ordinarily not break through Gandhi's defences, indicates the force of his feelings. He, however, regained his restraint to put across the argument pithily: 'You can only preach through your life.'[50] The scramble for

[47] Indirectly, however, something of this came out in Gandhi's comment: 'The last proposition–the crown of all the preceding ones–takes one's breath away. For it makes it clear that the other eight are to be applied in all their fulness to the poor Harijans.' Ibid. p. 457.

[48] For the propositions and Gandhi's response, see ibid., pp. 454–8.

[49] Gandhi's sequel to this question, though not addressed to Mott, was: '... if they wanted to convert Harijans had they not better begin to convert me?' Ibid. vol. lxiv, p. 73. If the Harijans as a mass, he argued, gave up Hinduism, they would do so because of the 'disabilities which brand them as lepers of Hindu society'. Nonetheless, they, a majority of them, did not know 'what change of religion can mean.' Ibid. vol. lxii, p. 281.

[50] Gandhi himself seems to have been taken aback by the fierceness of the outburst. The uncharacteristic 'well' with which he began the next sentence, as if seeking to soften the blow with a clarification, would suggest this. 'Well,' he said, 'some of the untouchables are worse than cows in understanding. I mean they can no more distinguish between the relative merits of Islam and Hinduism and Christianity than a cow.' Ibid. vol. lxiv, p. 37. The outburst can be explained in terms of Ambedkar's threat to leave Hinduism along with millions of other untouchables, and the readiness of Christian missionaries to angle for those prospective converts. 'I cannot help saying,' he told Mott, 'that the activities of the missionaries in this connection have hurt me. They with the Mussalmans and the Sikhs came forward as soon as Dr Ambedkar threw the bombshell ... and then ensued a rivalry between these organizations....' Ibid., p. 35. Even while leaving the missionaries to decide, in

converts, as reflected in the mass conversion of Harijans, was 'a blasphemy against God and the self'.[51]

The ultimate unknowability of the springs of genuine conversion apart, Gandhi had serious worldly reasons as well for being wary of conversion. Prominent among these was the damage done to the traditional fabric of a given society. Conversion, he was convinced, caused denationalization and cultural alienation. Though the conviction related to conversion in general, it rested almost entirely on what he believed to have been the effect of conversion to Christianity in his own time. In one of his many typical statements on the subject which, significantly, was addressed to an audience of Christian Indians, he said on 4 August 1925:

As I wander about throughout the length and breadth of India, I see many Christian Indians almost ashamed of their birth, certainly of their ancestral religion, and of their ancestral dress. The aping of Europeans on the part of Anglo-Indians is bad enough, but the aping of them by Indian converts is a violence done to their country and, shall I say, even to their new religion.... Conversion must not mean denationalization.... Is it not truly deplorable that many Christian Indians discard their own mother tongue, bring up their children only to speak in English?[52]

He formed these impressions as a schoolboy in Rajkot, where he first experienced what he then used to call 'beef and beer-bottle Christianity'.[53] Later on, he did occasionally describe this as his 'prejudice against Christianity'. But, in a classic confirmation of first impressions being also the last,[54] his sense of the impact of Christianity remained substantially unmodified, and reinforced his resistance to conversion.

A rather weird, but telling example occurred during the serialization of Gandhi's *Story* of his experiments with truth. When its tenth chapter appeared, describing what Gandhi remembered of missionary activities in Rajkot, Rev. H.R. Scott immediately protested to Gandhi:

---

the light of their conscience, if such proselytization was consistent with their mission, he did not miss to 'simply' state his 'belief that what the missionaries are doing today does not show spirituality'. Ibid., p. 38

[51] Speech to women missionaries, 6 June 1925, ibid. vol. xxvii, p. 205.

[52] Ibid. vol. xxviii, 1968, pp. 91–2.

[53] Interview to Dr Crane, 25 February 1937, ibid. vol. lxiv, p. 397.

[54] Indeed, despite occasional admission of prejudice, Gandhi insisted that his first impressions had not framed, but been confirmed by, his later impressions. Cf. the following in his letter of 16 February 1926 to Rev. H.R. Scott: 'I wish to add that my later experience does not improve the first experience. I have met thousands of Christian Indians. Many of them, if not a majority, I have found to be drinking and eating meat and wearing European clothes. When I have discussed these things with them, they have at least defended their meat eating and their European dress.' Ibid. vol. xxx, 1968, p. 19.

I was the only missionary in Rajkot during those years (from 1883 to 1897).... I certainly never preached 'at a corner near the High School' ... and certainly never poured abuse on Hindus and their gods.... During my time in Rajkot I baptised a number of Brahmins and Jain sadhus. They certainly had not to 'eat beef and drink liquor', either at their baptism or at any other time.

Gandhi's response to Scott's complete repudiation was an unambiguous reiteration: 'Though the preaching took place over forty years ago the painful memory of it is still vivid before me.' Then, in the space of one long sentence, he accepted 'Mr Scott's repudiation' and also added: '...I know very few [Christian Indians] who have scruples about eating beef or other flesh meats and drinking intoxicating liquors.' He admitted to a 'growing liberal spirit' among Christians and Christian missionaries, but also asserted his 'conviction that much still remains to be done in that direction'.[55]

As the utterance of a man for whom Truth was God, Gandhi's response to Scott's repudiation raises fascinating ethico-cognitive issues. Especially for those, like me, who cannot approach Gandhi, the man of truth, except from the vantage point of faith, even if that faith subsequently leads on to suspicion and criticism. Ostensibly, Gandhi's response to Scott is strangely contradictory and solecistic. He did not, obviously, draft it with the care it deserved. For once, his usual clarity of perception and articulation failed him. Still, in its substance his response holds good. Scott's testimony, it is true, significantly changed certain details in a specific instance. But it did not belie the overall indictment against the missionary enterprise in India. Hence the validity of Gandhi's acceptance of Scott's repudiation without repudiating his own position.[56] So self-evident, it seems, was in his mind the truth of his recall that he believed his response to Scott to ipso facto carry the same stamp of truth.

That was made possible by a certain want of criticality—something resembling blindness—vis-à-vis the presence of the Christian missionary. Gandhi may have suspected in himself a certain 'prejudice against Christianity'. But he had little idea of how it coloured his attitude towards conversion. To have affected one deeply influenced by Christianity and having Christians for friends and collaborators, the prejudice must have been very subtle. It must have lain deep and functioned imperceptibly, in spite of what he lived by.

[55] 'A Repudiation', *Young India*, 4 March 1926, ibid., pp. 70–1.

[56] I must, however, concede the admissibility of a more critical stance, and can imagine how exasperated Scott must have felt by Gandhi's response. I wish to be able some day to see the Scott papers at the British Library.

There was, perhaps, nothing in Gandhi's critique of Indian Christians and Christian missionaries that had, with equal or greater power, not been voiced by the more aware among the Indian converts to Christianity, some of whom have been named above. Since decades before Gandhi was born, they had warned, and worked against, the deculturation and denationalization that came inexorably in the wake of Christianity. They were clear that what they had renounced was their religion and not their culture. They had, in political and other fields, been pioneers of the newly emerging national consciousness. Indeed, their peculiar predicament as 'babes in faith', the supposition that they would under their white superiors serve an indefinite religious tutelage, had awakened in them the desire for ecclesiastical swaraj. They had, consequently, begun to work towards a national Church of India, one untrammelled by the sectarian, doctrinal, and organizational divisions of the parent churches which had little relevance to the cultural and spiritual requirements of Indian Christians.

They were also among the first to notice, and deplore, the deleterious connection—which Gandhi never tired of stressing[57]—between Christianity and imperialism. In an address that he appropriately entitled 'Searchings of Heart', Rev. Lal Behari Day had told a gathering of European missionaries:

I have sometimes thought it a circumstance prejudicial to the interests of Christianity in this country, that our Missionaries—at least, most of them— should belong to the very nation that has conquered us. English missionaries, who are but men, possessing like passions with other men, should, therefore, as members of a conquering race, guard themselves against the sense of superiority, that arrogance, if that be not too harsh a word to use, which a conquering race almost inevitably displays ...

Day was speaking in Calcutta, the seat of imperial power, and on 6 December 1858, in the immediate aftermath of 1857. His courage in speaking thus at that delicate juncture lent an extra edge to words like these:[58]

It is a fact ... that the relation subsisting between Missionaries and native Christians is not of a very satisfactory character.... This is a matter of the deepest regret. I have often thought, that this may be, for aught I know to the contrary,

---

[57] Like the following in his 28 July 1925 speech at the Calcutta YMCA: 'Christian missionaries come to India under the shadow, or, if you like, under the protection of a temporal power, and it creates an impassable bar.' Ibid. vol. xxvii, 438.

[58] The Rev. Lal Behari De, *Searchings of Heart in Connection with Missions in Bengal,* Serampore, 1858, pp. 9, 11.

one of the reasons why Missions in this country have not been so successful as they might otherwise have been.

Day claimed that what he had said publicly, perhaps for the first time, had long been privately admitted. This was confirmed seven years later by Rev. K.M. Banerji who, as the senior-most convert, had until then had thirty-four years of first-hand experience of the things he was talking about. The occasion, once again, was important. Banerji chose a funeral sermon, delivered on the tragic death by drowning of the Bishop of Calcutta, to express a deep-seated anguish:

It is useless to deny what is now a matter of history that from the beginning of missions in this part of the country, there existed but little sympathy between missionaries and their converts owing principally to misunderstandings occasioned by the conflict of widely diversified races.[59]

Just one more excerpt to span, from Duff's first conversions in 1832 to the time Gandhi emerged in Indian politics, the development of self-reliance among Indian Christians. Announcing what subject India needed after the termination of the first great war, Surendra Kumar Datta refused to believe 'for one moment' that her destinies lay in London. Even as Gandhi was shedding off his loyalism, and a year before he launched the Non-Cooperation Movement, Datta told Canon Tissington Tatlow:

... missionary and money are small matters as compared with the radical change of hearts we desire to see. Race hatred has become acute ... my belief is that the only solution lies in vesting authority in India .... This is true in all departments, whether in the State or in the Church. There will never be peace in India until Indians are masters in their own house and as such have authority to declare what type of foreigner they will use or refuse.[60]

Gandhi may not have known some of these details. But he appreciated the variegated contribution made by a whole galaxy of Indian Christians.

[59] *A Sermon Preached on Wednesday 10 October in St. Paul's Cathedral Calcutta Occasioned by the Sudden Death of Right Rev. Father in God George Edward Lynch Cotton D.D. Bishop of Calcutta and Metropolitan of India*, Calcutta, 1866, p. 14.

[60] Reflecting among Indian Christians similar intra-family political divisions as obtained among other communities, S.K. Datta'a aunt, Manorama, took a very different view of the political situation. She was critical of Gandhi and full of praise for the Punjab governor O'Dwyer. It may be noted that, true to the pattern common during the early years of the Congress, Manorama socialized with the top officials even as she enthusiastically reported the 1893 Lahore Congress in her diary, reserving her best praise for Surendranath Banerji's oratory. See Manorama's diary and Margarita Barns's manuscript history of the Datta family in *Datta Collection*, MSS Eur. F 178, India Office Library section of the British Library, London.

Speaking at the Calcutta YMCA, for example, he exhorted young Indian Christians to emulate the likes of Michael Madhusudan Dutt, Kali Charan Banerji, and Sushil Kumar Rudra, whose Christianity did not diminish 'their ardent love of mother tongue and national manners and modes of living'.[61] The exhortation, however, did not quite enable him to comprehend the significance of their efforts to work towards an autonomous and expanding Indian Christianity.

The idea of an indigenous Christianity in colonial India, as in so many contemporary Afro-Asian societies, had as its starting point the separation of Christianity from those who came to proselytize and stayed on to command. It sought to indigenize Christianity doctrinally as well as organizationally. Discussing the question of 'the independence of the Native Church in matters of doctrine and faith', 'A Hindustani' asserted in Lal Behari Day's *Bengal Magazine* in 1877: 'The Native Church derives its Christianity, not from the missionaries, but from the Bible.'[62]

Rather than appreciate, and highlight, the progressive growth of this idea among Indian Christians, Gandhi did the very opposite. Equating Christianity with the negative and exploitative aspects of its introduction under the colonial aegis—oblivious to the earlier centuries of Christian presence in India—he would not even distinguish the message of Christ from the lives of his followers. When Mott, wanting Gandhi's assessment of 'the contribution of Christianity to the national life of India' hopefully clarified that he meant 'the influence of Christ as apart from Christianity'—'a wide gulf separating the two at present'—Gandhi was unrelenting. 'Aye,' he exclaimed, and held forth:

There's the real rub. It is not possible to consider the teaching of a religious teacher apart from the lives of his followers. Unfortunately, Christianity in India has been inextricably mixed up for the last one hundred years with the British rule. It appears to us as synonymous with materialistic civilization and imperialistic exploitation by the stronger white races of the weaker races of the world.[63]

The tenability of linking the teachings of a religious leader with the lives of his followers can at least be debated. But it in no way squares with the logic Gandhi felt constrained to employ in critical times to salvage faith in his own fundamental tenets. For example, queried by faithfuls and sceptics alike, in the face of the violence that accompanied

---

[61] Lecture of 12 Aug. 1925, *The Collected Works of Mahatma Gandhi*, vol. xxviii, p. 57.

[62] *Bengal Magazine*, February 1877. Earlier in 1869, the year of Gandhi's birth, Day himself had delivered a lecture on the practicableness and desirability of a national Church.

[63] *Collected Works of Gandhi*, vol. xl, pp. 58–9.

the partition, about the truth of ahimsa, he cried hoarse that ahimsa could never be belied by the imperfection of its human instruments, including himself.[64]

Gandhi's image of Indian Christians as Europeanized and deracinated—a stereotype popular then as it is now—made him particularly alert and uncharitable about their outward appearance. He could be overwhelmed with joyous disbelief because a Kali Charan Banerji, not conforming to the stereotype, 'was dressed like an ordinary un-Europeanized Hindu Bengali', and his home 'was no different from an ordinary modern Hindu home'.[65] He could also recall, admiringly, how another of his exemplary Indian Christians, Principal Sushil Kumar Rudra, 'used often to express his grief that it was too late in life for him to change some of the unnecessary European habits to which he was brought up'.[66] True, dress and related modes of living, as his own sartorial and cognate transformation suggests, were for Gandhi more than matters of mere outward appearance. But, with regard to outward appearance, no Indian community was judged by him as harshly as the Christians.

Going by outward appearance, Rev. Krishna Mohan Banerji could have been matched only by W.C. Bonnerjee, the westernized Hindu barrister who became the first president of the Indian National Congress. As a leading figure in the emerging nationalist politics of the period, Banerji commanded a greater stature than Bonnerjee.[67] Besides, his pioneering doctrinal contribution to the making of an indigenous Christianity—as propounded in *The Arian Witness*—made him, in terms

[64] Written message of 15 June 1947 (that being Gandhi's day of silence), *Prarthana-Pravachan* (in Hindi), pp. 161–62.

[65] Here is Gandhi's account of the visit to Kali Charan Banerji whom, interestingly, he had been advised to meet for possible conversion to Christianity: 'Years ago I met the late Kali Charan Banerji. Had I not known before I went there that he was a Christian, I should certainly not have noticed from the outward appearance of his home that he was one. It was no different from an ordinary modern Hindu home, —simple and meagre in furniture. The great man was dressed like an ordinary un-Europeanized Hindu Bengali.' Though he notices at this point 'a marvellous change coming over Christian Indians', he laments that 'the process is too slow'. *The Collected Works of Mahatma Gandhi*, vol. xxviii, p. 92. The conversion dimension of the visit to Kali Charan in 1901 is described by Gandhi a quarter century later in his Calcutta YMCA speech in 1925. Ibid. xxvii, p. 435.

[66] Ibid.

[67] When the emerging educated middle classes in Bengal, chafing under the zamindar-dominated British Indian Association, founded, in quick succession, the Indian League and the Indian Association, K.M. Banerji was chosen to head them. But for his death in August 1885, it is tempting to speculate, he may as well have been asked to preside over the first Congress.

of nationalism and cultural rootedness, an even more significant presence than the un-Europeanized *Hindu*-looking Kali Charan Banerji. Gandhi seems to have missed the implications of Rev. Banerji's kind of westernization for assessing the nationalism of Indian Christians.

He seems to have had no such difficulty with the likes of Bonnerjee. Indeed, the eminent nationalist leader, Gopal Krishna Gokhale, whom he looked upon as his political guru, was in his outward appearance farther from Kali Charan and nearer to Krishna Mohan. Among the Parsis, he did not think any poorly of nationalists like Dadabhai Naoroji and Sir Pherozeshah Mehta on account of their westernized ways. Nor would he on that account pass an adverse verdict on the Hindus and the Parsis as communities.

The only 'answer' by way of 'self-defence' that Gandhi could imagine on behalf of Indian Christians did not relate to the coexistence of westernization and nationalism that they shared with other Indians. It was, instead, 'that many Hindus and even Mussalmans have become denationalized'. This was an answer that, given his sharp sense of right and wrong, could deserve not a moment's sympathy. So, he summarily dismissed the defence he had imagined for them: 'The *tu quoque* argument serves no useful purpose.' That done, he proceeded to reassure 'missionary friends and Christian Indians': 'I am writing not as a critic but as a friend who has enjoyed for the past thirty years the closest intimacy with hundreds of Christian Indians.'[68]

The man of truth—and brotherhood—could not have steered clear of what was invisible to him.[69] The Indian Christians he admired remained 'exceptional figures' who could not induce him to rethink his stereotype of their community. For Christianity, like Islam, his imagination could find no place in the Indian religious swadeshi.

Something similar marred his otherwise sublime exposition of principles with regard to conversion. Discursively he was, perhaps always, more than a match for the missionaries. There was often in their arguments a convenient slippage between high principles and mundane reality. In the typical example we discussed above, the first eight of the nine propositions stated abstract principles. Only the last one showed that the exercise was designed to defend mass conversions in a way that would avoid messy details. Gandhi, in that instance, was gracious

---

[68] *The Collected Works of Mahatma Gandhi*, vol. xxviii, p. 93.

[69] Intriguingly, Gandhi could appreciate the efforts of Chinese Christians to develop a Christianity that would counter the denationalizing tendencies associated with it. Ibid. vol. xxxv, pp. 249–50.

enough to stick to principles, which he enunciated with a rare subtlety born of intense introspection and reflection.

Faith in his own introspection and commitment to truth, however, also tended at times to blind him to the limits of some of his own insights. Falsity of conversion by human agency was one such insight. It carried about it an aura of spiritual invincibility. At any rate, Christians—with whom really the argument was on—could not assail the principle of the insight. But its application called for caution. What did human agency mean? In avoiding this question—a glaring omission—Gandhi managed to make the application of the insight practically limitless. He was possessed with an unexceptionable principle that, accepting conversion theoretically, made it in practice nugatory. Much more subtly, and for a diametrically opposite result, the same shift from the abstract to the concrete, as marked the nine propositions, was at work here.

As a Hindu familiar with the notion of *nimitta*, and struck by the nothingness of human beings in the presence of God, Gandhi should ordinarily have been alert to the Christian idea of divine grace, and to the tricky nature of human agency. What appeared as human agency could be divine instrumentality. Gandhi was, no doubt, right in seeing human agency at work in the proselytizing efforts of most Christian missionaries. However, at least some of them were inspired by the thought: 'Oh, what is man!' Nothing, for them, was accomplished by their might. Everything was done by the Spirit of the Lord. They could at best enlighten the mind of the prospective proselyte. But they had to ask the Lord to touch the heart. Which alone made conversion possible.[70]

Gandhi remained unquestioningly ensconced in his impressive enunciation of conversion by human agency with its valorization of silence and disinterested service. He also secured his position anecdotally, recounting past encounters in which people had come round to his point of view. A favourite story dated back to the South African years. One of his Christian friends, who had 'designs' on him, had introduced him to Rev. Murray with a view to effecting his conversion. The rest of the story was thus recounted by Gandhi to a group of women missionaries in 1925:[71]

We went out for a walk in the course of which Mr Murray cross-examined me by asking me a number of questions. When he had cross-examined me enough, he

---

[70] See *Memoir of the Rev. John James Weitbrecht of the C.M.S. Abridged from His Journals and Letters*, by His Widow. London, 1873, pp. 30, 68.

[71] *The Collected Works of Mahatma Gandhi*, vol. *xxvii*, pp.204–05.

told me: 'No, friend. I do not wish to convert you. Not only that, I will never try to convert anyone in future.' I was very much pleased.

Reporting Murray in the direct speech shows how vivid and accurate was for Gandhi the missionary's rejection of conversion. We do not have to doubt Gandhi's remembrance of what happened to wonder if Murray, too, remembered the incident exactly the way Gandhi did. We cannot decide in the absence of Murray's testimony. Still, it is not implausible that Gandhi imagined into the incident just that extra bit which would make it perfect for recall.

That his conscious concern for truth did not always guard him against crucial mnemonic shifts is illustrated by a discussion he had with Charles Frere Andrews in 1936. Gandhi held Andrews in such high esteem that he could tell the missionaries: 'Copy Charlie Andrews.'[72] Not least among the grounds for the esteem was Andrews's resolve not to proselytize. Gandhi imagined this to be opposition to conversion per se. Inversely, Andrews joined in the discussion with an underestimation of Gandhi's opposition to conversion.

The discussion having got off to an unpleasant start over the conversion of Harijans, Andrews switched over to what he called 'the fundamental position' to pose the question: 'What would you say to a man who after considerable thought and prayer said that he could not have his peace and salvation except by becoming a Christian?' For reasons we can appreciate at this stage in our enquiry, Andrews had confined the question to voluntary conversions in anticipation of a generally favourable reply, hoping that would give an agreeable turn to the discussion. He was in for a shock. Gandhi replied: 'I would say that if a non-Christian, say a Hindu, came to a Christian and made that statement, he should ask him to become a good Hindu rather find goodness in change of faith.'

This was a typical Gandhian position. But it had begged Andrews's question. He had to probe further and see where it led them. He had 'long ago' discarded the position that there was no salvation except through Christ. Still, he could not 'go the whole length' in what Gandhi had said. So he asked more pointedly: 'But supposing the Oxford Group Movement people changed the life of your son, and he felt like being converted, what would you say.' In a kind of *ignoratio elenchi,* rather than

---

[72] Ibid. p. 439. Gandhi's high regard for Andrews remained undiminished. Two years after this discussion, he remarked: 'It is better to allow our lives to speak for us than our words. C.F. Andrews never preaches. He is incessantly doing his work. He finds enough work and stays where he finds it and takes no credit for bearing the Cross. I have the honour to know hundreds of honest Christians, but I have never known one better than Andrews.' Ibid. vol. xxxiv, p. 262.

comment on the son's hypothetical decision to be converted, Gandhi reacted as if the question was about the missionaries' desire to convert. 'I would say,' he rehashed his earlier answer, 'that the Oxford Group may change the lives of as many as they like, but not their religion.' Then, mentioning a young Brahmin who had been inspired by Andrews's writings to embrace Christianity, Gandhi told Andrews: 'I said to him that you had never through your books asked Indians to take up the Bible and embrace Christianity, and that he had misread your book.'[73]

Not asking people to embrace Christianity was very different from asking them not to. Gandhi had forgotten the mysterious working of the rose.

Andrews, whom Gandhi had clearly misread, clarified: 'But I do say that if a person really needs a change of faith I should not stand in his way.' Ineffectually, for Gandhi shot back: 'But don't you see that you do not even give him a chance? You do not even cross-examine him.' And added self-righteously:

Supposing a Christian came to me and said he was captivated by a reading of the *Bhagvata* and so wanted to declare himself a Hindu, I should say to him: 'No. What the *Bhagvata* offers the Bible also offers. You have not yet made the attempt to find it out. Make the attempt and be a good Christian.'

Andrews saw the stalemate. 'I don't know,' he said resignedly, and attempted a last clarification:

If someone earnestly says that he will become a good Christian, I should say, 'You may become one,' though you know that I have in my own life strongly dissuaded ardent enthusiasts who came to me. I said to them, 'Certainly not on my account will you do anything of the kind.' But human nature does require a concrete faith.

The discussion ended, as it had to, with a last word from Gandhi. It was as unconvincing, messy, and unconnected to what was being said to him, as most of what he had said before.[74] If Gandhi, in the thick of a discussion with the man himself, could insist that Andrews's opposition to conversion went farther than it did, something similar may as well have affected his remembrance of the supposedly definitive rejection of proselytization by Rev. Murray.

Gandhi, obviously to the chagrin of a valued friend such as Andrews,

---

[73] Gandhi seems to have been unusually excitable during this discussion. After saying that the man had misread Andrews's book, he continued most offensively: 'unless of course your position is like that of the late Maulana Mahomed Ali's, viz., that a believing Mussalman, however bad his life, is better than a good Hindu.' Ibid. vol. lxiv, p. 19.

[74] For the discussion, ibid., pp. 18–20.

could get caught in a no-conversion tangle. But he could also author the profoundly moving response to the nine propositions. Similarly, under the immediate impact of Ambedkar's bombshell, he could favour the Harijans' freedom to leave Hinduism, wondering why more of them had not already availed of that freedom. Further, howsoever he may have reacted to his son's hypothetical conversion under the aegis of the Oxford Group Movement, when the son had earlier embraced Islam temporarily, Gandhi had issued a statement—'written with my pen dipped in my heart's blood'[75] —accepting true conversions: 'If his acceptance was from the heart and free from any worldly considerations, I should have no quarrel. For I believe Islam to be as true a religion as my own.' He had even claimed that Harilal, the apostate son, had known that he needed fear no resistance from the father because:

All my children have had the greatest freedom of thought and action. They have been taught to regard all religions with the same respect that they paid their own. Harilal knew that if he had told me that he had found the key to a right life and peace in Islam, I would have put no obstacle in his path.[76]

The premise that all religions are true sustained Gandhi's impassioned resistance to conversion. It also justified his acceptance of conversion. The paradox of Gandhi drawing from one truth diametrically different inferences may be seen as inconsistency. It makes greater sense, though, to locate the paradox in the potential of this particular truth to justify both resistance as well as acceptance of conversion.

Gandhi may have believed otherwise, but he does not appear to have resolved the issue of conversion in his own mind. Maybe, even as he kept speaking either way with conviction, he also felt the difficulty of being conclusive in the matter. This was 'not a matter,' he confessed, 'which admits of any conclusive argument especially from my side.'[77] This, we can see, applied forcefully to his interminable argument on the subject with himself.

Though the matter was never resolved, Gandhi's argument tended to be more often against than for conversion. The beauty of swadeshi reigned over his imagination. It lustred even more in the realm of religion. Freedom to incorporate other religions removed the very raison d'etre for renouncing one's own. It made the case against conversion so

[75] Gandhi said this to a Polish student three weeks after issuing the statement. Ibid. lxiii, 1976, p. 48.

[76] Ibid. pp. 5–7.

[77] Gandhi's response of March 1928 to W.F. Ireland of the Cambridge Mission. Ibid. vol. xxxvi, p. 137.

human and liberal. Still, Gandhi realized, in principle conversion could—must—not be banned.[78] He developed a strong resistance to conversion without quite rejecting it. The resistance alerted him to even subtle flaws and inconsistencies in pro-conversion positions. But it also produced the kind of blindness we have discerned. Perhaps never, not even in the discussion with Andrews, did he oppose the principle of conversion. The logic of this attitude made the expression of resistance, rather than acceptance, more frequent, elaborate, and impassioned. Only rarely would acceptance be voiced unhesitatingly or enthusiastically. Like it was at the time of Ambedkar's declaration, with its context of palpable injustice. Though, even then only spiritual considerations would justify transference of faith.[79]

This lifelong pattern of tension with regard to conversion, where resistance seemed to outweigh acceptance, is given a different perspective by what came from a much chastened and disenchanted Gandhi months before his assassination. He told a prayer meeting: 'A man, believing that he is doing the right thing, leaves his own religion and accepts another. I maintain that everyone is entitled to that.'[80]

This plain statement at a prayer meeting merits special attention. It was made at a time of deep churning within Gandhi. The eve of independence had brought him a nightmare. The country, all of a sudden it seemed, had never practised the values he thought had inspired its freedom struggle under his leadership. Even the much vaunted non-violence of that struggle, he realized, had been no non-violence. How could he have not seen all this?[81] Where had he gone wrong? His

[78] This conviction also extended to state policy. He assured the Conference of Missionary Societies in Great Britain and Ireland in 1931: 'I cannot stand for any kind of compulsion. Any suggestion that I should want legislation to prohibit all missionary enterprise or to interfere with the beliefs of other people is unthinkable.' Ibid. vol. xlviii, p. 121.

[79] Gandhi said to a Polish student who told him that he—the student—was a Christian convert: 'I can understand that. You are using the language of a truly converted Christian. You have a heart to lose or to keep. If the Harijans in India reach your intellectual and spiritual level, and experience your sense of original sin, I would bless them for voluntarily embracing Christianity.' Ibid. vol. lxiii, p. 47. Matters are, however, complicated by what he said around the same time to a Harijan who was impatient with some of his community's forms of worship: 'If ideals of Rama and Krishna are revolting to you, you should advise Harijans to forsake Hinduism, for I am quite sure that [if] a man does not believe in Rama and Krishna as God he is not a Hindu.' Ibid., p. 45.

[80] *Prarthana-Pravachan*, vol. I, p. 416.

[81] In a language that some may find irrational, Gandhi said with a pathos that even they will find moving: 'When God has to use someone for a purpose, He makes him a fool. I was blind until now.' Ibid., p. 275

prayer meetings were when every day Gandhi unburdened himself during this turmoil. Always conscious of the vitiating mediation of language, he was now practising a minimalist 'rhetoric' that aimed at utmost austerity of words. If Gandhi during that intense introspection came to value conversion more than before,[82] there is reason to re-evaluate the tension in his attitude towards conversion. Retrospectively, as it were, Gandhi's acceptance of conversion emerges as more important than would be warranted by its long subordination to his resistance to conversion.

It is also important, for acquiring perspective, to note that he was troubled by *shuddhi*, which claimed to bring back to the Hindu fold those believed to have been lured or forced into Islam and Christianity. It had, like much of conversion that he disapproved of, 'nothing to do with religion'. Ironically, the supporters of *shuddhi*, ignoring the complexity of Gandhi's views, claim that he was opposed to conversion. They also ignore his charge that *shuddhi* employed just the methods that were condemned in the case of Islam and Christianity.[83] Conversion, in his understanding, being 'a matter of heart and not of convenience',[84] he sought to save not only Hinduism, but Islam and Christianity as well, when he said: '... there is no sanction in Hinduism, Islam or Christianity for the *shuddhi*, *tabligh* or proselytization (respectively) as it is going on today.'[85]

Rejection of conversion *as it is going on today* just about sums up Gandhi's position. It presumes a suprahistorical ideal of conversion worthy, from a spiritual viewpoint, of universal acceptance. The ideal is framed within history and subjected to a temporal disjuncture. As the word 'today' implies, the ideal conversion has already given way to the impugned conversion of our day. The moment of the disjuncture remains unspecified. It is enveloped by an ahistoricity that shuts out—and also reveals—the glaring omissions that the ideal conversion needs must rest on. The greatness of the 'great' faiths of the world is assumed. How, unaided by preaching and mass conversions, they came to acquire great followings, never forms into a question. Gandhi shows awareness of the

---

[82] Gandhi expressed such sentiments at more than one prayer meeting. Earlier in the year, at another prayer meeting, he stated that conversion, which he rejected 'as an institution', 'should be wholly voluntary and must be based on a proper knowledge of the two faiths—one's own and the one presented for acceptance'. Ibid. vol. lxxxvi, 1982, p. 338.

[83] Ibid. vol. xxxiii, 1969, p. 8.

[84] Ibid. vol. xxx, p. 71.

[85] Speech at Nasik, 16 February 1927. Ibid. vol. xxxiii, p. 90.

process, as when he perceptively points to a time when the teachings of Buddha had not become Buddhism.[86] But that crucial transformation is assumed, assumed before the unhappy fall into today's—whenever that was—spurious conversions. Even the disappearance of Buddhism from India is explained in terms of its wonderful assimilation into Hinduism, and the indistinguishability of the two.

Gandhi is helped by yet another blindness. His imagined history protects the ideal conversion from the interrogation of 'real' history. We may see through that history and remain unaffected by that blindness. But that does not take away the power—the ideality—of the ideal conversion fashioned by him. Like what Gandhi said in justification of swadeshi and ahimsa, no practical considerations can belie the truth of this ideal of conversion. Not even the analytically paralysing implication of true conversion being a matter between an individual and God.

Unacceptable must be any view of conversion as denial of plurality that does not simultaneously admit of ideal conversion, no matter how

[86] Speech in reply to Buddhists' address in Colombo, 15 November 1927. Ibid. vol. xxxv, p. 246.

III
LIVING PLURALITY

Religious Plurality in the Chishti Tradition

A Case Study of the *Khanqah* at Salon in Awadh

SAIYID ZAHEER HUSAIN JAFRI

THE CONTEXT

'Sufi Islam' is often perceived and understood in juxtaposition with what is commonly constructed as 'Orthodox Islam'. This understanding emanates from the notion that the Sufi way of life went beyond the tenets of shariat. The rituals and practices that the Sufis adopted from time to time in the different regions of the subcontinent were often subjected to censor and criticism by the ulema and the qazis, the supposed custodians of Islamic jurisprudence.[1]

It was not in the realm of externals only that the Sufis faced the criticism of the orthodox; their belief system also came under scrutiny and was targeted. In the earliest history of Islam, the Sufis were seen as the people secretly in league with the Shi'a and the Ismailis, the main opponents to the Abbasid state.[2] In such a charged atmosphere, any digression from the accepted norms (formulated by the Sunni jurists) by an individual was enough to cause a hue and cry by the orthodoxy, thus putting the Sufis on the defensive.

[1] Some of the rituals at the Sufi centres, which were sanctified and made a part of their celebrations, can be shown to have an innocuous origin. An act or saying of the Sufi Shaikh was given such importance by his followers that it acquired a religious 'halo'. Continuous observance of the same in a prescribed manner created an aura around it. Thus originated some of the rituals at the Sufi centres which came to be denounced by the 'orthodox purists' as *bid'at* (innovations in religion).

[2] Seyyad Hossein Nasr, *Sufi Essays*, London: Allen and Unwin, 1972, pp. 104–20.

But apart from such external contestations, one notices substantial differences within the world of the Sufis themselves over questions of far-reaching consequences. We find that during the ninth century itself, the paradigm of *sukr* (intoxication) as against that of *sahw* (sobriety) became a dominant issue of debate among the Sufis. Abu Yazid Bestami (d. 875), who, through long austerity and meditation, 'reached a state of compelling awareness of merging his individuality into the Individuality of God' proclaimed *Subhani ma a'azam-ush-shani* (Glory be to me). Such a declaration did raise quite a few eyebrows, but a sharp reaction came only when Husain Mansur Al-Hallaj (d. 922) proclaimed *Ana'lhaq* (I am Truth) and was executed for the supposed blasphemy

The execution of Mansur created an atmosphere wherein the Sufis were compelled to reconcile with the orthodoxy. Initially, a number of texts were compiled by the Sufi masters to highlight the essential confirmation of Sufi doctrines with the Koran and Sunnah or in other words with Sunni Islam.[3] Having thus put themselves on a safe platform, a claim was later put forward by the mystics which posed a direct challenge to the orthodoxy. It was asserted by the Sufis that, 'the Ulema claim to be the successors to the Apostle. But we are his real successors. For, we have *faqr* (poverty), which he preferred. And in other virtues we have some share.' It is to be emphasized here that ulema and the Sufis were the products of the same system of education. Therefore, Muslim mysticism has rightly been described as 'a post-graduate creed of Islam'.[4] However, the antagonism between the ulema and Sufis was intensified to the extent that the term *Ulema-i Zahiri* (externalist) was used for the class of Ulema by the Sufis as a pejorative, while they thought of themselves as *Ulema-i Rabbani* or *Ukhrawi* (the pious).

These major trends and debates of early Sufism were transported in their entirety to Indian Sufism as well. The Chishti *silsila*, introduced in India by Khwaja Muinuddin Hasan Sijzi (d. 1236), became an important and popular mystic movement in the subcontinent during the thirteenth century. It attained immense popularity especially during the times of his successors, namely Shaikh Fareeduddin, known as Ganj-i Shakar or Baba Fareed (d. 1265) of Ajodhan, Punjab, and Shaikh Nizamuddin Auliya (d. 1325) of Ghiaspur, Delhi. These early Chishtis were severely criticized and opposed by the orthodoxy on account of certain practices, especially over the question of the validity and legality

---

[3] A. J. Arberry (tr.), *Muslim Saints and Mystics*, University of Chicago Press, pp. 4–5.
[4] *Collected Works of Professor Muhammad Habib titled as Politics and Society During the Early Medieval Period*, edited by Professor K.A. Nizami, PPH, 1974, pp. 277–8.

of sama' (literally, audition, but technically, singing of sufi poetry with musical instruments). This practice had been indulged in by the Sufis from very early on, and came to be adopted as an integral part of prescribed Sufi rituals. The debates on this issue ultimately compelled the Sufis to take a position against the codified law of the Hanafis (a school of jurisprudence of sunni Muslims, which prohibits the listening of music in any form) and even to denounce the notion of *Taqlid*, (literally, following; technically, the faithful adherence to any school of sunni Muslim jurisprudence)[5]

Although the stage was set quite early for the ensuing confrontation between the Chishti Sufis and the ulema, we find that, at a later stage, opposition to the Chishti came from within the other Sufi orders, namely the Naqshbandis and the Qadiris. By the time the Mughal empire was established in the subcontinent, the Chishtis were seen as group of people practising the tenets of plurality too liberally. It met with the disdain of those Sufis who claimed to be more in line with the Hanafi school of *fiqh* (jurisprudence).

But the story on the other hand was totally different. There had been quite meaningful encounters between the Yogis and the Chishtis since the time of Baba Fareed. Attempts were made to understand each other more closely.[6] This tradition continued in the other centres that Chishti mystics established subsequently. Unlike their counterparts, they paid equal attention to the masses. The rural elite in many places of Chishti activity constituted hostile and warlike Rajput chieftains, often inimical to the presence of the qazis and other ecclesiastical officers in their midst, as they were supposed to keep the officers informed about every incidence in the area which invariably invited the attention of the court. But the same elite adopted a strikingly different attitude towards the grantees and institutions with mystic predilections. Probably, this was because the Chishtis took pains to be seen as accommodative, with a fine sensitivity to local norms. They were just not tolerated but were shown enough respect by the local chiefs, who often bestowed on them land and cash grants.[7]

Within a century or so of Khwaja Muinuddin Hasan Sijzi establishing a *khanqah* at Ajmer, the cultural landscape of the subcontinent came

---

[5] Khaliq Ahmad Nizami, *Shaikh Nizamuddin Auliya* (in Urdu), Delhi: National Book Trust, 1985, p. 68, see also pp. 56–7.

[6] Muhammad Habib, *Hazrat Nizamuddin Awliya, Hayat aur T'alimat* (in Urdu), Delhi: Department of Urdu, Delhi University, 1970, p. 80.

[7] See my book, *Studies in the Anatomy of a Transformation: Awadh from Mughal to Colonial Rule*, Delhi, 1998, pp. 63–7. (Henceforth Jafri, *Awadh*)

to be dominated by a large number of *khanqahs* tracing their lineage from the great Shaikh and his successors. Centres of other Sufi *silsilas* did emerge, but it was rare to see any of them acquiring a long-lasting a status in its respective area as most of the Chishti *khanqahs* came to command. This initial phenomenal success is often explained in terms of the cosmopolitanism of the Chishtis and their ability to identify themselves with the concerns of the masses, rather than with only those of the elite or ruling classes. At the same time, one can notice a tendency to reject the religious exclusivism and the narrow limits set out by the jurists. These early Chishtis seldom practised adherence to a particular school of law.

Enough data exists from various Chishti centres in northern and southern India to enable a bold generalization on the issue of religious plurality, but that is not the purpose of this paper. What is intended here is an examination of the process of evolution of the various rituals, ceremonies, and practices, which were sanctified by the Chishti institution and were somehow given a 'halo'. It is also intended to examine the reaction of the religious orthodoxy to such 'innovations', thus getting to know the fault lines and the bottlenecks in such a process. At the same time, it is also important to see how the elite of the area viewed their presence in their midst. Was their attitude of open hostility or of indifference, of guarded welcome or respectful regard? It will also be worthwhile to see whether a hostile administration could make them abandon their ideological commitments. How faithfully did they follow the codified law and was there any flexibility vis-à-vis other schools of jurisprudence?

After writing my dissertation on the agrarian history of the Mughal province of Awadh[8] up to its annexation by the British, I started looking at the private and public records relating to Salon establishment, an important ecclesiastical institution of the province which had been enjoying substantial landed properties in the agrarian society of Awadh during the Mughal, Nawabi, and British periods. Here was a Chishti *khanqah*, deeply embedded in the Nizami-Siraji (the branch of the Chishtis popularized in the eastern part of the subcontinent by Shaikh Sirajuddin Usman [d. 1357], known as Akhi Siraj and Aina-e Hindustan, a disciple of Shaikh Nizamuddin Auliya) traditions and enjoying the income from quite a large number of villages as *madad-i maash* and *maafi*

---

[8] Awadh was a *suba* (province) under the Mughals, and came into being in the year 1580 when Akbar superceded the earlier divisions of the Lodi Sultans to make his own administrative arrangements. This set-up entailed the formation of provinces with subdivisions—*sarkars*—further subdivided into *parganas*. Jafri, *Awadh*, p. 30.

in the midst of a not-so-friendly and on occasions even a hostile, warlike Rajput-dominated society. Even in such an atmosphere, the *khanqah* continued to grow and made additions to its holdings by the grants made, among others, by these very Rajput chieftains. This is reason enough to prompt an examination of the elements that lent it such Catholicity and cosmopolitanism. The *khanqah* could also survive criticism for the practices and rituals it had come to adopt for ceremonial and ritualistic purposes as well as the onslaught of the Naqshbandi 'reformists' during the nineteenth century. By all accounts, the institution maintained its position as the only important Chishti institution in southern Awadh till 1857. After the suppression of the Revolt, the government policy changed diametrically to one of open hostility against the entire class of *maafi* holders. This changed policy created conditions which rendered the position of this institution quite precarious. Yet it has managed to maintain its creed of religious pluralism as against that of exclusivism till the present times.

THE EMERGENCE AND GROWTH OF THE KHANQAH

Tracing the history of the *khanqah* at Salon[9] makes it clear that several factors aided in its initial establishment: the familial and personal stature of its founder, the fame of his pir and the legitimacy acquired by both personal effort as well as appropriation of authority from already established local icons. It is also noticeable that the legitimacy acquired by personal effort is broad-based and not confined to the narrow limits of any particular Islamic *mazhab* (school of jurisprudence). The structure of the *khanqah* is, therefore, built, as it were, on pluralistic foundations.

The *khanqah* at Salon was established by Shaikh Pir Muhammad (AD 1585–1687). It belongs to the Chishti-Nizami tradition which can be traced through Shaikh 'Alaul Haq (d. AD 1398) of Pandua (West Bengal) and his son Shaikh Nur Qutb Alam (d. AD 1410), to Shaikh Husam-ul Haq of Manikpur (d. AD 1470) in Awadh. The seventh *sajjada nashin* of *Khanqah-i Husamiya*, Shaikh 'Abdul Kareem (d. AD 1647), selected Shaikh Pir Muhammad to lead his *silsila* in Awadh and nominated him as his successor. It is with this event that the shift took place from Manikpur to Salon.[10] The newly established *Khanqah-i Karimiya* by

---

[9] Salon is presently in district Rae Bareli, Uttar Pradesh. In Mughal and Nawabi times, it was in southern Awadh or *sarkar* Manikpur, *Suba* Allahabad. Jafri, *Awadh*, p. 50.

[10] Little information exists in contemporary sources about *Khanqah-i Husamiya*, Manikpur. For biographical notices of Shaikh Husamul Haq, see Shaikh 'Abdul Haq, *Akhbarul Akhyar fi Asrarul Abrar*, Delhi, AH 1309, pp. 171–3; K.A. Nizami, *Tarikh-i*

Shaikh Pir Muhammad (named after his preceptor) became the nerve centre of the Chishti-Nizami tradition in Awadh.

Shaikh Pir Muhammad came from an old and established family of Faruqi Shaikhs with their original home in Medina, settled in Yemen till they migrated to India, and came to Nagaur. The celebrated teacher of Khwaja Qutb ud-Din Bakhtiyar Kaki (d. 1235) of Delhi, Qazi Hamid-ud Din Nagauri (d. 1244), belonged to this branch of the family. During the times of the Sharqi Sultans, the family moved from Nagaur to Jaunpur. Makhdum Shaikh Bahauddin Nathan (d. 1540) and Shaikh Minallah Addhan (d. 1568) of the family acquired much fame in Jaunpur; the latter became famous as a Sufi, and from him the family began to use the nisba 'Addhani'. The next notable the family produced was Shaikh Pir Muhammad, born in 994/1585.[11]

After initial education at Salon, he was sent to Manikpur (known at that time as *Dar al-'Ilm*—the abode of knowledge) for higher studies in rational and traditional sciences at Kala Madrasa. But after an 'incidental encounter' with Shaikh Abdul Kareem, he enrolled as the latter's pupil. Even after completing the learning of the *Tafsir-i Baizawi* (a Koranic commentary incorporating the M'utazilite point of view as

---

Mashaikh-i Chisht, Delhi, 1953, pp. 203–4; John A. Subhan, *Sufism: Its Saints and Shrines*, Lucknow, 1960, p. 230. For a history of the *khanqah* and the family tree of Shaikh Husamul Haq, see Saiyid 'Abdullah Khan Alawi Qais, *Tarikh-i Kara' Manikpur*, Allahabad, 1916, pp. 260–6.

[11] A collection of eighty-nine letters of Shaikh Bahauddin Nathan was compiled by his son Shaikh Minallah Addhan in AH 869 titled as *Sahaiful Tariqah*. Probably the only surviving manuscript of this work is available at the British Museum (Add. No. 16848). The same has been published by Mian Muhammad Saeed with original fascimiles, summaries of the letters, notes, and a very useful introduction from Aiwam-i Adab, Urdu Bazar, Lahore, 1995. Similarly, the letters and *malfuzat* of Shaikh Pir Muhammad are available in manuscript form in the *khanqah* at Salon; see Saiyid Shah Ahmad Husain Jafri, 'Hazrat Shah Pir Muhammad Saloni ke *Malfuzat wa Maktubat*' (in Urdu), *Khuda Baksh Library Journal* No. 69–74, Patna, 1992, pp. 248–55.

Biographical notices of these ancestors of Shaikh Pir Muhammad exist in *Akhbarul Akhyar*, p. 44 and pp. 226–8. For him there are independent references in Muhammad Bakhtawar Khan, *Mirtul 'Alam*, Persian text, (ed.), Dr Sajida Alavi, Lahore, 1979, II, p. 417; Saiyid Shah Ghulam 'Ali Shah, *Mishkatun Nubuwah, mishkat-27*, MS compiled in AH 1212 (I am grateful to Professor Sulaiman Siddiqi, Osmania University, Hyderabad for letting me use this manuscript). Mufti Ghulam Sarvar, *Khazinatal Asfiya'*, Lucknow, AH 1280; Saiyid 'Abdul Hai', *Nuzhatul khawatir*, V. Hyderabad, 1911, pp. 97–8. For the history of the family, the institution, and the family tree see 'Abdullah Qais, *Tarikh-i Kara' Manikpur*, pp. 261–9; A Gazetteer of the Province of Oudh, Vol. 3., Lucknow, 1877, p. 290; H.R. Nevill, *District Gazetteer of United Provinces* (Rae Bareli), Allahabad, 1923. Vol. 39, pp. 101–3. For a complete list of the Sajjada nashins of the khanqah from the time of Shaikh Pir Muhammad till the present times, See Appendix I.

well) and the *Hidaya* (the digest of jurisprudence of the Hanafi school of Law), Shaikh Pir Muhammad remained for quite some time under the spiritual guidance and instruction of his preceptor.[12] He went back to Salon only when asked to do so by his pir.

According to a family tradition, Shaikh Pir Muhammad was advised by his pir to 'avoid the path of confrontation' and to 'try and become acceptable to all persons'. The following *doha* (couplet) in the Awadhi language survives as the 'motto' of the institution for all generations to come: [13]

> Piran Rasna tham key, kar miskini bhes;
> Mithey bolo nay chalo sab hai tumaro des.

> (O! Piran, hold your tongue, become a recluse, utter sweet
> Words, follow the straight path, the whole world will be yours.)

Following further the instructions of his pir, Shaikh Pir Muhammad undertook a *chilla* (meditation for forty days in a prescribed manner) at the tomb of Saiyid 'Abdul Shakur and Saiyid 'Abdul Ghafur (said to have been the companions of the legendary martyr Saiyid Salar Masud Ghazi, many of whose tombs are found in the region), popularly known as Piran-i Paratha. Upon the completion of this rigorous Sufi ritual Shaikh 'Abdul Kareem himself came down from Manikpur to declare Shaikh Pir Muhammad as his successor. Next, he asked Shaikh Pir Muhammad to take up abode with a sanyasi hermit. The family manu-scripts record many anecdotes of his spiritual prowess vis-à-vis these sanyasis. Quite expectedly, he defeated them spiritually and finally settled at the place where the *khanqah*, masjid, and maqbara of the family stand presently.[14] The 'spiritual jurisdiction' of the Shaikh of Manikpur over Salon was there for all time to come. As Shaikh Abdul Kareem reportedly told his successor:

---

[12] For details of this 'incidental meeting' see *wajib ul 'arz* of village Panahnagar Barai, *pargana* Bihar, and of village *Barwalia, pargana* Salon, in the *First Settlement Report of 1860*, *Nuzhatal Khawatir*, V, p. 97; *Tarikh-i Kara Manikpur*, p. 261. It is interesting that during the seventeenth century also a person, before being initiated into mysticism, was supposed to undertake extensive courses in the Koran, fiqh, and *m'utazilite* thought.

[13] These *dohas*, popular as astuts, survive with the musicians and the *Qawwals* (singers of sufi music) attached to the *khanqah*. Some of them have also been transcribed in the family papers and the manuscripts, which are being used here.

[14] Affidavit of Shah Muhammad Mehdi 'Ata, the seventh sajjada nashin of the *khanqah*, dated 26 September AD 1881. This has been published in full by Shah Muhammad Hadi 'Ata in *Musannif*, an Urdu Quarterly Journal, edited by Saiyid 'Altaf 'Ali Barelivi, Aligarh, 1945, III, no. 3, pp. 78–80.

Ayo Jayo Pirna hamar angan hoe jar
Dhelyan mar mohe jagayo ham Uth Lagab sar

(O! Piran keep coming to my place [whenever in trouble],
Wake me up [even if in a deep sleep] I will be on your side.)

Shaikh Pir Muhammad became a celebrity 'in the world of spirituality' during the lifetime of his Shaikh. The latter was highly enamoured of his successor's popularity and made frequent visits to Salon to witness the esteem in which his murid (disciple) was held by all. His sentiments are aptly expressed in one of his dohas:[15]

Chachar dekhan hum jo gain Piran Key darbar
Dekhat Naina jubh gayo besar gayo ghar bar

(Having gone to see the popularity of Piran at his durbar [the place];
The eyes could not stand the glitter, I forgot even my own place.)

Although he himself became a celebrity, Shaikh Pir Muhammad's regard for his pir remained undiminished and unflinching. This is aptly evidenced in the statement of Saiyid Abdul Sattar of Alipur (now in district Sitapur, Uttar Pradesh), one of the notable khalifas of Shaikh Pir Muhammad, referring to the occasions when the pir of his pir visited Salon:[16]

Masti-e Piram dar o diwar ra mastana kard,
Sad hazaran Alim-i Allama ra rindana kard;
Ibn Asif mast shud az deedan-i Pir Kareem,
Masti-i Ishqash ze sar ta pa wara deewana kard.

(The charm of my pir is manifest all over,
[due to his charm] scores of scholars and men of learning have
been spoiled;
The son of Asif got intoxicated with the glimpse of Pir Kareem;
intoxicated in his love people have gone crazy.)

Such appreciative attitude of the pir towards the *murid* when the latter had carved a niche for himself in social hierarchy has been the hallmark of Chishti tradition in India.

It is only when such persons have attained a certain degree of popularity in their area either as a scholar or as a holy men that we notice state patronage begining to flow. Evidently, this way the state tried to reach to the civil society by patronizing institutions and individuals

---

[15] Ibid.

[16] I am thankful to Shah Muhammad Shabbir 'Ata Nadwi of Salon, for saving me from the earlier slip.

commanding a social base. This can be seen in case of this establishment as well. But in case of this *khanqah*, the dynamics leading to state patronage is more interesting. In an obvious effort to build their social base from the grass-roots upwards, the Chishti mystics, in this case at least, have first accepted patronage from local officials and landed elite and only then sought imperial confirmation for it. Such prudence has only added to the appeal of their pluralistic teachings.

To continue, Shaikh Pir Muhammad soon acquired considerable prominence as a mystic and theologian. His fame reached the ears of the Emperor Aurangzeb who invited him to Delhi 'to pay a visit to the shrines of his pir so that the emperor could also meet him'. This invitation was politely refused. At the same time we find that the local jagirdar had made over to him, under his delegated powers, by way of *nazr-i khadiman-i haqaiq-wa m'aarif-i agah* (an offering for the servants of one knowing the mystic truths) a grant of 200 bighas of land in village Mirzapur Bakhtiyar, pargana Nasirabad, sarkar Manikpur, suba Allahabad. However, as it was made by an official of the Mughal empire, who was himself a holder of a jagir for a specified period, the grant could only be temporary in nature, coterminus with the tenure of the official concerned. Next, we find an imperial *farman* issued on fifth *Shawwal*, nineteenth RY/AD 1676 recognizing Shaikh Pir Muhammad directly as a grantee for the same piece of land. The Mughal chancery invariably designated such grants as *madad-i maash*, but the farman is probably unique in the sense that instead of the standard formula, the high-sounding description used by the jagirdar both in his *asnad* (deeds) and in the petition to the Mughal chancery, has been retained in the farman, in tune with the esteem in which the grantee was held locally.[17]

Patronage from the local landholding elite quickly followed state patronage. However, the considerations in this case seem to have been more complex than mere devotion to a mystic.

Shaikh Pir Muhammad died at an advanced age of 105 years in AH 1099/AD 1687. Even during his lifetime, his son Shaikh Muhammad Ashraf was assigned the revenues of a village, Singhwal (renamed Ashrafabad) in pargana Nasirabad by the zamindars of the village. A perusal of the *hasil* figures of the village from the fourth to the seventeenth RY, incidentally given on the *zimn* (reverse of the farman) shows that the revenue-paying capacity of the village had been greatly reduced. Hence, the zamindars transferred their rights to the mystic, who sought tax exemption from the Mughal authorities in the form of *madad-i*

---

[17] The letter of invitation by the Emperor Aurangzeb, the letter politely declining the invitation and the imperial farman have been reproduced in Jafri, *Awadh*, pp. 130–2.

maash. This was obtained in absolute perpetuity on 18 *Jamad* I, twenty-second RY/AD 1679. Shaikh Muhammad Ashraf must have been a minor when he was named a beneficiary in the grant in lieu of his father, who already held a grant. His young age might explain why no spiritual titles are put before his name and the standard formula of *madad-i maash* is employed to describe the grant, in contrast with the respectful address and an unusual description of grant for his father. Later on, Shaikh Ashraf became quite a legend and a sort of cult developed around his personality. It caught the imagination of an author like Mirza Qatil[18] and the Sufi poet of Awadhi language, Shah Qasim Daryabadi.[19]

After the setting of such initial precedents, the way seems to have opened up for ever-increasing patronage from all possible sources. We find that the rising graph of Shaikh Ashraf's popularity brought additional laurels for him. By the close of Aurangzeb's reign, we find him in possession of a vast area, spread over eight parganas in *suba* Allahabad and four parganas of *suba* Akhtarnagar, Awadh, either through imperial favours or through the local officials and the zamindars. All these were subsequently confirmed as *madad-i maash* by Bahadur Shah through his farman dated seventeenth Zilhij second RY/AD 1708. On the *zimn* of this farman a citation is made to the effect that;

... the grantee with a large number of mendicants is engaged in propagating the tenets of shariat and tariqat in the area and that in some of these villages he has established mosque, musafirkhana, and in the barren land has caused habitations to come up and has named them after his sons.

Probably the same considerations led to his obtaining yet another farman from Emperor Muhammad Shah on nineteenth Rabi I tenth RY/AD 1729.[20]

Shaikh Ashraf died in AD 1754. His tomb, with a very big egg-shaped dome was constructed in AH 1171/AD 1757 over his grave by an overseas

---

[18] Qatil mentions in AD 1812 that Shaikh Muhammad Ashraf was an important saint of the Chishti order. An anecdote he says that his disciples used to buy parrots and made the birds recite the Shaikh's name (obviously without his consent) and then leave the birds in the adjoining jungles of Salon. When the travellers and pilgrims listened to them, they were impressed with the 'spiritual prowess' and the 'saintly qualities' of the Shaikh. Mirza Muhammad Husain Qatil, *Haft-i Tamasha*, Urdu trans. Dr Muhammad 'Umar, Burhan, Delhi, 1968, pp. 168–9.

[19] Shah Qasim Daryabadi (AD 1731), *Hans Jawahir Bhakha*, Bombay, 1951, p. 4. There are three long alhas praising the 'saintly qualities' of Shaikh Muhammad Ashraf, his father, and his father's preceptor, Shaikh 'Abdul Kareem. The family tradition says that the poet was a disciple of Shaikh Muhammad Ashraf.

[20] For all documents mentioned above, see Jafri, *Awadh*, pp. 130–9.

merchant disciple named Saiyid 'Abdullah. According to a legend, Saiyid 'Abdullah's ship was saved from a disaster due to the spiritual intercession of his Shaikh. The chronogram of the tomb has been reproduced in William Beale's *Miftah-ut-Tawarikh*.[21]

Shaikh Ashraf's eldest son, Shah Muhammad Pir 'Ata, acquired a fame unparalleled in the history of the institution. It was through him that the branches of this *khanqah* were established at far-off places like Hyderabad Deccan by Shah Shuja'ul Haq Badakhshani.[22] The *Owaisiya* mystic order was popularized by him at Salon. As he died before his father, his younger brother, Shah Muhammad Panah was nominated to succeed as the future sajjada-nashin. It is said that he was held in high esteem by the Emperor Shah Alam II. When this emperor held a darbar (public audience) at Allahabad in AD 1764, the mystic sent a request for a new farman to be issued in the name of his son, the designated successor, Shah Karim 'Ata. The farman was issued on fifteenth Safar sixth RY/AD 1764. The significance of this act, i.e. seeking of an imperial farman in the name of the successor is seemingly hard to grasp, since all the *madad-i maash* grants had been made hereditary by Aurangzeb in his thirty-fourth RY/AD 1690. Was it that the nawab-wazirs were reluctant to honour such an order forever, and hence care was taken to safeguard the property in the manner as it was done by Shah Muhammad Panah?

By the Nawabi period, the *khanqah* had acquired a stature unique in the province. The grants held by it in the Mughal period seem to have continued more or less intact. It seems to have been the largest of its kind in the southern parts of Awadh. Its annual income was estimated by Donald Butter in AD 1836 at Rs 30,000, utilized in entertaining *bairagis* and *faqirs* without any distinction of religion: 'A large number of visitors flocked to the khanqah and at times there could even be about a hundred mendicants staying at the musafirkhana (guest house). These

---

[21] Besides giving the chronogram of the tomb, the chronograms inscribed at the main gate of the tomb (giving the dates of death for the first five sajjada-nashins) have also been reproduced in a chronological sequence. Similarly, the chronogram of the mosque of the *khanqah* is also given. Thomos William Beals, *Miftahut Tawarikh*, Agra, 1849, passim. It was the general belief that the tomb was a replica (*naql*) of the tomb of Shaikh Baha'uddin Zakariya of Multan.

[22] Apart from the recipient of such favours, the family sources point out cordial relationship between the nawabs and the sajjada-nashins of the khanqah. It is said that Burhanul Mulk and Safdarjung visited Salon when Shaikh Muhammad Ashraf was the sajjada-nashin. See Shah Panah *'Ata Fakhrul Fuqara'* (MS), AH, of 95. A number of *parwanas* were issued by the nawabs granting exemption of these grantees from the resumption. For the translations of some of these *parwanas* see my paper in PIHC, 47th Session, Srinagar, 1986, pp. 428–9.

were attended to and looked after by the sajjada nashin of the khanqah, whose reputation was such that any new chakladar appointed in the nizamat[23] of Salon promptly paid a visit and offered a few hundred rupees as nazr.'[24]

W.H. Sleeman, while undertaking a tour in the kingdom of Oudh (AD 1849–50) refers to this establishment as the prime mystic institution of the kingdom. Shah Panah 'Ata, the then sajjada nashin of the *khanqah*, was looked upon with great reverence by both Muslims and Hindus due to the sanctity of his ancestors and of the institution. He is said to have never left the *khanqah*: '(he) remained there to receive the homage and distribute food to the needy and the travellers belonging to all religions.' Sleeman estimated the annual income from the grant held by him in AD 1850 at about Rs 25,000.[25] In addition to this income, several local officials and princes from places as distant as Bhopal, Sironj, and Rewa had made substantial offerings. Taking all these into account, the actual income of the establishment, was calculated to have been about Rs 50,000 a year.

Relations of the establishment with the British were cordial to begin with. Complimentary letters were sent to Shah Panah 'Ata by the Governor General of India, and the lieutenant governors of the northwest provinces. When Colonel Sleeman was passing through the district of Salon, Shah Panah 'Ata sent him 'letters of compliments and welcome with a present of a tame antelope, some fruits and sugar'. This goodwill gesture was reciprocated by Sleeman, who records that 'his (the Shaikh's) character is held in high esteem by all classes of people, of whatever creed, caste or grade'.[26] However, such polite exchanges did not prevent the mystics reacting to the annexation of the kingdom of Oudh in AD 1856 with deep anguish. Shah Panah 'Ata thoroughly condemned the act of the British and expressed his feelings thus:Zulm-i Wajid beh ze adl-i Kampany ('The "oppression" by Wajid Ali Shah was better than the "justice" of the Company.')[27]

---

[23] Under the Treaty of 1801 between the Nawab of Awadh and the British, the province of Awadh was reorganized into new administrative units called nizamats and chaklas, put under the overall charge of the chakladar or nazim. Jafri, *Awadh*, pp. 33–4.

[24] Donald Butter, *Topography* and Statistics of *Southern Districts of Oudh*, Allahabad, 1836, pp. 139–40.

[25] W.H. Sleeman, A *Journey Through the Kingdom of Oudh in 1846–50*, I, pp. 232–4. An abridgement of this celebrated travelogue has been prepared by P.D. Reeves, as, *Sleeman in Oudh*, Cambridge, 1971, pp. 128–9, 131–2.

[26] Ibid.

[27] On a different occasion he criticized Wajid Ali Shah too for remaining a mute witness when Maulavi Amir Ali of Amethi led a jihad against the alleged high-handedness

Such open expression of hostile anti-British sentiments led to the moves to confiscate the properties of the sajjada nashin between the annexation of Awadh (February 1856) and the events of 1857, but due to his strong social acceptability and the respect in which the institution was held by both the Hindus and the Muslims, the punitive move had to be dropped. Major Barrow, the chief commissioner of Awadh after annexation, is said to have conducted an initial inquiry into the credentials of the grantee, but none of the files and papers pertaining to this inquiry are available. These were presumably burnt or destroyed during the events of 1857. A second enquiry could begin only during the first regular settlement of the province (AD 1860). The details of this enquiry conducted by W.C. Wood, the then deputy commissioner of Partapgarh, now forms a historical narrative, giving the history of landed properties accruing to the family since the period of Aurangzeb, the details of the buildings belonging to the institution and maintained out of the waqf fund, and the incomes and heads on which the expenditure were incurred. A distinction was made between the personal expenses of the sajjada nashin and the charitable expenses of the institution, including the madrasa.[28] On the basis of this report and on behalf of Lord Canning a sanad was issued on 26 September 1862, recognizing the allodial rights of Shah Husain 'Ata, the then sajjada nashin, over twenty-two villages of his grant. It is pertinent to point out that now the grant was a conditional one: it was to continue only as long as the income was devoted to the maintenance of the khanqah, buildings, tomb, mosques, and the running of a school of 'Muhammadan Education' and the continuance of the charities.

Till the promulgation of the UP Zamindari Abolition and Land reforms Act of 1952, the family continued to have possession of all these villages, though with some vicissitudes, especially through litigation. After the abolition of zamindari, an annuity was given by the Uttar

---

of the *bairagis* in Hanumangarhi mosque. He castigated the nawab as being directly responsible for the event. He also described Maulavi Amir Ali as *shahid* (martyr). These comments of Shah Panah 'Ata are spread over in his diary (MS with the present sajjada-nashin of the *khanaqah*).

In fact, it would be quite unhistorical to define the behaviour and 'loyalty' of sufi saints within any stereotype. Their 'responses and reactions' often came very close to popular sentiments. In case of Shah Panah 'Ata we notice his many 'identities' overlapping each other over a very small span of time, often defying logic.

[28] Letter No. 504 of 13 July 1861 from deputy commissioner of Partapgarh to the commissioner of Baiswara division resubmitting *m' aafi* register Nos 1–22 of Shah Husain 'Ata with his docket No. 1936 of 20 November 1860.

Pradesh Government only for the *maafi* villages and the amount fixed was Rs 14,800 (being the net rental of these villages as it was in 1952 excluding the cost of collection) per annum. The net result of such a policy has been quite disastrous for the upkeep of the institution. The present sajjada nashin of the *khanqah*, Saiyid Shah Ahmad Husain Jafri Islahi (himself a scholar) feels, 'It is unthinkable to manage such an institution in 2003 with the amount the government has fixed way back in 1952 without any consideration to the price index and the rising cast of living, but since the traditions of *darveshi* and *sultani* [mendicancy and royalty] in the institution have to be maintained irrespective of the grants, it is now being sustained by Him who provides everyone the ways He deems fit.[29]

RITUALS, PRACTICES, AND THE CEREMONIES AT THE KHANQAH

Adoption of local customs and accommodation of prevalent practices by Sufi institutions can be shown to have been an ongoing process, especially at places where large landed properties were attached by way of waqf or *madad-i maash,* more particularly in matters of succession and inheritance. Moerover, in the adoption and accommodation of rituals and ceremonies observed during public gatherings and other solemn occasions an eclectic attitude was generally displayed, for it was this that brought about a sense of belonging among the participants in the event. Such 'innovative flexibilities' were aimed at capturing the imagination of the masses and ensured sustained participation for a longer duration as well. The elaborate details of these ritualistics lent a 'sanctified halo' to them while, somehow, a punctual religiosity in their observance created an 'aura' around these ceremonies.

It should not be assumed that such 'innovative flexibilities' in ritualistics met with any approval by the 'ulema whose disapproval ranged from mild criticism to an all-out denouncement, often bracketing them with *bidat* (innovations in religion). But the orthodoxy never or seldom targeted the intrusion of local customs in matters of inheritance or succession of the landed properties, confining their attack to the 'external displays' popular among the masses, since the 'ulema too were appealing to popular sentiments in order to win over the same constituency from the hold of the Sufi institution. More than such opposition it is the ability of these institutions to withstand such persistent onslaught

[29] Personal Interview.

from many quarters that is important for us here. The Sufi institutions neither thought of abandoning their allegedly 'un-Islamic' practices under the pressure of the orthodoxy nor retaining that part of their constituency which was certainly going to the 'other side'. Here lies the crux of the matter: the Sufi institutions firmly believed that the rituals and rites at the elaborate ceremonial details adopted by them were representative of their ideological commitment to the philosophy of *Wahdat-ul wujud*, rather than just expediency or catering to popular demand or sentiments.

Sama' had been one of the major contentious issues between the Sufis and the orthodoxy in India since the days of Shaikh Nizamuddin Auliya. Neither had the orthodoxy reconciled itself to the very idea of *sama'* nor did the Chishti Sufis ever give up this practice. An incident attributed by Mulla Nizamuddin (d. 1748) of Firangi Mahal to Shaikh Muhammadi (d. 1696), confirms this stance in the case of this institution. Shaikh Muhammadi was a well-known *wujudi* scholar.[30] Mulla Nizamuddin reports the matter as it was reported to Saiyid Abdul Razzaq of Bansa (d. 1724), the famous Qadiri Shaikh:

Once in the khanqah of Shaikh Pir Muhammad of Salon, Sama' was in progress and compositions in Hindvi [Awadhi] were being sung. Those present were in the state of ecstasy [hal]. Shaikh Muhammadi also reached there. When the *raqs* and the *wajd* of the *Sufis* was over, he stood up and recited a few Quranic verses in the best of accent, but it had no impact on any of those present; neither *raqs* nor *wajd* overcame them. [Observing this] Shaikh Muhammadi said, 'It is strange that on listening to the *Quran* none became excited while the compositions in Hindi, which contradict Quranic themes, get you excited'. Upon hearing this, Saiyid Abdul Razzaq expressed his pleasure and approval of the conduct of Shaikh Muhammadi.[31]

While the original narrator of the story remains unnamed, it is highly unlikely for Shaikh Muhammadi, himself a *wujudi*, to have made this comparison between the recitation of Koranic verses and Sufi Awadhi poetry when sung with instruments, for both had different impact on the audience. Hence the reported incident per se becomes secondary. What is more relevant is the way in which it is used by Mulla Nizamuddin, the biographer of Saiyid Abdul Razzaq, and later commentators on this

---

[30] Shaikh Muhammadi's fame is attributed to his courage in defending, in front of Emperor Aurangzeb, the allegedly controversial points from the famous book *Al-Taswiya*, authored by his pir Shaikh Muhibullah of Allahabad (d. 1648).

[31] Mulla Nizamuddin Ansari, *Manaqib-i Razzaqia*, Lucknow, AH 1313, pp. 14–5; Muhammad Raza Ansari; *Tazkira Hazrat Saiyid Saheb Banswi,* Lucknow, 1986, pp. 70–1.

aspect, namely Mulla Qiyamuddin Abdul Bari (d. 1926) and Mufti Raza Ansari (d. 1990). Irrespective of the fact that they themselves were initiated into the principles of Qadiri and Chishti orders respectively, they have compared the *wajd* and *raqs* of Sufis to *tazwir* (simple lies) and *makr wa hila* (hypocracy). The house of Firangi Mahal, though otherwise known for its Catholicity, was unable to let an innocuous incident (which in all likelihood never happened the way it was retold) pass without an adverse comment.[32]

Similarly the other traditions inherited and the practices adopted at this *khanqah* continued to survive in spite of the claims of the biographers of Saiyid Ahmad of Rae Bareli for 'purging of Islam of the innovations (*bid'at*)'. In fact, the 'religious zeal' of these biographers/hagiologists prevented them from distinguishing between innovation in religion and an adaptation of the various practices in tune with the local customs adopted by the Sufi establishments. This inability to differentiate between the two and the failure to appreciate the spirit behind the ceremonies associated with the *khanqah* Salon appear to have caused misunderstanding between him and Shah Muhammad Karim 'Ata, the fourth sajjada-nashin of the *khanqah*, as the former's biographers indicate. He is said to have visited Salon at the time of the *'urs* and found that during the *sama'* gatherings, the *murids* indulged in *raqs* (dance) in the state of *wajd* (ecstacy), keeping earthen pots filled with water on their heads. Quite expectedly, Saiyid Ahmad is calimed to have objected to this ceremony as being un-Islamic. If one is to believe his biographer again, Shah Karim 'Ata is said to have admitted his 'faults and abandoned the practice altogether'.[33]

Holding for a while our comments on such a claim, let us first look at the practice referred to. It is that of *gagar* (lit. a small earthen pot) and involves the taking out of a procession from the *khanqah* led by the sajjada nashin who is accompanied by the disciples and musicians. The participants in the procession, carrying empty *gagars* on their heads, walked to the shrine of Piran-i Paratha, recite the *fatiha* on water in bigger earthen pots there and with that water fill their *gagars*. The practice is said to have originated during the time of Shaikh Husamul Haq (d. 1470) of Manikpur. The practice continues at Salon irrespective

---

[32] Ibid.

[33] The only authority for such story is Saiyid Muhammad Ali's, *Makhzan-i Ahmadi*, f.56 (compiled in AD 1865). This story is repeated uncritically by Ghulam Rasul Mehr in his *Saiyid Ahmad Shahid*, Lahore, 1954, pp.155–6. However, Saiyid Abul Hasan 'Ali Nadwi in *Sirat-i Saiyid Ahmad Shahid*, 2 vols, Nadwatul 'Ulema', Lucknow, 1939, has simply omitted the incident without any comment.

of the assertion of the biographer of Saiyid Ahmad. Moreover, the association of *raqs* with the *gagar* is also a figment of the biographer's imagination. It has only been people like this biographer of Saiyid Ahmad and others like him who have labelled such practices as *bid'at*. Not only this, according to the same biographer, even the well-known Sufi concept of *tassawur-i Shaikh* (perception of the preceptor) was said to have been compared with idolatry by Saiyid Ahmad when his own spiritual preceptor Shah Abdul Aziz (d. 1827) reportedly tried to teach it to him.[34]

On the other hand we find that the practice of gagar caught the imagination of other contemporaries, who found in it 'another chance of getting closer to *nur* (lit. 'light', 'reality', or 'truth') and a way of attaining *ma'rifat* (gnosis)'. One of them, Shah Kazim (d. 1806) the founder of a *khanqah* of Qalandariya order at Kakori (UP) paid a number of visits to Salon 'for the blessings and guidance' of Shah Karim 'Ata. The practice of *gagar* at Salon was well known to him and he refers to it in a respectful manner:[35]

> Aye ho Karim Ata kirpa rakh ham par
> Ham tose bari Aas Lagae,
> Nur sey bhar do gagar hamri
> Chunchi gagar ghar jat Lajai
> Kazim pai Karim Ata men,
> Rabb-i Karim key jyoti samai

> ('O! Karim 'Ata, have mercy on me.
> I have pinned my hopes on you;
> Fill my gagar with *nur*,
> as I feel embarrassed at taking the empty one to my house;
> O! Kazim I see the light of God in Karim 'Ata.')

Another poet of a later period has also expressed similar sentiments:[36]

---

[34] This is again from *Makhzan-i Ahmadi*. However, Saiyid Abul Hasan 'Ali Nadwi mentions the same thing in a somewhat diluted form with a degree of sophistication.

[35] Shah Kazim Qalandar (d. AD 1806), *Sant Ras or Naghmatul Asrar*, Awadhi text edited with introduction, notes, and translation in Urdu by Shah Mujtaba Haidar, Lucknow, AH 1376, pp. 72–3; doha nos. 484–9 (the numbering of the dohas is continuous). However, the editor tells us in the notes things which are quite different from what Shah Kazim himself says, besides making a factual error by stating that Shah Kazim has alluded to the 'blessing of the four pirs of Salon for overcoming his difficulties'. Hence they ought to be Shaikh Pir Muhammad, Pir Ashraf, Pir 'Ata, and Pir Panah instead of what we are told by the editor.

[36] A lesser-known poet of Salon, Ishtiyaq Ahmad Mushtaq, has composed a poem on the *gagar* procession. This is included in his collection, *Bagh-i Naim*, MS (compiled in AH 1350).

Ghairat-i saghar-i Jamshed Husami gagar

Mae Irfan sey hai Labrez ye nami gagar

(The bowl of Jamshed [the legendary king of Persia whose bowl was aid to have been inscribed with the World map] is envious of Husamul Haq's gagar; as it is filled with the wine of Irfan [gnosis].)

It would be quite unhistoric to think that the perception of the 'ulema about the role of the Sufi institutions and the customs they have adopted in various regions was in any way monolithic in nature. On the contrary, we notice substantial differences among them. This comes out clearly from the description given by another contemporary, Shah 'Abdur Rahman of Lucknow, known as *mawahhid* (monotheist), whose description of *tawaid* is considered to be a very stringent indictment of *shirk* (polytheism).[37] In the course of his sojourns to various parts of the country, he visited Salon and stayed with Shah Karim 'Ata for three months. He found in Salon the tradition of *darveshi* and *sultani* (mendicancy and royalty) going side by side and reported that nowhere else except in Salon *khanqah*, were the guests being looked after so well. He had reasons to be impressed by Shah Karim 'Ata because of the way in which he looked after the welfare of the destitute and mendicants at his *khanqah*. He entertained similar hopes for the future also, due to the sophistication, erudition, and scholarship of Maulavi Shah Panah 'Ata, the son and successor of Shah Karim 'Ata.[38] It appears that unlike the biographer of Saiyid Ahmad, Shah 'Abdur Rahman was looking for the things of *ta'at-i muta'adi* (man's obligations towards man), a cardinal principle in the Chishti tradition. This is what Donald Butter also emphasizes when he says that Saiyid Ahmad could not gain much in Salon, as he was told by the zamindars and the *miyan* (local title for the sajjada nashin) that for them relieving and aiding the poor, the lame and the blind was more pious than indulging in jihad. They also told him clearly that they intended to follow the examples of their forefathers.[39]

SPIRITUAL GENEALOGY AND LEGITIMACY AT THE KHANQAH

The Chishtis have always linked their spiritual genealogy to the person of 'Ali, the cousin and son-in-law of the Prophet, advocating the notion

[37] For the main arguments, see *Kasiratul Asnan* and *Kalimatul Haq*. See also *Anwarul Rehman Letanwirul Jinan*, his *malfuzat* compiled by Maulavi Nurullah, Kali Prasad, Press, Lucknow, AH 1270, p. 33.

[38] Ibid., p. 33.

[39] Butter, op. cit., p. 165.

that the spiritual legacy of the Prophet passed on to him. This aspect of their theology made them quite prone to criticism. The charge of *Tafziliat* (considering 'Ali superior to the other three Caliphs of the Rashidun period) was always made against them, and is something which they never denied. On the other hand, a branch of the Naqshband is faithfully adhered to the political chronology of the Rashidun period on the question of the spiritual legacy of the Prophet as well. We notice that although Salon received the Naqshbandi tradition directly from Shaikh Ahmad Sirhindi (d. 1624) through Shaikh Abdul Kareem of Manikpur (d. 1647), it never diluted its well-known position on the status of 'Ali, even in the face of hostile and adverse circumstances.

In a well-known passage, the eighteenth century scholar Ghulam 'Ali Azad Bilgrami (d. 1761) criticizes the shia rulers of the Mughal provinces of Awadh and Allahabad, particularly Burhanul Mulk (d. 1739) and Safdarjung (d. 1754) for resuming cash and land grants (*Wazaif-o Suyurghalat*) of the old and the new families. As a result of such a policy of indiscriminate resumptions, Muslim learning suffered heavily. Although he has not ascribed it explicitly to any sectarian motive on the part of the two nawabs but one can read between the lines that the author has those thoughts at the back of his mind. It has been argued elsewhere that the *aimma* villages of Salon establishment were resumed as a result of such a policy, though later on these villages were restored to the grantees selectively.[40] It has to be pointed out here that it was done on considerations other than that the grantees have fallen in line with the nawabs ideologically. No doubt such a policy had drawn a sectarian demarcation, yet the establishment at Salon did not budge from its earlier position in any respect, i.e. on the question of the primacy of 'Ali in the spiritual hierarchy and in observances and practices connected with Muharram etc. Not just in these 'external displays', the Sufis at Salon continued with their teachings and practices of invocatory prayers ascribed to and associated with Ali, and his grandson the fourth Imam Zainul Abidin and the sixth Imam Jafar Al-Sadiq, especially *Duae-Saifee, Hirz-e Yamani, Sahifae Sajjadia*, and *Hizbul Bahr* (these invocatory prayers are not a part of the Sunni traditions, while Shias have an altogether different version of these invocations than those of the Sufis, especially Chishtis).

Just as they did not give up their ideological commitments in the face of a hostile administration, they were least impressed with the agenda

---

[40] Ghulam Ali Azad Bilgiram, *Mathir ul Kiram*, Kanpur, 1913, vol. I, pp. 221–2; also see Jafri, *Awadh*, pp. 89–92.

of the 'reformist Islam' set out by the Indian *wahabis*, as Donald Butter specifically mentions while describing the little impact Saiyid Ahmad of Rae Bareli had on the Muslim population of the southern districts of Awadh. This was in sharp contrast to with the 'religious excitability'—of the Muslims—of Rohilkhand, in the Hydrabad states, or even in Bengal.[41]

On the question of pluralistic tradition practised as an ideological commitment, it is perhaps most illustrative to examine the career of Shah Muhammad Naim 'Ata[42] (d. 1966), the eighth sajjada nashin of the *khanqah*. He made his mark initially in the world of scholarship as a *muhadith* (a scholar of Hadith) and wrote commentaries on *Musnad-i Darmi*, a text of Hadith (AH 1316) and *Muntaqa ibn-i Jarut*, a text of Hadith (AD 1319). Although a follower of the Hanafi law, he deviated from it in a big way and did not agree with the issue of three talaqs in one sitting and also on the question of the legal prohibitions of Sufi music (*sama'*). In defence of the Sufi tradition of *sama'* he wrote a short treatise titled *Kashful Qina un Wajh-i Sama'* (AH 1320) where he forcefully argued for the validity of Sufi music. Similarly, he criticized the hanafi position on the issue of three talaq (the arbitrary pronouncement by the husband for the dissolution of marriage) in one sitting. He wrote *Al-Hajajun Nahidah ala an al Talaqat al Salasul Wahida* (AH 1329) and defended the anti-hanafi position on this issue and argued that such an act of the husband should not be taken as the final dissolution of the

---

[41] Donald Butter, op. cit., p. 165.

[42] Shah Muhammad Na'im 'Ata was a scholar, and a prolific writer on Hadith, *Fiqh, Tasawwuf,* and grammar. He was also a poet well known for his devotional poetry and anti-British feelings. He was a mystic with a high taste for sama' and music. Although a Hanafis, he was in many respects very imaginative and even innovative in his adoption of well-known principles from other schools of law, many of which were an anathema for the Hanafis. An authoritative biography of such a person will be a venture worth undertaking. For his early life see, Saiyid Taqi Hasain, *Nalae Anfas-i-Gham or Gham-iQiblae Alam,* Lucknow, AH 1318; for a list of his published and unpublished books (seventeen titles in Arabic and six titles in Urdu) and other biographical details, see 'Abdullah Qais, *Tarikh-i Kara' Manikpur,* pp. 267–9; Muhammad Usman Khan, *Yadgar-i-Naim,* Rai Bareli, 1966, which is in the form of an obituary by a disciple but also gives some interesting details. See the section of my book titled as, 'Aaj main wajh-i Iftikhar-i Salon', in *Masnad-e Fajr-o Irshad: Tareekh Khanwada-e Karimia Na'imia Salon* (in Urdu), Saqi Book Depot, Delhi, 2003, pp. 109–50, for a biographical note on him, his Sanad, detailing his works and obituaries. For his role in the peasant movement, though the analysis lacks sophistication, see M.H. Siddiqui, *The Agrarian Unrest in North India: The United Provinces (1918–1922),* Delhi, 1978, pp. 155–6.

As a man and mystic, there are very interesting aspects that have been highlighted by Claudia Liebeskind, *Piety on its Knees, Three Sufi Traditions* on *South Asian Modern Times,* Delhi: Oxford University Press, 1998, see especially the sections on Salon.

marriage, but only one of the three steps in the process of the dissolution of the marriage. Incidentally, this was the well known opinion of the anti-hanafi jurists also, variously knows as *Ghair Muqallids or ahle hadith*.[43] At the same time, from the point of view of just *Tafziliat*, he went out of the way to contradict the well-known Sunni position by openly criticizing Muawiya b Abu Sufyan, the rebel Governor of Syria who later established the Umayyad dynasty (AD 660–750), for he remains a controversial personality in Islamic history. Some sunnis in their anti–shia zeal tried to highlight him by exonerating his alleged acts of omission and commission. But Chishti Sufis and in this case Shah Na'im Ata never considered these arguments valid for consideration.

But he accorded considerable importance to the period of Rashidun Caliphate as well. He argued that the institution of the sajjada nashini was a replica (*fara*) of the Rashidun Caliphate. Hence, for him, applying to the shariat laws cannot regulate matters of succession to the office of the sajjada nashin. Keeping 'an idealized picture' of the Rashidun period in mind, he advocated that only nomination and in absence of that a consensus or *ijma* among the prominent people (*ahl-i hal-wa aqd*) should be invoked as the two possible methods for the selection of the future sajjada nashin of the *khanqah*.[44]

He ventured beyond the world of scholarship, into the realm of activism, when he criticized the British during the First World War and

[43] Urdu version of this *risala* was published in *Islam aur Asr-i Jadid*, Vol. XVIII, Special issue, part II, pp. 139–49, Delhi, 1986, with a prefatory note by Saiyid Naqi Husain Jafri, pp. 141–3.

[44] These perceptions have been spelled at an unusual place: a registered gift deed executed by Shah Muhammad Na'im 'Ata, the eighth sajjada nashin (1900–66) of the *khanqah* in 1938 in favour of his successor Saiyid Shah Muhammad Husain Jafri, ninth sajjada nashin of the *khanqah* (1966–79). The deed was executed in the office of the sub-registrar, tehsil Salon, Rae Bareli on 23 December 1938.

Since the nomination was made by Shah Muhammad Naim Ata in favour of Saiyid Shah Muhammad Husain Jafri (connected to Shah Naim Ata's family through the female line going upto Shah Karim Ata, the fourth sajjadanasheen) ignoring the other members of the family of the male line, thus pre-empting them from making claim to the office of the sajjadanasheen (which in fact they did make after 1966), Shah Na'im 'Ata had made the position very clear in favour of his action. The custom of nomination was so firmly established that it became difficult even for the contesting members of the male line to deny it in the court of law. After the death of Shah Na'im 'Ata, the title dispute was one of the most hotly contested cases in the chequered history of the family's Litigation. Finally, the court also accepted the action of Shah Na'im 'Ata in 1984 and the title was finally decided in favour of Saiyid Shah Ahmad Husain Jafri Islahi, the present sajjada nashin (Writ Petition No. 1682 decided on 12 July 1984 by the Hon'ble High Court of Allahabad, Lucknow Bench, Lucknow. The ruling was reported in *Allahabad Weekly* Cases, X, Allahabad, 1984, pp. 928–32.

sympathized with the Ottomon Turks. He also took up the cause of the peasant during the Kisan Sabha (Peasant Union) Movement, although he himself was affected by the 'No Tax' campaign of the Congress Party during the 1920s.

But these things were just a part of his multifaceted personality. Primarily, he remained a Chishti Shaikh with a very large circle of disciples and devotees. He displayed a high taste for *sama'* and composed devotional poetry as well. Though he raised a number of controversial issues of theology and law, he commanded immense respect among his contemporary Sunni/Shia and non-Hanafi scholars. Till the abolition of zamindari in 1952, he continued to enjoy superior land rights by way of *madad-i maash* and zamindari in over thirty-five villages, which were predominantly inhabited by the Rajput, Brahman, and other castes, all of whom considered him a holy man and a scholar.[45]

Probably in the recent past of the history of the *khanqah* he represented the best ethos of the pluralistic tradition of the Chishtis, where he stood firmly in defence of the earlier norms like the validity of *sama'* and venturing beyond the hanafi jurisprudence. He retained his *Tafziliat* in a big way, but at the same time gave equal importance to the Rashidun Caliphs also.

RURAL ELITE AND THE GRANTEES

Various Rajput clans were the dominant landowning classes in the agrarian society of Awadh, closely followed by the Brahmans. The Muslims constituted a small segment of the landholding classes even during the seventeenth century. These dominant castes of the landholders generally resented the induction of outsiders as aimmadars in their midst. Since some of the grantees were the holders of ecclesiastical offices as well, they had access to the local and Central administration. Apprehensive that the presence of such people close to the administration was likely to invite undue imperial attention to the stronghold of these castes, on occasion the locals tried to oust such grantees.[46] The situation was quite precarious in regions like Baiswara and the areas dominated by the Kanphuria chieftaincies.

---

[45] Hence, one is amused to see that in the recent historiography he is identified as a man having, 'subaltern mentality' and represented the 'ethos of the dispossessed'. See Gyanendra Pandey, 'Peasant Revolt and Indian Nationalism: The peasant movement in Awadh, 1919–22', in Ranajit Guha (ed.), *Subaltern Studies*, Delhi: Oxford University Press,1982, pp. 143–97.

[46] Jafri, *Awadh*, pp. 62–3.

A petition from the family of the qazi from pargana Pardeshpur (AH 1061/AD 1652) complains of the raid in their *aimma* by the Kanpharia Rajputs of pargana Salon:

They raided the *madad-i maash* villages of the petitions with a large number of their clansmen and carried away 940 oxen and buffaloes from the villages of Saleempur and Nizampur. This act was committed without there being any justification and with such impunity that they wounded even those two persons who had informed the Emperor of their misdeeds. The infidels are perpetuating such acts of oppression against the Muslims...[47]

A decade later, in AD 1662 Qazi Maudud, the qazi of pargana Asoha in Baiswara region, of sarkar Lucknow presents an even gloomier picture:

...the region of Baiswara happens to be the abode of infidelity and all the twenty one *parganas* are home and refuge of the Bais people. Out of these six *parganas* (Asoha, Harha, Dalmau, Moranwan, Sainpur, and Ranbirpur) have *qazis*, whereas fifteen *parganas* have neither *qazis* nor mosques, nor do the arrangements exist either for the *azan* [call for prayer] or for the congregational prayers. The fact that our ancestors exercised jurisdiction as *qazi* over all the twenty one *parganas* earlier, that there had been on-going clashes between our ancestors and the Bais Rajputs, this way eighty years have passed, consequently *qazis* lost their jurisdiction (*amal*), from fifteen *parganas*. None has cared so far to eradicate the source of infidelity, therefore, the petitioner, deemed it necessary to report the matter to the Emperor Aurangzeb.[48]

Such examples could be multiplied, but in no way it should be assumed that such harassment could dislodge the qazis or other imperial officers. They were extended the fullest protection by the government agencies. There are numerous instances when we find that imperial farmans were issued and those found guilty were awarded exemplary punishments, or, with a simple change of the area of the grant, the situation was rectified at the local level itself.

In the agrarian society of Mughal Awadh, which was marked with such tensions and even conflicts, it is worth examining how an establishment of the Chishti mystics could survive and flourish with substantial

---

[47] Abdul Qadir Collection of Acquired Documents, see No. 4, UP State Archives, Lucknow.

[48] National Archives of India; (OR Division) No. 2618/6. I first reported this petition with full translation at the Golden Jubilee Session of the Indian History Congress held at the University of Gorakhpur in 1989. This was published later on in the *PIHC*, (Fifty-first Session), University of Calcutta, 1990, pp. 354–60. Subsequently, the same has been used by Muzzaffar Alam, 'Assimilation from a Distance: Confrontation and Sufi Accommodation', in R. Champakalakshmi and S. Gopal (eds), *Tradition Dissent and Ideology*, Delhi: Oxford University Press, 2001, p. 167.

holdings for quite some time. None of the numerous villages they had was ever targeted and attacked by the dominant Rajput clans. Perhaps it was their mystic predilections that saved them from any onslaught; the pluralistic ethos they developed provided them not only protection but also earned for them a lot of goodwill from these very zamindars of the neighbourhood.

The manner in which the local chieftains bestowed favours upon these mystics can be culled from the *wajib al arz* documents prepared during the course of the first regular settlement of the province of Awadh after the events of AD 1857. These papers recorded the past history of the village from the earlier period. On the basis of such village-wise information, the history of families and clans of the various regions was arranged and incorporated in the settlement reports.

A few *wajibul arz* of the villages included in the *maafi* of the grantees are available. A perusal of these records gives us some idea of the favours bestowed on them by these chiefs:[49]

(a) Village Dhankesara, *pargana* Parshadepur, and village Barwaliya, *pargana* Salon, were in the estate of Raja Balbhadra Singh, the Kanpharia chief of Tiloin. He had donated the revenues of these villages in favour of Shah Pir 'Ata, so that he may be able to meet the expenses incurred in feeding of mendicants, destitute and the visitors to his *khanqah*. Since then till F 1174/AD 1763 the grantees held the possession of the villages on the strength of the *sanad* of the Raja; thereafter in F 1175/AD 1764 the imperial *farman* of Shah Alam II included these villages also in the grant of the grantees.

(b) The Raja of *taalluqa* Bhadri, *pargana* Behar has allotted two tracts of forest land to Shah Muhammad Panah. The grantee got the forest cleared and settled the area with the peasant castes especially the *kurmis*. One tract was named Panah Nagar and another Hayat Nagar (after his deceased brother Shah Muhammad Hayat).

The existence of a large number of the villages and *chaks* still having names based on those of the family members of the mystic establishment in pargana Salon, district Rae Bareli (UP) and pargana Kunda, district Partapgarh, suggests that many tracts of forest land have had a similar history and that these were also cleared by the grantees to settle the population and to raise their income.

Thus, in the case of this Chishti institution it is found that in developing

---

[49] This information is from the wajibul arz of each of these villages. The documents are the part of the *First Settlement Reports* of the pargana Salon and Parshadepur, now available at the Collectorate's Record Room, Rae Bareli.

a pluralistic ethos the main opposition came from within the Sufi circles, and in this case mainly from the Qadiris and Naqshbandis, while a hostile administration could only pose a marginal threat. Incidentally, the rural aristocracy seems to have shown greater understanding and maturity in the case of institutions having an eclectic ideology and Sufi predilections.

Perhaps it was the cosmopolitanism and the distinctiveness of the region (where Awadhi dialect was spoken) which made the pluralistic ethos possible. This very region had earlier produced personalities like Malik Mohammad Jaisi who wrote *Padmavat* in *Premakheyan* tradition; Kabir the great monotheist who lies buried at Maghar and who composed verses on love, devotion, and egalitarianism; the author of great epic *Ramcharitmanas*, Tulsidas.[50] It was in this region now, that the existence of a *khanqah* like that of Salon was possible. Here, there were few takers of the radical and puritan ideology of Saiyid Ahmad of Rae Bareli, while during the catastrophe of 1857, undoubtedly the most organized anti-imperialist struggle east of Suez, this region could boast of the most sustained and one of the most deadly fight against the British jointly waged by the Hindus and the Muslims. It is, indeed, quite unfortunate that the region and its people, who had such a glorious legacy of pluralistic past and at the same time have displayed such anti-imperialistic tendencies, have witnessed communal tensions and the rise of the movements of radical nationalism or nationalistic jingoism in the recent past, culminating in the demolition of the Babri Masjid (1992) and the attendant genocide.[51] Although these were quite an aberration from the norms, still when compared with the frenzy and holocaust in other regions of the subcontinent, especially in Gujarat and Maharashtra, these incidents and clashes will look less serious or even 'trivial' in spite of all the media hype and state-sponsored campaign of misinformation.

Though much water has flowed down the Ganga, the Sufi centers and their legacy in Awadh as elsewhere continue to be the standing symbols of a shared past. They continue to be venerated by all-irrespective of their affiliations and associations, who consider such places as centers of pilgrimage. For it is at these places that humanism, love and affection is taught without any preaching, thus making them the most visible signs of assimilation and pluralistic ethos.

[50] Jafri, *Awadh*, pp 17–18.

[51] For the tragedy at Ayodhya and its aftermath, see S.A.H. Haqqi (ed.) *Secularism under Seize, Ayodhya Tragedy in Retrospect and Prospect*, UP Rabita Committee, Aligarh 1993; see also Rasheeduddin Khan, *Bewildered India: Identity, Pluralism, Discord*, Har-Anand Publications, 1995.

APPENDIX I

Sajjada-nashins of Khanqah-i Karimiya at Salon

1. Shaikh Pir Muhammad (d. 1687), son of Shaikh Abdul Nabi, nominated as khalifa and *Jan-nasheen* by Shaikh Abdul Karim (d. 1647), the sajjada nashin of the *khanqah* established by Shaikh Husamul Haq (d. 1470) at Manikpur (the Nizami-Siraji branch of the Chishtis).

2. Shaikh Pir Muhammad Ashraf (d. 1754), nominated by 1.

3. Shaikh Pir Muhammad Panah (d. 1785), nominated by 2.

4. Shah Muhammad Karim Ata (d. 1833), nominated by 3.

5. Shah Muhammad Panah Ata (d. 1860), nominated by 4.

6. Shah Muhammad Husain Ata (d. 1880), nominated by 5.

7. Shah Muhammad Mehdi Ata (d. 1900), nominated by 6.

8. Shah Muhammad Naim Ata (d. 1966), nominated by 7.

9. Saiyid Shah Muhammad Husain Jafri (d. 1979), nominated by 8.

10. Saiyid Shah Ahmad Husain Jafri Islahi, nominated by 9, the present sajjada nashin of the *Khanqah*.

Spaces of Encounter and Plurality
Looking at Architecture in
Pre-colonial North India

MONICA JUNEJA

This article explores the workings of plurality in a field often bypassed by historians and social scientists—the history of architecture. Its focal point is the encounter of Islam as a cultural force with a range of building traditions and practices that proliferated in the Indian subcontinent during the thirteenth and fourteenth centuries. Can we recover some of the ways in which the structures and spaces of the built environment participated in the dynamics of conflict and coexistence, of processes of exclusion and assimilation that marked relationships between a host of communities and socio-religious groups that criss-crossed through the fabric of medieval societies in the subcontinent? Rejecting the polar extremities of conflict/iconoclasm and synthesis/ syncretism handed down by colonial and modern historiography, I seek to examine the workings of plurality and shifting cultural boundaries through the medium of buildings in a specific historical context.

The subject of architecture touches upon a number of issues that form the core of this collection of articles on the theme of religio-cultural plurality. As a form of symbolic representation, buildings are tied up with issues of political legitimacy, with the negotiation of identity and conflict. Back in the fourteenth century, the historian Ibn Khaldun perceptively observed that the uses of a building were both physical and social: it created spaces which could demarcate and separate, it constituted units, defined group and community from 'others'.[1] Through its ability to generate feelings of allegiance and solidarity, architecture has over time and across cultural distance been understood as a physical manifestation of a social and political order. The evident functionality of buildings allows them to enter into the sphere of practice, to interact in everyday life and cultural habits, and to become centrally implicated in the experience of difference and coexistence. As a space of encounter and lived plurality, the built environment participates in the negotiation of difference and tensions; it functions as a mediating factor both in setting up boundaries as also in rendering them porous or fuzzy.

Our understanding of architecture is equally rooted in the study of artistic form—of symbols and iconography, and of the acts of persuasion built into them. As a form of artistic-cum-scientific production, architecture is a field in which the iconic, the spatial, the functional, and the technical conglomerate. This would require giving equal attention to the modalities in which iconic form and practices are able to represent something else, in other words to the ways in which a building becomes a 'text'. Through what configurations are forms able to transmit certain meanings? A look at the mechanisms through which architectural form intervenes to make identities recognizable, to exhibit relationships, status, rank, to signify the coherence of a community, the force of an individual or the permanence of a power, would take us to the heart of issues clustering around the workings of architecture and the experience of plurality.

At the same time, inversely, the act of production, that of bringing a structure or a complex into being bears a fundamental relation to the distribution of power, the organization of society and the economy in a given historical setting. Building activity is as much a socio-administrative act in that it involves the control of an apparatus necessary to plan and design, mobilize resources and labour, organize the quarrying and transportation of building material. In monarchical polities, as those of pre-colonial India which form the focus of this article, patronage itself was a significant act: it spelt power, not only economic and political, but equally ideological, the potential to create utopian ideals of monarchy, to simulate the powers of God. At one level, as recent studies have underlined, patronage and creation of such structures were intrinsic to ideologies of power.[2] Plans, designs, and iconic forms all drew upon

---

[1] Ibn Khaldun, *The Muqaddimah: An Introduction to History*, trans. Franz Rosenthal, Princeton, 1967: vol. II, 357.

[2] See the useful collection of essays in Barbara Stoler Miller (ed.), *The Powers of Art: Patronage in Indian Culture*, New Delhi, 1992; also Romila Thapar, *Cultural Transaction and Early India: Tradition and Patronage*, New Delhi, 1987.

traditions and languages that can be classified as elements of a 'high' culture, at times articulated in complex, self-consciously constructed aesthetic-cum-philosophical treatises or statements, but more often through the forms and styles themselves. They formed part of a culture supported and propagated by the state or other institutions enjoying a position of authority, in other words a dominant or hegemonic culture of social and political elites.

Yet, to what extent is it legitimate to view this culture as autonomous, as existing in a 'pure' form? The endeavour to recover a history of architecture as a living space would involve paying equal attention to modalities of uses and appropriations of buildings and forms, to the shifting processes of construction of meaning, to seeing the connections between 'practices and representations'.[3] The location of buildings within a nexus and network of urban complexes, as also their use by large numbers of individuals, introduced a more varied cultural baggage within this nexus. This included cultures of non-elite groups who would have brought in an everyday *habitus* of work,[4] belief and ritual, caste and gender relations, through all of which groups saw themselves as particular communities and engaged with each other. Thus the meanings generated around the site of a building were necessarily heterogeneous. The multilayered complexity of a culture composed of such heterogeneous compounds undermines the assumption according to which products of the architectural activity on which this article will focus can be read as distinct cultural objects belonging to an elite or a particular religious group alone, and therefore demands different modes of analysis. Both interpretive and reconstructive techniques, still a largely unexplored and difficult terrain in medieval Indian studies, would be needed for a non-reductive investigation of the history of meanings at all levels. The search for such techniques rests on the premise that a range of diversely structured codes enter into the meanings of almost every building, public or ceremonial, courtly, ritualistic or domestic, in even the most self-consciously ideological and aesthetically refined artefacts of 'high culture'.

---

[3] As argued by Roger Chartier in a series of stimulating writings, *Cultural History: Between Practices and Representations*, London and Ithaca 1988; more recently, *Au bord de la falaise. L'Histoire entre certitudes et inquiétude*, Paris, 1998.

[4] The study of buildings as a space of 'everyday' interactions and transactions was suggested in the classic essay by Pierre Bourdieu, 'The Berber House' (1971), in Mary Douglas (ed.), *Rules and Meanings*, Harmondsworth 1973: 98–110; also Alf Lüdtke (ed.), *Alltagsgeschichte: zur Rekonstruktion historischer Erfahrungen und Lebensweisen*, Frankfurt/Main, 1989.

II

As in the case of every other discipline, the creation of a field of study designated as the architecture of the pre-colonial Indian subcontinent exists in a symbiotic relationship to cultural practice and belief. The academic production of knowledge about buildings through methods of classification, through fixing of attributes and the creation of a canon of values, all have impinged on the ways in which the functions and meanings of buildings have been perceived and further transmitted, often overlooking the complexity and disorderliness that the everyday use of built structures by a host of individuals and communities brings to bear upon their significance. Buildings then acquire a 'past' through the narratives created by historians about them, narratives centring on their origins, construction, symbolic apparatus, and uses. This implies a discursive use of architectural remains to 'build' collective pasts that generate emotions of stability, continuity, exclusiveness, or belonging, necessary to particular social configurations in particular historical contexts, and involving inventions and reinventions, concerted containment, elisions and forgetting, what Benedict Anderson describes as 'collective amnesia'.[5] It is important to address this hermeneutical issue, for buildings and their histories, exemplified through the case study discussed in this article, have over the course of the past century become a site of conflict and tension within political culture.

The history of pre-colonial Indian architecture as the discipline we know today came into being during colonial period. The earliest writings in this field were located in specific contexts of power and cultural concerns, both in the colony and the metropole. The pioneering achievements of these writings, while providing a copious amount of empirical and documentary material for subsequent studies, left a seemingly indelible stamp on many of the preoccupations and perspectives of more modern historians.[6] Together with the survey of archaeological sites by colonial administrators and scholars in the nineteenth and twentieth centuries, monuments became an important subject of study, to be described, analysed, and classified as part of a new discipline. This meant that apparently confusing and inchoate social and cultural relationships came to be transformed into categories sufficiently static and

---

[5] Benedict Anderson, *Imagined Communities: Reflections on the Origins and Spread of Nationalism*, London, 1991 (revised edition): 214.
[6] The following paragraphs are a summary of the extensive treatment of the colonial and nationalist historiographies of medieval Indian architecture in Monica Juneja (ed.), *Architecture in Medieval India—Forms, Contexts, Histories*, New Delhi, 2001: 7–35.

reified so as to be useful to colonial understanding and control. One way of making the alien familiar was to approach it through known models. In this case, the Graeco-Roman canon furnished European historians of Indian architecture with a language and a scale of values with which to classify and judge the aesthetic and cultural content of the buildings they sought to study. In addition, anthropological categories of race that had crystallized in the social sciences of the West over the course of the nineteenth century were deployed to impose a sense of order on a seemingly bewildering array of regional styles and idioms that had proliferated over centuries across the geography of the subcontinent.

The first systematic and comprehensive history of Indian architecture as a modern discipline was undertaken by James Fergusson. His *History of Indian and Eastern Architecture* the first edition of which appeared in 1876, has proved to be authoritative and influential in ways difficult to overestimate and has had far-reaching import. Fergusson had described the stylistic evolution of Indian architecture following the Turkish conquest of the subcontinent in terms of a 'fusion' or a 'mixture' or 'combining' of 'Hindu' and 'Muslim' forms. While he read these forms as an expression of the 'leading characteristics of the two races', the notion of race was now divested of its ethnological connotations and gave way to categories that postulated two homogeneous, well-knit religious communities whose often diametrically opposed beliefs, forms of worship, and rituals sustained architectural practices to create results that were highly successful and 'unrivalled' for their beauty. 'Indian Saracenic' architecture, as he labelled it, flowered through a large number of styles, thirteen in all, following the tastes and predilections of successive patrons—the Delhi Sultans, the regional Sultanates that emerged following the disintegration of the Delhi Empire, and the Mughals. He then proceeded to add two post-Mughal styles, those of the kingdoms of Oudh and Mysore, which he pejoratively termed 'bastard styles', thereby suggesting a paradigm of 'rise and decline'.[7]

A challenge to Fergusson's orthodoxy came from another colonial scholar, E.B. Havell, superintendent of the Government School of Art, Calcutta, from 1896 to 1906, and the author of a number of influential works on Indian sculpture, painting, and architecture.[8] Havell began his

---

[7] James Fergusson, *The History of Indian and Eastern Architecture,* London, 1876 : 490ff.

[8] Edward B. Havell, *Indian Architecture: Its Psychology and Structure from Muhammadan Times to the Present Day,* London, 1911: 1. Havell's views on Indian art and architecture were developed in a series of writings: *A Handbook to Agra and the Taj, Sikandra, Fatehpur Sikri and the Neighbourhood,* London, 1904; *Indian Sculpture and Painting,* London, 1908; *The Ideals of Indian Art,* London, 1911; *The Ancient and Medieval Architecture of India,* London, 1915. For

Indian Architecture with a polemic against Fergusson and colonial archaeology for their judgements on Indian art formed according to a European classicist canon, assumed to stand for a universally perfect taste. Indian art, he argued, needed to be understood and judged from within 'the tradition'. This 'tradition' was identified with 'Aryan philosophy',[9] whose essence was held to permeate every aspect of creative enterprise throughout Indian history. The Platonic notion of a transcendental Idea which stood for an inner truth, one often belied by material appearances, was used by Havell as an effective analytic device to build a bridge between Greek philosophy and the Vedic concept of *maya*.[10] The notion of 'Indianness', a unitary essence, created by Havell in order to characterize the art of the subcontinent had a definite bearing upon his analysis of Indian architecture following the Turkish conquest. For 'Indian' in his analytical schema came to be synonymous with a pristine Vedic tradition, a creative force that impregnated all of Indian art, 'until at last Arab, Persian and Central Asian art lost their own individual identities ... and merged into different local phases of Indian art of which the aesthetic basis was essentially Hindu ...'[11]

Common to both these apparently opposed examples of colonial scholarship was a concern with origins and essence that provided the key to understanding the significance of buildings. While earliest writings by Indian nationalist scholars sought to combat some of the most evident articulations of colonial prejudice—forms of racial or climatic determinism, or the dismissal of Indian art as a whole, through a denigration of forms which did not measure up to European canons of aesthetic worth—colonial critique was often responded to by leaning on another form of Orientalist interpretation, the more sympathetic judgements of Havell, inevitably imbibing, in the process, its specific canons, such as the privileging of 'Hindu' traditions. Writings of this kind became inextricably linked to a search for myths of origin to furnish underpinnings for the embryonic nation. The myth of a pre-colonial Golden Age found particular resonance in one stream of 'secular' nationalist writings, those concerned with the need to counter

an account of Havell's career, Tapati Guha-Thakurta, *The Making of a New 'Indian' Art*, Cambridge, 1992: 156–9.

[9] Havell, *Indian Architecture*: 2.

[10] The Platonic notion is the subject of a detailed study by Erwin Panofsky, *Idea: ein Beitrag zur Begriffsgeschichte der älteren Kunsttheorie*, Berlin 1989 (reprint); on Havell, Partha Mitter, *Much Maligned Monsters: A History of European Reactions to Indian Art*, Oxford, 1977: 271ff.

[11] Havell, *Indian Architecture*: 10.

interpretations of medieval India as a period which witnessed the spread of Islam in the Indian subcontinent through the use of force inflicted on a peace-loving, tolerant Hindu populace. Exponents of this latter position had sought to read all building activity during the centuries of 'Muslim rule' as an expression of the iconoclastic zeal of a 'foreign culture' seeking to forcibly superimpose itself within the Indian environment by a violent effacement of indigenous structures and traditions. The 'secular nationalist' response to such a separatist or 'communal' interpretation of the history of medieval Indian architecture found expression in the notion of a 'synthesis', a 'spontaneous blending of two styles'.[12] The natural fusion of the best features of 'Hindu' and 'Muslim' styles, a description which had its roots in Fergusson's analysis, was to become a powerful and enduring explanatory trope in a large number of writings:[13] the harmonious coexistence of elements drawn from two allegedly opposed religious traditions within the structure of a single building came to function as a mimetic device denoting a pre-colonial Arcadia.

One enduring legacy, then, of the earliest attempts to locate the study of Indian architecture within a disciplinary framework has been what Marc Bloch termed *le hantise des origines*, a preoccupation with the origins of forms. The search for and identification of sources as an end in itself could be described as the leitmotif of a large body of writings on the subject, whose paradigms, often irrespective of their position on the intellectual or political spectrum, draw in substantial measure upon the writings of Fergusson or Havell. Once the sources of forms, often selectively singled out from within a building, were identified as 'Hindu', 'Buddhist', 'Jain', or 'Muslim', they were believed to be capable of providing a key to the 'meaning' of that structure. At one level of analysis, the choice of these elements was read as an extension of the personalities of the patron: at its crudest, this would mean that the architecture of Akbar's reign would 'reflect' his 'liberal', 'generous', 'dynamic', or 'virile' personality, explaining thereby his preference for sandstone as a building material and the predominance of 'Hindu' elements in the buildings commissioned by him, while Shah Jahan's pleasure-loving, more 'effeminate' character was expressed through his predilection for marble as a building material and for vegetal and floral forms of decor, and finally, Aurangzeb's orthodoxy and austere

---

[12] Mohammed Mujeeb, 'The Qutb Complex as a Social Document', reprinted in Juneja (ed.), *Architecture*: 290–300.

[13] For references, see Juneja, ibid.: 33, note 127.

temperament meant not only a decline in patronage, but also an 'Islamisation of the Mughal style', implying its degeneration.[14]

The search for sources, in effect, becomes a search for essences. The construction of categories as 'Hindu' or 'Muslim' implies that these denote qualities which are fixed, unitary, and unchanging for all times to come. Moreover, it is blandly assumed that each of these stood for uniform attributes across the geography of the subcontinent, ignoring that, in fact, what we designate as 'Hindu' or 'Muslim' has acquired multilayered accretions and variations through interaction with innumerable traditions, grand and little, regional, sectarian, and tribal, all of which were then implicated in the shaping of forms and styles. Further, the legacy of colonial procedures such as classifying, labelling, and categorizing, upheld as important hallmarks of disciplinary rigour, has generated its own variety of essentialism in that the focus of study has frequently been to define the 'characteristic features' of dynastic building styles or of architectural genres, each viewed as a stable entity or archetype, for example, the mosque or the mausoleum or the 'Mughal garden'. This mode of elaborating typologies as an end in itself can become an obstacle to an engagement with the rich and diverse histories of the buildings of the medieval past. Historicizing the study of architecture would mean viewing form and structure as dynamic entities, as entities that not merely responded to historical phenomena, but were in themselves historical creations, and therefore subject to adaptation, change, resistance, or subversion. Equally significantly, it would mean according to architectural creations the potential to act upon history: by providing an arena for a range of activities of groups and individuals, of men and women, architecture intervened in the constitution and constant redefinition of relationships and identities among its users, and in this manner could be seen as participating centrally in processes of state formation, in the building and consolidation of empires and communities.

Finally, the search for sources has led to tangled disputes about symbols and structures, centring on issues as to whether certain buildings were 'originally Hindu' before other traditions took them over.[15]

[14] This is, surprisingly, the title of a chapter in Catherine Asher, *Architecture of Mughal India*, Cambridge 1992, rpt. Delhi 1999, which is otherwise scrupulous in avoiding clichés. Other writings often refer to the Bibi ka Maqbara at Aurangabad as the 'Mughal tomb gone to seed' or a 'crude caricature' of the Taj Mahal, Bamber Gascoigne, *The Great Moghuls*, London /New York 1971: 182. More recently, the use of a single material in Fatehpur Sikri has been described by an architect as an expression of 'architectural megalomania', Gautam Bhatia, *Silent Spaces and Other Stories of Architecture*, New Delhi, 1994: 63.

[15] See Ram Nath, 'Sources and Determinants of the Architecture at Fatehpur Sikri' in

The flaring up of religious conflicts in contemporary India, in the wake of a resurgent and militant Hindu Right, has meant that questions of this kind have acquired a particularly virulent resonance, where the history of architecture could be instrumentalized to legitimize desecration and violence. The invention of a collective past as embodied in its architectural vestiges continues to be achieved either through the singling of individual stylistic threads—Buddhist, Hindu, Islamic, or Jain— from out of an intricate patchwork quilt, or else by viewing the whole as a well-knit, cohesive unit, effacing either way the rich historicity of that past. That the meaning of a building is not fixed once and for all, but that an accretion of signification occurs throughout the history of its many uses, brought about by the plurality of traditions it engages with—these perspectives have unfortunately hardly been taken into account by scholarship in this field.

III

Efforts to impose a sense of order on different genres of buildings through categories understood as narrowly religious end up in ironing out the experience of processuality as well as of the multiple uses that buildings are more often than not put to by a cross section of individuals and communities. This has meant that certain buildings have come to be canonized as quintessential to a civilization in totality. The mosque provides a classic example of such a genre that lends itself most easily to conflation with the ideological and normative content of what gets to be described as 'the civilisation of Islam'. This is rooted in the premise that the acceptance of a certain core of beliefs central to Islam sought to cement diverse ethnic, linguistic, and regional components of a community into an 'umma, inevitably in tension with an array of inner differences, through shared norms and rituals. Reduced to their lowest common denominator, these meant faith in the revealed message of the Koran, acceptance of the essential duties of a Muslim, and a common image of the cosmos. The evident implication for architecture was the centrality of the mosque as a place for community prayer, as a demarcating space which held together the 'umma across geographical distance through a common axial orientation to the sacred centre in Mecca. Arabic calligraphy, the vehicle of divine revelation, developed as a primary art form

---

Juneja (ed.), *Architecture*: 563–83, which lends itself to such interpretations; by the same author, *The Immortal Taj Mahal: The Evolution of the Tomb in Mughal Architecture*, Bombay, 1972; *History of Mughal Architecture*, 2 vols, New Delhi, 1982–5.

that was among the most conspicuous visual elements characterizing any mosque, irrespective of location, size or stylistic attributes.

Yet it is difficult to identify a structure that may be described as a 'prototypical' mosque. Islamic texts do not lay down any fixed structural tenets nor do they prescribe any particular forms that were meant to orient the architecture of a mosque. Rather, building practices grew out of historical exigencies in specific contexts marked by the political and cultural presence of Islam. Art historians therefore tend to classify the architecture of the mosque in terms of regional styles—Arab, Iranian, Turkish, Mughal Indian, or East Asian—taking into account with varying degrees of sensitivity the high mobility of people and objects within the civilization designated as Muslim. Another classificatory model takes its cue from functional differences, emphasizing the distinction between the larger public mosque, *masjid-i jama*, associated with political power and ceremonial practices, and other smaller, simpler, and at times more private kinds of structures. Common to these varying classificatory modes is the perception of the mosque as a quintessential expression of the sacral-cum-theological premises that bind all Muslim communities. What tends to be overlooked is the remarkable fluidity of the frontiers separating the sacred and the profane in the politics and everyday lives of these communities: the location of a large number of mosques in dense urban structures and their constant imbrication in living cultures brought an additional layer of plurality to their meanings.

The remaining sections of this article attempt, through a case study, to suggest directions towards grasping the variegated histories of buildings inscribed in specific contexts—of warfare and consolidation, of the formation and constant redefinition of communities, of the contexts of everyday lives. Such a focus would take us beyond the contending claims articulated within narratives and discourses on architecture, to look at the evidence of the buildings themselves, and so ought to enable us to rethink categories and polar oppositions, such as that between 'sacred' and 'profane' architecture, often taken as fixed and unchanging. An attempt to reconstruct, wherever feasible, the myriad ways in which buildings, appropriated in contexts of warfare, were reappropriated and intervened in the lives of men and women, of different groups and communities may, in addition, help in historicizing the polarities between 'iconoclasm' and 'assimilation', and so sensitize us to the dangers of burdening pre-modern pasts with contemporary concerns and meanings. I shall attempt to develop these methodological reflections through a close look at a particular example, that of one of the earliest structures built in medieval Delhi in the wake of the Turkish conquest of the city: the *masjid-i jama* or public mosque where Friday prayers took place.[16]

The coming into being of Delhi's *masjid-i jama* can be seen as part of a pattern of conquest and 'symbolic appropriation' of an alien territory, processes which had precedents in the history of Islam's expansion in Arabia, North Africa, and southern Europe.[17] The expression of victory over a conquered land was effected through immediate visual acts and forms, often involving the seizure of the centres of power and most sacred sites of the indigenous populace: the ruler's palace was taken over, the main temples destroyed. As soon as possible, a *masjid-i jama*, the chief congregational mosque of the capital, was built, where the *Khutba* was read, proclaiming the new ruler. New coins were struck. Appropriation went beyond a simple annexation of territory or a geographical site; it included building materials, an existing labour force and a body of tradition and art forms belonging to the vanquished, which then got reabsorbed into the new structures in ways that were crucial to the (re)constitution of their meanings.

In other regions of the Islamic world, especially those who also possessed a tradition of community prayer, the wholesale destruction of extant buildings in order to construct a mosque was generally avoided, for basilica, churches, or synagogues all had large hall-like central spaces designed to accommodate large numbers of believers.[18] In the process of converting these buildings, with minimal adjustments, into mosques, the 'new' architecture absorbed many visual and structural elements—rows of columns, courtyards, arches, and domes—from the buildings it appropriated. In the Indian context, antithetical forms of worship in Hinduism and Islam—the one personal, introspective, and anthropomorphic, the other non-figural, inspired by an ideal of community, brotherhood, and surrender to an abstract truth—accounted for the distinct forms of religious structures, the temple, and the mosque, whose

[16] This mosque, which forms a main part of the so-designated Qutb complex in southern Delhi, has frequently been referred to as the *Quwwat-ul Islam masjid* or 'The Might of Islam'. For a critical appraisal of the use of this term, see Sunil Kumar, 'Defining and Contesting Territory: The Delhi Masjid-i Jami in the Thirteenth Century', (unpublished manuscript): 7–8.

[17] Oleg Grabar, *The Formation of Islamic Art*, revised edition, New Haven and London, 1987: chapter 3.

[18] Grabar, *The Formation*; Richard Ettinghausen and Oleg Grabar, *The Art and Architecture of Islam 650–1250*, New York/Harmondsworth, 1987; George Michell (ed.), *Architecture of the Islamic World*, London/New York, 1978; Henri Stern, 'Les origines de l'architecture de la mosquée Omeyyade', *Syria*, vol. 28, 1951: 269–79; Christian Ewert, *Denkmäler des Islam: von den Anfängen bis zum 12. Jahrhundert*, Mainz, 1997.

spaces could not be easily harmonized. Hence the necessity of dismantling the temples and redeploying their materials for the creation of an architectural space designed to accommodate a congregation of worshippers. The pulling down of the temples, hyperbolically claimed to be twenty-seven in number, at the Chauhan capital of Qila-i Rai Pithaura to construct a *masjid-i jama* on the same site, was, at the same time, part of the eulogization of conquest. This fact has been pointed out by every scholar who has worked on the subject, beginning with the colonial scholar J. A. Page's *A Historical Memoir on the Qutb*, published by the Archaeological Survey of India in 1926.[19] The central evidence for this is the proclamation of victory over the infidels made by the epigraph on the main portal.[20] The question however needs to be asked, whether the meanings that we believe to have been transmitted by Delhi's first *masjid-i jama* can be univocally reduced to a discursive statement of one kind—expressed through the medium of an extremely difficult and complex *naskhi* script whose access was limited to a handful of highly literate members of the orthodox ulama and nobility. Or whether the iconic evidence furnished by its architecture followed its own logic; and more significantly, whether the diverse possibilities of appropriation and use of this architecture by different social components within the emergent township of medieval Dilli allowed for a synchronic proliferation of multiple meanings within the spaces and forms of a single structure.

Any attempt to interpret the architectural evidence of the *masjid-i jama* would necessarily involve a reconstruction of the processes by which its structure and forms came into being, inscribed as they were within milieus and a specific repertory of genres, conventions, and building practices of the time. The *qibla liwan* or main prayer hall of the mosque oriented towards Mecca follows the Arab prototype made up of a hypostyle hall—a hall where the roof is carried by columns and pillars set in parallel alignment with the walls. The origins of this form go back to the visual memory of Islam's first mosque, the house of the Prophet at Medina, which had an inner courtyard with two shaded areas. The latter were made up through a thatched roof held up by rows of palm trunks. And so a visual form was created that soon became a sacred memory, one which crystallized in the minds of the faithful through the subsequent emergence of the hypostyle form and common to a large

[19] Reprinted in Juneja (ed.), *Architecture*: 143–170.

[20] Cited by Page ibid., as also by a number of modern scholars, see Robert Hillenbrand, 'Political Symbolism in Early Indo-Islamic Mosque Architecture: The Case of Ajmir', *Iran*, vol. 26, 1988: 105–17; Anthony Welch, 'Architectural Patronage and the Past: The Tughluq Sultans of Delhi', *Muqarnas*, vol. 10, 1993: 311–22; Kumar, 'Defining...': 18.

number of public mosques in Egypt, Tunisia, Syria, and Spain.[21] In addition, the courtyard of the Prophet's house was the place where almost all significant activities and decisions of the embryonic community took place; this space was then transmitted through to the collective memory of subsequent generations as more than a simple place for prayer.[22] That the earliest monumental mosque in Delhi relocated this memory within an Indian setting was a significant symbolic act associated with the inception of the Delhi Sultanate. It set a precedent repeatedly followed by rulers throughout the subsequent centuries: in the 1340s Sultan Muhammad-ibn Tughluq, to cite one instance, placed the *masjid-i jama* of his new capital Jahanpanah, also known as the Begumpuri Masjid, within the same tradition, hoping to assimilate its legitimacy to his ambitions. Similarly in Bengal, the articulation of political authority in the wake of the extension of Islam privileged the hypostyle plan in the construction of Friday mosques such as the Adina Masjid in Pandua of 1375.[23]

The advantage of the hypostyle model was that its space-creating elements, the rows of roof-supporting columns, could be added lengthwise and/or sideways to extend an existing building, without fundamentally disrupting its original conception, as in fact was done in the case of the *masjid-i jama* begun by Qutb ud-Din Aibaq and later extended by Iltutmish and Ala al-Din Khalji. The use of the hypostyle model moreover enabled subsequent Sultans to draw upon the aura of the previous site, consecrated through its use as the site of a hallowed structure symbolizing the presence of a new political and cultural force, and at the same time to make fresh additions marking their own claims to authority and glory.[24] In fact, the additions to the Qutb mosque made by Iltutmish transmit a message within which elements of continuity and discontinuity appear to coexist with little sense of strain. Under Ala

---

[21] Oleg Grabar, 'The Architecture of the Middle Eastern City from Past to Present: The Case of the Mosque', in Ira M. Lapidus (ed.), *Middle Eastern Cities*, Berkeley, 1969: 26–46.

[22] Grabar, *The Formation*: 102–4.

[23] Richard M. Eaton, *The Rise of Islam and the Bengal Frontier 1204–1760*, Delhi, 1994: 42–3, photograph by Catherine Asher.

[24] This practice was not confined to Delhi alone, it was followed in the mosques of Ajmer and Bayana, see Michael W. Meister, 'The "Two-and-a-Half Day" Mosque', and reprinted in Juneja (ed.), *Architecture*: 303–14; and also Mehrdad Shokoohy and Natalie H. Shokoohy, 'The Architecture of Baha-al Din Tughrul in the Region of Bayana, Rajasthan' in Juneja, ibid: 413–38. That it was a common architectural ritual among rulers to 'quote' from such monuments of the past which enjoyed a particular aura, and thereby add on another layer of legitimacy to their own ambitions, can be gauged from the interesting study by Ebba Koch, 'The Copies of the Qutb Minar', *Iran*, vol. 19, 1991: 95–107.

al-Din Khalji, the continuity sought to be established by the sultan stretches further backwards into history. Ala al-Din doubled the size of Iltutmish's courtyard, ordered the extended *maqsura* walls to be thicker and higher, and planned the construction of a second, even higher minar towards the northern end of the courtyard.[25] Moreover, he added a southern gateway to the complex, the exquisite Alai Darwaza. The complex epigraphic programme of the Alai Darwaza seeks to inscribe Ala al-Din's fame within the genealogy of earlier empire builders, including the great Alexander.[26] A central architectural component of the Alai Darwaza is its pointed horseshoe arch with its spearhead fringe, a feature which was introduced for the first time in an edifice on the Indian subcontinent. Its associations were unmistakeable: its visuality belonged to the memory of the Great Mosque of Cordoba, symbol of the power of the Caliphate at its highest. The horseshoe arch was subsequently emulated in other regions and structures of North Africa, subsequent to the decline of Muslim power in Spain and a large-scale emigration of artisans following the *Reconquista*.[27] This single image could then effectively function as a link, making up a chain of references that held together sites over a vast geographical area within the symbolic framework of a world empire.

To construct the Qutb mosque, the original temple was stripped of its *garba griha*, while the *vimana* was enlarged to form the central courtyard. The local *sthapati* was ordered to oversee the dismantling of the temple stones, held together through methods of dovetailing rather than cementing and therefore relatively easy to take apart without destruction or decimation, and their careful reassembling to form the pillars of the hypostyle *riwaq*. The visual and iconic evidence of the pillars does not, in fact, testify to any systematic iconoclasm. A similar practice seems to have been followed in the construction of the ceilings, where individual stones have been all put back together with great care taken to recreate the original motif of the lotus roof.[28] The result is unexpected and

---

[25] See Page, *A Historical Memoir*: 152.

[26] The inscriptions of the Alai Darwaza have been transcribed by G. Yazdani, 'Inscriptions of the Khalji Sultans of Delhi and their Contemporaries in Bengal', *Epigraphia Indo-Moslemica*, 1917–8: 23–30; for an interpretation of these inscriptions, Sunil Kumar, 'Assertions of Authority: A Study of the Dicursive Statements of the Sultans of Delhi', in Muzaffar Alam, Françoise 'Nalini' Delvoye and Max Gaborieau (eds), *The Making of Indo-Persian Culture*, Delhi, 2000: 43ff.

[27] Ronald Lewcock, 'Architects, Craftsmen and Builders: Materials and Techniques', in George Michell (ed.), *Architecture of the Islamic World*: 127, 133ff.

[28] For a similar process in the Ajmer mosque, see Meister, 'The "Two-and-a Half Day" Mosque': 311, Fig. 3.

unusual: a sacred space of Islam alive with the rich visual vocabulary of Hindu and Jain art forms. Rows and rows of pillars receding into the spatial depths of the *riwaq* resonate with the plasticity of the sculpted motifs that cover their surfaces—the *kalasa* and the lotus, *yakshas* and *yakshinis*, carved ceilings with figures connected with Jain Tirthankaras on the upper level of the *riwaq*. While a number of explicitly anthropomorphic motifs have been avoided by reversing the sculpted face of the stone towards an inner wall, others have remained visible and intact: representations of the ten incarnations of Vishnu can be seen facing the outside on the southern wall. Most striking, however, is a panel in the wall on the north side, portraying scenes from the birth of the infant Krishna.[29] The visual experience of this space, with its trabeate principles of construction and awkwardly shallow-domed interiors was far removed from the memory and associations of a prayer space created in accordance with arcuate principles of construction generally associated with a traditionally 'Islamic' aesthetic. It was in response to a need to recall and relocate some of those associations generated by a visual vocabulary familiar to Islam, that the construction of the *maqsura* or a free-standing screen of arches framing the *qibla liwan*, lending emphasis to its direction, and towering above the courtyard and its structures, was ordered. The entire screen façade, built through corbelling and smoothing the overlapping stones to form the outline of a pointed arch,[30] is carved in bands of low-relief patterns—calligraphic inscriptions intertwined with floral motifs, clinging creepers, and a stylized lotus design. Calligraphically rendered Arabic script is an art form found throughout the Islamic world, from Spain to India, from the earliest to the most recent times.[31] Religious inscriptions, primarily Koranic verses, make visible the word of God. They were also believed to act as a sort of talisman for the building or object on which they are inscribed. Inscriptions were mainly used as a frame along and around main elements of buildings, especially portals and cornices. Referred to in Arabic as 'geometry of the line', calligraphy provided at the same time a legible

[29] For an attempt to date this panel and locate it within the genre of scenes from the Ramayana and Mahabharata, see the brief article by R.B.K.N. Dikshit, 'A Panel Showing the Birth of Lord Krishna from the Qutb Mosque', *Journal of the United Provinces Historical Society*, vol. 17, 1944: 84–6.

[30] As has been pointed out at great length by Page, *A Historical Memoir.* 147; Percy Brown, *Indian Architecture: Islamic Period*, Bombay 1942, rpt. 1956:7, Plate IV, and Mujeeb, 'The Qutb Complex': 295–6.

[31] Wheeler Thackston, 'The Role of Calligraphy', in Martin J. Frishman and Hasan-Uddin Khan (eds), *The Mosque: History, Architectural Development and Regional Diversity*, London, 1994: 43–53.

message as a decorative motif. The scripts vary from the flowing, cursive *nasta'liq*, as in the *maqsura* of the first phase of the Qutb mosque, to the angular *kufic*, an earlier form which accentuates vertical strokes, bands of which cover the inner walls of Iltutmish's tomb located at the northwest corner of the same complex. The inscriptions on the *qibla* screen carry a selection of Koranic messages, distinct from those on the portal. Rather than making a statement about the punishments awaiting the infidel, they stress instead the importance of adherence to the tenets of the faith, piety in everyday life, of moral conduct, and brotherhood among Muslims.[32]

It becomes clear, then, that the architectural and iconic evidence of Delhi's first *masjid-i jama* carries a host of meanings, all of which cannot be reduced to a militant assertion of victory over a land of unbelievers. That the structure was addressed to the Muslim population of Delhi with a view to constituting its diverse components as a 'community' by reminding them of the political and moral virtues of their ruler—as opposed to those of other claimants to authority—was certainly one element of its programme. What needs to be investigated further is the polysemous character of this evidence—iconic, spatial, functional, and textual—which can be arrived at by looking at the possible forms of its circulation and assimilation, by trying to investigate the terrain where discursivity met with social practice and cultural experience, the determinations that would have come into play through the heterogeneous publics which made use of the spaces and structures of this significant complex. For the large majority of these publics, it must be emphasized, culture was accessible through media that were mainly oral or visual; the eclectic architecture and imagery of the mosque would have been interpreted by them in ways shaped by the particular structures of their competences, perceptions, aspirations, and anxieties, which may not necessarily have been controlled or constrained by the intentions of the various factions among warrior elites and the power struggles between them. We need, therefore, to look at the points of intersection and non-intersection between the functions of the mosque in the everyday lives of the urban populace who moved in and out of its spaces, the semiotics of its architecture, and the potential this had, in turn, to become a resource of one kind or the other for a range of individuals and groups.

[32] Anthony Welch, 'Qur'an and Tomb: the Religious Epigraphs of two early Sultanate Tombs in Delhi', in Frederick M. Asher and G. S. Gai (eds), *Indian Epigraphy: Its Bearing on the History of Art*, New Delhi, 1985: 261ff; Kumar, 'Contesting ...':38–40, though the latter seems to imply that these inscriptions belong only to the reign of Iltutmish, as part of a new discourse about the Sultanate as an embodiment of a 'unitary' Islam.

The centrality of a congregational mosque, the *masjid-i jama*, in the social life of the populace of a city has been well established by research.[33] From the very outset, a public mosque was more than a place for prayer. It formed the locus of community life: it housed a *madrasa*, a treasury—additions made by Ala al-Din Khalji to the *masjid-i jama* of the old *Shahr*—and was a place for meeting and transacting business. Sultans often decreed that the city's grain market and bazaars be located outside its portals, as Ala al-Din did in Delhi. Equally important were its political functions, as a place where the *Khutba* was read and legitimacy accorded to the ruling sultan, as also the site where protests were voiced, disputes adjudicated, and conspiracies hatched. As mentioned earlier, Islamic tradition does not lay down any specific plan or directives for the construction of a mosque; rather its architecture has evolved historically through the different phases of the expansion of Islamic empires in response to a variety of factors—climate, technology, regional traditions, and above all, the need to fulfil a range of communicative functions. At one level, the mosque is part of a larger whole, represented by Islam with its sacred centre at Mecca. Unlike a Christian church where every significant action converges at the altar, there is no liturgical centre in the mosque, for the sacred centre is not within the edifice but outside of it. It is this centricity which determines the orientation of every mosque in the Islamic world and that of every devout Muslim at the time of prayer, and becomes in this manner a physical reminder of belonging to a larger community transcending political frontiers. At another level, the congregational mosque was conceived as a closed unit at the time of prayer, a refuge from the outside world within which class antagonisms, dissidence, rivalries, and differences dissolve through the constitution of a homogeneous community held together by shared obligations, piety, and brotherhood. The horizontal axis of a mosque and the lateral organization of space within its interior sought to generate the experience of solidarity within an undifferentiated congregation. The hypostyle model owed its popularity in a large number of regions not only to its flexible ground plan (see above), but equally to its ability to fragment space in a repetitive manner, thereby creating identical units which

[33] Georges Marçais, 'L'urbanisme musulman', in *Mélanges d'histoire et d'archéologie de l'occident musulman*, vol. 1, Algiers, 1957: 219–31; Grabar, 'The Architecture of the Middle Eastern City...'; Kenneth L. Brown, *People of Salé: Tradition and Change in a Moroccan City 1830–1930*, Manchester, 1976; Janet L. Abu-Lughod, 'The Islamic City—Historic Myth, Islamic Essence, and contemporary Relevance', *International Journal of Middle Eastern Studies*, vol. 19, 1987: 155–76; Richard M. Eaton and George Michell, *Firuzabad: Palace City of the Deccan*, Oxford, 1988.

seemed to stretch into infinity, de-emphasizing any single unit of space which may draw attention to its uniqueness.

A variety of relationships could get cemented within and through this structure and its epigraphic programme. To begin with, one of an egalitarian brotherhood defined through submission and conformity to Islam and so, by its very definition, through an exclusion of those outside of that structure at the given moment of community prayer. In the context of north India, at the beginning of the thirteenth century, the 'Muslim community' was composed of a number of heterogeneous elements. Apart from a minority of Turks accompanying the Muizzi commanders, including their slaves, the ranks of the Muslims were expanded by considerable immigration from the regions of Afghanistan, Sind, and Khurasan, in the wake of the Mongol depredations of these areas. These groups were characterized by deep-rooted ethnic, socio-economic, and cultural differences.[34] And finally, a substantial section of 'Indian Muslims' were Hindu converts to Islam.[35] While certain kinds of Koranic prescriptions, as has been pointed out, formed one kind of programme through which all these groups could be collectively addressed as Muslims, the eclectic visual vocabulary of the mosque's decor was likely to be interpreted variously by the individual cultural and ethnic components of a community coming into being, each of whom

[34] Kumar, 'Defining...':37

[35] Mohammed Mujeeb, The Indian Muslims, London, 1967: 19–25. The question of what motivated Hindus, especially of the lower castes, to adopt Islam is a subject of debate. Richard Eaton has expressed doubts about the plausibility of what he terms a theory of 'social liberation' as it, he argues, fallaciously ascribes to medieval Indian society an appreciation of Enlightenment values of social and political equality, a view more recently echoed by Peter Jackson. See Richard Eaton, 'Approaches to the Study of Conversion to Islam in India', in Richard C. Martin (ed.), Approaches to Islam in Religious Studies, Tucson, 1985: 109–11; Peter Jackson, The Delhi Sultanate: A Political and Military History, Cambridge, 1999: 14–15. As opposed to this position, I wish to argue that the notion of brotherhood was not necessarily a category drawn from the European Enlightenment; rather it possessed a specific pre-modern complexion. Movements of religious revival in the Indian subcontinent have often espoused principles of syncretism wherein 'egalitarianism' or 'brotherhood' has been understood primarily in terms of a levelling of differences governing the access of individuals and certain communities, classified as 'outcastes', to God, to ritual practices and spaces, and to salvation and rewards within the cycle of births and rebirths. While conversion to Islam did not, obviously, bring with it a 'liberation' from caste hierarchies—on the contrary, these persisted amongst the new converts—it did open up to certain sections of Hindu society a sacred space within which an ideal of community and brotherhood found articulation. In the present state of research, however, it is still difficult to ascertain with greater exactitude the proportion of Hindu converts to Islam emanating from the lowest rungs of the Hindu social order in relation to those from the relatively prosperous and privileged echelons.

resorted to their own mechanisms to create a definition of the self in relationship to a larger whole. For 'identities' may be viewed as attempts, invested with varying degrees of success, to create and maintain a sense of coherence out of the inchoate and often inconsistent experiences and practices of everyday life. For Hindu converts to Islam, for example, often still tied to past beliefs and internalized structures of thoughts and perceptions, the access to a new sacred space and the forging of new bonds could effectively be mediated through a language of familiar forms that could then function as a meaningful resource in the constitu tion of 'identity'. Research has in fact established that conversion to Islam did not necessarily result in the discarding of older cultural practices, including distinctions of caste.[36] For those lower-caste Hindus, who had previously been denied access to the sacred sites of worship, the adoption of Islam, at a tactile level of experience, meant the entry into a sacred space alive with images and symbols of a divinity, union with whom had possibly represented the highest level of yearning.

Another question that needs to be addressed is whether and the extent to which the architecture of the Qutb mosque and complex intervened in the lives and perceptions of those sections of Delhi's inhabitants who were positioned outside of the fold of the Muslim 'community'. In other words, it becomes necessary to examine the functions of the mosque outside of the times of the Friday prayers, and the ways in which these were embedded within the socio-cultural fabric of thirteenth-century Delhi. As a locus of urban life, the mosque functioned as a pulse spot of the living city; the latter formed a dense and organic unity in which public and private, sacred and profane intermingled with little sense of strain. The mosque and the bazaar, two poles of urban life, were often located in close proximity. Ibn Battuta's descriptions of Delhi in the fourteenth century suggest that the first urban settlement of medieval Dilli, the old *Shahr* with the Qutb complex and the neighbouring *dargah* of Qutb al-Din Bakhtiyar al-Ka'ki, continued to retain its social and cultural pre-eminence, even after subsequent sultans had created their own capital cities, such as Siri and Jahanpanah.[37] The bazaar, with the grain market situated outside the portals of the mosque and the cloth market on the inside of the Badayun Gate, was then one important spine of the urban fabric, linking the *masjid-i jama* with the madrasas, the *haud*, the quarters of the Multani cloth merchants, and the *dargah*.[38] The

[36] Mujeeb, *The Indian Muslims*: 20.

[37] H.A.R. Gibb (ed.), *The Travels of Ibn Battuta A.D. 1325–1354*, 3 vols, New Delhi, 1993: III, 620–26.

[38] See map based on Ibn Battuta's description, ibid: 620.

extreme fluidity between the domains of the religious and the worldly has been repeatedly testified to by studies of various cities within the Islamic world, for which research has often arrived at a higher degree of sophistication than that relating to the Indian subcontinent during this period.[39] While knowledge about the architecture of the markets themselves is elusive, mainly owing to the disappearance of their structures and lack of descriptions in contemporary accounts, research seems to suggest that formal and functional parallels did exist with religious architecture. For example, the form of the Ottoman *bedesten* replicated the plan of Anatolian congregational mosques of Seljuq times.[40] The inextricable links between the sacred and the profane are also confirmed by the fact that revenue from commercial enterprises provided the financial underpinnings for many religious institutions, including their edifices, such as mosques, *madrasas*, and tombs.[41] It has been established beyond doubt as a general principle that the spaces of a public mosque, which on the one hand were used by members of the 'Ulama to inculcate within their disciples the norms of the Shari'ah, the rituals of prayer, and practice of piety, housed, on the other hand, a number of encounters and transactions between members of different communities and social classes outside of the times of the Friday prayers.[42]

Following conquest and appropriation, long-term exigencies had to be seen to: the authority of the new rulers had to be upheld, and this

[39] Brown, *People of Salé*: part II; Besim Selim Hakim, *Arabic-Islamic Cities: Building and Planning Principles*, London, 1986: chapter 2; Oleg Grabar, 'Cities and Citizens. The Growth and Culture of Urban Islam', in Bernard Lewis (ed.), *Islam and the Arab World*, London 1976: 89–100; Eleanor Sims, 'Trade and Travel: Markets and Caravanserais', in George Michell (ed.), *Architecture of the Islamic World*: 80–111; the most significant work on the Indian subcontinent is still C. A. Bayly, *Rulers, Townsmen and Bazaars: Northern Indian Society in the Age of British Expansion, 1770–1870*, Cambridge, 1983.

[40] Sims, 'Trade and Travel ...': 111.

[41] Ibid.

[42] Muslim normative literature did lay down that while it was permissible for the *dhimmis* to enter mosques outside of the times of the Friday prayers, it was undesirable for a Muslim to go into a temple as it would be 'infested with devils', cited in Mujeeb, *The Indian Muslims*: 70–1. The virulent fulminations of orthodox historians like Zia al-Din Barani against sultans who were wilfully 'gentle' in their treatment of the 'infidels' can be interpreted as an expression of orthodox anxieties that in everyday life, the tenets of the shari'ah were far from being a body of law that could be enforced. This was especially true in areas such as trade, markets, crafts, and inheritance. Barani's own position varies from one text to the other: while the *Fatawa-i Jahandari*, conceptualized as a normative text to advise rulers, adopts a stance of polemical rigidity on the question of the treatment of non-believers, the *Ta'rikh-i Firuz-Shahi* voices no protest against the concessions accorded to Hindu rural chiefs or nobles; see Irfan Habib, 'Ziya Barani's Vision of the State', *The Medieval History Journal*, vol. 2, 1999: 34–5.

required recognition and acquiescence by different social groups, the conquerors, the migrants, as well as the large majority made up by the indigenous populace. Ensuring the survival of new ruling groups meant that the economic needs of both old and new had to be met. The spread of new norms could not but go hand in hand with a peaceful acceptance of some of the older ones; interaction and the maintenance of exclusivity became part of a complex pattern of urban life. Its culture, often governed by a series of tensions between contradictory poles, was formed out of bonds between individuals, relationships between processes of different kinds—between the *qadi* and the Sufi, the *amir* and the merchant, between local particularism and the movement of peoples and ideas over continental distances. Practices governing the relationship between Muslim and non-Muslim communities in the Sultanate of Delhi often drew upon precedents from other regions of the Islamic world where Arab conquerors came into contact with communities of Jews and Christians. Orthodoxy on both sides clung to the principle of exclusivity as a mechanism for establishing and maintaining difference, and sought to place restrictions on forms of contact between Hindus and Muslims. Among orthodox Hindus it was the practice of untouchability that served this purpose: according to Ibn Battuta, Muslims were respected but the 'natives do not dine with them or admit them into their houses'.[43] Muslim orthodoxy, whose spokesmen were the *qadis* and the 'Ulama, prescribed that it was undesirable for Muslims held in esteem in their communities to be close to 'men of falsehood and evil' unless absolutely necessary. In everyday practice, however, the prescriptions of the Shari'ah could never become fully operative. Apart from a certain number of Muslim merchants engaged in lucrative long-distance trade, the majority of merchants, moneylenders, and shopkeepers were Hindus and to none of these communities were laws restricting commercial transactions ever applied. Relationships of mutual dependence thrived between the latter groups and members of the *'Umara*, who, next to the sultan, enjoyed the highest social status. Contacts, encounters, and the creation of new bonds and relationships were central to the processes by which empires came into being and state structures consolidated. Being a merchant, for example, required a knowledge of manners and an understanding of human beings and situations, for success hinged on the art of communication and cultivating contacts with potential patrons and customers.[44]

[43] Cited in Mujeeb, *The Indian Muslims*: 234.

[44] Travellers from Europe, like the Frenchman Bernier, pointed out that shops did not proudly display their wares, except for fruits and eatables or cattle. For customers of status

That the edifices and spaces—in this particular case the *masjid-i jama*—within which these encounters took place were mediating spaces that intervened in the processes of relationships coming into being, is a subject which historians of architecture have not adequately looked at. It is no doubt a slippery area, especially for this particular period of Indian history, and the difficulties involved in the recovery of experience belonging to the realm of the visual and the spatial ought not to be underestimated. Yet the question needs to be posed. In this particular instance, it may be postulated that 'symbolic appropriation' of a conquered land needed to be followed by attempts to relate meaningfully to the conquered world—the reabsorption of many of the religious and cosmological traditions and their visual forms, belonging to the vanquished, and their relocation by the new rulers within spaces which were both sacred spaces as well as the spaces of everyday life, could be read as one way of reaching out and assimilating different social groups within a complex of transactions and bonds. The reabsorption and relocation of motifs and symbols, it must be further pointed out, was not entirely arbitrary or idiosyncratic; rather certain principles of selectivity were at work. In the Qutb complex, two recurrent symbols, often fused into a single motif, are the lotus and the *kalasa*, symbols that occupy a central position within Hindu and Jain iconography. Both are replete with meanings related to life, fertility, and creation: the *kalasa*, an ancient Hindu and possibly Buddhist symbol,[45] used on pillars, was an auspicious receptacle for water, whose life-giving functions were suggested by a wreath of foliage that seems to grow out of it. The lotus, an expression of the totality of organic life, emerging from water and whose stalk connects it like an umbilical cord to the womb of the earth, could aesthetically function as a symbol of creativity at all levels. Symbols of this genre could effectively participate in the forging of links between different cosmological traditions: water was an equally central component of Islamic architecture whose uses were multiple—functional, symbolic, decorative, and ritual—used to irrigate gardens, as reflecting pool, to stand for the rivers of Paradise, to cleanse and purify. The *kalasa* and the lotus, separately or fused into a whole, reappeared

---

never came to the shops; rather the merchant or dealer went around, paying his respects to old customers, getting to know new ones, carrying samples of goods and bringing back orders, François Bernier, *Travels in the Mogul Empire*, (ed.) Vincent A. Smith, (second edition), New Delhi, 1992: 247–8.

[45] Ebba Koch, 'The Baluster Column—a European Motif in Mughal Architecture and its Meaning', *Journal of the Warburg and Courtauld Institutes*, vol. 45, 1982: 251–62, reprinted in Juneja (ed.), *Architecture*: 328–51, here 330.

and multiplied in an infinity of forms in buildings throughout the subsequent centuries—on the finial of domes, on columns and thrones, in pools, fountains, and marble basins. The form of the lotus itself, broken up into its component elements, could then be reworked into myriad inventions—as a bud or in full bloom, inverted or contained within a medallion, outlining a wagon vault or the interior of a ceiling— through processes of stylization and geometrization, so central to the principles of pattern in Islamic art, whereby a combination of geometric forms could be symmetrically repeated and extended into infinity. Such processes can be observed at work in a host of buildings that were constructed in different regions of the subcontinent from the thirteenth century onwards.

The proliferation of visual and structural forms across the geography and political regions of the subcontinent was thus built into historical contexts of encounter, of the demarcation and assimilation of peoples and traditions. In Bengal for instance, while the larger Friday mosques, representative of political authority, continued to be constructed according to the sanctified hypostyle plan, a large number of smaller mosques were modelled on simple hut-like structures, characterized by the curved cornice roofline that echoed the visual form of a thatched roof. This specific regional characteristic has been situated by Eaton within a devotional context of Islam in Bengal: the spread of faith and cultural practices in the countryside was not directly linked to the power of ruling elites, rather Sufi groups here functioned as mediating agents.[46] The movement of architectural forms does not however end here. From its unmistakeably popular context, the curvilinear 'Bengali roof' or *bangala* came to be re-appropriated in the opulent buildings commissioned by Shah Jahan in Delhi and Agra and to be re-canonized as imperial architecture.[47] Such continuous movements in many directions cannot be perceived as mere formalistic borrowings or be adequately characterized by the widely used art-historical term 'influence'. The dynamics of architectural practices, I have tried to argue, were directly implicated in movements of people, beliefs, and practices; they articulated processes of adjustment and absorption that were part of encounters between communities and traditions, and they participated in the erection of boundaries as also in their permeation and redefinition.

---

[46] Eaton, *The Rise*: 229ff.

[47] Pointed out in all art-historical studies of architecture commissioned by Shah Jahan, see Catherine Asher, *Architecture*: 180; Ebba Koch, *Mughal Architecture, A Outline of Its History and Development (1526–1858)*, Munich 1991, rpt. Delhi, 2002: 93, 115.

Transition from the Syncretic to the Plural

The World of Hindi and Urdu

SALIL MISRA

There is a tendency in social sciences to look upon plurality primarily in religious terms and often to equate plurality with syncretism or to treat them interchangeably. If, however, the concept of plurality were to be extended to the realm of language, particularly to the universe of Hindi and Urdu, as it existed in the nineteenth and the twentieth centuries, an interesting pattern of syncretism and plurality could be discerned. This article focuses on Hindi and Urdu in the last two centuries, specially on the development of their relationship with each other. It posits that here was a case, not of syncretism and plurality accompanying each other, but that of a syncretic and composite tradition giving way to a plural one. Simply put, the two languages, as we understand them to be today, formed a part of a common language amalgam or indeed one language[1] that transformed into two different and competing languages over a period of two centuries. The paper begins by tracing the history of this common language and then delineates the process through which it got bifurcated into two linguistic branches that not only developed their separate social, political, and literary trajectories in the course of time, but also constructed two separate lineages for themselves. It will also

---

[1] This indeed is the title of the interesting book written by Christopher R. King who argues persuasively that Hindi and Urdu were indeed one language written in two different scripts. King, *One Language Two Scripts: The Hindi Movement in Nineteenth Century North India*, Oxford, 1994.

comment upon the relationship that existed between language and politics and its implications for both Hindi and Urdu.

At the very outset it is necessary to emphasize that this article is not about language per se. It does not approach the question of language from a purely linguistic perspective. This disclaimer is necessary because any study of language and society is likely to become deceptive on the question of the relationship of language with society and politics. The essay argues that languages have a life trajectory whose destiny is not determined by their internal structure. Languages inevitably play multiple roles in society and politics but these roles are not shaped by the internal arrangements of the languages or their *linguistic* superiority or inferiority. The ultimate fate of a language is decided by factors and forces *outside* the domain of that language.[2] To that extent this essay may be said to follow an instrumentalist approach on the question of language. Therefore, in the interest of the argument pursued in this essay, it may be useful to look upon language not just as a linguistic artefact but primarily as an *identity* and as a feeder into various other identities.

I

That the two languages under discussion have a common lineage and a shared parentage is a point not likely to be contested by linguists and other scholars. In fact, the histories written specifically for Hindi or for Urdu read very similar to each other. Merely substituting the term Hindi for Urdu can easily convert an Urdu story into a Hindi story.[3] This story has been told by scholars but for the sake of clarity it is just as well to go over this background.

From the Aryan period till about the tenth century, Sanskrit acquired the status of a classic, standardized, grammatically uniform, and written literary language. However, at the level of speech a number of

---

[2] The argument can perhaps be expressed better in the words of Ernest Gellner: 'Language, man and the world are so intertwined that theories about any one of them inevitably presuppose a good deal about each of the others.' For an elaboration of the point, see his article on Chomsky in Ernest Gellner, *Spectacles and Predicaments: Essays in Social Theory*, Cambridge, 1979, pp. 111–16.

[3] For the Hindi story see Vasudha Dalmia, *The Nationalization of Hindu Traditions: Bhartendu Harishchandra and Nineteenth Century Banaras*, Oxford, 1997, pp. 146–61; for the Urdu story see Ram Babu Saksena, *A History of Urdu Literature*, Lahore, 1927, pp. 1–23; and Ali Jawad Zaidi, *A History of Urdu literature*, New Delhi, 1993, pp. 1–11; for a treatment of both the stories together, see Amrit Rai, *A House Divided: The Origin and Development of Hindi-Urdu*, Oxford, 1991.

regional variations continued to grow which could generically be called Prakrit (meaning natural). These Prakrits developed many regional variations called *apabhranshas* (literally meaning a corrupted version but implying improvised versions) one of which could be called western Hindi (a term coined in the late nineteenth century by the eminent linguist George Grierson in his famous *Linguistic Survey of India*), spoken in and around the area of present-day Delhi and western Uttar Pradesh. This area soon developed into a political and administrative mainstream. As a result, the dialect of this area, known as Khari Boli (again a term in currency only around late eighteenth-early nineteenth century but referring to a form of speech in existence since the eleventh-twelfth centuries) came into early contact with and incorporated many words from, the language of the rulers which consisted of a lexical reservoir drawn from Arabic, Persian, and Turkish. From here, this language was taken to new areas by the Sufi saints and soldiers. A greater exposure to new regions and cultures kept enriching its vocabulary. The grammatical structure however did not change very much. *This* language with its grammar constituted the base for many literary experiments that were undertaken in different parts of the country. Since it was different from Persian in grammatical structure and rooted very much in indigenous linguistic tradition, the rulers gave it the name Hindi. It was also called Hindavi/Hindui when its distinctiveness from Persian was to be highlighted. When compared to Sanskrit, it was called Bhasa or Bhakha. It continued to be written in both the Nagari and the Persian scripts and kept acquiring new names. In the southern territories of Bijapur and Golconda it flourished under the name Dakhani (literally meaning southern). It was also called Zabaan-i-Hindustan (speech of Hindustan) and around the turn of the eighteenth century, Rekhtah (literally meaning mixed or scattered because of the sparse presence of Persian words in it). Towards the end of the eighteenth century yet another term, Urdu, was added to the list. In spite of different names, the literary tradition of this language continued as an unbroken chain till at least the eighteenth century. Then at some point in history, the chain got disconnected and, after a process of differentiation and assimilation, re-emerged in the form of two separate linguistic streams that developed into modern Hindi and Urdu.

When did this common language reservoir get bifurcated into two languages? In other words, when did a composite, syncretic linguistic tradition begin to give way to a plural one? The beginnings of this trajectory have generally been traced to what has been called a literary purification attempted in the eighteenth century. Ram Babu Saksena, in his classic and probably the earliest attempt to write a history of Urdu literature in English, points out that under certain literary impulses the poetry written in the eighteenth century began to replace the indigenous words of Indic origin with expressions borrowed from Persian language. It was for this reason that the poetry written in the eighteenth–nineteenth centuries used a vocabulary very different from the earlier poetry of Amir Khusro (1253–1325), a thirteenth century poet from Delhi, or Malik Mohammad Jaysi, a sixteenth century poet in the Awadh region, and many others. Writes Ram Babu Saksena:

...the process of eliminating indigenous words continued and their place was filled by 'exotics'. Certain 'Bhasa' words were undoubtedly harsh and ungainly, not fit to rank in literary composition but the wholesale expulsion was undoubtedly harmful to the sturdy growth of the language of the soil.... It could not preserve its racy words received as a heritage from Sanskrit and Prakrit from the invasion of Persian. The early Urdu scholars were no scholars in Sanskrit or Hindi ...they ruthlessly rejected them [words of Sanskrit origin], supplemented them by others of Persian and Arabic origin. This process is called by them ...the process of refinement and crystallization of the language.[4]

Whether this was done under purely literary impulses or whether there were other factors at work is a little difficult to determine. Amrit Rai believes that this development (replacement of words of Indic origins by Persian and Arabic ones) was not purely literary but was also related to a loss of power perceived by the ruling elite and a consequent attempt to reinforce the connectivity with Persian literature.[5] Vasudha Dalmia agrees: 'This move to cement a culture that was already on the decline, came as an almost characteristic measure of defence, once the glory of the empire had begun to fade.'[6]

This argument of an eighteenth century literary reform has not gone totally uncontested. Shamsur Rahman Faruqi, a noted Urdu scholar, has made a rather strong critique of Amrit Rai[7] and posited an

[4] Ram Babu Saksena, *A History of Urdu Literature*, pp. 16–17.

[5] Amrit Rai, *A House Divided*, pp. 239–51.

[6] Vasudha Dalmia, *The Nationalization of Hindu Traditions*, p. 156. Also, 'It was a necessary cultural and spiritual compensation for the loss of Muslim political power in the 18th–19th centuries through the rise of the Marathas, the Sikhs and the British.' Suniti kumar Chatterji, *Languages And The Linguistic Problem*, Oxford Pamphlets On Indian Affairs, Oxford, 1943, pp. 17–18.

[7] Faruqi calls Amrit Rai's thesis of an eighteenth-century linguistic transformation 'full of inconsistensies, or tendentious speculation rather than hard facts, or fanciful interpretation of actual facts' but does not, at any point in his book, attempt a frontal confrontation with the eighteenth-century argument. Shamsur Rahman Faruqi, *Early Urdu Literary Culture and History*, Oxford, 2001, p. 21, fn.

alternative argument of a continuity of a single literary tradition till the nineteenth century. According to Faruqi, no dramatic ruptures took place in this tradition in the eighteenth century but it was broken and bifurcated only in the nineteenth century by the efforts of the College of Fort William, set up by the British. The composite language till then had been identified as Hindustani but the British preferred the term Urdu because of its obvious Arabic/Islamic connotation. The gap thus created was widened, according to Faruqi, by writers like Bhartendu Harishchandra who switched over from Urdu to Hindi and also began treating Urdu language and script disparagingly. In addition, leading nineteenth century Urdu poets and scholars like Altaf Husain Hali and Shibli Numani, writing the history of Urdu literature, began to overlook and exclude the Hindu contribution from it. All this was done under the influence of the 'standard theory of ... [their] British masters'[8] of equating Urdu exclusively with Muslims. However, by the 1930s, Muslims 'thrown on the defensive by the realization that Urdu might have no place in a Hindu-dominated India, proclaimed the folly and falsity of the "Urdu equals Muslim" equation, and began to assert the truth: Urdu was, and had always been, the language of both Hindus and Muslims.'[9] But it was probably too late and the damage, of a composite language being divided along communal lines, had been done by then. However, the two positions, Rai's and Faruqi's, do not question that a process of bifurcation *was* set in motion. They also do not deny the composite and common heritage of Hindi and Urdu. They only differ on when this process may have begun, in the eighteenth or the nineteenth century.[10]

This process of linguistic purification or refinement constituted the first stage in the creation of two distinct languages of modern Hindi and Urdu out of the composite Hindavi. By the new stress on purism it ceased to serve the function of a connecting link between the elite and

[8] Ibid., p. 49.
[9] Ibid., p. 51.
[10] However, it is difficult not to notice a bias in favour of Hindi in Amrit Rai's treatment, and in favour of Urdu in Faruqi's treatment. This bias is specially noticeable in the manner in which the two experts have treated Bhartendu Harishchandra and Sir Syed Ahmad Khan, two prominent actors involved in the nineteenth-century language controversy. Whereas Amrit Rai is critical of Sir Syed and sympathetic to Bhartendu Harishchandra (on Sir syed, see p. 269, and on Bhartendu, pp. 271–4, *A House divided.*), Faruqi does just the opposite (on Bhartendu, see pp. 46–7, and on Sir Syed, p. 58, *Early Urdu.*) It is also difficult to escape the conclusion that both Amrit Rai and Faruqi are not very far from actually sharing the prejudices of Bhartendu and Sir Syed, respectively.

the masses.[11] It also disowned its Indic heritage in preference for a Persian one. To quote Ram Babu Saksena again:

It was thus that the child forsook its parents and took its abode with its adopted parents who endowed it largely with *their* riches.... It must be admitted that the influence of Persian raised the dialect to the dignity of a language though it is to be deplored that it destroyed much of what was valuable in the dialect which it had obtained as a heritage from the parent tongue.[12]

The forsaken parents, to extend the metaphor employed by Saksena, did not disappear or go into oblivion. They resurfaced in the nineteenth century, under vastly different circumstances, and adopted a new child. It was actually this process of adoption and adaptation that invented parents and created new children out of a complex linguistic raw material.

The second major step in the creation of linguistic duality belonged to the efforts of the Christian missionaries and the activities of the College of Fort William established in Calcutta in 1800 to train the officers of the East India Company in Indian culture and languages. There would now appear to be a consensus, with a shift in focus, that the arrival of the British on the Indian soil, creation of the Fort William College, and a focus on modern education involving the creation of new schools and textbooks increasingly paved the way for a process in which Hindi and Urdu emerged as almost separated twins which had certain features in common along with some differences. Their grammar and morphology brought them closer; their scripts took them further apart.

Although no bifurcation had taken place in the eighteenth century, a lexical transformation (cleansing of the language, taking out of words of Indic/Hindavi origin and their replacement with words of Persian origin) did prepare the ground rules for its branching out into two streams. What concerns us here is that the vocabulary of the language was substantially Persianized which left a significant lexical residue. Its concrete manifestation was that in 1757, one Zuhuruddin Hatim brought out his *Deewanzada* from which words of a composite Hindavi origin were deliberately weeded out.[13] The words exiled from the literary written world did not disappear; they remained in oral circulation, waiting for an umbrella or an alternative literary patronage system.

[11] Tara Chand writes: 'Altghough it became the language of both Hindu and Muslim upper classes, its contact with the common people was weakened.' Tara Chand, *The Problem of Hindustani*, Allahabad, 1944, p. 57.

[12] Ram Babu Saksena, *A History of Urdu literature*, p. 4.

[13] Vasudha Dalmia, *The Nationalization of Hindu Traditions*, p. 157.

The early British efforts in India included an attempt at the codification of existing indigenous knowledge. This codification on the one
hand necessitated a certain standardization and on the other made script
very crucial as the indigenous knowledge could only be written in some
script. The Christian missionaries did much by extensive translations,
publications of tracts as well as school books and setting up societies in
different parts of UP for the promotion of Hindi written in Nagari
script.[14] They seemed to operate with the impression that Hindi written
in Nagari was the language of Hindus and therefore all missionary work
among Hindus had to be done keeping this in mind. The British, brought
up and conditioned into looking upon language as a mirror to ethnicity,
began to form an impression that Hindus and Muslims, constituting
different religious groups, must speak different languages. Chamberlain,
a Christian missionary who arrived in India in 1803 to spread the gospel
of Christianity, wrote in a letter:

The language called by Europeans Hindusthani and the language of Hindus are
diverse. The latter is 'Hinduwee'. The 'Hindusthani' which is spoken by the
Mussulmans is a compound of Hinduwee, Persic [Persian] and Arabic; it is
much spoken as a popular tongue and is used in all civil and military proceedings; but I suspect that if we would do good to the major part of the Hindoos, *we
must have the scriptures in their own vernacular languages, and must preach to them in
that language too.*[15]

It would appear that this understanding of Hindus and Muslims being
divided along linguistic lines was fully shared by the functionaries of the
Fort William College. The College appointed John Bothwich Gilchrist
as a professor of Hindustani. John Gilchrist wrote in his book: 'In a
country where pedantry is esteemed as a touchstone of learning, the
learned Moosulman glories in his Arabic and Persian ... the Hindu is
not less attached to Sanskrit and Hinduwee.'[16] Such thinking influenced
the choice of the script in which different literary works were to be
written, translated, and printed. Hence, works like *Betal Pachisi, Sinhasan
Battisi,* and *Prem Sagar,* with a Hindu association, were printed in the
Nagari script. Mir Amman's famous work, *Bagh-o-Bahar,* written in the
tradition of Arabian Nights, was produced in Urdu.[17] This, along with
the possibility that the residual vocabulary of the Hindavi tradition

[14] Ibid., pp.169–75.
[15] Quoted in ibid., p. 169, emphasis added.
[16] Quoted in ibid., p. 164.
[17] Neeraj Goyal, *Fort William College: Ek Itihas* (in Hindi), Meerut, 1986, appendix iii, p.
89.

would have been employed in the creation of new literature, texts, and the school texts, would certainly have imparted a duality or a two-ness to the same language.

Another factor of some consequence was the decision of the East India Company to replace Persian with English and the vernacular as the language of official and court proceedings in the areas under its control. Thus, in 1837, English became the official language of the Bengal Presidency (in Bombay and Madras Presidencies in 1832). This dealt a severe blow to Persian which had till then enjoyed the status of the official language. Gradually, Hindi written in Nagari script was introduced in Bihar and Central Province. In UP (North-West Province and Oudh) however, it remained Hindustani written in Persian script. This meant that whereas English replaced Persian as the court language at the top, leading regional languages like Bengali, Oriya, and Hindi written in Nagari became the prevalent court languages in Bengal, Orissa, Bihar, and CP respectively. Therefore, a common language (Hindi) began to be identified as two different languages mainly on account of different scripts: In Bihar and CP, Hindi was written in the Nagri script and was established as the language of court and administration. In UP, on the other hand, the same language written in the Persian Script became the court language.

II

Why was it that in the nineteenth century people suddenly began to attach so much importance to their language? Why was it that the question did not remain confined to language but invariably fed into people's political and ideological universe? How did language, a matter of functional necessity, acquire the power to shape and determine people's politics and ideology? Part of the explanation lies in the very arrival of modernity which imparts a new role and capacity to language. Language, as a form of speech, had accompanied mankind in various phases of its history and development. Never before, however, did it acquire the power on humanity that it came to exercise in the modern and modernizing world. Prior to the arrival of modernity it only had a functional relevance. Now it emerged as an organizing principle and a great source of human bonding. Under the impulses of modernism, modern groups and communities begin to be brought and held together not so much by land, clan or caste as earlier, but by common language. Language emerges as a powerful vehicle of identity formation, promoting group solidarity. Language, under modern conditions (defined by, among other things, ideas of perpetual growth, literacy, and mobility) acquires a power that it did not possess before. Along with culture and religion it emerges as a serious candidate for being a motivator of group formation and solidarity. When language combines with religion and culture it becomes an irresistible force capable of creating and also destroying states. Conversely, in a situation where language communities and communities based on culture and religion are not congruent with each other, they make every effort to become so. This modernist insistence that language communities should be more than just language communities, that apart from common language they should also share a common culture and politics, has been a contributor to the process of the creation of two languages of Hindi and Urdu.

This new power of language (in which language is not just the written or spoken word; it is the maker and marker of new solidarities) has also been identified by another concept, called linguism. Linguism may be defined as the belief that 'language is the product of a mystic folk unity and its speakers have, therefore, an inalienable right to govern the region which they occupy. It identifies language with culture and equates culture with political frontiers.'[18] The growth of this linguism in different societies has followed a trajectory that has three phases. One, it expresses itself in efforts to enrich one's regional language. Two, it then creates around it a hallow of sanctity, and, three, it invents a history and an antiquity along with a passion for its greatness. Finally, it sets in motion a motive force that develops expansionist tendencies and seeks to create political boundaries with total disregard for existing social or geographical realities.[19]

Applying this principle to Central and Eastern Europe, Schuman writes:

If a language group does not possess independence, it must achieve it. If, having attained independence, it does not include within the nation-state all those who speak the mother tongue, efforts must be made towards their annexation even at the cost of dismemberment of neighbouring States. If there are those within the State who do not speak the mother tongue, they must be taught, assimilated and, if necessary, coerced into abandoning their own language and culture in the name of national unity and power.[20]

Let us see how this monster of linguism translated itself in the Indian situation as existed in the nineteenth century.

[18] K.M.Munshi, *Indian Constitutional Documents: Pilgrimage to Freedom, 1902–50, Vol. I,* Bombay, 1967, p. 222.
[19] Ibid., p. 223.
[20] Ibid., pp. 224–5.

III

It would be futile to deny the existence of two separate linguistic entities called Hindi and Urdu in the nineteenth century. But they did not initially correspond to the demand of linguism that language communities should be congruent with cultural and religious ones. Urdu in particular continued to defy any possible language-religion congruence in both the possible ways: a substantial number of non-Muslims continued to read and write in Urdu and an equally substantial number of Muslims did not.[21] Although attempts had begun to broadly identify Hindi with Hindus and Urdu with Muslims, they were rare. There were many factors that did not allow a simple Hindi-Hindu and Urdu-Muslim equation to develop. For one, the term Hindi continued to be used in a generic sense representing both the languages. Amir Khusro, undisputedly the first recorded poet of the Hindavi literary tradition, had said in a Persian couplet: 'I am an Indian rose finch, if you ask me the truth. If you wish to hear some subtle verses, ask me to recite in Hindui.'[22] Abul Fazl, the court historian of Akbar, called Hindvi the language of *Doab* (the area between the two rivers Ganga and Yamuna) in his *Ain-i-Akbari*. Ghalib, the leading nineteenth century Urdu poet, called a collection of his letters *Ood-i-Hindi*, and Mir Taqi Mir, famous eighteenth century Urdu poet, continued to persist with the old practice of calling Hindi the language of the people of the land.[23] Ayodhya Prasad Khatri, writing his *Khari boli Ka Padya* (Poetry in Khari Boli) in the second half of the nineteenth century, referred to five types of Hindi spoken in the region: Pandit Hindi (Sanskritized Hindi), Maulvi Hindi (Persianized Hindi), Munshi Hindi (composite Hindi), Theth Hindi (pure Hindi without excessive Persian or Sanskrit words), and Eurasian Hindi (Hindi with a mixture of English words spoken in

---

[21] There are many instances to deny Urdu's exclusive identification with Muslims in the nineteenth century. Three major caste groups among Hindus—Kayasthas, Kashmiri Brahmins, and Khattris—were all traditionally brought up in Urdu and had a strong association with it. Arya Samaj, a strong Hindu proselytizing movement, did much of its propapaganda in favour of Hindi, in Urdu language. For more instances of this kind see Salil Misra, 'From the Mainstream to the Margins: Urdu in North India' in *Contemporary India,* (Journal of the Nehru Memorial Museum and Library, New Delhi), Vol. 1, No.2, pp. 123–4.

[22] The original Persian couplet is: *Chuman tooti-i-Hindam, ar rast pursi; Ze man Hinduipurs, ta nagz goyam.* Syed Ehtisham Husain, *Urdu Sahitya Ka Itihas* (in Hindi), Aligarh, 1954.

[23] Here, is his famous couplet: *Kya Janun Log Kehte Hain Kisko Suroor-i-Qalb; Aaya Nahin Hai Lafz Ye Hindi Zaban Ke Beech.* Gopal Rai, *Hindi Bhasha Ka Vikas* (in Hindi), Patna, 1995, p. 11.

official circles).[24] In this typology, in the second and the third category (Maulvi Hindi and Munshi Hindi, respectively) he was referring to chaste Urdu of Lucknow and a somewhat more mixed Urdu of Delhi.

The term Urdu, on the other hand, is of a later date. Urdu is a Turkish word meaning camp and its usage for a language or a group of languages is not recorded earlier than eighteenth century. The term that was used for the language was *Zaban-i-Urdu-i-Mualla-i-Shahjahanabad*, literally meaning the language of the exalted city of Shahjahanabad. From there it shortened to Zaban-i-Urdu-i-Mualla, then to Zaban-i-Urdu and finally to Urdu.[25] Till as late as the eighteenth century, the term Urdu implied not a language but a territory, or a city, where the language was spoken. Insha Allah Khan, in his classic *Dariya-i-Latafat* (Ocean of Subtleties, written in Persian in 1807) wrote: 'The languages of the camp [Zaban-i-Urdu] include a few languages such as Arabic, Persian, Turkish, Braj etc.'[26] It is said that the shortened name Urdu owes itself to its usage in a couplet by the eighteenth century Delhi poet Mus-hafi sometime in the 1760s. From then onwards only the term Urdu began to be used for the language. With more and more literary usage, the language acquired grammatical and lexical standardization, and also a fixed and stable name Urdu. It could be defined as a language with a grammatical base of Khari Boli, a vocabulary drawn from Arabic and Persian on the one hand and a host of local dialects on the other, and a Persiani script. Likewise Hindi came to be identified as a language that drew its grammatical structure from the same source as Urdu did, a vocabulary drawn from Sanskrit and other languages/dialects of Indic origin, and a Nagari script. Hindi and Urdu, in their increasingly systematizing and formalizing nineteenth century versions, were like two overlapping circles consisting of both a shared territory and separate domains. Grammar united them and script divided them. Some part of their vocabulary was common and the remaining was specific to each language.

Thus it was that at the beginning of the nineteenth century, various terms that had been in usage at different points in time in different areas, like Hindui, Hindavi, Dehalvi, Dakhani, Bhasa, Zaban-i-Hindustan, Zaban-i-Urdu-i-Mualla, had gone out of circulation. Hindi and Urdu emerged as two terms without any definitional ambiguity.[27] However,

[24] King, *One Language Two Scripts*, p. 30.

[25] Shansur Rehman Faruqi, *Early Urdu: Literature, Culture and History*, pp. 25–6.

[26] The original Persian quote is: '*Zaban-i-Urdu mushtamil ast bar chand zaban yani Arbi va Farsi va Turki va Biraj Vaghairah.*' Quoted in Ali Jawad Zaidi, *A History of Urdu Literature*, p. 10.

[27] Yet another name that made an appearance from the eighteenth century onwards was

the use of the term Hindi has still carried some semantic complications for scholars. Whereas Hindi was probably one of the earliest expressions used for *the* language, Urdu was certainly the last. Having been in existence for much longer than Urdu, the term Hindi has obviously been employed in a variety of ways. At one level it can be defined as a generic, catch-all term for a group of languages/dialects written/spoken in the area of north and central India since the twelfth century. Amir Khusro, in his Persian epic *Noor Sip-har* (Nine Skies) written around 1318, called Hindavi the language of most parts of India, and distinguished it, on the one hand from Sanskrit ('language of Brahmins which the common people are not familiar with') and Persian and Turkish on the other ('Hindavi is more popular in comparison with Persian and Turkish because of the pleasantness/sweetness of its words').[28] But in a more specific sense it is also the name of a language that emerged as a formidable candidate for the status of national language in the era of nationalism. In the latter capacity it was involved in a serious contest with Urdu and to a lesser extent English. Hindi therefore is a term employed both at a generic and a specific level. It is interesting to see how this dilemma has been handled by linguists and other scholars. Eminent linguist Suniti Kumar Chatterji, uses the term Hindi for the original and High Hindi or Nagari Hindi for the specific.[29] Alok Rai chooses to demarcate the two by writing one as Hindi and the other as 'Hindi' (within quotes).[30] His father Amrit Rai uses the term Hindi/Hindavi for the language amalgam and modern Hindi for the denominational one.[31] Terms like old Hindi and new Hindi have also been employed to highlight the distinction between the two.

Hindustani. Hindustani was to develop a chequered career in the subsequent centuries and its story will be dealt with slightly later in this essay.

[28] Gopi Chand Narang, *Amir Khusro Ka Hindavi Kavya* (in Hindi), New Delhi, 1990, pp. 24–5.

[29] Suniti Kumar Chatterji, *Indo Aryan and Hindi*, Calcutta, 1960, pp. 138–40.

[30] Alok Rai, *Hindi Nationalism* (a part of Tract of the Times series brought out by Orient Longman), Hyderabad, 2000.

[31] Amrit Rai, *A House Divided*. This duality about the term can be deceptive. It has made leading linguist Suniti Kumar Chatterji take apparently contradictory positions in two of his works. In his earlier works of the 1930s he called Hindi the recognized language of practically the whole of Aryan India, excluding Bengal, Assam, Orissa, Nepal, Sind, Gujarat, and Maharashtra. He considered it the third-largest language in the world after Chinese and English and acknowledged its presence in most parts of country. (Chatterji, *Bharteeya Arya Bhasha Aur Hindi* [Hindi translation of eight lectures originally delivered in 1940 at the Gujarat Vernacular Society, Ahmedabad], Patna, 1977, pp. 150 and 157–9). Then, three decades later, in another series of lectures delivered at Mahatma Gandhi Memorial research Centre, Bombay, in 1973, he did a complete volte face and declared that

This semantic puzzle regarding the term Hindi is important in as much as it has actually created a largely false polemic among scholars. As mentioned earlier, both Amrit Rai and Faruqi agree that modern Hindi and Urdu are products of the same root. But the debate really is whether this root language should be called Hindavi or early Urdu. In other words, is it the case that modern Hindi is the offshoot of some form of early Urdu, or is Urdu a product of the original Hindavi? Purely at the level of nomenclature, this should not constitute any problem since both the terms, Hindavi and early Urdu, can be treated as synonymous. But the two authors, mentioned above, have insisted on making an issue of it. Amrit Rai says:

...what I must stoutly contest is Urdu's claim to being a common language of the Hindus and the Muslims, *that* modern Urdu is not—and old Urdu (if one should insist on that name, since the language was in those times called Hindi or Hindavi or Dehlavi or, when it moved to the Deccan, Dakani and Gujari) most certainly was. It is no use pretending that modern Urdu is the same language, and there is no getting away from the fact that modern Urdu acquired its present character by deliberately throwing out words of Indian origin, i.e., Sanskrit words and their derivatives, from the naturally growing common language of the Hindus and the Muslims, and by substituting them, as far as possible, exclusively with Persian and Arabic words. It may therefore be pertinent to say that modern Urdu, far from representing the unity of the language, represents the willfully brought about cleavage in the natural unified character of the language.[32]

Faruqi's effort, on the other hand, is to turn this understanding upside down, from saying that Urdu is a descendent from Hindi, to asserting

---

'Hindi the *Rashtra Bhasha* is nowhere spoken in Bihar' and other places where people speak their area-specific speeches different from Hindi. He openly questioned Hindi's claim to represent various dialects and considered it unfit for the status of the national language on the ground of being unrepresentative (Chatterji, *India: A Polyglot Nation and Its Linguistic Problems vis-à-vis National Integration*, Bombay, 1973, p. 158). It would be interesting to make a study of this transition in Chatterji's understanding. It is possible that in the pre-independence period he may have looked at Hindi's role as a potential national language and, after 1947, may have been disappointed by the undue haste displayed by the Hindi chauvinists to impose it on the rest of the country. But it is clear that in his two positions, Chatterji was employing two different meanings of Hindi, the generic and the specific. This semantic confusion has been handled best by Tara Chand who provided three different definitions of the word Hindi, one, in the generic Hindavi sense; two, in the sense of 'tertiary Prakrits' or the new Indo-Aryan languages (the various dialects spoken in north and central India since the medieval times, like Bundeli, Kanauji, Braj, Bangru, Khari Boli, Dehlavi, Awadhi, Bagheli, Chhattisgarhi, Rajasthani, and Magahi); and three, as modern Hindi in its modern incarnation during the nineteenth century. See Z.A.Ahmed (ed.), *National Language for India: A Symposium*, Allahabad, 1940, pp. 133–5.

[32] Amrit Rai, *A House Divided*, p. 288 (italics and brackets as in the original).

that modern Hindi is nothing more than a stylistic version of Urdu.[33] The difference between the two arguments is only skin-deep. It is obviously possible to argue both ways. If Urdu can be equipped with an extended lineage (in the form of early Urdu or Hindavi), modern Hindi can be easily projected as its modern product. It can also be done the other way (as Amrit Rai does), i.e., to treat Hindi, or Hindavi, as the root language from which sprang Urdu and modern, or high, or Nagari Hindi. But the basic point remains the same: the two modern languages (Urdu and Hindi) are a product of the same language base, whatever be its name, Hindavi or early Urdu.

The question then is: What was the process, or what were the processes, through which Hindi and Urdu came to be identified with Hindus and Muslims, respectively. It is evident that battles on behalf of Hindi and Urdu were fought by men who were Hindus and Muslims, respectively. Did they just happen to be Hindus and Muslims divided along linguistic lines, or were there larger forces working to ensure this? It is also evident that the language scenario prior to the eighteenth century did not correspond to a Hindu-Muslim divide. So what happened in the eighteenth and nineteenth centuries?

The eighteenth century process of linguistic purification referred to earlier (replacing words of Indic origins with Arabic and Persian ones) was accompanied by another process of Islamic reformism. The spiritual leader of this reform was Shah Wali Ullah (1703–62) who attempted to bring about a return to pristine Islamic glory by eschewing non-Islamic practices and traditions brought into Islam by converts from other faiths and by Sufi saints with their stress on syncretism. Shah Wali Ullah, in this sense, was a precursor to the nineteenth century Wahabi and Faraizi movements. His reform efforts have been conceptualized in a simple formula: *Sunna* plus *Sharia* minus *Bidaa*.[34] It meant that the trodden path of Islamic tradition (*Sunna*) should be combined with the rules of high Islam (*Sharia*) and purged of the un-Islamic influences and practices brought by interaction with local traditions (*Bidaa*). Shah Wali Ullah's initiatives were carried on by his disciples in the late eighteenth and early nineteenth centuries. This was purely a reform movement intended to standardize and purify Indian Islam. But a similar process was underway in the realm of Urdu language. The formula there was: Khari Boli plus Arabic and Persian vocabulary minus words of Indic

---

[33] Faruqi, *Early Urdu*, pp. 54–5.

[34] Hafeez Malik, *Sir Sayyad Ahmad Khan and Muslim modernism in India and Pakistan*, New York, 1980, p. 256. Also see P. Hardy, *The Muslims of British India*, Cambridge, 1972, pp. 28–30.

origins. There is no evidence that the two processes, of religious and literary purification, went together or were intended to go together. But given the similarities of the projects and also among the actors undertaking these projects, the two could not have remained separate for long. Urdu was thus bound to be identified with high Islam.

Very similar processes were underway in the realm of Hindi in the nineteenth century. The process of the creation of a standardized Hindi language involved achieving internal standardization and external differentiation. The former involved displacing established languages like Braj and Awadhi from their territory and appropriating the same.[35] The external differentiation was obtained by demarcating Hindi as *Arya Bhasha* (Aryan language) as against the language of the Muslims. Like Urdu, this too was a development more religio-cultural than purely linguistic. Vasudha Dalmia writes:

The homogenization of language which followed ran parallel to the similar movement taking place in the constitution of modern Hinduism. Here the process involved was the absorption of 'sects' (corresponding to the position of dialects) regarded not as autonomous in their religious authority and tradition, but as deviations from the one central strand, the sanatan dharma (corresponding to the notion of arya bhasha), which had apparently always remained constant, though the principles that make for cohesiveness at the core were themselves in the process of being negotiated.[36]

Thus, it was probably inevitable that the processes creating modern Hindi and Urdu on the one hand, and those leading to the formation of structured Hinduism and Islam on the other, would result in the identification of Urdu with Islam and Hindi with Hinduism. The question then is: why did the protagonists of the two languages fight each other? Duality or plurality is not a sufficient precondition for conflict. The conflict between Hindi and Urdu cannot be explained merely by the *presence* of Hindi and Urdu or their identification with Hinduism and Islam, respectively. Why then did the two enter into a conflict with each other?

---

[35] On the displacement of Braj and Awadhi, there is an alternative argument that needs to be taken seriously. Hazari Prasad Dwivedi, eminent Hindi scholar, has argued that this standardization was more a result of a voluntary merger on the part of Braj and Awadhi into Hindi, rather than any appropriatiary imperialistic tendency on the part of high Hindi. It was a part of an attempt to merge the language of poetry (Braj) and the language of prose (Khari Boli-based high Hindi) to create one literary tradition of both prose and poetry. Hazari Prasad Dwivedi, 'Hindi aur Anya Bhashaon Ka Sambandh (Relationship between Hindi and Other Languages)', in *Hazari Prasad Dwivedi Granthavali*, Vol. 10, pp. 218–19.

[36] Vasudha Dalmia, *Nationalization of Hindu Traditions*, p. 151.

IV

The context for the strife was provided, though probably not voluntarily, by the British government. As mentioned earlier in this essay, the decision taken by the East India Company in 1837 to replace Persian with English at the top and vernacular in lower courts set the stage for a prolonged battle between the two languages. For all practical purposes, Urdu along with English became the language of the administration in UP. This development led to what has been called the Hindi/Nagari movement. The original aim of the movement was to petition the British government to introduce the Nagari script in the proceedings of the courts. Over the years, however, it developed into a powerful movement committed to achieving social prestige for Hindi. Understandably enough, Urdu, and not English, was seen as the rival language that was competing for the same space. The British government was accorded the status of arbiters in this movement and so the supremacy of English was not challenged at all. The movement was conceived of as an internal battle to gain supremacy for Hindi as a template of cultural regeneration. Let us briefly go over this movement.

Started roughly in the 1860s, the Hindi (or Hindi-Nagari) movement flourished in UP in the second half of the nineteenth century and rested on three pillars: 1) a number of applications and petitions (1868, 1873, 1898 being the major ones) submitted to the government to allow Nagari characters in the court language of UP; 2) creation of a number of literary works (plays, stories etc.) written in favour of Hindi and popularizing the need to preserve Hindi; and 3) formation of a number of organizations to propagate the cause of Hindi—Nagari Pracharini Sabha, formed in 1893 in Banaras and Hindi Sahitya Sammelan, formed in 1910 in Allahabad, being the most prominent. Through its activities the movement served to highlight, and sometimes exaggerate, the differences between the two languages and scripts. The defence of Hindi also provoked a similar defence of Persian/Urdu script by Urdu protagonists. The upholders of Hindi emphasized separateness; those of Urdu urged integration, denying a separate status to Hindi.[37] Hindi protagonists used the democratic argument (benefit to the majority of people)

---

[37] Interestingly, these projected roles were reversed after independence, once the supremacy of Hindi over Urdu was established and ceased to be a contentious issue. Hindi protagonists refused to look upon Urdu as a separate language and considered it as a mere dialect of Hindi. Sampurnanand declared emphatically: 'I don't agree that Hindi and Urdu are two languages.' Jyotirindra Das Gupta, *Language conflict and National Development: Group Politics and National Language Policy in India*, London, 1970, p. 141.

and their Urdu counterparts stressed the need for continuity and the political importance (as against the numerical one) of the Urdu–speaking people.[38] Hindi protagonists accused Urdu of being 'illegible and ambiguous'; their Urdu counterparts looked down upon Hindi as 'slow and clumsy'. Multiple other such qualities, sometimes linguistic but often purely non-linguistic, were attributed to each other. And so, Hindi was pure, Urdu was impure; Hindi was national and indigenous, Urdu was foreign; Hindi was like an austere housewife, Urdu was like a prostitute. The Urdu protagonists claimed Urdu to be refined, pure, legible, and also a language representing aristocratic taste and elegance whereas Hindi was declared to be just the opposite—crude, impure, illegible, slow to write, and a language of the rustics.[39] Its result was to set in motion a process of the creation of separate identifiable linguistic communities with the possibility of their subsequent transformation as political ideological communities. Urdu's normative identification with Muslims (done as much by Hindi protagonists as their Urdu counterparts) made sure that there would be fewer and fewer Hindus in the Urdu community and few Muslims in the Hindi community. The Kayasthas, Khattris, and the Kashmiri Brahmins—all trained and brought up mainly in Urdu—might initially resist the principle of linguistic communities being congruent with religious communities, but they all would have to eventually fall in line.

The process of Hindi–Urdu conflict being equated with a Hindu–Muslim one was also facilitated by the behaviour and anxieties of the major actors involved in the conflict. Sir Syed Ahmad Khan, Bhartendu Harishchandra, Raja Shiva Prasad, and Madan Mohan Malaviya played an active role in the language controversy but from different sides. Harishchandra campaigned vigorously for the introduction of Nagari characters, and Sir Syed was just as vigorously opposed to this. Raja Shiva Prasad moderated between the two stands though in the end he sided with Harishchandra. Madan Mohan Malaviya's open advocacy of Hindi and Hindu cause was something that continued in the twentieth century as well. Their political behaviour and anxieties on the language question tended to reinforce the language-religion convergence mentioned above. Their activities also helped to popularize the idea of Urdu's identification with Muslims and that of Hindi with Hindus. For

---

[38] See Paul Brass, *Language, Religion and Politics in North India*, Cambridge, 1974, pp. 132–3; and Christopher R.King, *One Language, Two Scripts*, pp. 128–9.

[39] Christopher King has prepared an interesting chart of the allegations hurled against the two languages by Hindi and Urdu protagonists respectively. King, *One Language, Two Scripts*, p. 184.

instance, commenting on the Nagari movement, Syed Ahmad wrote to a friend:

'I understand ... Hindus are roused to destroy the Muslim [cultural] symbol embodied in the Urdu language and the Persian script.... This ... would destroy cooperation between the Hindus and the Muslims. Muslims will never accept Hindi and if Hindus persistently demanded the adoption of Hindi in preference to Urdu it would result in the total separation of Muslims from the Hindus.'[40]

At the other end of the spectrum was Bhartendu Harishchandra who was willing to moderate his advocacy of Hindi by an acknowledgement that 'there is no real difference between Hindi and Urdu' and that the cause of Hindi had been ruined by the war between the Maulvis and the Pandits.[41] Yet he was convinced that Muslims stood to benefit by the government decision to retain the Persian script just as Hindus would have benefited if Nagari was made the official script. In a journal named *Kavi Vachan Sudha* that he had started, Bhartendu wrote: 'The Muslims ... it is true might suffer by the change [from Persian to Nagari script] but they are only a small portion of the community and the interests of the few must always yield to the many.'[42]

Even Raja Shiva Prasad, considered to be much more reasonable on the language question and a great advocate of retaining much of Persian vocabulary in Hindi language, was convinced that the question of language was, in the ultimate analysis, a question essentially of nationality:

The Persian of our day is half Arabic; and I cannot see the wisdom of the policy which thrusts a Semitic element into the bosoms of Hindus and alienates them from their Aryan speech; not only speech, but all that is Aryan; because through speech ideas are formed, and through ideas manners and customs. To read Persian is to become Persianized, all our ideas become corrupt and our nationality is lost. Cursed be the day which saw the Muhammedans cross the Indus; all the evils which we find amongst us we are indebted for to our 'beloved brethren' the Muhammedans.... I again say I do not see the wisdom of the policy which is now trying to turn all the Hindus into semi-Muhammedans and destroy our Hindu nationality.[43]

[40] Hafeez Malik, *Sir Syyad Ahmad Khan and Muslim Modernism in India and Pakistan,* p. 246.

[41] See his statement before the Hunter Commission on Education, 1882, in Ram Gopal, *Swatantrata-Poorva Hindi Ke Sangharsha Ka Itihas*(in Hindi), Appendix II, Allahabad, 1967, pp. 128 and 132.

[42] Quoted in Francis Robinson, *Separatism Among Indian Muslims: The Politics of United Provinces Muslims, 1860–1923,* Oxford, 1973, p. 71. In the same vein, another person wrote: 'It is not too much to conjecture that with the extinction of Hindi, the death-knell of Hindu nationality will begin to ring.' Ibid., pp. 71–2.

[43] Quoted in Christopher R.King, *One Language, Two Scripts,* p. 131.

The net result of the Hindi movement was the permission by the UP government in April 1900 for permissive (though not exclusive) use of the Nagari characters in the courts. This decision, intended to impart parity to Nagari along with Urdu, remained only partially operative and did not substantially affect the administrative dominance of Urdu till 1947. Nonetheless, it became the catalyst to different perspectives on the question of language.

Hindi movement, it may be important to emphasize, was not just motivated by self-seeking individuals out to enhance their career prospects by insisting on the introduction of Nagari scripts in court and government usage. The leaders of the movement were also gripped by a genuine, though unrealistic, anxiety about the possibility of the extinction of their language and *thereby* their culture. Language was not seen only as a component of culture but as something that shaped and determined culture.

Very similar fears characterized the activities of Urdu defenders. After the UP government's April resolution allowing simultaneous use of Nagari along with Urdu, a Muslim wrote in a letter to the editor:

'This new calamity... hangs over our head. We are required thereby to wander amidst the zigzag of the strange and horrible characters of the Deo-Nagri and to bid farewell to the language that reminds us [of] the glory of our forefathers.... Is it not the severest suffering for a man of the slightest sentiment?'[44]

Another one wrote:

'Let us consider that if Urdu were to be substituted for Gujarati in the Bombay Presidency, what would be the result? Each and every person will, the next day the resolution is passed, be seen with an Urdu primer in his hands, and will not in the least care if Gujarati is to live or to perish, as his existence, so to speak, depends on his knowledge of Urdu.'[45]

It is essential to get a grip of the predicament the Urdu and Hindi protagonists found themselves in. It was not just a battle for jobs; much more was at stake. It was believed by both that the government recognition was crucial to the preservation and survival of the language. And language did not just mean jobs; it was seen as the key to a cultural universe. It was largely for this reason that a superficial and largely inconsequential decision of the government was invested with such grave implications.

---

[44] Quoted in King, *One Language, Two Scripts*, pp. 156–7.
[45] Quoted in ibid., p. 159.

This language scenario was of some consequence for the main political actors of the twentieth century, both of the nationalist and the communal variety. To begin with, it is important to recognize that they did not invent the idea of a language-religion-culture congruence; they *inherited* it from the nineteenth century. But this language-religion-culture alliance had different implications for different political actors. It did not in any way handicap the functioning of the communal leaders who were working towards the transformation of religious communities into political constituencies. In fact they stood to politically benefit by the idea of a religious community being endowed with one language and culture. Urdu language could thus become a handy tool in the politics of Muslim League, of mobilizing Indian Muslims on an exclusively Muslim platform. Likewise, Hindi could be used by Hindu Mahasabha in its politics of Hindu mobilization. The question is: how did the language scenario inherited from the nineteenth century sketched above, affect the leaders of the Indian National movement who were involved in the task of creating a nation of Indian people? Was it any longer possible for them to define or evolve an Indian nation endowed by one common language? The idea that nations are formed by languages along with other features, had arrived from Europe. What implications did it have for Indian nationalists? Also what implications did it have for the possibilities of linguistic syncretism and/or linguistic plurality?

V

The idea of lingua franca held a very special importance for many leaders of Indian nationalism from the nineteenth century onwards. Bal Gangadhar Tilak was a great believer that a nation should have its own language and in the Indian context that language could only be Hindi on the ground of being the language of a majority of the people and also for being a link language. The idea of a language being the bedrock of a nation had many advocates, but perhaps its most representative and unambiguous defence can be found in the words of Premchand, leading twentieth century Hindi litterateur, who originally wrote in Urdu but later shifted to Hindi:

We believe language to be an important component of nationality. It is impossible to get a sense of nation without a national language. Where there is a nation, it is essential to have a national language. If the whole of India has to be welded into a nation, she will have to base herself on one language.... Language constructs nation, literature and culture and also gives birth to morals.... A nation, in spite of a common culture, can never be stable if it is not based on a national language.... This only goes to prove that language plays the most important role in the formation of a nation.[46]

Likewise, Suniti Kumar Chatterji, said in 1943: 'We feel that we ought to have a common language for the whole of India as the symbol of a common Indian nationality, which would both check the centrifugal or fissiparous tendency of the provincial languages and meet the unsympathetic argument that India cannot be a single nation with so many languages.'[47]

It is actually in this context (a linguistic divide pregnant with political possibilities, the idea of language feeding into nation formation, and the project of nation building undertaken by the nationalist leaders) that the emergence of Hindustani should be viewed. Hindustani was generally understood as the Khari Boli without the excessive use of Persian or Sanskrit words, to be written in either the Nagari or the Persian script. Gandhi, more than anyone else, laid stress on Hindustani as the language that could develop into the language of Indian people. The usage of the term went back to the eighteenth century when the popular language that was neither Persian nor Sanskrit was called by the European writers *Lingua Indostanica* or *Hindustanica.* [48] The term Hindustani was coined by Gilchrist in 1787 who eventually became a professor of Hindustani at the College of Fort William. From then onwards the exact meaning of the term kept shuttling between being some form of Urdu and a composite language of the people of north and central India. The College of Fort William treated Hindustani as a form of Urdu. But Grierson defined Hindustani as the common language of the people in his *Linguistic Survey of India*: 'Hindustani is primarily the language of north Doab and is also the lingua franca of India capable of being written both in the Persian and the Nagari characters and without purism, avoids alike the excessive use of either Persian or Sanskrit words when employed in literature.'[49]

Gandhi's ceaseless and persistent advocacy of Hindustani is now well known and requires no elaboration.[50] He also saw in it the possibility of

[46] Amrit Rai (ed.), *Vividh Prasang* (A collection of non-fictional writings of Premchand) (in Hindi), Vol. 3, Allahabad, 1962, p. 275

[47] Suniti Kumar Chatterji, *Languages and the Linguistic Problem*, p. 3.

[48] Ram Babu Saksena, *A History of Urdu Literature*, p. 7.

[49] Quoted in the Census of India Series, Census of the United Provinces of Agra and Oudh, 1931, Part I, Report, (by A.C.Turner), Allahabad, 1933, p. 487.

[50] Gandhi founded the Hindustani Prachar Sabha in Wardha, though rather late in the day, in 1942. The Indian National Congress, at its annual session in 1925, resolved to carry out its proceedings in Hindustani, to be written in either of the two scripts. The organization

bridging Hindu-Muslim differences. Interestingly, in his championing the cause of Hindustani, he found an unusual ally—the British government in UP. The position of the UP government on this question was a little ambiguous. The Census of 1911 in UP employed categories like Hindi on the one hand and Urdu or Hindustani on the other, while enumerating the language of the people of UP. This may have given the impression that the government did not distinguish between Urdu and Hindustani. This form of categorization was obviously problematic and was given up by the time of the next census in 1921 when it was decided to record only Hindustani as the language of the people. The UP Census Report of 1921 noted three possible yardsticks for recording the language. Grierson's linguistic survey had mentioned four languages in the province: Central Pahari spoken in the hilly tracts of Kumaun and Garhwal; Western Hindi spoken in the areas of Meerut, Agra, Kanpur, Rohilkhand, and Bundelkhand; Eastern Hindi spoken in Awadh, Faizabad, and Allahabad; and Bihari Hindi prevalent in the divisions of Gorakhpur and Banaras. But the Census noted that this classification was not familiar to the people of UP who considered Hindi and Urdu to be the two vernaculars of the province. The Census therefore decided to go by the third method which was to enter Hindustani as the common speech of the province. The superintendent for UP Census understood the four categories employed by Grierson to be the vernaculars of the same language and not four different languages: '...to me the difference between speaking to a villager of Gorakhpur and to a jungleman of Jhansi is precisely the difference between speaking to a peasant of Devon and to a crafter of Aberdeen.'[51] He also noted that the Hindustani language had actually begun developing in the twentieth century after the language controversy of the nineteenth century had subsided. It had also begun adopting many English words and needed to be standardized in order to develop further.[52]

---

also upheld Hindustani as the lingua franca of the Indian people. But it agreed to accommodate other languages in its famous Karachi resolution in 1931. The Congress resolution on fundamental rights laid down its commitment to the 'protection of the culture, language and scripts of the minorities'. Jawaharlal Nehru, in his capacity as the president of Congress, prepared a long statement called 'A Question of Language' in which he advocated the adoption of Hindustani as the common language of the Indian people. S.Gopal (ed.), *Selected Works of Jawaharlal Nehru*, Vol. 8, pp. 829–45. For Gandhi's position on the language question, see Z.A. Ahmad (ed.), *National Language for India:A Symposium*, pp. 31–44.

[51] Census Report of United Provinces of Agra and Oudh, 1921, Vol. XVI, Part I, Report (by E.H.H. Edye), Allahabad, 1923, p. 130.

[52] Ibid., p. 131.

This thinking may have led the UP government to open a Hindustani Academy in Allahabad in 1927. There was some confusion on the objective of the Academy, whether it was to create a common language called Hindustani or to promote Hindi and Urdu separately so as to enable the two to come closer to each other. UP's Governor Sir William Marris said in his address at the inauguration of Hindustani Academy:

The Government resolution which created the Academy recognises Urdu and Hindi as twin vernaculars of the province and embraces them both in the possibly unscientific but admirably innocuous title of Hindustani.... I am not going to dogmatise upon the question whether Hindi and Urdu are one language or two. I confine myself to the safe and unexceptionable statement that they have some things in common and some things not in common.[53]

The government position of acknowledging Hindustani as the language of the people continued in the Census of 1931 and the enumerators were given instructions to '[e]nter the ordinary language of the province as Hindustani. Do not write "Urdu" or "Hindi". "Pahari Boli" should be entered as Hindustani.'[54] The government decision of not acknowledging Hindi and Urdu separately for the purposes of census enumeration and persisting with it in the next census of 1941 antagonized both the Hindi and Urdu enthusiasts. By this time, the Muslim League had formally declared Urdu to be the lingua franca of Indian Muslims.[55] Before the census operations were to begin, Jinnah issued an appeal to all the Muslims to make the right entries in the census enumeration. These 'right' entries were to be: Muslim against race, tribe or caste, Islam against religion, and Urdu against mother tongue.[56] But the census instructions in UP did not allow Muslims to follow Jinnah's instructions. As a result, the City Muslim League of Kanpur expressed the deep resentment 'of the Urdu speaking people and Muslims in particular' at their mother tongue being recorded as Hindustani because of the general impression that all entries recorded as Hindustani would eventually be treated as Hindi.[57] Similarly, Gandhi's espousal of Hindustani was treated in a similar fashion by Urdu protagonists as amounting to

[53] 'Why Hindustani', Editorial in *The Leader*, Allahabad, 15 February 1941.

[54] UP Census, 1331, Part I, Report (by A.C.Turner), Allahabad, 1933, p. 485.

[55] 'Urdu is our national language and we should strain every nerve to keep it unharmed and unpolluted and save it from the aggressive and hostile attitude of our opponents.' Jinnah's message to Urdu conference, 13 February 1941, no. 427, Khurshid Ahmad Khan Yusufi (ed.), *Speeches, statements and Messages of Quaid-e-Azam*, Lahore, 1996, p. 1318.

[56] Jinnah's Statement on Census Operations, 11 January 1941, no. 419, Ibid, p. 1309.

[57] 'Why Hindustani', *The Leader*, 15 February 1941.

nothing more than an attempt to 'develop Hindi and undermine Urdu in this garb [of promoting Hindustani]'[58] Another Urdu partisan wrote: 'An attempt is made to make confusion worse confounded by trying to solve this question by giving a new name "Hindustani". This is a pure myth. *There does not exist any such language as Hindustani.* There is either Urdu or Hindi.'[59]

The Hindi enthusiasts were just as discontented with the decision of the government to record only Hindustani as the language of the province. An angry Hindu wrote to the editor of the *Leader.* 'This order of the Government surpasses all previous attempts of the Government to suppress Hindi and install Urdu in its place in the guise as Hindustani.'[60] And the Hindi Sahitya Sammelan, formed in 1910 to popularize Hindi, stated categorically at its annual session: 'There could not be any compromise with Hindi. No admixture could be permissible as it would be harmful. Neither should the script be altered as Devanagari was scientific and contributed towards the growth of Hindi.'[61] The Hindi Sahitya Sammelan also decided to hold a 'Hindi Day' as a day of protest against the UP government's instructions to the census officials. Public meetings were held in parts of UP and resolutions were passed to request the government to enter Hindi as the language of the Hindi-speaking people.[62]

Hindustani thus carried the risk of antagonizing both the Hindi and the Urdu supporters. In spite of the fact that it was truly a language from India's composite linguistic tradition and was supported by no less a person than Mahatma Gandhi, it found few takers and actually had more enemies than friends. Neither British government's administrative authority nor Gandhi's moral authority was able to carry Hindustani towards a position of respectability. It failed to establish an identity of its own and continued to be suspected by Hindi chauvinists of being disguised Urdu and by Urdu chauvinists of being disguised Hindi.

Under persistent pressure from both the extremes, the census authorities decided to give up not only Hindustani but refrained from giving any language statistics in the census report of 1941. The census report recommended against recording the language of the people in future

---

[58] Editorial in *Star of India* (an English Daily from Calcutta, functioning as a mouthpiece of All India Muslim League), 14 February 1940.

[59] 'The Camouflage of Hindustani' (emphasis added), in ibid., 5 July 1940.

[60] Letter to the editor, *The Leader*, 31 January 1941.

[61] Ibid., 7 February 1941.

[62] Ibid., 16 February 1941. For more protests by the City Hindu Sabha of Lucknow and the Kanpur city Hindu Sangh, see ibid, 18 February, 19 February, and 23 February 1941.

also: '... if communal passions are running high ten years hence the language question should be given up.' The census noted that the language question in many parts of India was 'completely corrupted by political influence.... Muslims were told to return their mother tongue as Urdu and many cases were brought to may [sic! my] notice where men who manifestly knew nothing of that language but were Muslims by faith persisted in returning it [Urdu] as their mother tongue admitting that they had been "told" to do so.' And then the census report prophesied: 'If this is how leaders imagine they can misuse a census then there is not much hope for India.'[63]

A few years later, other supporters of Hindustani also decided to give up their preference for that language. The question came up before the Constituent Assembly constituted to frame a Constitution for independent India. The partition had eliminated the possibility of there being any serious claim being put forward on behalf of Urdu. With Urdu out of the way, Hindustani should have stood a better chance of removing misunderstandings and establishing its justified credentials of being India's lingua franca. But what happened was just the opposite. Hindustani found very little support anywhere. The Constituent Assembly did not seem very interested in the question. The Congress members of the Assembly were evenly divided between their support for Hindi on the one hand and Hindustani on the other. Leaders like Nehru and Maulana Azad put up a token defence on behalf of Hindustani but, sensing the general mood in the Assembly, did not press for its acceptance. Hindi, written in Devanagari script, was declared as the official language of the Indian Union. Urdu found a place along with other regional languages mentioned in the eighth schedule. Hindustani was relegated to a small mention in article 351 of the Constitution as a possible source that could provide some enrichment to the official language Hindi.[64]

Just as Hindi written in Nagari script became the official language in independent India, Urdu, predictably enough, became the official language of Pakistan. Although it was the mother tongue of no more than 4 per cent (3.8 to be exact) of the people of Pakistan and stood fifth in the list after Bengali, Punjabi, Sindhi, and Pashtu,[65] its role in the making of

[63] Census of India, Vol. I, Part II, Administrative Report, (by M.W.W.M. Yeatts), Simla, 1942, p. 21.

[64] For details of the language question as it was taken up in the Constituent Assembly, see B.Shiva Rao, *The Framing of Indian Constitution: A study*, New Delhi, 1968, pp. 781-801.

[65] However, after the formation of Bangladesh, the proportion of Urdu-speaking people in Pakistan went up to 8 per cent. Interestingly-a large part of the Urdu, speaking community consisted of *muhajirs* who had migrated from UP and Bihar to Pakistan. Quite

Pakistan was highlighted in glowing terms by Urdu enthusiasts. Abdul Huq, a leader of Anjuman-i-Taraqqi-i-Urdu and recognized generally as *Baba-i-Urdu* (grand old man of Urdu) spoke thus on a formal occasion: 'Pakistan was not created by Jinnah, nor was it created by Iqbal; *it was Urdu that created Pakistan*. The fundamental reason for the discord between the Hindus and the Muslims was the Urdu language.... Therfore, Pakistan owes a debt of gratitude to Urdu.[66] This indeed was a generous compliment being paid to Urdu.

Hindustani, by comparison, suffered serious reverses. In the census of 1951 in UP, around 6.7 million people (6,742,937 to be exact) registered Hindustani as their mother tongue. The number of Hindustani speakers, though more than Urdu speakers (4,300,425 to be exact), was considerably lower than those who enlisted themselves as Hindi speakers (well over fifty million, 50, 454, 217 to be exact). However, by 1961, the size of Hindustani-speaking community had shrunk to less than 2 per cent of what it was in 1951 (only 100,530 as against 6,742,937 in 1951). In the urban areas, a total of 731,677 were enlisted as Hindustani speakers in 1951. By 1961, not a single person was enlisted as Hindustani speaker from UP's urban areas.[67] Predictably enough, both Urdu and Hindi showed an increase in the number of their speakers, from 1951 to 1961. The size of the Urdu-speaking community actually swelled by a remarkable 152 per cent in UP's rural areas. This phenomenal growth of the Urdu-speaking community was the result neither of any natural increase in the number of Urdu speakers nor of any migration, but primarily that of a linguistic displacement from Hindustani to Urdu.[68] It was also not as if people had shifted from one language to another because, as we have seen, Hindi, Urdu, and Hindustani were not very different from one another. Some differences existed at the literary level,

---

clearly, Urdu's status as the national language of Pakistan had nothing to do with its numerical status. Athar Husain, 'Peregrinations of Pakistani Nationalism' in Michael Leifer (ed.), *Asian Nationalism*, London, 2000, p. 141.

[66] Quoted in Amrit Rai, *A House Divided* (emphasis added), p. 264. Interestingly, prior to 1947, Abdul Huq had upheld Urdu's claim to be the national language of India precisely on the grounds of Urdu being a composite language of both Hindus and Muslims. He called Urdu 'the only language which is really common, having been born of the joint efforts of the Hindus and the Muslims' and thought that Urdu was 'far better qualified to be recognised as the common language' of India compared to any other language. Z.A. Ahmad (ed.), *National Language for India*, p. 86.

[67] All these figures have been gathered from Ashish Bose, 'Some Aspects of the Linguistic Demography of India', in *Language and Society* (Proceedings of a seminar held at Indian Institute of Advance Studies, Simla, in 1969), pp. 40–1.

[68] Ibid.

but at the level of speech it was virtually impossible to distinguish one from the other. It was just that people who, in 1951, had identified themselves as Hindustani speakers, later declared either Urdu or Hindi to be their mother tongue. It was an ideological rather than a linguistic shift. It was for this reason that the number of people willing to identify themselves as Hindustani speakers dwindled dramatically to a mere one lakh (100,530 to be exact) in UP's villages and a big zero in urban areas, by 1961. The number of Hindi and Urdu speakers registered a corresponding increase.

Why did Hindustani prove to be so unacceptable? Unlike Urdu it had never attempted to threaten Hindi's domination or projected itself as a language rival to Hindi. It certainly had the potential to develop into a link language for the whole of India. Why did it get reduced to a mere tokenism? Part of the explanation lies in the nineteenth century linguistic scenario referred to above. The fate of these languages, whether Hindi, Urdu or Hindustani had become tied to the nineteenth century mentality of 'linguism' which saw languages as the exclusive carriers of religious and cultural communities. It was a continuation of the nineteenth century anxieties that the frontiers of a language should also bring with it the culture and religion of the language into the mainstream. In this battle both Hindi and Urdu appeared to be better placed as they found their accompanying religions and also invented their specific cultures and suitable pasts. Hindustani lost out not because of being ambiguously defined but because it lacked the accompanying baggage of culture and religion.

VI

The transformation of one language into two, a great conflict between them, failure of a compromise being worked out between them, and banishment into oblivion of a language that had promised to bridge the gap between the two, call for an explanation. There is not much evidence that these developments could possibly have been brought about by the language policy of the colonial rulers. The usual charges of 'divide and rule' do not apply to the world of language, not directly at least. Modern Hindi and Urdu enthusiasts did not seem to need the British government to divide them in order to rule. They fought on their own and resisted efforts at a reconciliation. Is there an explanation for the developments mentioned above?

Some of the explanations for this must be sought in the modernist tendency to link language to ethnicity; to view language as belonging to an exclusive ethnic domain; to necessarily look for ethnic roots of language or linguistic roots of ethnicity. This insistence can be seen in sharp contrast to the pre-modern tendency, prevalent in India at least, to link language to territory.[69] The early terminology, employed for language prior to its standardization, referred actually to a territory where the language was spoken. Hence, words like Hindi or Hindavi, Dehalvi, Dakhani among others. Even the term Urdu, as we have seen, was used for the *area* where the language was spoken. It was thus possible for a language to cover many speeches spoken in one geographical area.

The modernist inability to view language in a context other than the one marked by religion or ethnicity would lie at the heart of the language divide under discussion. There is some evidence that one of the earliest attempts to look for separate languages of Hindus and Muslims was made by the functionaries of the College of Fort William. John Gilchrist made a distinction between the 'Islamic languages of Urdu, Persian and Arabic and the languages of Sanskrit, Bengali and Hindi'. He actually hoped that his works would help establish the precise similarities and differences between 'Muslim and Hindu languages'.[70] The various departments of the College included Arabic, Persian, Hindustani, Sanskrit, and 'Hindu languages' (Sanskrit derivatives).[71]

A related tendency was to see language as a vital component in the making of a nation. This obviously posed, and still does, irresolvable problems for a society like India, which had a huge number of dialects and also many languages that had developed over the last few centuries and were not likely to easily merge into one major language.[72] It was simply not possible, in the Indian context, for many languages to blend

[69] In the context of Hindi, Suniti Kumar Chatterji had noted that often in the past the term Hindi was referred to not simply for a language but rather for a group of speeches in currency in the area of north and central India. During the census operations of 1891 in UP, the enumerators found that often people employed terms for the dialects that were unfamiliar to the experts and had been derived from the names of the area. Some of these names given to their speeches were Doabi, Saharanpuri, Muzaffarnagari, Rohilkhandi, Kateharia, Moradabadi, Azamgarhia, Mirzapuria, Sarwariya, etc. (Census of India, 1891, Vol.XVI, North-West Provinces and Oudh, Part I, Report by D.C.Baillie, Allahabad, 1894, pp. 264–65.) It appears that naming a speech by the territory and identifying it on that basis was a practice prevalent, not just among the experts but also among common people.

[70] David Kopf, *British Orientalism and the Bengal Renaissance*, Berkeley, 1969, p. 83.

[71] Ibid., p. 64.

[72] According to Grierson's *Linguistic Survey of India*, India had 179 languages and 544 dialects. Not all the languages have emanated from the same source. Four major language families—Austric, Sino-Tibetan, Dravidian, and Indo-Aryan—have generated all the Indian languages and dialects.

and create a new composite one, for the purpose of nationality formation. Quite apart from the fact that such a project would have involved a
clash of high cultures, it also appears to be contrary to laws of linguistic
evolution, as has been pointed out by some philologists. Amrit Rai
writes:

The mixture of two languages, or of two altogether different speech communities, is not known to result in the birth of a new third language; what really
happens is that the grammar of the conquering language (which does not mean
the language of the conqueror) forms the base, and the other language merges
with it.[73]

A fusion of two distinct high cultures—Islamic and Brahmanical—did
not appear very feasible in the context of the nineteenth century. The
argument here is not that these high cultures were defined and shaped
by Urdu and Hindi respectively (the high cultures existed prior to the
emergence of the two languages in their modern, segregated form), but
that the proponents of these high cultures tended to promote Urdu and
high Hindi, respectively.[74]

By contrast, Hindustani stood a much better chance of emerging as
the acknowledged common language of the Indian people. It was the
speech of the large parts of north and central India. The British government recognized it as the main language of UP and Gandhi made great
efforts to promote it. He made it quite clear that by encouraging
Hindustani he was not seeking any merger of Hindi and Urdu which
were entitled to their separate existence. He defined Hindustani as a
language which, upon being established, could bring about the much
needed linguistic unity without the cost of sacrificing any language. But

---

[73] Amrit Rai, *A House Divided*, p. 51. Rai also quotes Shaukat Sabzwari, an Urdu linguist
from Pakistan: 'A misconception which I consider most dangerous and one that leads us
astray from the realities of linguistics is that by mixing two or more languages a new third
language can be created which is different from and independent of the other two. By
mixing two or more colours one certainly creates a new colour different from the other two,
but it is impossible to construct a new third language in this fashion.' Ibid.

[74] The term 'high culture' is used here in a sociological rather than evaluative sense. By
high culture is implied, not necessarily a superior culture, but a well-codified, literate,
formally transmitted, exclusive culture based on formal social norms, serviced and
imposed by a corps of clerics in possession of literary skills. In the eighteenth- and
nineteenth-century India, these high cultures were engaged in a process of bringing the
uninitiated members of the cultures living at the cultural periphery, into the orbit of high
cultures. On a general discussion of 'high culture', see Ernest Gellner, 'The Coming of
Nationalism and Its Interpretation: The Myth of Nation and Class', in Gopal Balakrishnan
(ed.), *Mapping the Nation*, London, 1996, pp. 102–3.

Gandhi's Hindustani, a carrier of the old Hindavi tradition of many centuries and as the symbol of national unity in modern times, did not find any acceptance among the very people who ironically continued to speak Hindustani. In the end the large number of Hindustani-speaking people divided themselves into Hindi- and Urdu-speaking peoples. The two languages also found themselves two suitable homelands in the form of independent India and Pakistan. Hindustani made a quiet and unceremonious exit from the normative emotional universe of the new Hindi and Urdu speakers of north India and Pakistan who have, nonetheless, continued to speak that language without identifying with it.

Telling the Story of Communal Conflicts in South Asia

Interim Report on a Personal Search for Defining Myths[1]

ASHIS NANDY

Most theories that have changed cosmologies and most paradigmatic histories of discovery acquire their cultural location partly through a popular foundational myth or an arresting story. Sometimes the stories are apocryphal, sometimes not. But they always sum up for the laity—and at times for the theorists themselves—the larger cultural meaning and organizing principles of the breakthrough and what the theory's public constituency is likely to read into it. Can those who hate psycho-analysis and grudge its powerful presence in our times describe the discipline without invoking the tragedy of King Oedipus? After all, even those like Vladimir Nabokov, who choose to believe that Sigmund Freud was a Viennese charlatan, have to battle the Oedipal metaphors associated with psychoanalysis and confront the tragic grandeur and alluring hermeneutics of the myth. Even those who have introduced major deviations into psychoanalysis or changed the way we think of the discipline have not been allowed to forget the myth.[2]

[1] An earlier version of this paper was delivered as the 2001 Annual Ethnic and Racial Studies Public Lecture, London, 3 May 2001 and published in *Ethnic and Racial Studies*, January 2002, 25(1), pp. 1–19. It in turn was based on the Inaugural Lecture at the Institute of Postcolonial Studies, 29 March 1999.

[2] For instance, Gilles Deleuze and Felix Guattari, *Anti-Oedipus: Capitalism and Schizophrenia*, trans. Robert Hurley, Mark Seem, and Helen R. Lane, New York: Viking, 1972.

As crucial is the story of the falling apple in the Newtonian world view. Generations of ordinary consumers of the history of modern science and western civilization have seen the story as a doorway to Newton's world in which we have now lived for more than two centuries. There may be many versions of the story. Indeed, one of the jobs of myth, as opposed to history, is to keep open the scope for multiple interpretations and allow play to diverse exegetic traditions. Thus, some have said that Newton's story acquires its meaning not from the fall of the apple but from Newton's sudden recognition that the force that reached the top of the tree to ensure the fall of the apple might also reach the moon to hold it in its orbit.[3] That has not cramped those who live with the more conventional meanings of the story. The issue they know cannot be settled by data; it has to do with the way public imagination adapts to—and, at the same time, tames—esoteric knowledge.

Sometimes such myths acquire public presence despite scanty details. They can even be close to being one-liners that hint at the personality of the discoverer and the romance of the discovery. So much so that, after a while, neither can be thought of without the myth. Can the Archimedes principle or, for that matter, the world of Hellenic science be imagined without that famous cry from a bathtub—'eureka'? Archimedes may not be the whole of Greek science; Pythagorean mysticism might have been a major coordinate of Greek knowledge systems. But the popularity of the story of discovery in a bathtub remains a clue to the way in which the history and mythology of Greek science has been integrated in contemporary common sense. By using the imagery of an eccentric, self-oblivious genius, the story stresses individual creativity and downplays the idea of creativity as a divine gift. It prioritizes Greek positive sciences over alternative traditions of Greek science. It fits the intellectual history of an entire civilization within the Enlightenment vision to further consolidate and legitimize the Baconian idea of scientific knowledge.

Till now, I have given examples from the natural sciences and the western world. But such myths abound in social theories and in other parts of the world, too. Let me summon a few examples from areas adjacent the one I am going to cover in this article. Rammohun Roy (1772–1822), the nineteenth-century social and religious reformer is popularly known as the father of modern India. Virtually everyone who has written on him, and his victorious battle against sati, tells how his sister-in-law's ritual suicide after the death of her husband had moved him and how that experience—with its mixture of sorrow, anger, and

[3] Lynn White, Jr., 'Science and the Sense of Self: The Medieval Background of a Modern Confrontation', *Daedalus*, 1978, *107*, pp. 47–59.

awe—powered his movement against sati. Some have admitted that the story might be apocryphal, but that has not stopped them from telling it. Others, including this writer, have gingerly related various aspects of his ideology of reform—especially, the 'odd' mix of virulent opposition to the *practice* of sati *and* respect and admiration for the *mythology* of the rite—to that story of self-destruction in the family.[4] It allowed him to offset the courage and self-sacrifice symbolized by the rite in epic times against the sadism, greed, anomie, and economism that powered the act in colonial times.

Who can write about Mohandas Karamchand Gandhi and his theory of militant non–violence without mentioning that lonely encounter at a South African railway station between a formally dressed Gandhi, still trying to be a brown Englishman, and a White railway official who would not honour a presumptuous Indian barrister's first-class train ticket? When the official threw out Gandhi on the platform along with his baggage, he did not know he was writing a story that would survive as a myth and inspire generations of activists all over the world to defy mighty war machines, arrogant modern nation-states, and hollow tyrants.

As revealing is the story of Swami Dayanand's (1825–83) early encounter with everyday Hinduism. It features in almost all accounts of his life and the religious reform movement he built, the Arya Samaj. Young Dayanand, we are told, was deeply disturbed when he woke up in an especially auspicious night, Shivaratri, to find rats eating the food offered to gods. The embarrassing spectacle—embarrassing because others thought that the gods accepted the offerings—convinced Dayanand of the poor state of Hinduism at the time, particularly when compared with that of Christianity and Islam, two faiths that had been close to central political authority in India in the previous few centuries. He was to spend the rest of his life trying to rid Hinduism of its irrationalities and its closetful of gods and goddesses, and give the Hindus a proper religion in the form of canonical texts, an evangelical priestly order, and a rational and internally consistent set of moral codes. Some ungrateful thinkers and scholars have, however, held the Arya Samaj and its ratio- nal, neat, puritanical, closed-ended Hinduism responsible for the growth of both Hindu-Muslim and Hindu-Sikh distances and for freezing the boundaries of faiths in India. Indeed, Dayanand's attack on popular religion—which has for centuries supplied South Asia with a flawed but trusted basis for easy, chaotic, often creative, religious tolerance—is a

---

[4] Ashis Nandy, 'Sati: A Nineteenth Century Tale of Women, Violence and Protest', in *At the Edge of Psychology: Essays in Politics and Culture*, New Delhi: Oxford University Press, 1983, pp. 1–31.

key to the appeal of the ideology of Hindu nationalism among the modernizing, urban, middle classes.

It is all in the story—the fear of the commonplace and the lowbrow, the belief that others believed what they did because they did not know any better, the shift in emphasis from unexamined performance to the content and intensity of belief, the search for respectability and acceptance in the modern world, the attempts to systematize and homogenize a fluid, open-ended faith through tough-minded, rational, masculine, moral cleanliness. The story captures the argument that the efforts of religious reformers like Dayanand and Anagarika Dharmapala (1864–1931) during colonial times—as also that of their contemporary Islamic modernizers—might have been well intentioned and justified up to a point, but their long-term impact has sometimes been disastrous in South Asia. Dayanand's otherwise innocent story hints that ethnic cleansing may begin in one's own self and acquire its demonic public form when the cleansers begin to project the same model of cleanliness outwards. Dayanand's rats remind one of Gandhi, a self-proclaimed *sanatani* or traditional Hindu, who claimed that in the long run the nineteenth-century reform movements had done more harm than good to Hinduism and India.

These organizing myths or apocryphal stories work in two ways. Sometimes they supply a shorthand description of the primary concerns of the new theory; at other times they tell the story of the discovery in a way that hints at the latter's social relations and status in popular culture. In either case, they do what a physical or social theory by itself can never do; they ground it in the shared culture of a community; they humanize and socialize the theory.

Against the background of these mythographies of breakthrough, this paper reports an incomplete personal search. It assembles fragments of a few stories to serve purposes that the stories I have told you do, often by default. For the last few years I have been working on genocides, mainly on a major study of the mass violence that accompanied the birth of India and Pakistan and, later, Bangladesh through the construction of life histories. I work with a large team of about thirty researchers belonging to at least eight disciplines and three countries. Each of us in this project has his or her own slant and private search. The research, too, has changed us in different ways and pushed us towards strange directions. One of us, for instance, found out that his family was presided over by one of the roughly 100,000 women who had been abducted during the period.

I have been looking for stories that would epitomize the complex experiences, interpretations, and insights that sensitive scholars and writers have amassed on ethnic and religious violence in general, but particularly in South Asia. I am looking for stories that simultaneously describe a hydra-headed phenomenon and venture clues to interpretations that are at the margins of our awareness. We are not always keen to accept these interpretations, but they are the ones in conversation with the categories that many victims and perpetrators of such violence use. Why do some communities, cities or regions chronically suffer from such violence, whereas others have been more or less free from it over the decades? When communities live in peace, what resources do they depend upon—culturally and psychologically? Do communal stereotypes and essentialist constructions automatically lead to violence in the region or do these stereotypes and constructions operate within a complex system of checks and balances?[5] Can the right to moderate use of essentialism that Gayatri Chakravarty Spivak claims for our kind be extended to ordinary citizens too?[6] A complex set of answers is emerging from the ongoing works on caste, ethnic and religious violence in South Asia.

Many acute observers and researchers in South Asia, over-socialized to their disciplinary histories, work with models that reflect pre-war studies of social distance and racism in the West.[7] When it comes to ethnic and religious strife, they work with constructions of South Asian society that in other contexts would look like caricatures to them. I have been searching for stories that bypass such over-socialized interpretations and theories and capture something of the rich, complex answers the empirical data, 2500 years of tradition in theorizing on violence, and less guarded researchers' comments themselves suggest, especially when one cares to read them in between the lines.

I

My search began accidentally. Some years ago, a journalist and human rights activist in Pakistan told me of her grandmother, a victim of the

[5] Ashis Nandy, 'Time Travel to a Possible Self: Searching for the Alternative Cosmopolitanism of Cochin', in *Time Warps: The Insistent Politics of Silent and Evasive Pasts,* New Delhi: Permanent Black, 2000, pp. 157–209.

[6] Gayatri Chakravarty-Spivak, 'Can the Subaltern Speak?', in Cary Nelson and L. Grossberg, *Marxism and the Interpretation of Culture,* London: Macmillan, 1988, pp. 271–313.

[7] The hoary Social Distance Scale of Emory Bogardus is used more frequently in India than in the United States, where it was developed some sixty years ago. *The Authoritarian Personality* by T. W. Adorno and his associates, New York: Norton 1950, remains the last word on such problems till now.

great partition riots in 1946–8. The grandmother used to often wake up at night with terrible nightmares and scream that Sikhs were coming and killing everyone. For she had seen a mob of Sikhs butcher her closest relatives. Shortly before her grandmother died, my friend said to her, 'Grandmother, you must be very angry with the Sikhs.' Grandmother, traumatized most of her life by memories of loss, replied, 'No, at the time we had gone mad and so had they.'

Everyone's journey has to begin somewhere. Mine began here. Was this an instance of personal morality, an individual's capacity to transcend stereotype and hatred? Was the grandmother trying to make peace with her private ghosts in her final days? Was she pretending to a forgiveness that her granddaughter would approve of? Or was she trying to free the next generation of the burden of avenging her suffering? I do not know. But I was to later find out that many other victims considered the carnage and the exodus a period of madness. This helped them locate the violence outside normality and disown the relevance of its memories. Others call the period evil times, when all humanity and all ethical concerns were jettisoned. They prefer not to recount those times lest they contaminate their present life. The spirits of the victims and perpetrators, they fear, will enter the life of the living, once the clandestine memories are reactivated:

Daughter, why talk about evil days? In our religion, it is prohibited to even utter or think about evil acts. If you do so, it is like actually committing the acts....

If one discusses such acts, one also internalises them in one's blood and bones.... There is a saying that if you discuss ghosts and snakes, they tend to visit you. This talk is about dead people. Why invite their ghosts?[8]

Indeed, many respondents seem to speak from within an encapsulated self, sometimes hermetically sealed, with which one cannot live

---

[8] Meenakshi Verma, interview with Rajinder Kaur, formerly of Rawalpindi, now at Delhi, in February 1997. Kaur adds: '... By the grace of Vahe Guru, we are quite comfortable ... and do not need anything. The misfortune did not happen just to me and my family. Millions of people and families have been devastated.... Why I do not want to speak about partition? The reason is that the murderers could not be caught, nor were they punished. People who killed and looted were strangers. No one could have recognised them. When you do not know the murderers, why this complaint or lamentation?' Cf. the remarks of a Hebrew writer who survived the Nazi concentration camps: 'After liberation the one desire was to sleep, to forget and to be reborn. At first there was a wish to talk incessantly about one's expereiences; this gave way to silence, but learning to be silent was not easy. When the past was no longer talked about, it became unreal, a figment of one's imagination.' Aharon Appelfeld, quoted in Martin S. Bergmann and Milton E. Jucovy (eds), *Generations of the Holocaust*, New York: Columbia University Press, 1982, pp. 5–6.

comfortably in normal times.[9] Based on his conversations with Sikh participants in violence that accompanied the Partition, Suketu Mehta describes the guilt-ridden silence that has come to be associated with the memories of the carnage.[10] They, too, think of those times as essentially sinful, not worth remembering. 'I shall tell you what is *pap, gandagi* ... when a man lusts for another man's blood, and that too without any personal animosity, when a man has a woman at home and yet defiles helpless other women. Don't you think that is *pap* [sin]?'[11]

Some other questions these memories raise are more difficult to answer. For instance, was the response of my friend's grandmother a means of distancing herself from the hatred within, a cultivated forgetfulness that defied the empiricism of history?[12] Did the presumption of madness allow her to live with memories of one's own days of hate and ensure forgiveness? I could not decide, but I wished I knew.

A year or so after that experience, I started working with some friends on the Ayodhya imbroglio, the one that led to the demolition of a sixteenth-century mosque by well-organized groups of Hindu nationalists. As is well known, that story had a tragic ending in December 1992.[13] During one of our field trips, I was reminded of my friend's story by an apparently unrelated story, when I heard that two lawyers who had fought for years in the courts for the Hindu and Muslim rights in connection with the disputed Babri mosque often travelled together for the court hearings at Lucknow. When contacted, one of them said that they were childhood friends and the case could not embitter their relationship. The other said that petrol was becoming more expensive and they did not want to waste money.

Did everyday life tame passions that were otherwise untameable? Did the primordial ties of friendship have primacy over xenophobia or did they coexist peacefully in the same heart? Did the pragmatics of petrol price override ideologies? I had no way of knowing; I could only guess. I now decided to look more seriously for characteristic narratives of

[9] Cf. Henry Abramowitz, 'There are no Words: Two Greek-Jewish Survivors of Auschwitz', *Analytic Psychology*, 1986, 3(3), pp. 201–16.

[10] Suketu Mehta, 'Partition', *Communalism Combat*, April 1998, (420), pp. 8–12.

[11] Verma's interview with Kaur, August 1997.

[12] On the reaffirmation of a moral universe through the defiance of formal history, used both as a culturally specific ego defence and a coping mechanism, see Ashis Nandy, 'History's Forgotten Doubles', *History and Theory*, 1995, Theme Issue 34: *World Historians and Their Critics*, pp. 44–66.

[13] Our version of the story is in Ashis Nandy, Shikha Trivedi, Achyut Yagnik, and Shail Mayaram, *Creating a Nationality: The Ramjanmabhumi Movement and Fear of the Self*, New Delhi: Oxford University Press, 1995.

communal violence and individual and cultural resistance to it in the region. (The resistance is important because, when compared to the Jewish experience in Europe, it seems to have been widespread in India in 1946–8.) In this essay, I want to give you some idea of the nature of my search—through stories that show some promise as foundational myths.

II

My first candidate is a story Tapan Raychaudhuri tells in his Bengali autobiography, self-deprecatingly titled—this is a rough translation— *Chewing the Cud or Reminiscences of a Senile Gossip,* presumably to differentiate the product from his serious historical scholarship in English.[14] However, Raychaudhuri's history is peopled by standardized or predictable figures that we can all recognize; the autobiography is peopled by a different set of political actors, less identifiable even to its Bengali readers and its author. The story I retell is so incongruent in tone with the historian's own understanding of the communal problem that he can only put it in a Bengali memoir, the intellectual stature of which he himself discounts.

The story involves one Shahjahan Chaudhuri, whom Raychaudhuri knew in his childhood as Sajukaka or Uncle Saju. Over the years, Raychaudhuri saw him graduate from the Revolutionary Socialist Party to local leadership of the Muslim League and participation in anti-Hindu riots in the 1940s. Those were dark days for Bengal; politics was quickly getting communalized, bitter, and violent. Shahjahan Chaudhuri was sucked into the vortex. After the riots died down, Shahjahan as usual came on the Vijayadashami day during the annual Durga Puja to touch the feet of Raychaudhuri's parents and seek their blessings at their ancestral home at Barisal. Tapan's mother, who knew Shahjahan from the age of two, blessed him and then commented, 'Saju, after Puja, you have come to a Hindu home to touch feet!' Shahjahan, a giant of a man, suddenly broke into sobs. Through his tears, he said, 'Boudi, you are more than a mother. You have always spoilt me by your affectionate tolerance. Whether I do something good or bad, you do not say anything. If the doors of your house close for me, where shall I go?'[15]

The autobiography does not go out of its way to build up the event or the person. It recognizes that ideology is a double-edged weapon and

[14] Tapan Raychaudhuri, *Romanthan athaba Bhimratipraptar Paracharitacharcha,* Calcutta: Ananda Publishers, 1993, pp. 78–9.
[15] Ibid.

collective hate and personal relations can bypass each other. The author mentions that Shahjahan sided with the Pakistani army in the freedom struggle of Bangladesh in 1971 and died during the tumultuous events. His political loyalty had not wavered since the days when Tapan's mother confronted him. To his credit, for once Raychaudhuri lowers his guard and admits his bewilderment that he cannot but mourn one who, by all criteria, was an enemy. The discipline of history might have lost in the process, but our insight into the dynamics of communal violence has certainly gained.

Who was Shahjahan Chaudhuri? Was he one who retained a sector of sanity even when turning rabidly anti-Hindu? Was he an innocent, rustic, Bengali Muslim recruited by scheming political ideologues for use as a canon fodder? Did his heart-rending statement 'Where shall I go if the doors of this house close for me'—and the sense of loneliness and abandonment it invokes—have anything to do with his acquired ideology of hate? Did he separate his personal relations from his political life because he *had* to use the latter to give meaning to a meaningless life and, yet, protect his personal relations from his other life? Was he articulating the pain of transcending personal relations for the sake of ideologies in a society where, by most accounts, politics previously had been peripheral?[16] Were the double ledgers he kept more typical of those consumed by political hatred in South Asia? Raychaudhuri recognizes—and here lies the real pull of the narrative—that there can be no final answers to these questions. His bewilderment is the final marker of his narrative success. As if he recognized that, in this case, there could only be interpretations, and interpretations of interpretations. Whether the story changes the listeners or not, it has already changed its author. We have come close to a genuine candidate for a foundational myth for understanding communal conflicts in South Asia.

Dipesh Chakrabarti had some years ago told, as part of a larger narrative, a story that is my second candidate for a foundational myth.[17] It involves two highly creative Bengalis: Mrinal Sen, the famous film-maker, and his childhood friend Jasimuddin, perhaps the best-known 'folk poet' of Bengal in this century. Sen is not only a distinguished film-maker; he is also a radical, known for his political sensitivities and activism.

[16] For instance Rajni Kothari, *Politics in India*, Boston: Little Brown, 1970, Chapter 9.

[17] Dipesh Chakrabarty, 'Remembered Villages: Representation of Hindu-Bengali Memories in the Aftermath of the Partition', *Economic and Political Weekly*, 10 August 1996, pp. 2143–51. Chakrabarty bases himself on Mrinal Sen, *'Chhabi Karar Ager Dinguli'*, in Pralay Sur (ed.), *Mrinal Sen*, Calcutta 1987, p. 11.

Jasimuddin, on the other hand, became a strong votary of a separate homeland for the Muslims of united India.

Sen's story, too, is set in the 1940s, in the last days of British empire, when things were coming to a head politically, as a prelude to independence and the creation of two brand-new nation-states, India and Pakistan. At the time, Jasimuddin used to regularly visit Sen's home at Faridpur in East Bengal (that later became East Pakistan and then Bangladesh) and often ate with the Sens. During these visits, he would often argue the Muslim case, while Sen's father, otherwise close to the nationalist movement, would pick up cudgels on behalf of the Hindus.

There would be furious arguments and counter-arguments.... One day Jasimuddin said to my mother, 'Mother, if it is true that I am one of your sons, why do you when feeding me seat me outside? Why is it that you never let me sit with your sons to eat from the same plate?'

Sen continues:

My mother found herself in difficulty. What Jasimuddin said was not untrue after all. But mother was helpless. She explained to him that she had no objection to his seating inside while she fed him, but the servants of the household would not accept this argument. Her eyes glittering with tears, she said, 'Sadhu, you may not know this, but it is me who washed up after you.'[18]

There is much to recommend in the story. There is a humiliated hero seeking equity and dignity facing an aging authority, unable to acknowledge the grievances of an emerging political community. There is an innocent but relatively powerless mother unable to control either her husband or the unnamed foot soldiers of an oppressive order in the form of domestic helps, the lowest in the hierarchy and, therefore, defensively and aggressively reproducing that order. Finally, there is the silent spectator in the form of a son sympathizing with the wronged but 'misguided' ethno-religious chauvinist and getting radicalized by the encounter. In fact, listeners *have* identified such *dramatis personae* whenever I have used the story. For the moment, however, I bypass the possible diverse interpretations to raise a different kind of question regarding the voice and the language of dissent. The story has four dissenters, not one. We know from other sources that Sen's father was a nationalist lawyer who had suffered under colonial rule for his beliefs. He was very impressed by Jasimuddin's talents and he was the one to encourage the young poet to become a member of the household. Only, his dissent did not range wide enough. He was a captive of his time and

[18] Chakrabarty, 'Remembered Villages', pp. 2150–1

the ideas floating around in his class. It is also obvious from even the brief narrative that Jasimuddin considered himself as a wronged member of the family rather than an outsider. For even when making his claim for separation, he addressed Mrinal's mother as mother. He was actually claiming that he had been treated as a wronged stepson of the family. Young Jasimuddin and his friend Mrinal, identifying with Jasimuddin and sensitive to the inequities in the system, are obviously rebels against not only the system but his father's version of nationalism and the standardized frame of dissent offered to them. Were the tears of Mrinal Sen's mother only a sign of embarrassment, as his modern son seems to believe? Or were there in them also encoded a tragedy of incomprehension between two world views, not Hindu and Muslim, but modern and non-modern. Was Jasimuddin, despite his ethno-nationalism and sectional allegiance, being more fully modern in demanding absolute equality? Was Sen's mother, in washing Jasimuddin's plates and doing what even her servants would not do, representing a form of nurture and maternity that transcended social hierarchies but had no more place in modernizing Bengal? Was her confusion and pain also a confession of secret defiance of the traditional hierarchy?

Once again, the story has the makings of a prototypical myth. There is the wronged hero subjected to humiliation and distancing, the rebellion of the underdog, the ineffective self-justification of authorities, and the distribution of just desserts. The story as recounted by Sen even bears a vague imprint of the dilemma of the ultimate mythic hero of modern India, Karna of Mahabharata. The hero fights maternal rejection and seeks a recognition that would go beyond his ascribed social status; yet, he has to himself reject maternal acceptance to defend his acquired status. However, there is also the minor tragedy of one whose identification with the wronged hero, defiance of social codes through generosity and largeness of heart go unnoticed. While Jasimuddin thought he was rebelling against an unjust system, his poetic sensitivity failed to alert him to the silent, uncelebrated, maternal love that was to go unrequited at the end.[19]

The two stories I have told both involve middle-class political awareness and its ambivalent affair with ethno-religious nationalism. They are helpful but limited by the social background of the characters who seem

---

[19] On the emergence of Karna as pan-Indian hero in the Mahabharata in modern times, see Ashis Nandy, *The Ambiguous Journey to the City: The Village and Other Odd Ruins of the Self in South Asian Imagination*, New Delhi: Oxford University Press, in press, The Jerusalem Lectures in Indian Civilization, 1997, Ch 1.

primarily engaged in ideological battles. Some of their actions subvert ideological postures but the frames of the protagonists, which dominate the stories, remain ideological. Let me now try to get out of this structure and end this section with a story where there is no effort to transcend, bypass, or compartmentalize ideologies, simply because the main, categories of our politically correct universe of discourse—nationalism, communalism, composite culture, and secularism—just do not enter the picture. The context I have in mind, especially as it involves the relationship between the ideological and the religious, is beautifully anticipated in a recent paper of Valentine Daniel, in turn influenced by, according to Daniel himself, by the work of S. N. Balgangadhara.[20]

Let me now briefly tell the story of Jaipur's Gangadevi, the humble wife of one nondescript Babulal Bijwala, of whom I came to hear through political anthropologist Shail Mayaram. The story still does not answer Arjun Appadurai's question about when and how a neighbourhood sours, but probably prepares the ground for an answer. Recounting her family's close relation with a Muslim Manihar family she had been protective towards, Gangadevi told us:

For twenty years we lived together in the *basti* below in huts. They [the Manihar family] had a hutment and so did we. Then they were allotted a plot .... We came here in 1973 and lived together after that. There was affection between us. When I faced a problem—for instance, when my child had an accident on Moharrum— Munna [their eldest son] rushed her to the big hospital. She had come under a truck when she was going with her grandfather to see the *tazia*. She was saved but her foot was cut; she has an artificial foot. So we shared each other's sorrows and joys.[21]

Like many others, Gangadevi was shocked that religious violence came to Jaipur. 'This is the first time I've heard of such a thing [the riot]. But nothing happened in our neighbourhood.' She feels that the violence did not touch her neighbourhood because it had a certain social solidarity: 'We were all together, the people of this colony. We'd been together for twenty years.' A shared sense of being forsaken by larger and more powerful forces—the police and the politicians—cemented this solidarity.

But who listens to poor people? Our daughter was killed for dowry. It is now one

[20] E. Valentine Daniel, 'The Arrogation of Being by the Blind-Spot of Religion', Paper presented at the Conference on the Twentieth Century: Dreams and Realities, organized by the Graduate School of Social Science, Hitotsubashi University, Tokyo, 2 December 2000; and S. N. Balagangadhara, '*The Heathen in His Blindness...*': Asia, the West and the Dynamic of Religion, Leiden: E. J. Brill, 1994.

[21] Nandy, Trivedi, Yagnik, and Mayaram, *Creating a Nationality*, p. 153.

and a half years; the police don't listen. She was hanged by her husband and in-laws, Agarwals of our own caste. Who bothers? ... Our Muslim neighbours left the colony even though we did not want them to. But when our daughter was killed by her in-laws, they all came to share our sorrow.[22]

However, the almost surrealist interweaving of relationships and unfolding of selves are best revealed in the case of Jamil. When religious riots came to the colony and the Bijwalas heard that Jamil was stranded,

we jumped across and fetched him. We were so scared, we thought someone might kill us.... My elder son had gone to Ayodhya for *karseva*—he ran away.... I had the responsibility of my daughters-in-law and grandchildren. I don't go anywhere, to any temple. My temple is in my home where I worship all gods. For Ram and Rahim I light *agarbattis* [incense sticks], for Sayyad baba I light an *agarbatti*.

Gangadevi told Jamil, 'See son, you are just like this son [of mine] here.' She then gave him tea and dinner. If anyone asked, she said, 'He is our guest, my daughter-in-law's uncle from Delhi.' When next day her nephew came to sell newspapers, she told him to leave Jamil at a safe place. After eight or ten days, Jamil's mother and relatives came to thank Gangadevi and bless her. Gangadevi says, 'Possibly it is due to their *dua* (blessing) that my son returned from Ayodhya where so many died. His mother said, "You have saved my son, your son will also come back safe". He [the *karsevak* son] is not in the BJP but went because of his friends; he was only twenty. The police came to leave him in a car. He said, "I was put in jail". I said, "Good, even better if they'd broken your limbs. Here you come back after twenty-two days, and you knew your wife was going to have a baby".'

I have told this story in some detail not only because the details are available, but also because it partly allows us to relive the fear and the trauma of a communal riot, as witnesses or as researchers vicariously experiencing the violence, whether sitting in classes or newsrooms, in slums or middle-class homes. The story is also obviously of the kind that allow the victims to celebrate their survival through their community ties cutting across religious boundaries. Such modest forms of resistance cannot be glamourized or given high moral or philosophical status; they are all too obviously a part of the 'trivia' of everyday life. The ties on which the story pivots cross ideological divides—the mother of a *karsevak* protects his declared 'enemy', and the enemy's relatives in turn come to offer their blessings for the safe return of the *karsevak* from his mission of destroying the enemy's place of worship.

[22] Ibid., p. 153.

There are many possible ways of reading these negotiations. One can be dismissive about them and read them as an inferior form of religion—crude, insufficiently self-aware and, therefore, more open-ended or chaotic. One can declare them irrelevant because they bypass the 'standard' formats of religious beliefs and practices, even though there is no empirical evidence to believe that they are any less standard than the beliefs and practices the urban middle-class believers consider standard. One can even read them as individual moral acts, idiosyncratic in the way acts of individual Germans who protected Jews during the Nazi terror. Studies of such rescuers in Germany, too, have shown that the behaviour of the rescuers had something to do with their strong religious beliefs.

I cannot ignore the possibility that the apparent absurdity of the situation, in which Jalil and Gangadevi found themselves, only under-scores the different moral frames and concepts of responsibility and obligations that permeate the lives of the likes of Gangadevi and her friends. These frames and responsibilities are neither fully accessible to the social science community nor to the urban, middle-class media persons thinking with the aid of standard concepts of ideology, stereo-types, and prejudices.

Some years ago, economist Stephen Marglin differentiated between two types of knowledge, techne and episteme. With a wealth of data he made the claim that while *techne* was inescapably defined by local experience or practice, episteme was primarily universal, transferable, generalizable knowledge.[23] Though Marglin confines his analysis mainly to systems of knowledge, could it have wider cultural applicability? Can it capture the differences between a theory of life grounded in—or in continuous conversation with—local practices and community ties, and a theory of life grounded in abstract, more universal, political ideology? Did the discomfort that Marglin's classification aroused in some come from the suspicion that Marglin was stealthily empowering and equating what might be called an 'unexamined life', which we are told is not worth living, with the painfully crafted, philosophically sophisticated theories of social life inherited through social science texts? Perhaps there is a *techne* of resistance to communal violence, too, beyond the reach of those immersed in and theorizing about its episteme from a distance.

[23] For instance, Stephen A. Marglin, 'Farmers, Seedsmen, and Scientists', in Frederique Apffel Marglin and Stephen Marglin (eds), *Decolonizing Knowledge: From Development to Dialogue*, Oxford: Oxford University Press, 1990, pp. 185–248.

During the last fifty years the widening influence of the whole range of interpretations of fascism and racism inspired by the critical theory of the Frankfurt school—a school that deeply influenced my own work for many years—has slowly seeped into the southern world. This has sanctioned a degree of ambivalence towards popular culture and everyday life, seen as analogous to mass cultures in developed societies.[24] Many have looked for and found, like Wilhelm Reich, 'little men' naturally prone to violent ethnic and religious bigotry.[25] But the South has not been massified in the way the North has been. While communities are breaking down everywhere, the process certainly is not complete in the South. The operational definitions of communities and even ideologies are not the same here. Demystifying popular culture in the North may unearth the fascism of the little man and the oppressive, non-self-reflexive aspects of the dominant public culture. That is not what popular culture is all about in the South, which retains some flavour of the marginalized, defeated cultures of the non-modern and the non-canonical. Could there be a modest celebration of the lifestyles of the millions who have ensured that, in South Asia at least, genocidal ethnic and religious passions remain, firstly, a personality feature of a minority, even when invoking ancient religions and, secondly, such passions are counterbalanced by other psychodynamic forces—even if inadequately—within those afflicted? I am afraid the readers will have to give the answer to themselves, outside the earshot of their sane, rational, professional academic colleagues.

Finally, it is also becoming obvious—and the stories I have told you underscore this—that nearness, rather than distance may have more to do with the venom in ethnic and religious violence in South Asia. Stanley J. Tambiah, who has worked on such violence for years, has recognized this explicitly and some of our recent empirical works, too, support his insight.[26] Participation in communal violence, when it is not

---

[24] The theories of mass culture ventured by the likes of Theodor Adorno and Max Horkheimer have not become debatable in South Asia the way they have become in the West. Partly because they also serve as a shield for the social élite in this part of the world and their claims to guardianship of classicism.

[25] Wilhelm Reich, *The Mass Psychology of Fascism*, New York: Orgone, 1946.

[26] Stanley J. Tambiah, 'Obliterating the "Other" in former Yugoslavia', pp. 7–8. Also Ashis Nandy, Shikha Trivedy, Achyut Yagnik, and Shail Mayaram, *Creating a Nationality: The Ramjanmabhumi Movement and Fear of the Self*, New Delhi: Oxford University Press, 1995; and Ashis Nandy, 'The Invisible Holocaust and the Journey as an Exodus: The Poisoned Village and the Stranger City', in *The Ambiguous Journey to the City: The Village and Other Odd Ruins of the Self in the Indian Imagination*, New Delhi: Oxford University Press, in press, Chapter 4.

professionally conceived, strategic intervention in politics, is often an exorcism—a determined attempt to banish from the self its unacceptable parts exteriorized and represented by hated enemies who live next door in the guise of neighbours. A person who had killed during the great Calcutta riots in 1946 once told a researcher in our team how, during the violence, he saved the life of a Kabuli from a mob because, though a Muslim, 'he was not one of us'.[27]

I leave it to more serious academics to work out the full implications of these.

III

A few closing comments on the strange record of a quest for myths in a world that prides itself on its ability to transcend myths and live with a demystified world.

I am not committed to any of the stories I have told here as an adequate, self-sufficient, or representative myth. The ones I have narrated have been chosen mostly intuitively and also because they were available to me readily. But there are in them some of the qualities that I am looking for in the candidate myths. And these qualities have something to say about both the nature of communal and ethnic conflicts in South Asia and their relationship with other aspects of politics, particularly the state and the content of Indian nationalism and some parts of the Indian's cultural self.

However, this does not mean that I do not have some tacit demands that the stories must fulfil to qualify as candidate myths. First, all the candidate myths have to have an element of healing built into them. Partly perhaps because I started life as a student of clinical psychologist and that identity has left its sediments. Partly because, I guess, I was a witness at the age of nine to the communal riots in Calcutta that set off the genocidal religious violence in northern India in 1946–8 and did see many acts of inhuman cruelty but also courage and resistance to violence, too. Often from the same people who were responsible for the violence. Even though in a few instances they came close to it, these were not industrialized, assembly-line killings—of the type in which the twentieth century specialized—and killers and victims involved in them had not been reduced to being cogs in a killing machine. While speaking of this violence, everyone speaks of the roughly 100,000 women who

[27] Samik Goswami, interview with Dutt, 2002.

were abducted. Some scholars have written sensitively about the 30,000 odd women who were identified and in many cases restored to their families. They even mention that many of them resisted repatriation, knowing that their new social and familial status would be uncertain. May I be politically incorrect and point out that in a large number of cases, the resistance to repatriation was also because the abductors married their victims and integrated them within their family and the abductors' families too accepted them? It need not detract from the personal tragedies of the violated women if I stress that something like this would have been unthinkable in Nazi Germany, though in both cases their were elaborate theories of purity and impurity, touchability and untouchability. On the face of it, untouchability in modern Europe can sometimes go farther than in countries identified with ritualized untouchability.

Second, these myths should not endorse the idea that there are no 'genuine' communal hostilities in South Asia and such hostilities are only artificially created by nasty, conspiratorial politicians greedy for short-term political gains. Such politicians exist, but the larger picture must capture the animosities as well as the amity and locate them within the same cultural world. Some years ago, while doing a study of Cochin, an old city remarkably free from religious and ethnic violence, despite all the 'right' ingredients, I found that tolerance and resistance to violence were often built on carefully, almost lovingly nurtured hostilities, prejudices, and stereotypes.[28] Perhaps in an epic culture, one can ritually neutralize even demons into a predictable, regular, and necessary presence within one's world view. Indeed, the world view is incomplete without them. What kind of a Ramlila is it in any case, if it includes only a Rama and not a Ravana?

Hence, the chosen myths should not mechanically underwrite the thrust of social analyses that suggest a direct, almost one-to-one relationship between social distance and racial, ethnic, and religious violence. I have in mind a whole range of studies, from the social-distance-scales-based ones done in North American universities to some of the psycho-dynamic ones on the holocaust. I do not deny their relevance and I have learnt much from them. But they seem inadequately sensitive to the issue of nearness that has often been at the heart of some of the recent genocidal efforts—in Rwanda, Bosnia, Sri Lanka, perhaps in the whole of South Asia, and West Asia. These are places where the lives of the warring communities are intertwined in love and hate. The

[28] Nandy, 'Time Travel to a Possible Self'.

venom comes from splintered proximity, not distance. The crucial question still remains the one Arjun Appadurai raises, though in a somewhat different context: when does proximity implode and turn into hate.[29]

Third, there has to be in the myths intimations of the limits that the protagonists would not normally cross but are tempted to, and which they sometimes actually do in extreme situations. These are recognized and shared. They give confidence and trust in extreme situations to both victims and rescuers; they even perhaps restrain the killers. Sometimes, however, they can also seriously mislead the actors to tempt their fate. My colleague in the ongoing study of partition violence, Saleem Ahmed is a writer who has been for some years collecting stories of resistance to communal violence during 1946–8. He was inspired to begin his work when he heard of an old Sikh who warned his young hot-blooded son not to touch the Muslim woman he had abducted. In those times, when thousands of young women were being abducted, the young Sikh was not likely to obey his aging father's admonition. He did not. The father took out the family gun and shot his son.

Finally, the candidate myths must reflect something of the empirics of political life in South Asia. Not the life as it is routinely narrated in the textbooks of social sciences, but life as it is captured in the same textbooks if you care to read between the lines or scan their tables without wearing ideological prescription lenses. I have already told you enough stories. I shall be more tiresome at the end and read out some data in a belated bid at respectability. I propose that each myth to qualify must reflect the following three odd details of popular culture and politics:

One, during the last fifty years in India, roughly 80 per cent of Indians have stayed in villages. (The figure presently is roughly 75 per cent, though it is expected to go up in the current census.) However, if you add up the number of the dead in communal violence in the last fifty years, only 3.6 per cent have died in villages. Within urban India, eight cities account for about half the deaths in communal riots. There are also at least ten states in India where communal riots are virtually unknown. These include, unbelievably, Punjab and Kashmir, both of which have seen militancy and politics divided along religious lines. In both cases, efforts have been intermittently made to precipitate communal riots,

[29] Arjun Appadurai, *Modernity at Large: Cultural Dimensions of Globalization*, Minneapolis: University of Minnesota Press, 1996.

[30] For more details, see Ashis Nandy, 'Coping with the Politics of Faiths and Cultures: Between Secular State and Ecumenical Traditions in India', in Joanna Pfaff-Czarnecka, Darini Rajasingham-Senanayake, Ashis Nandy, and Edmond Terence Gomez, *Ethnic Futures: The State and Identity Politics in Asia*, New Delhi: Sage, 1999, pp. 135–66.

unsuccessfully.[30] Hindus and Muslims might be fighting each other from the beginning of time but, apparently, a vast majority of them have not had much time or energy to indulge in their favourite pastime in places where traditional lifestyles and faiths reign.

Two, the colonial-style, official census continues to enumerate the religious and ethnic communities with its customary neatness and zeal, so that the Hindus come to exactly 82.2 per cent of the population, the Muslims 11.9 per cent, Christians 2.1, and Sikhs 1.9 per cent. However, there are other ways of viewing a society in which communities may be under stress, but have not yet collapsed. As late as in 1994, a census of communities, as opposed to that of individuals, was done by the Anthropological Survey of India under the leadership of cultural anthropologist K. Suresh Singh. It revealed that roughly 15 per cent of all Indian communities still had more than one religious faith. This does not mean that they included people from different faiths; this means that each person in these communities can be classified in more than one faith. Thirty-seven communities had three faiths.[31] These findings can only surprise a western readership, modern Indians, and the Hindu nationalists. For in the entire region of East Asia, South-east Asia, and South Asia, this is common. In the Japanese census, when it adds up the percentages of different religions, the total usually comes close to 200 per cent. For a huge majority of the Japanese are both Shinto and Buddhist. The situation in China is not radically different.

Three, no Hindu nationalist party has ever won a majority of Hindu votes in India. Only about 10 per cent of all those who vote for the Hindu nationalists do so on ideological grounds and the base of such parties is mainly urban in a country still predominantly rural. I also know that a majority of Indians—according to a survey, 62.8 per cent of all those who have an opinion on the subject—disapproved of the demolition of the Babri mosque in 1992, but a majority (54.6 per cent) of the Hindus did so too. This was true for both urban and rural respondents. Also, the opposition came from 64.9 per cent of lower caste, tribal, and dalit communities, and from 43.7 per cent of the upper castes. In the elections held four month after the demolition, in March 1993, in eight out of the nine constituencies in Faizabad district, where the mosque was located, the BJP lost the elections. They were all predominantly Hindu.[32]

---

[31] K. Suresh Singh, *Peoples of India*, Calcutta: Anthropological Survey of India, 1994, Vol. 1.

[32] The data come from various public opinion surveys of the Centre for the Study of Developing societies, Delhi, mainly from studies of the Mid–Term Elections 1993 and the General Elections 1996.

All these details are known to everyone working on religious violence in South Asia. I have not unearthed anything even vaguely new. However, many researchers view any emphasis on such data as a form of lotus-eating or day-dreaming. Especially in the Southern world, research in religious violence is expected to be gory and stark in its details—an unrelieved catalogue of what human beings can do to each other. Any effort to return agency to ordinary citizens or look for forms of resistance outside the small modern sector in these societies is invariably seen as reactive, backward-looking romanticism. For the still-colonial knowledge systems that dominate social knowledge have equipped us with the expertise to export to history our living, functioning, next-door neighbours, whose presence, lifestyles, and categories are an uncomfortable reminder to us that they retain the capacity to subvert the favourite values, frameworks, and theories of progress of their well-wishers. We want them to be perfectly transparent and like to write about them in our way, with great sympathy but in the past tense. The stories I want to tell should capture something of this new slave trade of our times.